Writing Business Bids & Proposals

for dummies

A Wiley Brand

Writing Business Bids & Proposals

for dummies®

A Wiley Brand

**by Neil Cobb, APMP Fellow,
and Charlie Divine, CPP APMP Fellow**

Published in association with The Association of Proposal Management

Professionals (APMP), Rick Harris, Executive Director

Writing Business Bids & Proposals For Dummies®

Published by: John Wiley & Sons, Ltd., The Atrium, Southern Gate, Chichester, www.wiley.com

This edition first published 2016

© 2016 by John Wiley & Sons, Ltd., Chichester, West Sussex

Registered Office

John Wiley & Sons, Ltd., The Atrium, Southern Gate, Chichester, West Sussex, PO19 8SQ, United Kingdom

For details of our global editorial offices, for customer services and for information about how to apply for permission to reuse the copyright material in this book, please see our website at www.wiley.com.

For general information on our other products and services, please contact our Customer Care Department within the U.S. at 877-762-2974, outside the U.S. at 317-572-3993, or fax 317-572-4002. For technical support, please visit www.wiley.com/techsupport.

Wiley publishes in a variety of print and electronic formats and by print-on-demand. Some material included with standard print versions of this book may not be included in e-books or in print-on-demand. If this book refers to media such as a CD or DVD that is not included in the version you purchased, you may download this material at http://booksupport.wiley.com. For more information about Wiley products, visit www.wiley.com.

A catalogue record for this book is available from the British Library.

Library of Congress Control Number: 2016940591

ISBN 978-1-119-17432-5 (pbk); ISBN 978-1-119-17433-2 (ebk); ISBN 978-1-119-17436-3 (ebk)

Printed and Bound in the United States by Bind-Rite Robbinsville, Robbinsville, NJ.

10   9   8   7   6   5   4   3

Contents at a Glance

Introduction 1

Part 1: Understanding Proposal Development 7
CHAPTER 1: Introducing Bids and Proposals 9
CHAPTER 2: Understanding Different Types of Proposals. 25

Part 2: Focusing on Your Customer 53
CHAPTER 3: Building Customer Relationships. 55
CHAPTER 4: Giving Your Customers What They Ask For (And More). 77
CHAPTER 5: Sizing Up Your Competition 103

Part 3: Planning Your Approach 123
CHAPTER 6: Developing Your Proposal Process 125
CHAPTER 7: Setting Yourself Apart From Your Competitors. 155
CHAPTER 8: Keeping Your Proposal on Track 169

Part 4: Creating Your Proposal 193
CHAPTER 9: Developing Your Proposal. 195
CHAPTER 10: Applying the Principles of Good Writing:
　　　　　 Structuring Your Argument. 221
CHAPTER 11: Making Your Proposals Look Good 251
CHAPTER 12: Getting Your Proposal Out the Door. 275

Part 5: Taking Your Proposal to the Next Level 297
CHAPTER 13: Using Tools and Templates to Accelerate Your Proposals 299
CHAPTER 14: Leading Proposal Teams Effectively 323
CHAPTER 15: Making Each Proposal Better than the Last. 345

Part 6: The Part of Tens 363
CHAPTER 16: Ten Templates for Building Your Proposal. 365
CHAPTER 17: Ten Common Misconceptions about Bids and Proposals. 371

Appendix: Online Resources 379

Index 383

Table of Contents

INTRODUCTION 1

About This Book. 2

Foolish Assumptions. 3

Icons Used in This Book 4

Beyond the Book 4

Where to Go from Here 4

PART 1: UNDERSTANDING PROPOSAL DEVELOPMENT. . . . 7

CHAPTER 1: **Introducing Bids and Proposals**. 9

Defining Bids and Proposals 10

Looking at the differences between RFP responses
and proactive proposals. 11

Understanding why organizations request proposals. 13

Preparing to Propose 14

Starting before the beginning 14

Developing your proposal from cover to cover 18

Proposing better all the time. 21

Becoming More Professional. 22

CHAPTER 2: **Understanding Different Types of Proposals**. 25

Responding to a Request for Proposal (RFP). 26

Joining the game: The invitation to bid. 26

Following instructions: Compliance and the case
for responsiveness 28

Facing the third degree: The challenge of Q&A-style RFPs 30

Writing a Proactive Proposal 38

Getting sponsored: The value of customer concern 39

Supporting a strategy: The proposal as a means
to your long-term goals 40

Building a win theme: Motivators, issues, and hot buttons 41

Organizing your proposal: A repeatable structure. 43

Comparing Small and Large Proposals 45

Scaling the process: Modifying to meet the opportunity. 45

Constraining yourself: Overcoming the challenge
of limited content 47

Understanding Procurement: The Differences Among Segments. . . . 48

Going global: Developing proposals outside your region 49

Going green: Electronic versus print. 50

PART 2: FOCUSING ON YOUR CUSTOMER 53

CHAPTER 3: **Building Customer Relationships** 55

Getting to Know Your Customers 56
    Getting real: Your customer's business is your business 56
    Starting right: Asking opening questions 57
    Digging deeper: Understanding the needs of your readers 59
    Winning customers: It's all about them 61
Handling Customer Engagement: Your Sales Process 67
    Stage 1: Finding the right market 69
    Stage 2: Planning a common approach for your accounts 70
    Stage 3: Identifying and qualifying your opportunities 70
    Stage 4: Planning for every opportunity 71
    Stage 5: Developing your proposal plan 72
    Stage 6: Writing your proposal 73
    Stage 7: Negotiating and closing the deal 73
    Stage 8: Sustaining the relationship 74
Managing Customer Relationships 74

CHAPTER 4: **Giving Your Customers What They
Ask For (And More)** 77

Following Your Customers' Instructions 78
    Clearing the first hurdle: The proposal qualification
    questionnaire 78
    Reading the instructions: Customers say the
    darnedest things 81
    Managing questions: When the RFP is unclear 82
Complying with Your Customers' Requirements 84
    Shredding the RFP: Parse your way to compliance 85
    Watching out for gotchas: Instant disqualification 87
    Creating a compliance matrix: An annotated index of your
    response 88
Enhancing Compliance with Responsiveness 94
    Reading between the lines: The problem with
    unstated needs 95
    Selling everywhere: The compliance matrix as
    responsiveness tool 98
    Maintaining a customer focus: Sidestepping obstacles 99
    Using knowledge about your customer to win
    the advantage 100
    Speaking your customer's language 101

CHAPTER 5: **Sizing Up Your Competition** 103

Gathering Information About Your Competitors 104

Assessing your competition: Asking the right questions. 104

Gathering intelligence: The first line of defense 106

Hosting a competitor review 109

Understanding what you know: Two tools for
getting a clearer picture 110

Unseating Incumbents 114

Ghosting Your Competition 117

Highlighting your strengths 119

Drawing attention to your competitors' weaknesses. 120

Compensating for your weaknesses 121

PART 3: PLANNING YOUR APPROACH 123

CHAPTER 6: **Developing Your Proposal Process** 125

Understanding Where the Proposal Process Fits In. 126

Pre-Proposal Stage: To Bid or Not to Bid? 128

Making the bid/no-bid decision. 128

Getting your act together. 130

Proposal Development Stage: Delivering on Your
Proposal Strategy 131

Setting the overall strategy 132

Planning the proposal. 137

Writing the proposal 144

Producing the proposal 149

Post-Proposal Stage: Getting Ready for Another Round 152

Responding to customers' questions 152

Preparing for oral presentations. 153

Capturing lessons learned 153

Harvesting reusable content 153

CHAPTER 7: **Setting Yourself Apart From Your
Competitors** 155

Presenting Features and Benefits. 156

Describing your proposal's features. 157

Clarifying benefits 159

Applying the "so what?" test. 160

Quantifying the value of benefits with discriminators. 161

Backing Up Your Claims with Proof 163

Using past projects to back up your claims. 164

Making your proof persuasive. 165

Making your proof tangible 166

Making your proof credible 167

CHAPTER 8: **Keeping Your Proposal on Track**......................169

Coming Up with a Schedule That Works 170
Beginning at the end and working backward 171
Breaking big assignments into manageable chunks 178
Maximizing parallel tasks and minimizing sequential tasks 179
Learning from your experiences...........................180
Managing the moving parts...............................181
Budgeting Your Funds and Resources 182
Budgeting your funds...................................182
Budgeting your time....................................185
Choosing Your Proposal Team 186
Understanding roles and competencies 187
Managing virtual proposal teams 188
Supporting global teams 188
Working with external partners...........................189

PART 4: CREATING YOUR PROPOSAL.........................193

CHAPTER 9: **Developing Your Proposal** 195

Crafting the Executive Summary................................196
Knowing what an executive summary is 196
Knowing what an executive summary isn't 196
Focusing your message on your customer 197
Building a compelling summary 198
Creating a good impression...............................199
Writing a Transmittal Letter..................................200
Describing the Customer's Situation 201
Setting up the scenario..................................202
Expressing the problem and the pain 203
Illustrating the customer's environment 203
Describing problems in the customer's own language 204
Answering Your Customer's Questions 204
Responding to an RFP's questions 205
Answering the questions plainly...........................206
Linking your answers and win themes......................207
Writing the Solution for a Proactive Proposal....................208
Developing a structure that's easy to understand 208
Creating a vision of the outcomes you'll provide 211
Establishing Value in the Pricing Section 213
Expressing the value of your solution 213
Quantifying your claims with data 217
Building the Experience Section 217
Documenting your team's know-how........................218
Choosing relevant past-performance examples...............219
Closing with a Call to Action.................................220

CHAPTER 10: **Applying the Principles of Good Writing: Structuring Your Argument**.........................221

    Outlining to Guide Your Writing 222

        Using topical outlines to build content.....................222

        Using descriptive outlines to guide your readers (and your writers) 223

        Outlining the RFP response 225

    Writing Clearly 225

        Telling stories to your customers 226

        Writing like you talk.....................................232

        Writing concisely 236

        Showing your document's structure.......................240

        Revising your work 243

    Writing Persuasively 243

        Knowing who you're writing to 244

        Applying the principles of rhetoric 245

    Using Headings to Guide the Reader through Your Proposal 248

        Understanding heading styles.............................248

        Accenting benefits and discriminators.....................249

        Making sure your headings work 250

CHAPTER 11: **Making Your Proposals Look Good** 251

    Designing Eye-Catching, Accessible Documents..................252

        Designing right . . . from the start.........................253

        Distinguishing your proposals with consistent document styles..254

    Applying Basic Design Principles to Make Your Proposal Stand Out...264

    Using Graphics to Help Readers Understand Your Proposal 267

        Persuading better than with words alone 267

        Making abstract ideas more concrete 268

        Enhancing the power of your graphics 269

        Connecting your text and graphics.........................272

CHAPTER 12: **Getting Your Proposal Out the Door** 275

    Getting Fresh Eyes On Your Proposal...........................276

        Structuring your final proposal reviews.....................277

        Scaling final proposal reviews 278

        Putting together the final proposal review 279

    Readying Your Proposal for Delivery 284

        Scaling production to meet your needs.....................284

        Using checklists to ensure quality.........................285

        Planning for the worst 286

Responding to Electronic Submissions 287
    Understanding how electronic submissions
    differ from paper. 288
    Adapting your messages accordingly. 289
Giving an Oral Presentation. 289
    Planning your approach. 290
    Helping your message stick. 293
    Practicing good public speaking skills 293

**PART 5: TAKING YOUR PROPOSAL TO
THE NEXT LEVEL** 297

CHAPTER 13: **Using Tools and Templates to
Accelerate Your Proposals** 299
    Tooling Around with Proposals. 300
        Mechanizing the pre-proposal process 301
        Using tools to enhance the proposal development stage. 305
        Preparing for the next one. 311
    Creating Foolproof Processes and Outputs 314
        Planning smarter with templates 314
        Writing to spec with templates 317

CHAPTER 14: **Leading Proposal Teams Effectively**. 323
    Leading Long Before the Project Begins 324
        Leading by doing. 324
        Engaging your colleagues at every level. 325
        Knowing where your resources lie 329
    Guiding Your Team from Start to Finish 331
        Embracing the leadership role 332
        Timing your feedback. 336
        Tracking your team's progress 336
        Motivating your team 337
    Taking a Virtual Approach to Proposal Team Leadership. 338
        Considering the positives and negatives 338
        Creating a virtual proposal center 339
        Laying the groundwork for clear communication 341
        Conducting virtual kickoffs and reviews. 343

CHAPTER 15: **Making Each Proposal Better than the Last** 345
    Improving with Every Opportunity 346
        Learning from your customers 346
        Learning from your colleagues 349

Collecting Content for Reuse 352
    Building your content repository 353
    Choosing your content objects 354
    Applying knowledge to the next proposal .356
Getting and Staying in Proposal Shape 357
    Joining a professional organization 358
    Earning professional certifications 359
    Getting trained by the best 361
    Mentoring and coaching for leadership 361

PART 6: THE PART OF TENS 363

CHAPTER 16: Ten Templates for Building Your Proposal 365
Creating a Compliance Matrix 365
Proving Your Past Performance 366
Standardizing the Proposal Model 367
Keeping Up with Your Costs 367
Tracking Your Customer Contacts 368
Scheduling Your Process Milestones 368
Deciding Whether to Bid 369
Checking Off Production Activities 369
Checking the Checker 370
Capturing and Sharing Lessons Learned 370

CHAPTER 17: Ten Common Misconceptions about Bids and Proposals 371
Engaging the Customer Early Isn't Important .372
An Executive Summary Only Summarizes Your Proposal 372
Features and Benefits Are All the Same 373
If You're the Incumbent, You've Got Nothing to Worry About 374
Always Use Business Speak and Buzz Phrases in Your Proposals . . .375
Sales Is a Game of Numbers, So Bid on Everything 375
You Can Skip the Reviews if You're Short on Time 376
Collecting Information about Your Competitors Is Unethical 377
After You Decide to Bid, Stick to Your Decision to the End 377
Debrief Sessions Help You Single Out Underperformers 378

APPENDIX: ONLINE RESOURCES 379

INDEX 383

Introduction

This may come as a bit of a surprise to you, but some people write proposals for a living *and enjoy it.*

We don't mean people who have to write proposals to sell their products and services as an obligatory part of their roles as business owners, salespeople, and entrepreneurs. We mean people who write proposals as their profession — it's their primary role. They delight in this intricate, detail-oriented, thought-provoking work. They toil for businesses big and small, and all they do all day (and all night at times) is write proposals. Some write proposals that are a handful of pages, while others write proposals with hundreds of pages in multiple volumes. Some write them pretty much on their own, while others coordinate the efforts of anywhere from a couple of specialists to hundreds on a single deal. They propose to every kind of business and government entity you can imagine, because most publicly owned or regulated enterprises buy goods and services through proposals.

It may not matter to you personally, but proposal writing is a profession — a growing and increasingly important one. It's an essential part of a broader group of business development professionals who plan and execute strategies for businesses to obtain new customers. Proposal writers have a professional organization — the Association of Proposal Management Professionals (APMP) — whose best practices are the foundation for this book. This group of more than 7,500 practitioners from around the world knows that proposal writing is a skill you can learn, practice, and master, and, ultimately, prove your mastery of through a professional certification process.

Here's what does matter to you: *Writing Business Bids & Proposals For Dummies* is your easiest and best ticket for finding out what these professional proposal writers know and for applying it to your own business. You have in your hands the collected knowledge and skills of the professional proposal writer — without having to be one.

About This Book

This book is primarily for small- to medium-size business owners, first-time proposal writers in medium-size companies, or sales representatives who need to represent their companies in the best light possible. A written proposal, whether it's delivered in print or digital format, is still one of the most common, personal, and effective ways to win business, even in this age of near-instant online communications, social media marketing, and live-action websites.

Proposal writers have an old saying: "The best proposal won't win the business outright, but a bad one will certainly lose it." This means that a proposal doesn't work in a vacuum. Developing a successful business is a complex and difficult process, with lots of interworking parts. You have to have useful and reliable products, dedicated people providing a dependable service, and innovative thinking that can solve unique problems. But even if you have the best products, the best people, and the best service record of anyone in your industry, if you can't express those advantages clearly and persuasively in terms that truly mean something to your customers, your business will never be as successful as it can be.

If you adopt the concepts, implement the processes, practice the techniques, and adapt the tools in this book to meet your unique needs, you'll improve the way your business captures new customers and communicates with existing ones. This book can help you to

>> Establish a process for finding and assessing business opportunities.

>> Create repeatable plans for responding to opportunities.

>> Understand your customer's business and its needs.

>> Assess your and your competitors' strengths and weaknesses.

>> Build and manage teams to develop compelling proposals.

After you have a process and the required resources in place, this book can guide you to

>> Structure your proposals in proven, effective ways.

>> Write them in the clearest and most compelling terms.

>> Design them for maximum readability and visual impression.

>> Create practices for doing a better job each time.

We also use a few conventions throughout the book to make finding what you need easier:

>> If you see a word in *italics,* it means that the term has a unique meaning in the proposal world. We define it right there for you.

>> If you see a sidebar, you can skip that information if you're in a hurry. It's there to provide background information or other supporting content.

Foolish Assumptions

As we wrote this book, we assumed a few things about you, dear readers:

>> You need to write a proposal, and sooner rather than later. You may be an inexperienced salesperson who inherited an account with a pressing need. You may be a newly named proposal resource in your company, and a Request for Proposal (RFP) has just landed on your desk with the clock ticking. Maybe you've written a proposal before, and you want to do a better job on the next one. Whatever your immediate need, we assume that you want to do this job right, and that's what we aim to help you do.

>> You know how to use a computer and word-processing software. You can't write a proposal on the back of an envelope or napkin and be taken seriously. The leading word-processing programs on all platforms provide enough layout and graphics capabilities that you can easily create a professional document that follows basic design principles. If you don't know how to use them, you can always grab another *For Dummies* book and improve your skills!

>> You know how to convert a word-processing file into PDF format, which allows you to create a digital copy of your proposal that is more tamper-resistant. Leading word-processing tools have menu selections that can do this in a couple of clicks.

>> You'll eventually work your way through the entire book and will understand that there's still more to learn. That's where the APMP comes in. If you do need to know more, an APMP membership provides a legion of mentors and volumes of references. The APMP also offers a professional certification program for those who want to demonstrate mastery of the craft. Go to www.apmp.org for more information.

Icons Used in This Book

We use a few icons throughout this book to call out important information that you may otherwise miss.

TIP

This icon provides extra information for applying proposal-writing techniques or alternative ways of doing things.

REMEMBER

This icon points out important information that you may want to note down or highlight, or that you may want to keep in mind as you try your hand at the task.

WARNING

This icon highlights potential pitfalls and danger spots.

EXAMPLE

This icon indicates examples that we provide to illustrate what we're talking about as you work through the book.

Beyond the Book

We've created a handy, access-anywhere Cheat Sheet, which provides high-level reminders that you can easily reference when you don't have the book on hand. For instance, are you looking for a reminder of some of the key reviews you can undertake to help develop and perfect your proposal process? The Cheat Sheet helps you remember at a glance. To access this Cheat Sheet, go to www.dummies. com and search for "Writing Business Bids & Proposals For Dummies Cheat Sheet" in the Search box.

We've also created a one-stop-shop for all digital content related to this book. Check out the appendix at the end of the book for the URL and a list of the online templates and checklists.

Where to Go from Here

Writing Business Bids & Proposals For Dummies takes you from the basic concepts behind proposal writing and the practical techniques you apply to create winning proposals to advanced concepts you may consider after you've mastered the basics.

We recommend that you check out the table of contents for the complete list of topics, and then read Chapter 1 to get the end-to-end story from 30,000 feet.

You don't need to read this book in any particular sequence. Each chapter is self-contained, tackles a single proposal-related subject, and, like a good proposal, has cross-references to related information. Just pick a chapter that addresses an immediate problem you have, and read, think, and apply. For example, are you already responding to an RFP? Look to Chapter 4 for advice on identifying all the customer's requirements, or jump to Chapter 9 for ways to collect and structure your past-performance records.

And last (or maybe first), to get a general "lay of the land" in proposal writing, be sure to review our simple proposal process in Chapter 6. This list of major steps provides an "at-a-glance" view of the many duties a proposal writer performs over the span of developing either a proactive proposal or an RFP response.

1

Understanding Proposal Development

Find out what proposals are and why everyone in business needs to know how to write them. Take a peek into the world of professional proposal writers and how they do their jobs. Look at the bigger picture and how proposals fit into a business's sales process and a customer's buying process.

Discover the similarities and differences between proactive proposals and reactive proposals (or responses to a Request for Proposal [RFPs]). See how to avoid the traps lurking in RFPs and how to make sure the customer finds what it's looking for. Understand how creating a consistent structure and format for your proactive proposals can help customers choose you over your competitors.

IN THIS CHAPTER

Getting the intel on bids and proposals

Gearing up for your proposal

Developing a professional approach

Chapter 1

Introducing Bids and Proposals

This book is about writing business bids and proposals. Why bids *and* proposals, you ask? Aren't they the same thing?

Many proposal professionals would say so. Others favor one term over the other, especially when used to modify another term. For example, in the United Kingdom, they may say *bid manager* and *tender*; in the United States, we say *proposal manager* and *Request for Proposal (RFP) response* — and we mean pretty much the same thing.

Some people think of bids as something we'd call a *quote* — a line or two about the offer and a price — something you can write on the back of a napkin. Some may even call that a proposal. The more people you talk to, the more confused you can get.

As we use the terms, *bids* and *proposals* are more formal, more thorough, more informative, more persuasive, more descriptive, and more professional than *quotes.* They're more about communication than selling, more about value than price, and more about relationships than a single deal. Throughout this book, we use them interchangeably because it's how proposal professionals talk: A *bid* is a *proposal*; a *bidder* is someone who submits a proposal or bid (and we'd never use the word *proposer*).

In this chapter, we introduce you to the world of bid and proposal management — what proposals do, how they work, and how you write one — drawing from the best practices that bid *and* proposal professionals use worldwide.

Defining Bids and Proposals

In the broadest sense, *business proposals* are formal, written offers by businesses or individuals to perform work on the behalf of other businesses, government entities, or other individuals. Proposals set out in clear, concise language what you'll do for a customer, how you'll do it, how much it will cost, and the business benefits the customer will realize after the work is done. Proposals aim to both inform and persuade. And that makes them pretty unique.

In some industries, business proposals are precursors to contracts. That's why many proposals stipulate how long certain offers or prices are valid. Some government entities require the proposals they receive to be authorized by a bidder's officer to underscore their legal status. Some proposals even become an integral part of the final contract.

REMEMBER

Business proposals come in two main flavors:

>> **Proposals submitted further to a formal request from the customer:**
These are sometimes referred to as *solicited* proposals. You may also hear them called *reactive proposals,* because you can't really anticipate all their requirements. More often, these proposals are called *RFP responses,* because the customer issues a *Request for Proposal*. We opt for that term throughout this book.

>> **Proposals that you give the customer independently of any request:**
These usually follow deep discussions about the customer's business needs and are called either *proactive* or *unsolicited proposals*. Instead of the customer requesting a proposal, you ask the customer to accept your proposal. We prefer the term *proactive* because it indicates that you write these on your own initiative (plus, it's easier to say).

Both types consist of a series of textual and visual components that form an *argument* in support of your approach to solving a customer's problem.

In the following sections, we discuss the differences between RFP responses and proactive proposals — their structures and some of the rules around writing them — and then discuss the reasons why organizations issue RFPs.

Looking at the differences between RFP responses and proactive proposals

Before we go any further, we cover how you construct RFP responses and proactive proposals and why they're different.

REMEMBER

For all their differences, when you look closely at RFP responses and proactive proposals, you see that their deep structures are more alike than different. That makes sense, because they both argue for one solution over others. Therefore, what makes one type of proposal successful applies to the other.

Turn to Chapter 2 to find out more about the similarities and differences between RFP responses and proactive proposals.

Understanding the structure of RFP responses

RFPs are the procurement method of choice for most governments and large organizations. Most RFPs, regardless of the source, have similar structures. Government RFPs have elaborate number schemes and consistent, required sections. Commercial RFPs may have these as well, but the formats and sequences can vary widely from industry to industry and from RFP to RFP.

TIP

RFPs always have one thing in common: Whoever releases them expects your response to follow the prescribed structure to the letter. RFPs are designed so evaluators can easily compare bidders' various responses. They also tend to reflect whatever structure has worked before, which is why you can anticipate repeated elements when you respond to RFPs from certain customers.

Though RFPs can have many surface differences, most contain individual sections that do the following:

>> Describe the background of the customer and its business problem.

>> Lay out the rules that the customer expects all bidders to follow, including any terms and conditions of a potential contract.

>> List the specific requirements that the customer needs you to address as you solve the problem. These requirements often take the form of questions. They may cover not only how your solution will work but also how your company will implement and manage the solution.

>> Specify pricing components (usually in separate spreadsheets, depending on the complexity of the project).

Many RFPs instruct you to include in your response an executive summary, which you need to do whether instructed to or not (unless the RFP explicitly forbids you to). As you see in Chapter 9, an executive summary is your best chance to explain your solution and its value to the customer's highest ranking decision maker (who won't normally read the entire proposal). You never want to miss out on the opportunity to communicate directly to a customer's leaders.

Understanding the structure of proactive proposals

Proactive proposals, more or less, also follow a standard structure. The difference is that with proactive proposals, you control the structure, although you should always use a structure that customers find comfortable, satisfying, and compelling. The standard sections include

>> An *executive summary* that recaps needs and benefits, win themes, and value propositions in language that speaks to decision makers

>> A description and illustration of the *current environment* or *problem*

>> Your *recommendation* for creating a new, improved environment or for solving the problem, comparably illustrated to show the changes in the customer's world

>> A *statement of work* that describes how you'll set up the solution and maintain it

>> A *pricing summary* that focuses on benefits, value, and return on investment

>> A final recap of benefits and an action close to outline next steps

Adjusting your process for RFP responses and proactive proposals

High-level differences exist between RFP responses and proactive proposals that involve how you adhere to the rules, work with time frames, and handle the competitive landscape.

PLAYING BY THE RULES

REMEMBER

RFP responses have to mimic the structure of the RFP they respond to. They echo the numbered sections and subsections (sometimes four or five levels deep) of the RFP. They populate structured forms that the customer includes for pricing information. They adhere to customer-mandated page and format restrictions. Fortunately, they don't have to copy the normally stilted, bureaucratic language of the original, although you must be careful to repeat key terms so you sound responsive (we talk about responsiveness and compliance in Chapter 4).

TIP

You can insert the original RFP into your response template to put a brand wrapper around it, but you'd better not stray from the format prescribed. Read the RFP closely to see what you can and can't do. If your RFP says "don't use color images," make sure you don't. If your RFP says "insert your response directly after each question," do as it says and highlight your response so the reader can tell the question from the answer.

Proactive proposals have only the rules a customer sets when you offer to submit one. Your customers will hopefully be intrigued enough by your solution to put aside their hard-and-fast rules and allow you to present your solution in your preferred format. Proactive proposals can look like, well, whatever you think your customer wants them to look like: magazine articles, business letters, glossy brochures, or even (ugh) RFP responses.

STICKING TO A TIMELINE

RFPs are deadline driven. If you miss the deadline, you're usually eliminated. That may sound harsh, but it's not necessarily a bad thing. With an RFP response, at least you have an engaged customer setting a clear deadline.

With proactive proposals, you may have nothing more than a customer's promise to consider your idea. Your salesperson may set a date with the customer to deliver a proactive proposal, but you may find that the date slips as other sales initiatives take precedence or if the salesperson gets distracted and doesn't provide you what you need to finish the proposal by the due date. And your customer won't be as obligated to review your proposal when it does arrive.

WORKING AROUND THE COMPETITION

Salespeople try to avoid RFPs because they are, by design, more competitive than proactive proposals. By releasing an RFP, customers consciously pit competitors against each other. You present proactive proposals after you've worked with customers long enough to see inside their operations and discover areas where your business's expertise can benefit them. And although a customer may entertain multiple proactive proposals to solve a problem, you usually have much less competition, if any, to worry about.

Understanding why organizations request proposals

Knowing how to write proposals well is important because most mid- to large-size organizations acquire services and products through proposals. Many regulated industries and government entities must, by statute, set up an RFP competition so they can create a fair basis for comparing vendors and solutions. Others release RFPs because they know pretty much what they want and are trying to find the best, lowest-cost provider. Still others release RFPs because they're unhappy with their current provider's performance and know that an RFP can remedy the situation, one way or another.

WARNING

Some companies request proposals to validate a prior decision (when they've already chosen a vendor) or merely to apply pressure to a current provider to lower its price. The better your relationship with the customer, the better your chance of avoiding being used as a tool for making an incumbent more responsive.

Preparing to Propose

Well-written proposals are a product of a well-defined and closely followed process. That's why we spend so much of this book walking you through the three major phases of proposal development:

» Pre-proposal stage

» Proposal development stage

» Post-proposal stage

REMEMBER

If you look at the bigger picture, proposal development is just a part of the overall sales or business development process in a company. You acknowledge that relationship by starting the proposal process long before an RFP is released or a salesperson has uncovered that proactive opportunity — back in what some sales organizations may call their *pre-sales process* (when they create and formalize their sales strategies for a customer). And we recommend staying involved long after the proposal is delivered, the contract is signed, and the work is underway, so you can be ready to do even better before the next opportunity (whether with either the same customer or a different one). (To better understand the scope of the proposal process, turn to Chapter 6, where we take you through each stage in more detail.)

The following sections introduce this three-stage proposal process to give you a big-picture view from the proposal writer's perspective.

Starting before the beginning

We begin before you even know you have an opportunity: The pre-proposal stage. It's where you make many key decisions that can make or break your efforts to build a winning proposal.

Your goal is to get involved well before a proposal is a certain outcome. In some segments (like government), it's easier — you may receive a draft RFP to work with, sometimes with significant lead time before the final RFP is released. In other cases, you get a warning from the sales representative that a customer is gearing up for a procurement or that the rep has discovered an opportunity for a proactive proposal. The best scenario is when your sales clients invite you to their sales planning sessions to ensure that you're engaged as soon as you see an opportunity on the horizon.

Here's why getting ahead of the game is so important: If you don't get involved early, you may never recover. RFP responses are "reactive" proposals, and you don't want to be the only bidder who's reacting when an RFP is released. If you have no prior warning, that's about all you can do. It's hard enough to win an RFP — you don't want to see the competition two goals ahead before you take the field.

The following sections consider how you can gain — and keep — the advantage ahead of the proposal development stage.

Becoming the trusted advisor

The best way to get engaged early is to become the trusted response resource who brings serious value to your sales organization's planning during its pre-sales process. Start capturing historical records about your engagements with your customers: The strategies you use, the win themes you develop, and the lessons you learn. Make those available, along with archived prior proposals for the customer and even some that you've created for other companies with similar problems. Your colleagues will start seeing you as an essential part of their success.

Looking for the right opportunities

As a proposal writer, you want to be included in the sales strategy sessions that determine when and how you'll be engaged on a proposal project. You also want to be involved when the sales team assesses whether an opportunity is winnable or not. This is where your archive of information and even your personal experience can influence decisions.

REMEMBER

Your resources are limited (indeed, you may be the *only* resource). You have to focus on only those deals that your company has a real chance of winning, or you'll become stretched too thin, or your work may be marginalized because you're seen as ineffective.

Influencing your sales team to get involved early in the right opportunities can mean the difference between success and failure. It means you may be able to influence the questions a customer asks in an RFP. It may mean that you get to pose questions directly to the customer for a proactive proposal. Chapter 3 looks at the value of having a strong relationship with your customer and how this can influence the proposal process in your favor.

Making it all about the customer

If you take away only one golden nugget from this book, make it this one: **Your proposal is all about your customer — it's *not about you*.** Use your customer's terms to describe its problem and your shared vision for a solution. Place your solution into the customer's environment — customize your proposal's look and language so it reflects the customer's brand, its colors, its imagery, and its logo. Go easy on the boilerplate, and customize your source material to better reflect your customer's working environment.

TIP

One way to "think customer" is to identify the pain the customer goes through as a result of the problem you want to solve. When you identify the most pressing, emotionally charged needs and clearly depict the pain they cause, you're said to be pushing the customer's *hot buttons* (for more about hot buttons, see Chapter 2). These are the most meaningful issues to your customer and the reasons a customer will buy. Downplay your solution's features (what it does) and play up the benefits (what your customer gets or can do from the solution) instead. If you can show that you alone can provide that single benefit that solves the customer's hot-button problem, you'll win the deal (see Chapters 7 and 9 for guidance on how to develop and write feature and benefit statements).

Gathering and providing the right information

REMEMBER

Seeing things through your customers' eyes is the difference between complying with your customers' requirements and truly responding to their needs. Compliant proposals *can* win; responsive proposal *do* win. How do you figure out what your customers need? You ask a lot of questions.

You won't know your customer's hot buttons if you don't gather the right information. How do you do this (especially when you're not the salesperson and never escape the back office)? If your opportunity is proactive, you ask questions. You ask the customer. If your company won't let you, you ask the customer rep or the customer support tech. You ask thoughtful, probing questions that get to the heart of the customer's problem, and you listen closely to the answers so you can write like the customer talks.

If you're responding to an RFP, you do all the above and *shred the RFP*. By *shredding*, we mean parsing, or separating, every requirement as a stand-alone topic to address in your response. Sometimes, that's easy: Just follow the number scheme that the customer provides in the RFP. But sometimes, customers are sneaky. They bury requirements, using trigger words like *will, shall, must,* and *should* to indicate that a requirement follows. Some sophisticated proposal groups use parsing software to find all the incidents. Some still use multicolor highlighters as a shredding tool. Either way can be effective (and one is definitely cheaper, if a lot slower). For a detailed look at shredding an RFP and building a compliant *and* responsive proposal from the results, see Chapter 4.

Getting the better of your competitors

Competitive analysis is a legal business discipline that uses a variety of public sources and tools to help you choose the right strategy for setting yourself apart from your competitors. Check out your competitors' websites to discover their latest product information and market strategies. Use social media to track your competitors' claims and trending interests. If you have the funds, subscribe to competitive assessment research sites or reports.

TIP

Another way to capture knowledge about your rivals is to hold a *competitor review* with employees in your company who compete with or perhaps even work alongside them. You can explain the opportunity and collect insights and new perspectives. Your business may be one of those that finds new employees by luring them away from competitors. Ask around and talk with any colleagues who have recently worked for a competitor to discover whatever you can about the way it does business.

Your goal as proposal writer is to shine a bright light on your competitors' weaknesses while subtly touting your strengths. We proposal writers call that "ghosting" the competition. You can take the information you gather from your sources and prepare a *SWOT analysis* (which assesses strengths, weaknesses, opportunities, and threats) to create powerful discriminators for your solution and ghosting statements for your proposal. For more on creating persuasive content from your competitive analysis, see Chapters 5 and 7.

Using the proposal as a communication platform

Your goal in gathering customer and competitor information is to build tactics for creating a long-term and mutually beneficial business relationship, not just a one-and-done customer-vendor agreement. Use your initial work on a given opportunity to help establish a comprehensive communication plan for a particular company or even industry. For instance, what you learn from one engagement may

>> Uncover a need for conceptual proposals for longer-range and multi-staged projects

>> Enable you to establish customer-focused content for private websites and social media messaging

>> Open doors for producing executive-level communiqués that open a dialogue with senior management perhaps, providing status on in-progress projects and forecasting future needs — both of which can result in more winning proposals

Deciding to bid (or not)

The *bid/no-bid decision* is the last action you take in the pre-proposal stage. It's the last chance for you to bail before putting your resources behind a deal. You need to use the information from your customer investigation and SWOT analysis to make this either/or decision.

REMEMBER

You need to make sure you have the following:

>> A solution that can win over all others

>> Proof that you can deliver the solution as your customer requires

>> A strong win theme that addresses your customer's hot buttons

>> Commitment from your company to dedicate the resources you need to develop the proposal and win the bid

You can find more about bid/no-bid decisions in Chapter 6.

Developing your proposal from cover to cover

Next comes the *proposal development stage*. This is where you do the bulk of your work over four phases — strategizing, planning, writing, and publishing.

During the *strategizing* phase, you take the needs and vision of a customer, the products, services, and vision of your company, and the skills and insights of a team of specialists, and blend them into a cohesive argument that satisfies both the intellect and the heart of the decision maker. *Planning* is where you establish the structure of your proposal argument and the material you'll use to support your argument. *Writing* is where you craft your descriptions, arguments, and get them ready to be published. And *publishing* is creating the physical or digital copies of the proposal and delivering it to the customer.

REMEMBER

Proposal writers bring value to an organization in many ways, but none more so than by directing proposal development resources in the proposal development stage, working within the time constraints of a particular opportunity. Proposal writers may be better termed *proposal managers* at this point because they're the glue that holds the whole operation together.

The following sections take you on a whistle-stop tour through each phase.

Strategizing: Making the case for success

The strategizing phase is multilayered, so we take you through this step by step.

GETTING READY TO PROPOSE

You need to distill the preliminary fact-finding and speculative thinking of the pre-proposal stage into a specific strategy for this one opportunity. You have something tangible to work with: A final RFP or a diagnosed problem that can drive real work, helping your sales team to create real solutions.

TIP

Having a consistent structure and format for your RFP responses and proactive proposals will help you assemble a customized proposal for your customers and help them choose you over your competitors.

Here's where the real writing begins, too. You have to create tangible references to guide your contributors: win themes, value propositions, hot buttons, and discriminators. Better still, here's where you work with your sales lead to write the executive summary (yes, you write it first), to lay a foundation for messaging that resonates throughout the proposal. See how to do all of this in Chapters 6, 7, and 9.

PUTTING THE RIGHT RESOURCES ON YOUR PROPOSAL

Creating a proposal takes at least a village — sometimes a small metropolis. Depending on your circumstances, a village may be a sole sales partner and a few specialists or a hundred or more individuals with unique skill and knowledge sets. Some specialists will be your sources for technical and messaging content, while others will be your resources for putting together the professional proposal: graphics specialists, production specialists, editors, and the like. Still others will be the objective, expert reviewers that all proposals need to reach their potential. Get more information on proposal roles and responsibilities in Chapter 8.

TAILORING THE PROCESS

Each proposal is unique because each solution for a customer is unique (if it's not, your proposal probably won't succeed). For that reason, you need to be ready to adjust your standard proposal process to fit the circumstances of each particular opportunity. It's natural to think that responding to an RFP and creating a proactive proposal would follow two distinct processes, but that's really not the case.

TIP

Your proposal process should be a standard to follow in every instance, with the flexibility to expand or contract like an accordion so you can respond professionally to large and small opportunities alike.

All proposals deserve the full rigor of a standard process. However, you may not need to customize the product description as much each time, or go through as many reviews, or you may not have enough time to do everything to the extent you normally would.

REMEMBER

Always start with the gold standard. Your proposal process is your road map to success (but every road map allows for detours and shortcuts as necessary). Chapter 6 walks you through the details of building your standard process.

Planning: Scheduling the process

When you have all your process steps in place for this particular opportunity, devise a schedule that ensures you have time to do your work as you manage the efforts of your contributors. This may sound a little selfish, but no one outside the proposal business really understands what you go through to deliver an error-free, single-voice, professionally published proposal. You have to leave yourself ample time to review, revise, edit, and proofread the work.

Discover more about building an effective and suitable schedule in Chapter 8.

Writing: Crafting the story of your proposal

A proposal is an argument — but it's also a *story* about how people help other people overcome problems and achieve their goals. Readers like stories, especially when they can relate to a character in that story. Stories are easier to read, and they motivate people to act in ways that other forms of writing can't.

REMEMBER

A proposal story is basically about benefits and value. Every portion of your proposal needs to focus on the business outcomes, not the means by which you deliver the outcomes. A proposal is about your customer — not your company, not your products, not your industry accolades, and not your history. Don't take this the wrong way; those items have their value as proofs that you can do what you claim — proofs like past performance, testimonials, and recognized innovations. But they're there only to show that you can help your customer do what it wants and needs to do.

In Chapters 9 and 10, you discover how to write strong proposal stories, using a direct, active writing style that has actors performing actions to accomplish results. You see how to write win themes, compelling value propositions, and concrete benefit and proof statements. You find tips on what to do and what to avoid when you pull your content into a presentable shape, and how to make your proposal easy to read, easy to understand, and easy to accept. We even show you how to use all these tips to write a winning executive summary and clear, concise, and responsive answers to your customers' questions.

Proposal writers usually "grow up" to become proposal managers. They add project management skills to their researching, authoring, and reviewing skills, and take the burden off sales and other specialists to make sure the proposal is responsive, compelling, and on time. Getting the proposal out the door is often an extraordinary challenge — setting up and managing reviews, creating and executing multimedia productions, and ensuring timely delivery to wherever the proposal must go. And the job doesn't end with delivery. You may have to lead clarification efforts or coach oral presentations to help secure a win.

The proposal manager's responsibilities may differ from company to company, but a true proposal manager is game for any job that ensures a successful submission. To find out more about how to submit your proposal successfully, see Chapter 12.

Publishing: Making your proposal visible

Proposals need to stand out in a crowd (or on an evaluator's or decision maker's desk or desktop). That doesn't mean that you have to doll them up like the Griswold's house at Christmas. It does mean that you find ways to tell your story visually as well as in words.

TIP

Make your proposal *look like* your customer. Start with the cover. Put the customer's name and logo (if appropriate) in the first place they'll look (that is, the top-left corner for Western audiences). Create visual themes that complement your verbal themes. Carry those themes throughout the proposal. You can create accessible content by using professional layout techniques. Use white space to unite similar content and separate the rest. Use bold headings that let your readers scan your proposal to get a sense of the storyline.

REMEMBER

The writing techniques we discuss in the preceding section work even better when you illustrate them. Try to tell your story through graphics, refer to them in your text version of the information, and reinforce both with an *action caption* (that explains the relevance of the graphic) beneath the illustration.

You can find out more about creating eye-catching proposals in Chapter 11.

Proposing better all the time

The hallmark of a professional proposal writer or manager is a commitment to continual improvement. You can display that commitment in many ways:

>> Through the tools you create or acquire to reduce the mundane, tedious, or repetitive aspects of the job

>> By the manner in which you lead kickoff meetings, daily status checks, review sessions, and executive briefings (consider strategies for improving your leadership skills in Chapter 14)

>> Through the way you assess how well the process is working and how it affects your contributors

Our recommended proposal process includes continual improvement as its third and final stage. We make it part of the overall process for a reason: If you don't plan for it and make it a habit, it won't happen.

REMEMBER

Every time you work a proposal through your proposal process, you're going to learn something. For example, you may discover that

>> A process step is unnecessary in some situations.

>> A process step is ineffective as or where it stands.

>> A tool isn't getting the job done.

>> A contributor is more successful when doing something a different way.

Your job as a proposal professional is to offer opportunities for these lessons learned to be voiced, captured, and distributed to the right people to improve the process. You have to champion this effort, because most of your colleagues will, by necessity, go back to their regular roles after the proposal is completed and submitted. But you'll also have to work at it, because your next proposal is never more than minutes away.

You can find out more about harvesting and sharing lessons learned in Chapter 15.

Becoming More Professional

As a proposal writer, one of your best sources for improving your writing and management skills is the Association of Proposal Management Professionals (APMP). In Chapter 15, you find out about how APMP can help increase your professional status by providing educational opportunities, networking venues, a three-tier certification path, professional mentoring programs, and programs for building and sharing knowledge.

The APMP's Body of Knowledge (BoK) is the source for most of the information you find in the rest of this book, including the ten templates, worksheets, and checklists in Chapter 16. These are just a few of the many helpful tools available within the BoK. For even more, go to www.apmp.org.

TIP

Before you explore the rest of this book, here are a few things we want to plant in your head as you use this resource to help you build better proposals. These are the attributes of true proposal professionals, regardless of the size or makeup of an organization. These are the attributes we looked for when building our proposal teams. As you can see, proposal professionals are a special breed:

>> **Lead up, down, and sideways.** Proposal professionals must lead their teams, their peers, and even their bosses during a proposal project.

>> **Write like an angel and edit like the devil.** Proposal professionals hone their writing and editing skills more than all the other skills they use because what the proposal says is ultimately all that matters.

>> **See the forest *and* the trees.** Proposal professionals understand their company's overall business as well as the detailed techniques and processes of proposal development.

>> **Be a good cop and a bad cop all in one.** Proposal professionals, like project managers, do whatever it takes to coax the finest work from proposal contributors.

>> **Believe in the process, but know when to cast it aside.** No two proposal projects are the same, so a proposal professional has to know when to bend or even break the rules to succeed.

>> **Do what few can and fewer want to do.** Proposal professionals have a wide range of skills that, frankly, a lot of businesspeople either can't or won't learn. Doing what others can't or won't can make you indispensable.

>> **Listen twice as much as you talk.** Proposal professionals depend on others to get their jobs done. Understanding others' perspectives and needs is crucial to proposal leadership.

>> **Stay cool no matter what.** One clear differentiating characteristic of proposal professionals is their ability to accept and manage the stresses of urgent, important bids.

>> **Think three to five years ahead.** Technology paradigms shift in months, and successful proposal professionals are also futurists: They know technology trends and how those trends will affect their profession.

>> **Be a disciple of change.** Proposal professionals are change agents because customers are always changing what they want and how they want it.

How do you match up?

IN THIS CHAPTER

Delivering on a proposal request

Initiating a proactive proposal

Looking at the difference between small and large proposals

Creating proposals in different environments

Chapter 2

Understanding Different Types of Proposals

Business proposals come in two major flavors: *reactive* (or *solicited*) and *proactive* (or *unsolicited*). Reactive proposals, also known as RFP responses, are the way most mid- to large-size businesses acquire new products and services; these companies know precisely what they want and have the clout to formally ask suppliers to deliver on these requirements.

Proactive proposals can work for any size of business (some large companies run proactive campaigns for particular industry or solution sets) but are more suitable for midsize and smaller companies. Bidders write them on their own initiative with no guarantees that their efforts will succeed.

In this chapter, you discover the differences between these two major types of proposals and some other considerations that can complicate the primary differences. You also find out how to develop strategies and tactics for writing proposals in each situation.

Responding to a Request
for Proposal (RFP)

You write a solicited proposal when a prospective buyer formally requests solutions from you and a number of other bidders. This type of proposal is also known as a *reactive* proposal because you have to react and respond to the customer's topics and specifications rather than prescribe a solution in the manner you may prefer (see the section "Writing a Proactive Proposal," later in this chapter). Your goal with this type of proposal is to get "out in front" of the request — to be collaborating with the customer so you know when a problem is about to reach a breaking point and force the customer to seek a solution — and not be scrambling to pull together a response under duress. To win this type of bid, you need to know as much as possible about the customer as you can and as much about the specific opportunity before your competitors get wind of it.

REMEMBER

You normally write a reactive proposal in response to a *Request for Proposal (RFP)*. The RFP identifies the buyer's current problem and needs in specific terms and requires you to solve the problem in whole or in part. Think of an RFP as a game where the buyer sets all the rules. The buyer may already think you're the right company to solve its problem, but it may not be able to legally give you the business without you meeting the requirements of an RFP. You have to abide by the buyer's rules if you're going to win the business.

TIP

An RFP is sometimes known as an *Invitation to Tender (ITT)* or *Invitation to Bid (ITB)* depending on your location.

In the following sections, we take a look at the RFP, some of its sibling request types, and ways for you to stay ahead of the curve and play within the ever-changing rules of the game.

Joining the game: The invitation to bid

An RFP is an invitation to do business. Some are open invitations, posted publicly so any company can respond. Some are private invitations, sent to a select few providers. And some require that potential bidders prove their mettle by meeting strict requirements in a qualification step before being formally invited to submit a bid.

RFPs can be simple and small — a few pages that identify a need and ask for a solution in relatively broad terms — or they can be complex and large — hundreds of pages of precise requirements, often in the form of nested questions. Bidders must read the RFP carefully and be on the lookout for requirements meant to disqualify careless, would-be suppliers. Bidders must answer each question thoroughly, preferably in a consistent manner, and read between the lines to discover unstated requirements that can mean the difference between winning and losing the business.

REMEMBER

RFPs are not for the faint of heart. In some cases, they can mean future employment of participants or even the long-term viability of a company.

RFPs are the standard way of doing business for many industries for several reasons, including the following:

>> They establish a supportable and repeatable rigor for procurement.

>> They create tangible and comparable views of alternative approaches to solving a business's problems.

>> They quickly weed out the pretenders from the viable providers.

RFPs are a way of business life throughout the world. What was once a staple of doing business with only the largest companies and government entities is now a recognized standard throughout all industries and markets.

Sometimes, the RFP isn't the first stage of the process. You may need to work through a Request for Information (RFI) or a Request for Quote (RFQ) first. You may even find that you have to undergo a pre-qualification step before you can move forward. In the following sections, we outline these possibilities in more detail.

Understanding requests: RFPs, RFQs, and RFIs

As you gain experience in business development activities, you may run across some relatives of the RFP. Table 2-1 lists the different types of requests that potential customers may have, listed in the sequence they normally follow, and what they mean to you.

TABLE 2-1   **Common Types of Customer Requests**

Request Type	Situation
Request for Information (RFI)	A customer has an idea what it needs but seeks potential solutions from qualified suppliers. An RFI may later lead to an RFQ or RFP.
Request for Quote (RFQ)	A customer knows what it wants but seeks information about how a supplier would deliver the solution and how much it would cost.
Request for Proposal (RFP) or Invitation to Tender (ITT)	A customer doesn't know how to solve a problem. The RFP (or ITT) supplies detailed information so suppliers can offer viable solutions. The ITT is also referred to as an Invitation to Bid, or ITB. The RFP format may allow a bidder more flexibility in designing a solution.

TIP

We provide some examples to guide you — see the appendix for more information.

Narrowing the field: The infrequent pre-qualification step

Although some RFPs are open to all bidders, some companies whittle down the competition by requiring prospective bidders to fill out a pre-qualification form. These forms are usually questionnaires — some actually call them PQQs, or Pre-Qualification Questionnaires — but they come in a variety of sizes, formats, and structures, and you can count on them requiring the following:

>> Information about your company, including its size, location of offices, scope of resources, type of company, and how long you've been in business

>> References and evidence of how well you've performed on similar jobs in the past

>> Human resources data, such as minority ownership and sustainability programs

TIP

You need to always be ready to respond to qualification questionnaires, because they're gatekeeping devices designed to reduce the number of bidders and they tend to pop up at the most inconvenient times. If you respond quickly and thoroughly (and with the least amount of effort), it may offer you a competitive advantage — the less time you spend dealing with these pre-qualification forms, the more time you can spend crafting your solution and responding to the RFP itself. If you receive a lot of qualification questionnaires, consider building a customer-facing website that provides pre-approved, standard questions and answers. While your customer may not use the site, simply publishing the questions and answers will give you a legup on responding.

Following instructions: Compliance and the case for responsiveness

To win with your RFP response, you must comply with your customer's requirements. If you fudge, hedge, or dodge, you lose. It's that simple.

A compliant proposal is one that clearly and directly

>> Meets the customer's detailed requirements

>> Follows all the customer's submittal instructions

>> Answers the customer's questions

TIP

The most important aspect to responding to an RFP is that you carefully read it from beginning to end, note all statements and even hints of need, and build your proposal to clearly respond to every one of them.

To maximize your chances, you need to

>> Respond to and meet every requirement your customer identifies

>> Structure your proposal exactly as your customer instructs

>> Adhere to all the formatting and packaging guidelines that your customer specifies

>> Stay within the page limit your customer sets

>> Build a compliance matrix to show your customer where in your proposal you respond to a requirement (see Chapter 4 for how)

And then there's responsiveness. Being responsive does compliance one better. Responsive proposals address overarching goals, underlying concerns, and key issues and values that your customer may not spell out in its RFP.

TIP

Responsive proposals help customers achieve their business goals, not just their solution needs or procurement objectives. Examples of responsiveness include

>> Understanding and addressing your customer's stated and implied needs

>> Describing the benefits your customer will gain from your solution

>> Pricing your proposal within your customer's budget

>> Editing your response so it reads like your customer talks

REMEMBER

Your goal as a proposal writer is to comply with all your customer's requirements and express how your company goes beyond those requirements to help meet its business goals. Compliance alone won't win in an increasingly competitive marketplace. You have to work with your customer before the RFP is released to understand its *hot button*s. Hot buttons are singularly important issues or sets of issues that are likely to drive customer buying decisions. They're emotionally charged, and your customer will repeatedly bring them up because they inhibit success. You can think of hot buttons as benchmark issues — issues that ultimately determine whether the customer selects your solution. You must clearly address them in your proposal — and doing so is what we mean by going beyond compliance and being truly responsive. So while compliance can prevent your proposal from being immediately eliminated, responsiveness edges out your competition in the long run. For more about hot buttons, see Chapter 3.

Facing the third degree: The challenge of Q&A-style RFPs

Most RFPs consist of a series of questions that you must answer thoroughly while wrapping a story line or set of messages around the answers. A question-and-answer (Q&A) style of RFP provides specific directions on how to structure your response: You follow the organization of the RFP to the letter and answer each question one by one as it appears in the text. Deviating from this approach can cost you business.

Q&A-style RFPs often have short deadlines and are notoriously demanding. Procurement organizations and consultants use Q&A-style RFPs to develop line-by-line assessments for comparing each bidder's capabilities and solutions. Q&A-style RFPs not only ask many direct, compliance-oriented questions but also ask challenging, open-ended questions that you really can't answer satisfactorily without a consistent *win strategy*. A win strategy is the collection of tactics you use to help you win a specific opportunity — written and dispersed to everyone on the proposal team. Clearly defining your win strategy and its components ensures that your contributors consistently echo your main messages throughout your proposal.

To devise a consistent win strategy, you must understand the entire scope of the opportunity (which is why you read the RFP cover to cover) and be able to answer every question with an eye to how it relates to all your other answers. A win strategy is something you'll create early in your process for every opportunity (see Chapter 6 for a full discussion) and includes the following:

>> A succinct statement of your overall solution and benefits so all contributors think about your strategy as they write their answers.

>> Expressions of your solution's most important, overarching benefits (these are sometimes called *win themes* and must contain a need, a pain statement, a feature, a benefit, and a corresponding proof point). You need to echo your win themes at every opportunity within a proposal (see Chapters 6 and 7 for more on writing win themes).

>> Clear descriptions of your customer's hot buttons (those compelling reasons to buy). Including your customer's hot buttons in your win strategy ensures that you consistently address your customer's most pressing and emotionally charged issues. Check out the preceding section for more about hot buttons.

>> A *SWOT analysis* of your and your competitors' products and services (*SWOT* stands for strengths, weaknesses, opportunities, and threats). A SWOT analysis will help you align your solution with your customer's needs while evaluating how well you stack up against your competition (see Chapter 5 for more on SWOT).

>> Your company's *key discriminators*. These are the things that matter to the customer that you can do that your competition can't, or things you do better than your competition.

Win strategies are easier to create and implement when you know as much as possible about your customers, their needs, and your competitors *before* an RFP is released. If you've had a meaningful dialogue with your customers before they release an RFP, you have time to gather the right people, exchange knowledge about the customer's hot buttons and how you've solved similar problems, craft meaningful win themes by using that shared knowledge, and hit the ground running when the RFP is released.

WARNING

If you haven't talked with your customers, you have to do the same strategic preparation during the time you should be honing your response, and you'll be in what we call *reactive mode* — you'll be *reacting* to new information instead of *acting* to shape the outcome of the opportunity. Industry research bears this out: You win more when you start early.

TIP

GETTING AHEAD OF THE CURVE

So how do you stay ahead of the curve and avoid falling into reactive mode? A lot of this book is devoted to answering that question, but in brief, you should

- Find out as much about your customer as you can. See Chapters 3 and 4 for ways to do this, but the idea is to establish a relationship long before the customer releases an RFP.

- Create a comprehensive, repeatable process for responding to RFPs. Having a documented, proven approach for your responses gives you a better chance of assembling the resources and people you need to win. Chapter 15 offers ways of putting knowledge and resources on standby for a rapid response.

- Tailor your standard proposal processes to meet the deadlines and unique requirements of each opportunity. Chapter 6 also addresses this topic.

- Create a standard template for responding to RFPs. Your customer may require that you use its template, but often you have the liberty to plug in the customer's RFP within your response template, so you can distinguish your response from your competitors' responses through branding, textual, and visual elements. We have lots more about this in Chapter 11.

- Gather as much information about your likely competitors as you can, using insights from salespeople who have competed against them before. Chapters 5 and 7 help you do this.

The nearby sidebar "Getting ahead of the curve" points you in the direction of some useful advice for avoiding reactive mode.

To craft the ideal Q&A-style RFP response, you access all the information you need to answer your questions and then write a dazzling persuasive document around these answers. A customer's Q&A-style RFP can be daunting because of the sheer number of questions and their varying degrees of complexity. You need an efficient way to make your way through the questions. The following four sections break down this process into stages — from easiest to most complex and strategic — so you can take purposeful steps toward developing a complete, compliant, and responsive proposal.

Getting the easier questions out of the way

Answering a customer's questions properly is hard and tedious work, especially if you have hundreds to answer with a short turnaround. To be successful, you have to allocate to each only the time it warrants. To help you work your way through the questions successfully, use the following strategy to classify the questions by degree of importance and difficulty.

1. **Place the customer's questions into your proposal template so you'll have a familiar framework for responding while still adhering to the customer's prescribed structure.**

   Number the questions exactly as in the RFP. Create visual distinctions between sections, using descriptive headers, color schemes for contrasting between questions and answers, and theme statements so you can echo and highlight your win themes and your solution's benefits. Using a standard template will also let your contributors see the proposal take shape as the process unfolds (to access a sample reactive proposal [RFP] response template, see the appendix).

2. **Answer the easy questions first.**

   Identify the questions that you can address without too much noodle-baking (just worry about getting in the answers at this point; you'll fine-tune the content later).

   TIP

   If you aren't responding on your own to the RFP, assign "owners" to each question and a due date (see Chapter 14 for a method to track your assignments). Many questions will require subject matter experts to answer them.

   To identify and assemble your answers to the easy questions:

   - Scan through the questions.

   - Highlight those that you can answer easily and directly.

- Insert bullet points beneath the easy questions to collect ideas for your responses.

- In your first bullet point, state how you comply with the requirement, echoing the question's language as much as possible.

- In the next few bullet points, list the main ideas and themes that you want to express in the order of their importance to the reader.

- Follow that with a bullet entry identifying your proof points (*proof points* are facts that prove your claims: statistics, documentation, testimonials, and so on).

- If appropriate, include a bullet item describing any imagery you want to support your answer.

- Finish off your answer with a key takeaway or point statement for your reader.

TIP

TIP

Using this approach to assemble your answers anticipates our recommended four-part response model, which we explain fully in Chapter 9. You can review an annotated template for this response method in Chapter 13.

Make each answer stand on its own merits by stating supporting proofs within the response. As a rule, avoid cross-referencing. For example, instead of responding to a question about your financial stability with "see our attached annual report," provide the pertinent proof point in the body of your answer: "As proof of our financial stability, Standard & Poor's verifies that our company has had 20 consecutive profitable quarters. No other bidder can match this record of stability." This tactic does two important things: It helps you consistently echo win themes (such as financial stability) with specific proofs (20 profitable quarters) while making your response easier for readers to evaluate (no jumping to another part of the bid for proofs).

3. **Distinguish between the least and most important questions.**

   Run through the questions again to decide where your priorities lie:

   - Identify the questions that will have the most influence on the evaluators who assess and score your proposal. Set them aside for now because they will take more thought and effort.

   - Respond to questions of lesser importance by using the bullet point method that you used in Step 2.

   - Classify any question that directly relates to the customer's hot buttons or to your key discriminators as having high priority (for more on this, refer to the earlier section "Following instructions: Compliance and the case for responsiveness"). Your answers to these questions will usually require more research (or reliance on your subject matter experts) to craft your strongest proof points.

Working with more challenging questions

Time now to plan content for the difficult and most important questions that you identified in the preceding steps, such as those that directly relate to hot buttons.

A question may challenge you for several reasons. For example, it may

>> Be one you've never answered before

>> Require official documentation or other hard-to-find proof

>> Ask you to calculate or analyze some data

We recommend that you answer the difficult questions in reverse order of importance. Distinguish which of the difficult questions are less important than others, and take the following steps to deal with these questions:

1. **Approach the less important questions by using the bullet point approach outlined earlier in this section.**

   Refer to Step 2 in the preceding list in this section.

2. **Determine the most minimal response that complies with your customer's requirements.**

   Refer to the earlier section "Following instructions: Compliance and the case for responsiveness" for more information on what you can do to maximize compliance.

3. **Figure out how much time you need to get the minimal response.**

   Your minimal response can be one of only three possibilities: "We comply," "we do not comply," or "we partially comply." You may need to contact someone else for a definitive answer (for example, an engineer, a lawyer, or an executive), so quickly determine what expertise you need to fully answer the question, and either add the expert to your response team or email the expert (so you can get a written response). Send them the actual question from the RFP and a statement describing the context of your response and your win theme strategy. Ask the expert to reply by a specific date and time ("ASAP" is not specific!).

4. **Lock down your sources and finalize the content as early as possible.**

   No answer is final until you sufficiently explain *why* and *how* your solution is better than anyone else's on this particular requirement. *Never* simply say, "we comply" and leave it at that. Make the bullet point method from the previous section your mantra: Comply with the requirement, echo your win theme, provide concrete proofs for your claim, illustrate your solution if possible, and plant a key takeaway in your reader's mind. You can't do this unless you have sources who will supply the proofs and benefits, so locking down your sources, if they're not already part of your proposal team, is crucial.

TIP

You should spend 80 percent of your time and allocate 80 percent of your proposal's strategy on the important questions. This may sound obvious, but people tend to go all out on every response, and that approach simply won't work for Q&A-style RFP responses. It's why we recommend getting the easy and least important questions out of the way early and quickly. You have limited time and resources, and you must allocate them to the responses that will mean the most for a successful outcome.

Responding to the most important questions

After you've handled the less important of your challenging questions, use your win strategy (see the earlier section, "Facing the third degree: The challenge of Q&A-style RFPs") to build answers for the most important and strategic questions:

>> **Focus on determining levels of compliance.** A Q&A-style RFP will (usually) provide a numbered series of questions by categories identified through main and subheadings. Be on the lookout for *nested requirements* (one or more customer needs buried within the sentences that comprise a numbered question), signified by the verbs *will, must, should,* and *could*. Make sure you respond to each of these trigger words. To make sure you respond to them all, search for these terms by using the Find or Search function within your word-processing software.

>> **Highlight your key discriminators.** What makes your company the best-right choice in this particular matter? What do you offer that no competitor can or will? Highlight these attributes and tailor them to fit the specific question being asked.

>> **Establish how you understand the customer's needs, goals, and issues.** Keep your customer's hot buttons in mind as you respond. Every word you write should pertain to your customer's hot buttons and what your solution brings that others' don't.

For more on hot-button issues, refer to the earlier section "Following instructions: Compliance and the case for responsiveness."

>> **Illustrate your responses first, and then write what you see.** Sometimes proposal writers find it difficult to understand a highly technical or overly complex response provided by a subject matter expert. In these cases, a picture is not only worth a thousand words but can also launch a thousand words (well, hopefully not a thousand for a single response!). One way to get a clear description of a technical concept is to have a subject matter expert

sketch the steps making up a process or draw the components of a solution in relation to one another. Use this effective technique to get highly technical content from subject matter experts and then create a more professional version of the drawing for the proposal to make that content more accessible to less technical evaluators. Discover more about this technique in Chapter 11.

>> **Prove your assertions.** Demonstrate your capabilities and support your claims with brief, pertinent examples. If you've installed a similar solution recently, one having a similar or even greater scope, cite that experience and supply enough detail to ensure that the reader sees the similarities.

>> **Remember to be responsive.** Think hard about what you've learned about your customer through close reading of the RFP and visits with the customer. Echo the customer's own language to indicate your empathy and understanding.

Fine-tuning your responses into a narrative

Gathering the information for and drafting your answers may seem like the hard part, but turning thorough answers into effective responses and compiling them into a coherent and compelling proposal narrative is just as challenging and even more important.

Consider the following advice when writing your responses:

>> **Outline your content before finalizing it.** Before you start writing or ask others to write, build an outline to direct your response. In other words, think before you write!

- At the macro level, your customer's RFP structure supersedes your preferred proposal outline. Follow that structure to the letter unless the customer says otherwise. Still, many RFPs allow leeway in organizing some proposal sections (such as executive summaries, pricing sections, and reference sections), so prepare an overall outline to your response that adheres to the customer's structure and guides writers through the more flexible sections.

- Develop your outline within the first 24 to 72 hours, depending on your deadline. Share it immediately with your response team.

- At the micro level, populate the outline with visuals, bullet points, and notes. (You'll have accumulated this information as you gathered the relevant materials for your answers — refer to the earlier section, "Getting the easier questions out of the way.")

TIP

- Make your outline-in-progress available for stakeholders and management to review, amend, and approve. This way you'll quickly gain consensus on your strategy and raw content plan.

Assign every question to your writers (or yourself) with clear, firm deadlines for all content — answers, images, forms, and attachments.

TIP

Establish a systematic way for contributors to deliver content so you can keep track of what's been done and what hasn't and what needs to be revised or supplemented.

>> **Use lean and concise content.** Evaluators appreciate clear, factual, and concise content, even if they haven't set page restrictions. Remember that your bid is only one of many, so your most conscientious evaluators will be pressed for time. Also be aware that, based on their evaluation criteria, evaluators may be more interested in "checking the box" than in assessing the technical merits and details for responses to certain questions. So always aim to deliver the briefest yet most evocative content you can. This doesn't mean leaving out words to save space, cramming processes into jargon that only you can understand, and listing your points in interminable bullet lists. Tell your customer that you can do the work, how you'll do it, and why you think it matters.

For instance, evaluators may only care that you meet a particular quality standard, while quality processes may be something you think clearly differentiates you from your competitors. If you meet the standard and supply documented proof, you comply and that's that. Going on and on about your quality team and processes may not help your score.

If you need to make your quality capabilities a discriminator, respond to the question with a visual and a caption that relays your strategic message, but keep the text as short as possible.

>> **Immediately and directly answer every question.** The most important rule in Q&A-style responses is to ensure that the first sentence of every response directly answers the question. This rule isn't always easy to follow, especially if compliance isn't clear. But with a strong strategy and an understanding of which questions are the most important, you should be able to score well on the critical questions and establish enough separation between your company and others to remain competitive.

Following the advice outlined in this section, as well as using the steps in the preceding section to gather your raw data, will help you to continually improve your responses to Q&A-style RFPs.

SETTING YOURSELF FREE: THE JOY OF THE FREE-FORM RFP

Some RFPs are quite the opposite from the tight structure of the Q&A-style RFP. A free-form RFP describes a problem, asks for a solution, and sets a time frame for delivery, leaving you the freedom to structure your response to best represent your company's particular take on the solution. If you have a format that you've used successfully for proactive opportunities (see the section "Writing a Proactive Proposal" for more information), you may find that a free-form RFP is a cause for celebration. You can use the standard structure and any proactive material you have to quickly develop a response that is already custom-fitted for your strengths.

Use your own format for free-form RFPs, but look for any requirements in the RFP that limit your freedom, and by all means, err on the side of conservatism if you're in doubt as to what to do. The free-form structure doesn't necessarily supply a license to do whatever you want.

TIP

If you respond often to Q&A-style RFPs, we strongly recommend that you create an easy-access archive of strategy documents, templates, and reusable, pre-approved Q&A-based content that you can use to jump-start responses.

REMEMBER

Time is either your biggest enemy in RFP responses, or your best competitive advantage. If you have to start from scratch every time, you'll waste precious hours, even days, and put yourself at a competitive disadvantage. On the other hand, if you can draw from previous work you will have more time to adapt and customize rather than research and compose. Using your head start, you can consistently create more compliant and responsive proposals.

Writing a Proactive Proposal

We call the unsolicited proposal a *proactive* proposal because you undertake the work completely on your own initiative, with no guarantees that the buyer will even read it. A proactive proposal normally results from you or your sales representative discussing an unmet need or unsolved problem with a customer during a sales visit or over the phone. In the best cases, your customer contact is interested in your solution and ideally becomes your proposal coach or sponsor, advising you as you prepare your proposal. If you can get a customer executive to sponsor your proposal, your chances for success go up considerably. If you can connect the success of your proposal with the personal success of your sponsor, you have the perfect scenario.

But the best thing about proactive proposals is that they are non-competitive. You jointly discovered the problem with the customer, and you have an early, and likely unopposed, shot at solving it.

TIP

A proactive proposal is best built to a schema or blueprint that you can replicate for every opportunity and every customer. Training your customers to consider your argument in a certain structure is great for not only convincing them to buy from you but also building long-term customer relationships. Repeat readers know exactly where to go to find just what they're looking for, speeding their assessment process, just as reusing your proven structure speeds your development process.

REMEMBER

You may hear people refer to proactive proposals as white papers, analytical studies, feasibility reports, and advisories. They're also known as sales proposals, executive briefings, and letter proposals.

In the following sections, we look at four aspects of proactive proposals:

>> Gauging customer interest in your solution

>> Choosing the right strategy

>> Building themes from your customer's hot buttons

>> Following a standard, repeatable schema

Getting sponsored: The value of customer concern

Without a concerned or invested audience, preparing and submitting a proactive proposal has about the same probability of success as a mass or bulk mailing — near zero. However, your success rate for proactive proposals rises far above those for reactive proposals (your response to an RFP) when one or more of the following conditions are met:

>> One or more people who work for your customer, especially decision makers or influencers, have expressed interest in your proposal (these are potential sponsors).

>> You have confirmed your customer's hot buttons, and your sponsor has confirmed that addressing them in the proposal with your customer's decision makers and their influencers is appropriate (recall that hot buttons are those emotionally charged, key issues that compel your customers to buy).

>> The value of obtaining a prompt solution outweighs the cost of soliciting solutions from others and the savings that may come from competitive bids.

>> The customer's purchasing guidelines permit awards without competition. You should already know if this is the case through your preliminary fact-finding discussions with the customer (see Chapter 3), but as a rule, the smaller the company, the more flexible the purchasing guidelines.

Proactive proposals can also be a good, long-term sales strategy. Proactive proposals can improve your win probability on subsequent bids with the same customers because they

>> Create opportunities for building relationships with key decision makers

>> Demonstrate your ability to solve your customer's problems

>> Show that you truly understand the customer's business, almost as well as an employee

TIP

The higher up your sponsor, the better chance you have of selling a proactive proposal. An executive sponsor can introduce you to key subject matter experts and ensure through that introduction that you have an ally in the trenches.

The best proactive proposals are those where you have a *sponsor* — an insider in the company coaching you toward success. Gaining a sponsor — preferably a highly regarded voice in your customer's company — is like being on a date and having your date's best friend in your corner, pointing out your good traits, rationalizing your mistakes, and downplaying your inability to choose the right fork at a restaurant.

Supporting a strategy: The proposal as a means to your long-term goals

The overarching objective of a proactive proposal is to advance a sale. But to develop the most effective proactive proposal possible, you must define your objectives more precisely. Do you want to persuade your customer to

>> Agree to a subsequent meeting?

>> Issue (or not issue) a bid request?

>> Reconsider its purchasing process?

>> Enter negotiations without further competition?

>> Issue a purchase order?

Your specific objectives determine how you develop your proactive proposal. Here are two of the aforementioned scenarios and strategies for each:

>> If your objective is to persuade your customer to meet so that together you can qualify the opportunity, don't propose a complete solution. Your proposal should define the problem, create interest in solving it, and define your solution only to the extent that the customer knows it's feasible.

>> If your objective is to persuade your customer to forgo competitive bidding, focus your proposal on the cost of delayed implementation. Your proposal should clearly illustrate the amount of money the customer is losing each day, week, or month of inactivity, and suggest that delaying the decision may cause further damage and cost.

Building a win theme: Motivators, issues, and hot buttons

After your meeting with the customer, you'll know who will read and evaluate your proposal. With this knowledge, you create a win theme that matches the priorities of those key decision makers (for more on win themes, check out the earlier section "Facing the third degree: The challenge of Q&A-style RFPs").

A good win theme statement contains need, a pain statement, a feature, a benefit, and a corresponding proof point. While a good proposal has a single, overarching win theme, it can also have supporting win themes that reinforce other key messages and address multiple hot buttons. Here is an example of an overall win theme statement — a single sentence that summarizes the main message — and a supporting win theme:

>> **Main win theme statement:** "Our transaction monitoring software will reduce your online revenue losses from fraudulent charges by an average of 34 percent, based on installations similar to yours."

>> **Supporting win theme statement:** "Real-time notices integrated with our monitoring software relieve your card holders' concerns and reinforce your 'Always on Guard' brand messaging."

Win themes may be even more important in proactive proposals than in reactive ones, because proactive proposals are essentially narratives. A proactive proposal is a story: a story of how you (the hero) will save your customer (the person in peril) from the villain (the problem or need the customer faces). Narratives of all types — novels, screenplays, and, yes, proposals — need theme statements to consistently deliver key messages across multiple structural elements (chapters, scenes, and proposal sections). Creating win themes and corresponding theme statements is crucial to your proposal's coherence and its success.

You derive your win themes from three elements:

>> **Motivators:** These are things that compel your customer to act. They may be corporate (reduced costs or improved customer service) or personal (advancement by demonstrating thought leadership).

>> **Issues:** These are the things that worry your customer. They stem from the problem you discovered in meetings with your customer, such as potential out-of-service conditions or production delays.

>> **Hot buttons:** These are a combination of issues and motivators. Hot buttons are the singularly important issues that are likely to motivate your customer to act. (You can find out more about hot buttons in the earlier section "Facing the third degree: The challenges of Q&A-style RFPs" and even more in Chapter 3.)

TIP

In your proposal, cite the origin of your customer's hot buttons to provide context for evaluators other than your sponsor and your main contacts. If you found out about a critical need from the head of IT operations, say so. This will not only show unfamiliar readers that you clearly understand the present situation but also validate the theme statements that you sow now and again throughout the proposal.

Here's how you might set up your discussions of customer hot buttons:

>> In our recent meeting, you mentioned that your key requirements are . . .

>> In your quality circle, several workers complained of . . .

>> Acme Vice President Mary Jones recently said . . .

You want to echo your win theme throughout your proposal but especially in these sections:

>> **Transmittal letter:** Use here to grab attention!

>> **Executive summary:** Include here to reinforce the value of your proposal with decision makers.

>> **Recommendation:** Share here to address the *why* that supports the *what* and *how* of your solution. Win themes add "sticky" reminders of the pain and urgency related to factual descriptions and make the proofs more persuasive.

>> **Pricing:** Add here to reinforce your solution's overall benefits when your reader is evaluating the cost.

Organizing your proposal: A repeatable structure

Most proactive proposals are highly structured documents with standard major sections. You may find the following sections in a typical proactive proposal:

>> **Transmittal letter:** Every proposal needs a cover letter to introduce the proposal and associate it with the opportunity. It's also a good place to start selling your solution.

>> **Executive summary:** Aimed at executives with short attention spans, this section reduces the entire proposal to a single page.

>> **Current situation:** This section shows your reader that you've done your homework and that you understand the reader's business, industry issues, operations, and the needs or problems you're addressing with your proposal.

>> **Recommendation:** This section identifies your solution, explains how it works, describes the benefits of implementing it, and shows the future state after the solution is implemented.

>> **Pricing:** This section summarizes the cost of the solution with a particular focus on value and the rationale for choosing this solution over others.

>> **Implementation plan:** This section clearly depicts who will do what and when. This is sometimes referred to as the statement of work, or SOW.

>> **Qualifications:** Sometimes referred to as the "Why Choose Us" section, this provides brief bios or résumés of the people working to design and install the solution and provide support after installation. Use this section to express the advantages of doing business with your company.

>> **Next steps:** This section launches the project, pushes for a contract if necessary, or expresses follow-up actions for the customer and solution provider.

You don't have to follow this structure, but you should aim to establish a repeatable model, or *schema*, for all your proactive proposals, so a customer who receives a second, third, and fourth proposal — even if they're for different solutions and months apart — knows what to expect and where to find what they seek. This way you're subtly training readers to conform their way of thinking about proposals with yours.

TIP

Persuading others to get on board can be difficult, even when they've already expressed interest. In the nearby sidebar "Persuading your readers: A lesson from antiquity," we look at some timeless persuasion tips that help you to sell your proposal. Check out Chapter 10 for more techniques for writing persuasive proposals.

PERSUADING YOUR READERS: A LESSON FROM ANTIQUITY

A proposal is a written argument — the good kind of argument, not the issue-avoiding, mud-slinging nonsense of modern political debates. It's an appeal to get someone to agree with you, coupled with an offer to partner with you to solve that person's problem.

Okay, a brief history lesson to set up some practical takeaways. Aristotle (yep, the old philosopher who suffered from some of that same political nonsense) noted three elements of persuasive arguments: *logos* (the appeal to the audience's reasoning ability), *ethos* (the appeal to the ethics or integrity of the audience), and *pathos* (the appeal to the audience's emotions). And although Aristotle argued orally thousands of years ago, his methods still work for those of us who write to persuade.

You can use Aristotle's fundamental elements of persuasive writing in your proactive proposals (and for that matter, your reactive ones, too). The following table provides some questions you can ask yourself and your colleagues to ensure that you're using these elements in all your proposals.

Element	Questions
Logos (logical appeal)	Have we clearly explained the rationale for change?
	Do we help them see the potential benefit to their organization?
	Do we provide demonstrable proofs for our claims that are meaningful to them?
Ethos (ethical appeal)	Do we give insights and examples that show we understand their organization and business?
	Do we give them reasons to think we are trustworthy?
	Do we show how ours is a true win-win solution?
Pathos (emotional appeal)	Have we expressed the consequences of not acting in monetary and operational terms?
	Do we describe the current problem or conditions in a way that they can feel the pain their employees feel?

Whatever proposal structure you use — one of your own design, a standard schema (such as the proactive proposal structure described in the section "Organizing your proposal: A repeatable structure"), or one required by the customer — make sure your content includes some or all of these elements of persuasive arguments.

WARNING

If your customer contact requests a particular proposal organization, make sure that you understand the structure and that you comply with the request! Ignoring instructions or requests projects a noncompliant, arrogant tone.

Comparing Small and Large Proposals

As you work through this book, you find that the proposal techniques we recommend work on all types and sizes of proposals — responding to small or large opportunities is simply a matter of scale. But all our recommendations hinge on one key principle: If you initiate business through proposals, you need a repeatable, end-to-end process for developing business opportunities — from identifying and selecting appropriate opportunities to developing solutions and the proposals that describe and sell those solutions.

Your business development process should be in place long before you write the opening words to either a proactive or reactive proposal, and your proposal development process should be a distinct stage of the business development process. But not every step in your proposal process is needed or even feasible in every instance, based on the size, scope, and value of the opportunity.

With this in mind, we review some of the unique situations that can influence how you adjust your standard business development and proposal processes to meet the needs of your opportunity (depending on the industry you work in and the markets you target).

Scaling the process: Modifying to meet the opportunity

The key to scaling the process you use for a given opportunity is knowing your audience's expectations. Every industry has its traditions and special requirements. All governments have their own set of rules. For example, United States procurements are governed by FAR, or Federal Acquisition Regulations. Even commercial opportunities may take on complex and rigid requirements, especially those managed by consultants.

You need a flexible proposal process — you may call it an *accordion process* — that expands like the bellows to encompass every possible preparation step and contracts to fit within the tightest of deadline time frames. Otherwise, you can't hope to create a proposal capable of winning every time. Here's how you can create such a process to accommodate opportunities of different sizes and degrees of complexity.

Starting with your most comprehensive process

The best approach is to start big and work down. For your largest, most complex opportunities, you need a master process with each step broken into stages and each resource mapped to the required deliverable or outcome. If you build a comprehensive process for your largest opportunity, you'll have every possible step available for every less complex, smaller opportunity you encounter — then you merely pick and choose what's right for each project. Chapter 6 goes into much more detail if you need it, and if your process must be even more rigorous, you can always check out the techniques in *Project Management For Dummies,* 4th Edition, by Stanley E. Portny (Wiley).

Looking at the due date and working backward

A deadline for an RFP response is just what it says: You cross the line, and you're dead (well, your opportunity is, and you may be out of a job). Your timeline is always at the mercy of the customer's deadline. An RFP states a firm deadline — for example, "Your proposal is due on (date) at (time, usually including the time zone, such as GMT) at (address)."

TIP

Sometimes a customer extends the due date if a bidder or number of bidders request more time to respond, but you can't count on it, even in the government segments where it's much more common — and you *never* want to be the bidder who asks for more time.

A proactive proposal also has a deadline — it's the time within which your customer expects you to offer a solution to the problem it may not have known it had until you brought it up. If it's an urgent problem, you may have a shorter deadline.

TIP

If you're the salesperson who discovered the problem and you have to write your own proposals, you can create a reasonable time frame for getting something in writing to your customer. If you're a proposal writer working on a proactive proposal with an anxious salesperson, you may be more under the gun than with an RFP response.

REMEMBER

Whatever the situation, the plan is the same: Start at the end and work backward. Consider the following list of development questions to help you decide which ones are relevant to your opportunity and talk them over with your salesperson or proposal team, or, if you're a salesperson writing the proposal yourself, use them as a mental checklist to ensure that you get the proposal out on time:

>> When is the proposal due?

>> How much time will you need to deliver the proposal?

- » How much time will you need to print and package the proposal and related media?

- » How much time will you need to proof the final copy?

- » How much time will you need to assess comments and revise the content?

- » How complex and time-consuming will your reviews be?

- » How many review cycles will you need?

- » How long will your solution designers need to develop the solution?

- » How long will you need to assemble your team to develop the solution?

- » How long will your team need to assess requirements?

- » How long will management need to assess the opportunity and decide to bid?

- » How long will you need to analyze the RFP and assign work?

- » How long will you need to read the RFP and build your work plan?

TIP

As with the list of project stages in the preceding section, you won't have to address all these questions on every engagement (indeed, some are RFP-specific, as you can see). Run through them all on the first few proposals you work on, and they'll become second nature to you. These questions should be comprehensive enough to get you through any opportunity you face.

Constraining yourself: Overcoming the challenge of limited content

Having more steps in your process to consider than you have time for is just one of the challenges you face as a proposal writer. Along with time constraints, customers often set limits to the amount of content allowed in an RFP response. For instance, they may set specific page limits for executive summaries and past performance entries, and total page limits for volumes and entire responses. Automated response platforms may even set character limits by answer or section to eliminate long-winded sales pitches. And as for proactive proposals, this is the age of limited attention spans, so being long-winded is not a prescription for success. Your best strategy in all circumstances is to limit your content on your own.

TIP

Less is definitely more when it comes to content. Evaluators want a direct response to their questions: Full of meat, short on fluff. Consider creating a strict response model for all your content. Base even your proactive proposal content on responses to general and specific questions you know that your customers may have about your solutions.

Constrain the answers to these general and specific questions on a tight authoring model. You can use the following steps and the accompanying examples as a guide:

1. **Start with a clear, short compliance statement.**

"We understand and comply with your requirement for three independent quality checks during the installation period."

2. **Offer a brief answer to the question.**

"Our installation process already includes two internal quality checks — one at the midpoint and the second at the end of the process — so adding a third and opening them up to an independent assessor will be easy, although we will need to add a new interval to our timeline to comply."

3. **Provide a description of method or example of proof.**

"As you see in the flow diagram, we can easily insert a third checkpoint either at equipment drop date or during offline testing. Again, the degree of testing you require will dictate the increase in overall implementation time."

4. **Confirm the key takeaway message.**

"Our flexible implementation process helps ensure your complete satisfaction with our solution. This flexibility extends beyond installation to system support."

5. **Use graphics instead of words.**

For example, you may be able to customize the standard process flow diagram to show callouts at the optional checkpoints proposed by the bidder.

TIP

Consider setting limits to the number of characters for each of your responses before you write or assign writers to work on the proposal. You may still have to whittle down your content to meet a strict customer's specification, but using a tight writing model sets you well on your way to the clearest, most direct depiction of your solution.

Understanding Procurement: The Differences Among Segments

Every industry has unique requirements for proposals, both reactive and proactive (and some outright refuse to accept proactive proposals). Depending on the size of your customer's business, you may be dealing with procurement departments that govern what and how that company buys products and services.

Depending on the segment, you may have strict published rules and regulations to follow. For instance, before you consider bidding on a government procurement, be sure you understand acquisition rules and regulations. Most government proposals must follow a strict organization and response methodology, wherever you are in the world. You must adhere to the rules or you'll find yourself eliminated from the contest. Or you may just be dealing with the preferences of individuals in key positions. The following sections provide a brief guide to some of the more prominent segments you may encounter.

Going global: Developing proposals outside your region

Global procurements teams, including public sector and large commercial organizations that frequently make large purchases, also follow a rules-driven process. All buyers want to make the evaluation process easier. Forcing standardized responses helps achieve this goal, whichever region you're looking toward.

Play by the rules

Bid requests issued as part of a formal, rules-driven purchasing process normally advise and guide bidders on the structure they should follow. Some rules are industry-specific. In the United Kingdom and Europe, for example, PAS 75 provides detailed lists of headings for pre-qualification questions for bidders in the construction industry. Although rules are not standardized across legislatures, you can expect procurements to be transparent and fair, with some type of bidder instructions provided. Some U.K. government agencies now offer detailed guidance that makes forming a content plan easy but meeting page counts difficult.

Understand the subtleties

Depending on current political trends, bidding and partnering with companies based in multiple countries can be perceived either positively or negatively by international audiences. If you're responsible for assembling a multinational response team, you need to keep up with current political scenarios and understand how they relate to your company, your home country, and the opportunity at hand.

TIP

When writing proposals for customers in different countries, pay special attention to proposal instructions, local customs, and audience expectations in terms of language, paper size, binder size, media production and playback capabilities, and actual delivery methods and time frames. Also consider the customs requirements and legalities surrounding information and technology export restrictions.

Be(a)ware of cultural differences

Cultural awareness is especially critical when doing business in different countries, so be sure to research your customer's traditions before you make an unintentional faux pas that may undermine a bid.

Closely consider your customer's use of color, imagery, metaphors, and tone to avoid miscommunication or a worse offense. For example, when submitting a proposal to a South African company, know that red can be associated with mourning. When proposing a solution to any country's military, avoid photographs of another government's soldiers (unless they are obviously relevant to the proposed solution).

REMEMBER

Keep in mind that the cultures of readers in other countries shape their communication styles, just as your culture shapes yours. Neither style is inherently wrong or right, but failing to adjust your style to match that of your readers may build a barrier that the best technical solution can't overcome.

TIP

Find out as much as you can about your audience's expectations and culture to prevent miscommunication. Check to see what, if any, style guidelines your employer recommends from a branding perspective. See if your company style guide includes lists of prohibited words and phrases that put vendors at risk. If not, create one as you prepare your first proposals for customers in other countries.

Going green: Electronic versus print

In recent years, commercial and government buyers have inclined toward running greener procurements, requiring that bidders submit proposals and follow-up documentation and discussions electronically. Procuring organizations use a variety of platforms and methods.

Examine the areas on the submission platform carefully and ask questions if you're unsure about where to place documents and proposal artifacts. Leave plenty of time in your schedule for

>> Converting word-processing files to PDF format

>> Consolidating documents based on platform requirements

>> Pasting individual answers into database fields

For electronic submissions, allow extra time for uploading your content:

>> Avoid waiting until the last minute, because uploading usually takes longer than you anticipate.

>> Remember that your competitors are uploading along with you, and capacity and network issues can affect the system's performance at crunch time.

>> Upload any documents that you consider final "as is" (for instance, standard policies and certificates) days or even weeks in advance to reduce work as the deadline looms.

>> Get the required signatures on documents early on because you need to scan them, or convert them to PDF files, before submitting them.

REMEMBER

Electronic proposals can also present a challenge because the system may restrict content precisely. Your responses must be tight, to the point, and with clear, direct proofs. Your ability to use persuasive techniques, even graphic depictions, may be limited or excluded. The goal of most of these systems is to turn your products and services into mere commodities, where price is prince and value a pauper. Use every communicative technique allowed to gain a competitive advantage wherever possible. (Turn to the earlier section "Constraining yourself: Overcoming the challenge of limited content" to find some tips for maximizing your word count.)

2 Focusing on Your Customer

Find out why a proposal is all about your customer and not about you. Acquire tactics for creating a strong business connection, not just a customer-vendor agreement, and see how you can turn that connection into a long-term, mutually beneficial relationship. Use your customer's words to help cement that relationship.

Understand the difference between complying with your customer's requirements and truly responding to its needs. Practice shredding a Request for Proposal (RFP) to ensure that you address every customer need. Discover how to read between the lines of a customer's RFP to identify its unstated needs.

Scope out the competition with research tips, analysis techniques, and tools that help you shine a light on their weaknesses while subtly touting your strengths.

IN THIS CHAPTER

Tailoring your proposals to your customers

Engaging with your customers

Managing the relationship with your customers

Chapter 3

Building Customer Relationships

Customers, no matter who or where they are, tend to behave in predictable ways: They choose to work with other people and companies that they know, like, and trust. In certain markets, like in governments, your customers have to follow closely monitored procurement regulations, evaluate you against specific formal criteria, and even publish the results for the world to see. But despite these constraints, if they know, like, and trust you, they'll figure out a way to pick you over other businesses. Conversely, if they don't know, like, and trust you, they'll figure out a way not to pick you.

As you begin the process of writing your proposal, keep this mantra firmly in mind: Your proposal is not about you — it's about your customers. It looks like them. It sounds like them. It follows their line of thinking. It reflects the relationship you have with them. Therefore, you need to get to know your customers long before you deliver your proposals, and you continue to develop your relationship with them long after they've read the last sentences or crunched the last numbers.

In this chapter, we help you establish and enhance relationships with your customers, use those relationships to create more persuasive and effective proposals, and use those proposals to continually improve relationships with your customers so they'll know, like, and trust you better than they do your competition.

Getting to Know Your Customers

Quick — off the top of your head — what's the most important part of a proposal or Request for Proposal (RFP) response? The executive summary? You may say that because the broadest audience of evaluators and decision makers will almost certainly read it. How about the pricing section? You'd be right to suspect that some readers will bypass the rest of your proposal for a close look at the bottom line (don't you hate it when they do that?).

And guess what — both viewpoints are right. Both sections are critical for your proposal's success but not necessarily for the reasons you may think. As important as your solution and numbers are, they're less important than how your customers perceive you and your company. If you're going to propose anything beyond a simple commodity, your customers' decision-making process may come down to how well they like doing business with you and how much they trust you.

REMEMBER

As a proposal writer, you may or may not be responsible for the customer relationship, but you are responsible for how that relationship is represented in the proposal.

The following sections explore how you win over your customers — how you craft your proposal to show that you understand their needs and how their business works. We also introduce some useful questions that you can ask to tailor your approach to your customers and to help you discover their deeper business needs.

Getting real: Your customer's business is your business

Every proposal writer has to find out as much as possible about the customer — its business, decision makers, and all the evaluators and influencers who will assess your proposal. You can do this by asking questions. If you personally know the customer through sales visits, you can get answers directly. If you don't get to meet with the customer, you have to get someone else to ask for you and then give you the answers.

TIP

Don't assume that the customer contact knows the answers to your questions. Although many of the questions are basic sales questions, some salespeople don't know to ask them. Some salespeople will tell you that the answers aren't important, but understand this: If you don't get the answers you need and get them into your proposal, your proposal will fail.

Getting a customer to agree to accept a proposal is like asking someone to go on a first date. You have to ask a lot of questions before you know whether your date is someone you want to start a relationship with. It works the same way with a business relationship. You have to

>> Set up the sales meeting (ask for the date)

>> Figure out how the customer's business operates (ask what your date likes to do)

>> Identify the customer's business goals (ask where your date wants to go)

>> Uncover the customer's problems and needs (ask what your date dislikes)

>> Determine when changes are needed (ask when your date needs to be back home)

>> Offer to develop a proposal (ask for a second date)

You need to have a good relationship with someone before you decide to propose marriage — and before that someone may consider accepting your proposal. Business is similar. An unsolicited proposal to a company you don't know well will fall on deaf ears almost all of the time.

You may be thinking, "So you're saying there's a chance . . ." — yes, but it's a slim chance. Your unsolicited proposal has about as much a chance as someone walking up to a complete stranger at a bar and proposing marriage. The result: at best, an incredulous laugh, and at worst, a slap in the face. And that's about what you can expect from submitting a proposal that a customer hasn't asked for or isn't expecting.

Starting right: Asking opening questions

You've asked for the sales meeting. How do you prepare for that meeting with the end game in mind? The process is twofold, even if you're both the customer contact and the writer of the proposal.

Table 3-1 contains two sets of questions. In the left column are ten starter questions that you (or your sales rep) need to ask your customer to start the conversation, move the discussion to a meaningful dialogue about the customer's needs and your abilities, and set up an opportunity to develop a relationship and ultimately propose a solution and close a sale.

TABLE 3-1   **Asking Your Customer Some Initial Questions**

What the Salesperson Asks the Customer	What You Ask the Salesperson
What markets do you serve or want to serve?	Are our services available in this market?
	What prior solutions can we reference?
What are you trying to achieve, short term?	Do our solutions match the customer's immediate goals?
What are your long-term goals?	Do our strategic goals align with those of the customer?
How do you operate your business today?	What insights can we bring from working with other customers in this business?
	Do we have resources that understand this customer's operations?
What operations problems concern you?	Can we describe these problems in the customer's language?
	Can we prioritize these problems for the customer?
When and how do these problems occur?	Can we raise FUD from these issues? (FUD is proposal-writer shorthand for *fear*, *uncertainty*, and *doubt*. These are the kinds of pain points that can turn problems and needs into *hot buttons* — emotional reasons to buy.)
	Do we have experience solving these kinds of problems?
	What are the financial repercussions?
What have you done to remedy the situation?	Can we ghost this approach? (See Chapter 5.) How can we improve upon this remedy?
Who do you do business with today?	What do we know about this competitor?
	Have we performed a SWOT* analysis? (See Chapter 5.)
	Can we ghost this competitor? (See Chapter 5.)
Is your current provider solving problems as quickly and effectively as you would like?	Do our assets indicate we can respond faster than the incumbent? If so, how specifically and to what degree can we improve on the incumbent's performance?
When can we meet again?	How fast can we build a preliminary assessment of the prospect's situation and follow up with a proposal?

Strengths, Weaknesses, Opportunities, Threats

Getting answers to the questions in the left-hand column prompts you to assess the potential of having a relationship with this customer. The right-hand column then lists the questions that your proposal writer (or the proposal writer in you) will need answers for if you're going to take the relationship to the next level.

Digging deeper: Understanding the needs of your readers

While a salesperson is normally concerned with understanding the customer's business needs, a proposal writer needs to know this information, too, plus some additional information to help build a proposal that meets the individual communication needs of all readers within the customer's organization. To get this extra detail, you need to dig a little deeper into the personalities and preferences of the proposal decision makers and evaluators. (Yeah, more questions.)

The process for writing any sales, financial, marketing, or technical document (a proposal is a unique blend of all of these) begins with a comprehensive analysis of your readers. Knowing your readers (rarely just one, mostly many) affects what you say and how you say it. If you're a salesperson, you have the greatest insight into your readers — hopefully you've spoken to the decision maker and any influencers multiple times. If you're a proposal writer who doesn't get out much, you have to get that information from your salesperson. If you're sending your proposal out cold, you'll have to research your customer through third-party sources to find out all you can about who'll be reading your proposal.

Regardless of your situation, the questions in Table 3-2 can help you to discover all you can about the person or people who'll read your proposal, evaluate your offer, and decide whether to accept or reject it.

TIP

Some proposals are oral presentations, but they're usually supported by some kind of presentation slideware. The reader analysis questions in Table 3-2 can easily apply to presentation audiences as well as readers.

TABLE 3-2   **Reader Analysis Questionnaire**

Question	Comments	Strategy
Who is your decision maker?	This is the person or persons most likely to have the final say about your offer.	Use the words and anecdotes you heard this audience use to describe the current needs and the pain suffered. Address the kinds of problems that keep leaders awake at night (such as market share and top-line revenues).
Who are the influencers?	These are the people who help the decision maker make the final decision — the technical staff, finance team, or selection committee.	Think about all the voices that weigh in on the decision and design content elements to address their concerns. Include features and specifications for the technical staff and ROI (return on investment) for the finance team.

(continued)

TABLE 3-2 *(continued)*

Question	Comments	Strategy
What is each reader's level of education?	This determines the balance of text and visual material you supply. For multiple audiences, make sure your text and visual elements can stand on their own.	Opt for more text the higher a reader's education and technical knowledge; opt for more visuals the lower a reader's education and the higher the reader's level in the company (time issue).
What is each reader's level of technical expertise?	This tells you what technical terms you can use and whether you'll need to explain concepts.	If your primary audience is non-technical but has technical advisors, write your body text to the non-technical reader and supply technical details in a sidebar or appendix.
What is each reader's professional experience?	This tells you how much background material and detail you need to supply.	Provide a brief summary of the need and move directly to the recommendation; provide needs, pain points, features, and benefits within your recommendation.
What is each reader's familiarity with the subject?	This tells you whether you'll need to explain the reasons for the proposal.	If your reader is your decision maker and familiar with the subject, quickly remind him or her of the need that prompts the proposal and outline your solution and costs. If your reader is less familiar, fully explain your understanding of the situation and review alternatives before presenting your solution.
What are each reader's expectations?	This helps you anticipate resistance by one or more readers up the chain of command.	This is where you can use a technique or argument to address any issues you know your advocates will expect and your adversaries may throw at you. You can place these under a separate heading in your current situation/problem section.
How enthusiastic is each reader about the project?	This determines the priority your readers will place on reading your proposal.	The less enthusiastic your reader, the greater the need to create a good executive summary that spells out current and future pains and the costs of not acting. You need vivid pain statements to capture your reader's attention.
What is each reader's urgency for finding a solution?	This relates directly to costs — the losses mounting through inactivity versus the cost of fixing the problem.	Highlight costs in the transmittal letter and the executive summary. Provide graphic proofs of payback period, ROI, and bottom line improvements, if possible.
What is each reader's reading environment?	This determines how you package and lay out your proposal to simplify evaluation.	Include a compliance matrix if not already required by an RFP. Consider a separate executive summary so decision makers can read in parallel with technical evaluators.
What do your readers need to do or understand?	This helps you facilitate faster action by your readers.	Make any customer actions, such as implementation considerations and leasing/buying issues, clear and actionable. Make sure you highlight this content and clearly indicate who will do what.

Table 3-2 doesn't list all the questions you need to ask to understand your customer, but it's a great reference that has helped fledgling and seasoned writers customize their proposals to better speak to their customers. Combined with the information your salesperson gathered from the questions in Table 3-1, these questions help you build a strong foundation for establishing a relationship that can lead to a winning proposal.

Winning customers: It's all about them

Before you hand over the proposal, you need to understand some principles of customer relationships and how they translate into successful proposal elements. If you want your customer to know, like, and trust you, you have to master — and genuinely demonstrate — these principles in your customer interactions and especially in your written proposals.

We don't tell you how to talk business to your customers; that's not our job here. The next few sections do, however, help you take what you hear and say at a customer visit and turn that information into content that reinforces the relationship you build with your customer.

Make the message about them

The first principle for getting your customers to know, like, and trust you bears repeating: Your message has to be all about them, not about you. This is especially true of proposals. Many proposal writers — often at the insistence of their own organizations — create self-centered documents. They reflect the branding, colors, and public personas of their business, not their customers' business. As a result, their proposals all look and sound the same, regardless of the customer.

Customers prefer that the proposals they receive be customized for their needs. They want to believe that each proposal they receive has never been submitted to another company because no other company is like theirs. Rightly so, they believe that no other company shares their distinctive business approach, their unparalleled products, or their unique set of problems. Think about it: If they were like other companies, why would they be in business? So this first principle surpasses all others: A proposal is a one-of-a-kind, customer-focused message.

What does this mean in practical terms? Here are three key ideas to keep in mind:

>> **Place yourself in a subordinate position to your customer.** Many companies emblazon their proposals with their corporate logos, colors, and imagery. They see proposals as another marketing tool for the

masses, like a corporate website or a brochure on steroids. But they're not — proposals are customized sales messages that have to persuade individual customers to pony up their hard-earned funds to buy something from you. One way to show that you care about your customer is to place your branding in a position subordinate to its branding — for instance, in the bottom-right corner of the proposal cover and in footers instead of headers on pages. Using your customer's logo, brand colors, and imagery in superior positions sends a not-so-subtle message that it's all about them.

WARNING

If you decide to use your customer's logo and other brand indicators, make sure you ask permission before you display this copyrighted information. Never disrespect a customer's branding.

>> **Accurately describe your customer's current environment.** Another great way to show your customers that you care is to do your homework about their business. Start by researching industry challenges. For a medical office, that may mean patient privacy concerns or rising fraud claims. For a university, that may mean campus security or cost-control efforts. Knowing your customer's business thoroughly is a great way to instill confidence that you've got its best interests at heart. And much of that knowledge is just an Internet search, an annual report, or a trade magazine article away. Your self-education in your customer's business reaps great benefits when you get your face-to-face meeting and get the customer's personal story about the business.

>> **Go easy on the boilerplate.** *Boilerplate* is reusable content that explains products, company histories, and even solutions in generic marketing terms. Nothing screams, "I don't really care about you and your problems" like boilerplate that's all about your company, your products, and generalized situations where those products can supposedly help.

WARNING

True, boilerplate saves time and repetitive work, and it often contains content that's appropriate for many different proposals. But you must always customize any boilerplate you use to fit your customer's unique situation.

TIP

Apply this approach to any communications with your customers — whether emails, sales letters, or brochures. Keep the boilerplate text to a minimum and tailor it effectively each time.

You can find out more about writing to meet your customers' requirements in Chapter 10.

Echo your customer's needs

As you talk with your customer initially, or as you debrief your company's rep who talks with your customer, you'll hear unique descriptions about what the customer's business needs to improve to achieve specific outcomes. These are the cornerstones to a great customer-focused proposal. Being able to convince your customer that you understand industry issues and individual needs gets you well down the road to winning your customer's trust.

TIP

You can do this in part by accurately echoing your customer's words in your proposal. One proven technique is to reference those face-to-face meetings in your description of the current situation, using a phrase like, "In our meetings with your department heads, they told us. . . ." You fill in the blanks with the actual words your customer uses to describe the problem or situation. So, if the procurement manager uses the phrase "herding cats" when she describes her efforts to manage vendors, use it as you describe her problem. For example, you'd say, "In our talk with your procurement manager, she told us that managing vendors is like herding cats." If the CFO (chief financial officer) says, "the revenue we lose because of these disruptions is like a slow leak in the pipes," you can work that phrase into your description of the current situation as follows: "We met with your CFO, Ms. Spalding, and she said, 'the revenue we lose because of these disruptions is like a slow leak in the pipes.'"

TIP

Your customers may respond even better if, along with describing needs in their own words, you also display empathy. Being subtle is key. You don't need to say, "We know how you feel" or "We feel your pain." Save those empty clichés for sympathy cards.

You can show true empathy for your customers' needs in two main ways:

>> **Describe the pain associated with the need.** A major part of every proposal is describing the needs or problems that are prompting your proposal. As you talk about a need or problem, provide details about the pain it causes. For example, use a quote from a worker to spell out the pain caused by a tracking system, such as "I waste four hours a week checking and manually revising the automated reports." By merely expressing the need or problem in terms of the pain it causes, you show you truly do know how it feels.

>> **Discuss possible approaches to ending the pain.** When you say that you have the only solution to a problem, you may instill doubt rather than confidence. First off, it sounds arrogant. And remember, your goal is to make the customer like you. Take some time to acknowledge alternate solutions — state them, but then refute them. This is a classic, effective argument technique dating back to the ancient Greeks. Explain why the other solutions won't work at all (or as well) in the customer's environment. This tactic helps you to build trust because it shows that you're not trying to sell a solution but rather trying to solve a problem.

Push your customer's hot buttons

Hot buttons are the singularly important issues or groups of issues that compel customers to buy a product or service (refer to Chapter 2 for more details on hot buttons). You can tell a customer's hot buttons because they come up repeatedly in conversations and usually relate to persistent issues or problems that inhibit the success of the business.

You derive your customer's hot buttons from two sources:

>> **Motivators:** What your customer is trying to achieve short term to realize a long-range vision. For example, a car dealership may be trying to streamline its inventory procedures to become the volume leader for its region.

>> **Issues:** The things that your customer is worried about. They may stem from an existing problem or be driven by an upcoming revenue or operational opportunity. To continue with the car dealership example, imagine that updates to the inventory database haven't occurred in real time, leading to confusion, repetitive work, and angry customers (who thought they'd found their dream car, only to discover it had been sold out from under them).

TIP

You express a hot button by combining a motivator and pertinent issue. For example:

> You need to streamline your inventory process and modernize your new- and used-car database before you can hope to compete for top sales in the region. Yet database latency has slowed your progress and caused nightmares, literally and figuratively. And your fears are well founded; you actually had one salesperson almost come to blows with another by selling the same car twice. Any solution must eliminate the latency and ensure that your inventory is up-to-date all the time.

TIP

Before you express a hot button, you must have validated the motivators and issues with the customer's representatives or your customer sponsor (refer to Chapter 2 for more on getting a sponsor).

Focus on benefits, not features

Want to turn off a prospective buyer? Provide an exhaustive list of your product or solution's features. Customers care less about the discrete features of your products and more about what those features can do to solve their business problems.

REMEMBER

Don't get us wrong: Features are important. They may reach a loftier status if a customer sees them as providing an advantage over a competitor's similar features, but they still take a back seat to the tangible benefits a customer will realize from your solution. Features are the *what* of your solution; benefits are the *so-what*.

Table 3-3 shows the differences between a couple of products, a key feature of each, and their respective benefits. One example's pretty commonplace, while the other is more high-tech.

TABLE 3-3   **Product Features versus Product Feature Benefits**

Product	Feature	Feature's Benefit
Alarm clock	Automatic time setting	Adjusts from standard to daylight savings time so you don't have to manually reset it.
Fiber network	Quick turn-up interval	You're back in business 60 percent faster than if you stay with your current provider.

We go into greater depth about the relationship among needs, features, and benefits in Chapter 9, but the examples in Table 3-3 help to show you the big differences between features and benefits. In the meantime, just hang on to this concept: Features do things, while benefits are the things of value that result.

TIP

Technical gurus love to read the technical specs and thrive on feature lists, but they're the minority, and they rarely make final decisions on proposals. Give them their features, but don't let those features get in the way of your real story — the business benefits that your solution brings to your customer.

Differentiate your offer from all others

What makes your company or your offer different, and better, than your competitors' offering? Consider the following questions:

>> Is it your world-class product line?

>> Is it your form-fits-function design?

>> Is it your unmatched customer support?

REMEMBER

Proposal writers call the things that you bring to a customer that your competition can't your *key discriminators*, the features of your offer that differentiate you from the competition and that the customer acknowledges as delivering a benefit.

Although these three examples can be effective key discriminators if you back them up with proof, the most effective key discriminators have more to do with the way you behave than what your products do. For instance, how quickly do you respond to requests for information? Do you deliver on time every time? Can your customer trust that you'll always stand behind your product because you have every time there's been the slightest glitch?

Think about how your customers will feel if you tout "unmatched support" as a key discriminator, yet you take two days to call them back, deflect blame for any problems, and hedge when answering a question about the contract. You're not walking the walk.

If you listen to your customers' concerns, repeat those concerns so they know that you get it, and work hard to solve their problems based on what you've heard, they'll see how you behave and grow to trust that you'll continue to deliver on your promises, no matter what the issue.

Here are some examples of how this approach may work for you in a proposal:

>> **Your key discriminator is unmatched customer support.** Tell a story in your executive summary about a similar situation when you and your company went far beyond the terms of a contract to ensure customer satisfaction. Add repeat references to that story in your implementation plan or statement of work. Tack a reference to your story in the pricing section of your proposal to reinforce ongoing value.

>> **Your key discriminator is your dedicated account team.** Create a list that covers each team member and provide complete and up-to-date contact information to close out your proposal. Identify the chain of command within the account team, with contact information for all escalations.

Use discriminators the right way

In any competitive situation, you try to set yourself apart from your competition in ways that are truly meaningful to your customer. In the earlier section "Focus on benefits, not features," you discover the power of benefits over features. Now, think of a positive *discriminator* as a benefit that only you can rightfully claim.

In your proposals, you need to echo your discriminators in every interaction, and these discriminators should be significant enough that your customer can use them alone as a justification for selecting your solution over all others. So if features are the *what,* and benefits are the *so-what,* your positive discriminators are the *why us.*

When determining your discriminators, always look at things through the customer's eyes. All too often, companies fall into the trap of drinking their own marketing Kool-Aid, believing that what they offer is unique simply because "we're so-and-so brand." Relying on your brand as a discriminator is a common mistake in proposal writing.

REMEMBER

No one else can offer a solution with your logo on it, but that alone is never a benefit. And though your past performance may support your claim, the way you've applied your people, processes, and tools to successful customer engagements are your discriminators, not your brand.

The discriminator *sweet spot* is where your customer's needs, your competitors' capabilities, and your own capabilities intersect. It's the perfect combination of factors or qualities to achieve a goal. An example would be a customer needing a one-hour response time for repairs: You offer that and your competitors don't. Chapter 7 looks at positive discriminators and the sweet spot in more detail.

Discriminators lie in the single segment where you offer something that no one else does, and that something matters to the buyer. No other set of conditions fully qualifies as a discriminator. However, you can convert a feature that both you and a competitor have to a discriminator by offering a benefit around it that's unique to your business.

Consider the example of the fiber network turn-up feature in Table 3-3. The benefit read: "You're back in business 60 percent faster than if you stay with your current provider." You can turn that benefit into a key discriminator — if installation interval is truly an overriding concern of your customer's and if only you can deliver the solution that quickly — by boldly declaring, "No other provider can deliver this solution as quickly because no other provider has a node on its fiber ring so near your campus."

Handling Customer Engagement: Your Sales Process

The principles discussed so far in this chapter are crucial for getting your customers to know, like, and trust you. But they don't work unless you apply them often and consistently, preferably within a strategic, end-to-end plan for capturing, winning, and retaining business. Some professionals refer to this as the *business development lifecycle*. That's a fancy name for *sales process*. Good proposal writers prefer simplicity; go with the simple term.

Before diving in, take a look at Figure 3-1.

REMEMBER

A key goal of any sales person or team is to advance a business opportunity and move from an unknown position toward being in a favored position from the customer's perspective. Advancing an opportunity through these sales stages helps to move an organization in the market to a known position. That term *favored* is the kind of term business developers use. Replace *favored* with *known, liked, and trusted.*

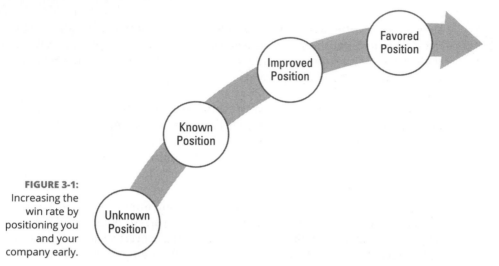

FIGURE 3-1:
Increasing the
win rate by
positioning you
and your
company early.

Source: APMP Body of Knowledge

Don't let the formal language throw you off. A formal sales process is just a systematic approach for handling customer engagement from start to finish. It works whether your customer is the largest of corporations with offices around the globe or a small retail shop around the corner. You just have to tailor your sales process to fit your opportunity.

Figure 3-2 shows the eight stages of the sales process. As with Figure 3-1, don't let this chart overwhelm you. As in all proposal-related matters, you have to scale sales processes like this through your personal filter. Not all these stages apply in every situation, so look at them in relation to a real proposal opportunity so you can assess what's right for you in any given situation. Discipline at each of these stages improves win rates and leads to repeatable processes that help you win again and again.

TIP

Writing a proposal is one stage in the sales process. Some may say it's not even the most important. We believe that every other stage in the process either leads to a proposal or sustains work initiated by a proposal. But then again, we write proposals! With this relationship between the proposal process and the sales process in mind, take another quick glance at Figure 3-2 and then turn to the three-stage proposal process in Chapter 6. You can see that the proposal process aligns with the overarching sales process beginning in Stage 3 (opportunity assessment) and extending beyond proposal submission into Stage 7 (negotiation) and even further into Stage 8.

The following sections take a look at each of the eight stages in more detail.

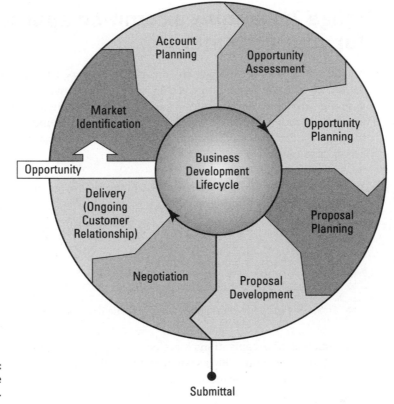

FIGURE 3-2:
The eight-stage
sales process.

Source: APMP Body of Knowledge

Stage 1: Finding the right market

The sales process starts before a proposal is even a glint in your eye. To have a successful business, you must decide on the markets you intend to pursue and penetrate. Doing the upfront work during this stage helps you to ensure that you spend marketing dollars and resources on the most profitable business targets.

Still, what you learn about your markets in this phase is very important to the success of your proposals. Insights into the way the market works and its key players drive bid/no-bid decisions on RFPs, and the industry issues you uncover can help flesh out your descriptions of current situations.

TIP

Constantly assess and re-evaluate your markets, identifying new market segments and validating current markets. Whether to enter a specific market is a key *decision gate* (a point in a process where you decide to go on or stop) at this phase of the sales process.

Stage 2: Planning a common approach for your accounts

An *account* can be a prospective customer, an existing customer, an entire organization, or a single buying unit within a large company. Account planning is an ongoing activity across the sales process, requiring adjustments as opportunities progress through the sales pipeline or as new opportunities arise. This stage includes marketing activities that position you in the market and with specific target customers.

You can easily see the value that account planning brings to a proposal because it contains information on the account's

>> History

>> Buying patterns and budget cycles

>> Executives, decision makers, and influencers

>> Strategies for penetrating or growing a particular customer

Many successful organizations store account-planning data in a customer relationship management (CRM) system and keep data up-to-date so proposal writers like you can get information for analyzing readers and understanding earlier successes and failures. If you don't have access to a CRM system, consider building a database or even a spreadsheet to keep this information.

Stage 3: Identifying and qualifying your opportunities

This is the stage where you or your leadership makes a key, proposal-related decision: the preliminary bid/no-bid verdict on a specific opportunity. This decision is heavily influenced by decisions made during the two prior stages, because strategic planning and market positioning (and segmentation) can often dictate how you identify opportunities and put them into the sales pipeline. Your situation will be unique to your company's approach and any systems or software that you use.

Qualifying your opportunities — that is, determining whether opportunities have a good chance of paying off — is a key stage for improving the win rate of your proposals. If you fail to adequately qualify your opportunities, you're likely to overspend on your marketing and sales budgets and pursue too many opportunities that you have a low probability of winning. This dilutes your response resources: Desperate companies divert resources from more winnable deals and from delivery of projects that may lead to renewals. A good way to avoid this scenario is to ask a few strategic questions about a potential opportunity:

>> Who is the incumbent, and how has it performed?

>> Who are the known competitors, and may others be behind the scenes?

>> Can you win and still make money?

>> Do you need to team up with another organization?

>> Will bidding for this opportunity better position you for future opportunities?

>> Does this opportunity fit within your strategic plan and vision?

Assessing your competitors' strengths and weaknesses as they relate to an opportunity is critical during this stage. You discover more about assessing your competition in Chapter 5.

Stage 4: Planning for every opportunity

Opportunity planning — that is, the process of preparing a plan specific to an opportunity and identifying actions and strategies to position your company to be the customer's preferred provider — starts early in the lifecycle and continues through proposal submission. This planning process involves working closely with customers to understand their needs and issues. Its output is an opportunity strategy, which will feed into your proposal plan.

You can remember the key components of opportunity planning by the mnemonic "the 4Cs and P":

>> **Customers:** Continue to work with your customers so you know and understand their situation, needs, hot buttons, issues, and biases.

>> **Competition:** Thoroughly analyze your competitors — especially the incumbent. Are you at a competitive advantage or disadvantage? Might the customer decide to do nothing, spend money on other things, or do the work in-house?

>> **Cost:** Analyze the opportunity and decide on the price that will win. As you gain more information, adjust the price as needed.

>> **Contemplation:** Take a hard look at how your customer will perceive your solution, how you've done on similar projects in the past, how the opportunity will affect your reputation if you lose, and the risks you're willing to take to win.

>> **Portfolio:** Look at all your opportunities and treat each one like an investment. Prioritize them according to the resources that each opportunity will require and how the ROI of each one compares with the probability that you'll win it.

TIP

You may be thinking that opportunity planning is pretty much everything discussed in the earlier section "Getting to Know Your Customers"; if so, you're right. What your salesperson finds out during this time is pivotal to your work, which begins formally in the next stage.

Stage 5: Developing your proposal plan

Inserting your proposal planning process into your company's sales process saves your company time, resources, and money. It also saves you time in the final stages of proposal preparation (not to mention aggravation, headaches, heartburn, and maybe even your sanity!). There's a reason the proposal writer's standard dinner is cold pizza (and sometimes breakfast, too).

REMEMBER

Before the bid request or proposal opportunity arrives, you need to prepare a proposal plan focused on five activities. You need this plan to cover the customer's issues and needs (that you identified during your opportunity planning; refer to the preceding section) in your proposal:

>> Move data from the opportunity plan to the proposal plan (or to proposal planning tools, if you have them).

>> Draft a proposal strategy based on your opportunity strategy. A *proposal strategy* states your company's stance on the opportunity and how it plans to make each point in its proposal. Document the strategy by drafting an executive summary.

>> Refine your solution and the price-to-win from Stage 4 (refer to the preceding section).

>> Engage the right resources for the proposal team and secure executive support.

>> Host a proposal kickoff meeting to share your plan with the proposal team.

The kickoff meeting is a good time to review, validate, and suggest improvements to the proposal strategy. While you have all the experts together, have them review the technical, management, and pricing solution against the customer's needs and requirements. This is also a good time to check how it aligns with your opportunity strategy and to appraise your competitive focus. We work you through a kickoff meeting in Chapter 6.

TIP

Keep a close eye on the solution while you're in this phase. The proposal has to describe the solution, and you want to continually update your content about the solution as your colleagues make their inevitable changes to your proposal plan.

Stage 6: Writing your proposal

It's your turn to shine. At some point, the opportunity will become an active proposal project, either reactive or proactive (refer to Chapter 2). The planning documents you prepared in Stage 5 (refer to the preceding section) now become working proposal development documents. During this stage, the strategy and solution should be set in concrete. Everyone needs to be on board. The proposal schedule should be untouchable.

WARNING

Ongoing changes waste time and resources and most certainly lead to a mediocre proposal.

Luckily, you have at your disposal a variety of tools and techniques to keep things on track. During this stage, you implement compliance matrixes (see Chapter 4), response assignment checklists (see Chapter 8), and reviews to ensure that your contributors are meeting the proposal requirements. You use communication tools to validate progress, troubleshoot proposal content, and address concerns. You invoke short check-in calls or meetings to monitor progress and to ensure that you meet your schedule's milestones.

Then you set up reviews, and, depending on your situation, you can go as light (a substantive review followed by a proofreading) or as heavy (with multistaged reviews and executive sign-offs) as your proposal requires. See Chapter 6 for details on how to manage reviews of all types and when to schedule them.

You may think that when the proposal is published and submitted, you're done. Ha! Gotcha! A proposal writer is never done (at least it seems that way).

Stage 7: Negotiating and closing the deal

Submitting a proposal doesn't signal the end of the sales process. During this stage, business decisions become intense and more real. We know that you think your proposal was perfect, but now it's time for your customers to ask their questions, such as the following:

>> What did you mean by that?

>> Is that the best price you can offer?

>> Where is the part about warranties?

These questions can go on and on. You may have to modify your proposal to answer them all. You may have to help prepare final revisions, follow-up presentations, or any further documents the customer needs to decide on a provider.

During this stage, your company needs to refine its opportunity plan information and keep to a simple strategy by

>> Responding fully to customer questions and concerns

>> Reinforcing the customer's trust in your solution and organization

>> Optimizing the deal to the benefit of bidder and customer

TIP

What else can you do during this time (if another opportunity hasn't come in already)? Consider hosting a *lessons-learned review*. Document the things you did right and not-so-right. Add the good things to your processes. Discuss how to improve and adjust your processes accordingly. Contact people who struggled to meet deadlines and fell short of expectations, and ask what you can do to help on future opportunities. Store what you found out during your account planning (in Stage 2) for others to access and reference for future opportunities.

Stage 8: Sustaining the relationship

Effective sales processes continue after your solution has been sold and delivered. Winning the contract is an opportunity to prove your value and position your organization for subsequent opportunities. This stage is so important that it deserves its own section (which we provide next).

Managing Customer Relationships

After you've archived your winning proposal, documented and discussed the lessons learned, and reaped whatever reusable knowledge you can from the engagement, it's time for the proposal writer to move on to the next proposal. If you're the salesperson or the sole proprietor, now comes the task of managing the customer for life (you can hope it lasts that long). This is the daily responsibility of the main customer contact. And this responsibility is where the real work begins.

You won your customer over with your charm, but you need to keep listening, meeting its needs and solving its problems (if possible, it helps to anticipate those needs and problems too). You need to stay in frequent contact. And when you do get in touch, you'd better COMMUNICATE effectively (all caps intended).

This last point reminds us of Edmond Rostand's play *Cyrano de Bergerac*. In the early stages, your proposal writer was your Cyrano — he wrote your proposals to the object of your desire (your prospective customer). Cyrano not only helped Christian win Roxane's favor, but he also continued to write letters to help him keep her. Is there something similar your Cyrano can do after helping you to secure your new customer?

As it was with Cyrano, your proposal writer's initial work is just the beginning of a comprehensive communication plan. Although executing effectively on a contract is the best way to position yourself for future business with a customer, managing the customer relationship is all about ongoing communication with the customer. That means regular visits to the customer, product demonstrations and upgrades, social marketing campaigns, and participation in relevant industry and trade events. Communicating these actions is something your proposal writer can do better than anyone else, mainly because of the work he's already done on the proposal.

TIP

Here are just a few ways that proposal writers can help maintain customer communications:

>> Create conceptual proposals for setting the stage for future proposals that relate to a recent winning proposal.

>> Write internal communications for your contact to sell ideas within the customer organization.

>> Establish customer-focused content for private extranet sites and social media messaging.

>> Produce executive-level communiqués that provide status on in-progress projects and forecast future needs that can result in more winning proposals.

These activities, to name just a few possibilities, demonstrate an ongoing interest in your customer's business and success and help to position you and your organization for future opportunities. And they're all things that a proposal writer can help you achieve.

IN THIS CHAPTER

Paying attention to your customers' expectations

Meeting your customers' requirements

Being responsive to your customers' needs

Chapter 4

Giving Your Customers What They Ask For (And More)

I n this chapter, we turn our attention almost exclusively to reactive proposals — those you write in response to a Request for Proposal (RFP; refer to Chapter 2). You'd think an RFP response would be as simple as asking for a date: They ask; you answer. But that's hardly the case. A lot of history, emotion, and anxiety exist between the asking and the answering.

This chapter provides strategies and techniques for responding to the varying degrees of complexity you may encounter. You discover how to avoid the pitfalls of complex and confusing customer instructions — giving you the *how* of your response. You also find tools to help you demonstrate that you can comply with your customers' needs — providing the *what* of your response. Lastly, you discover ways to go beyond the *how* and *what*, getting to the *why* behind the bid and demonstrating your responsiveness beyond that of your competitors.

Following Your Customers' Instructions

An RFP provides you with a formal way to discover what potential customers want, how they want it, and when they want it. You can think of an RFP as being like a prenuptial agreement. Your would-be spouse writes down everything he or she wants and you agree to all the "must-haves" as is. You may take exception to a few items on the "nice-to-haves" list and offer alternatives, but you do so at the risk of blowing the whole deal. Just as an incumbent may feel if a long-standing customer released an RFP for services it already provides, you may be offended if your true love puts such a document in front of you, but you may find it hard to stay in the relationship if you don't agree to the terms of the agreement.

TIP

Throughout this chapter, we refer to the customers' employees who read and assess the RFP responses that you and your competitors submit as "evaluators." They may be the decision maker(s), procurement professionals, technical specialists, or managers who run the departments affected by your proposed solution. They are a major audience for your proposal, and the more you know about them, the better you can craft your response to meet their needs.

REMEMBER

An RFP, like a prenuptial agreement, isn't a lot of fun for anyone (except maybe the lawyers). But it's an increasingly standard way to start and sustain a business relationship, even for small to midsize businesses. And some small-business RFPs are as stringent and challenging as those for the big kids. At times, you may scratch your head and wonder how customers can turn something as basic as "they ask; you answer" into something so difficult and frustrating, but such is the life of the proposal writer.

With an RFP, you're at the mercy of your customers, and some customers (and especially their consultants) have devised tricky ways to use the RFP as a way to weed out undesirables, test the mettle of even the most established providers, and squeeze every ounce of innovation and value from all bidders. And a few of them do a poor job of writing the RFP in the first place!

The key to success here is being able to follow directions — the *how* of doing business with your customers. The following sections look at the RFP in more detail and provide advice on staying in line with your customers' expectations.

Clearing the first hurdle: The proposal qualification questionnaire

As we note in Chapter 2, some businesses develop extensive questionnaires to make sure unqualified bidders don't waste their time by submitting RFP responses that they can't live up to. You may find yourself faced with such a Pre-Qualification

Questionnaire (PQQ) at some point, and you have to meet the requirements of this "mini-RFP" before you can expect an invitation to bid.

The following list contains topics from real-life questionnaires that a large telecommunications company had to respond to before being eligible to bid for an opportunity (think about it: All this information is required from an internationally valued brand before it can bid!):

>> Corporate information:

- History, experience, and financial condition

- Key personnel résumés

- List of corporate officers

- Legal issues (citations for violation of laws at any level, litigation, or breaches)

- Subcontractor due diligence

- Union affiliations

>> Corporate policies:

- Ethical code compliance

- HR policies (background checks, hiring procedures, and drug testing)

- Insurance coverage

- Quality management programs

- Risk management competency

- Safety policies

- Sustainability programs

>> DUNS number (Dun & Bradstreet 9-digit ID used in the United States and the European Union) and most recent rating/report

>> Government certifications

>> Security issues

- Business continuity and disaster recovery programs

- Information security (privacy policy)

- Network security (formal standards adherence, hardware, software, and redundancy)

- Physical security

How do you deal with such a broad list of ever-changing content and be ready to respond quickly with the least pain possible? Following are five approaches you can take to be ready for the PQQ (the more of these you do, the more prepared you are):

>> **Harvest prior responses.** You've probably used some of the information the questionnaires ask for in prior proposals. Take some time to review your proposals, especially around your corporate history, quality programs, security, and compliance with government agencies and policies.

>> **Create a network with content owners.** If you have HR specialists, reach out to them to access documented hiring policies, drug-testing programs, and other policies. Ask your business's IT specialists to share their approaches to data security and adherence to standards. Set a time, annually or biannually, to reconnect and note any changes that have been made to the documents or policies.

>> **Build and populate a standard résumé.** Work with your key personnel to create a consistent model for listing their qualifications, education, and experience. Ask your HR contact for your executives' résumés and bios. Work with project managers and lead engineers directly so you can highlight their skills to match the types of solutions customers seek.

>> **Capture and store seldom-changing content.** Some of this content, like your business's origins, never changes; some, like your financial results, changes annually or quarterly. Classify your content according to how frequently it changes and keep copies in clearly named folders on a server or on your PC. If your organization has a knowledge repository or SharePoint infrastructure, store it there so it's accessible to your colleagues.

>> **Ensure that you include any active certifications or registrations.** Sometimes you need to go digging for certain types of information (like the DUNS number). When you find them, document your sources (employee or title, website, internal document) and get the pertinent information (phone number, email, or URL) into your content repository so you can verify or update the information periodically.

TIP

If your industry uses PQQs, be prepared to respond quickly. PQQs come in all sizes and levels of complexity, so as we recommend with your *accordion proposal process* (that flexible, expandable, and contractible process we outline in Chapter 2), build your responses to prepare for the most comprehensive of questionnaires, so you can respond to any PQQ that may hit your desk.

Reading the instructions: Customers say the darnedest things

RFP response requirements cover a lot of ground and can affect how you put together your proposal in a variety of ways:

TIP

>> **Format requirements:** For digital or paper submissions, customers may request that you use a certain typeface and/or color to write your question-by-question responses. Or they may require you to respond in a spreadsheet with macros and limit your responses to numbers or other prescribed data formats. They may even prevent double-sided printing.

Government RFPs usually dictate the layout and even the format of headings.

>> **Packaging requirements:** Customers may ask that you place your printed proposal in a 5-inch, 3-ring white binder or place all your volumes in a box that you have to label a certain way and address to a particular person or office location. If the proposal is digital, you may have to submit as a single or multiple PDFs or in a specific package through a procurement system.

>> **Delivery requirements:** For printed proposals, customers may ask you to stamp one copy as "original" and the remaining copies as "duplicates." They most certainly include a "drop-dead" due date and time, which you miss at your own peril. For digital proposals, you may have to submit through email, through an online portal or tool, or through a file transfer service.

>> **Structural requirements:** Some customers may prevent you from including an executive summary or appendixes. Structural requirements usually dictate the precise sequence of your response.

>> **Content requirements:** You may be asked to limit the number of pages in your response or to submit your response in a certain digital format, like email or in PDF files. These requirements can be the most taxing, because they constrain how much space you can use to depict your solution and express your discriminators.

REMEMBER

Your job as proposal writer is to read each RFP thoroughly. Don't ever assume that someone else will (in fact, most busy salespeople and subject experts won't have time to read the entire RFP, only the parts that concern them directly). If you fail to find every requirement or fail to insist that the response team follows them to the letter, your business stands a good chance of being disqualified, and you may be held responsible.

RFP response requirements usually are listed in a section clearly marked at the beginning of the RFP. However, an RFP may place a requirement elsewhere in the RFP, to make sure you're paying attention. You can be certain to catch all hidden requirements by following the *shredding* techniques that we introduce in the later section "Shredding the RFP: Parse your way to compliance."

After you've scrutinized the RFP for all submission requirements, make sure they're in your compliance matrix and review them with your proposal team. Everyone on the team needs to know and understand the customer's expectations.

Managing questions: When the RFP is unclear

In many procurements, customers define a period after they've released an RFP in which bidders may submit questions about it. Customers benefit when bidders fully understand their requirements, and they understand that their requirements may be a little vague (after all, they're seeking expertise to solve a problem they can't solve on their own). Giving bidders a chance to ask clarifying questions can benefit all bidders while improving the customers' odds of solving its problem. Customers may also hold a bidders' conference to kick off the procurement, where all invited bidders can ask questions and the customer can clarify issues with everyone present.

The customer sets the degree of formality to the question-and-answer process. Always anticipate that your organization will have questions to submit, even if you thought you understood the customer, and the requirements, before the RFP was released.

Never underestimate the importance of a customer's question-and-answer process or the skill required to manage it effectively. Failure to pay attention to this process undercuts your chances of winning and weakens your team's ability to take advantage of a strong, customer-focused, competitively intelligent win strategy (for more on win strategies, turn to Chapter 2).

Aim to limit your questions to those topics and issues that may prevent you from submitting a fully compliant proposal, and follow all these best practices for managing this critical situation:

>> **Assign a single point of contact to submit questions and receive responses.** You want to ensure that your customer sends and receives consistent information during the procurement.

TIP

Assign a backup to help out in a crunch.

>> **Be aware of deadlines for questions and answers, and don't procrastinate.** Many RFPs set deadlines for receiving bidders' questions; after the deadline, no further questions are accepted. Some RFPs schedule anticipated dates for releasing answers. In other cases, customers set up question-and-answer calls for bidders to anonymously ask questions. In any case, take note of when answers will be provided so you can include these dates in your proposal schedule (see Chapter 8).

TIP

>> **Be quick to collect, log, edit, submit, and track your questions.** Often, customers seek to respond to batches of questions — that is, your questions and those of other vendors — together. In other cases, it's "first come, first served." Getting your questions in early — especially your important questions — may provide you with a competitive advantage.

Track your competitors' questions as well as yours with a customer question tracker. To access our example customer question tracker, see the appendix.

>> **Engage your entire organization to create and review questions.** Proposals are an organization-wide commitment — everyone has a stake in understanding the solicitation process and the technical and business risks involved. Even a well-written RFP may require clarification.

TIP

As soon as you receive the RFP, encourage your technical and business specialists to review it and to submit questions. For major proposals, schedule meetings with the entire proposal team to build your question list.

>> **Cite the specific section of the RFP and the wording you need clarified for each question you submit.** To help the customer understand the context of your question, be specific. For example:

> Instead of asking: "What does 'a reasonable amount of time' mean in Section 2.3?" Ask: "In Section 2.3, 'Challenge Tasks,' Item c, you state that a vendor would lose points for failing to 'complete the challenge course in a reasonable amount of time.' Can you specify the time interval?"

>> **Ask questions, using your customer's preferred terms or generic language.** Using your customer's language to craft your questions demonstrates customer awareness and focus. It also reduces the risk of identifying your organization if you want to remain anonymous or avoid revealing a new and critical technology to competitors. Avoid including your organization's name or your product's names in questions, and avoid "testing the waters" on a solution that goes beyond compliance.

>> **Keep questions short and on point.** Try to ask only one question at a time. A question with multiple parts may indicate your lack of understanding of the customer's needs, or it may be seen as an attempt to alter a requirement.

>> **Don't ask questions just because you can.** More questions mean more work for your customer. Let your customers know ahead of the question due date that you don't have questions. This allows them to focus on other matters.

The question-and-answer process is sometimes highly formalized and highly constrained, sometimes informal and open. Sometimes customers share questions and their answers with all bidders. Sometimes they answer each bidder individually, and you'll never know what another bidder has asked. You need to know upfront whether they do or don't share your questions with other bidders, so you can be careful about what you ask. Remember that questions you ask may provide clues about your solution, and if they're shared with your competition, they may be able to ghost your solution better. In general, assume that all bidders will see all questions, and pose them accordingly.

WARNING

The questions you ask can provide your competitors with clues about your strategies and tactics (and vice versa).

Between the release and submission of the RFP, your ability to contact your *sponsors* (strong influencers on the decision maker, friendly toward your business, with a stake in the outcome) may be constrained. Before anyone contacts your insider sponsor, make sure the customer allows any communications outside of the formalized bid process (you'll probably find that information somewhere in the RFP). For more on customer sponsors, refer to Chapter 2.

WARNING

Ask questions to discover information, not to instruct or manipulate. Never use questions to challenge — overtly or subtly — what the customers want to acquire or how they should determine the best product or service.

TIP

Customers send and receive most question submittals today through email. Take care to see that the more conversational tone of email doesn't open the door for imprecise or impolitic language. Keep your language clear, positive, and professional at all times, regardless of the medium.

Complying with Your Customers' Requirements

The preceding sections consider following your customers' instructions concerning *how* to bid. In this section, we tackle customer requirements: the specific *whats* that can solve their problems.

Winning a proposal is possible, in most cases, only if you fully comply with your customers' requests. For every question your customers ask, you have to

>> Declare that you understand and comply with the request.

>> Describe how you can meet each need and solve each problem.

>> Express the benefit and value of every aspect of your solution.

This is the rigor of the RFP response, and we dive deep into how to write these responses in the coming chapters. But it all starts with capturing your customers' requirements in one place. We call this the *compliance matrix*. The compliance matrix is a table that lists all the requirements you glean from the RFP and provides an indication as to whether you comply with them or not. It's a great tool for communicating at a glance how well you meet your customers' needs.

The compliance matrix is a product of identifying all the requirements from the RFP — a process we call "shredding." It is a vital part of your response process, and can keep you from missing key requirements that can instantly disqualify you. The following sections cover how you shred your RFP, how to avoid being disqualified instantly, and how you move on to create your compliance matrix.

Shredding the RFP: Parse your way to compliance

REMEMBER

Proposal writers call the process of reading the RFP closely and documenting customers' requirements *shredding*. Shredding can be an arduous — yet crucial — process because some customers nest their requirements deep within long paragraphs. Shredding is an appropriate metaphor, because you chop up the proposal — question by question, line by line, and even word by word — until you have a listing of every need, every want, and every wish you can find. You can then use that list to create your compliance matrix, which will help you decide how well you can respond and what information you need to gather to respond effectively.

When shredding an RFP, you must separate every requirement into individual entities so you can address them in your response. The comprehensive list not only allows you to assess how well you can comply with the customer's requirements but also provides a way for tracking your progress as you craft your responses.

TIP

Follow these steps to shred your customer's RFP and build your list of requirements.

1. **Convert the customer's RFP into a searchable, changeable format.**

   You may use your preference of word-processing or spreadsheet software.

2. **Create an entry for every topic heading in the RFP.**

   You may categorize content by volume, section, and so forth, based on the unique structure of the RFP. If the RFP is in a question-and-answer format, create an entry for every question.

3. **Search within each section and each question for the words *shall, will,* and *must*.**

   These are trigger words for buried requirements.

4. **Place each *shall, will,* and *must* phrase or sentence in a separate line beneath the section or question where you found it.**

5. **Set the requirements list aside for a period and then work through the RFP again to make sure you haven't missed anything.**

   Better still, have someone else repeat the process for you, if you have the resources.

TIP

Some RFPs come in PDF format, and you may need Adobe Acrobat Pro to convert the file to text that you can shred digitally. Some RFPs are still delivered on paper to control the number of issued documents, so you either have to scan those and shred digitally or shred the original by hand, copying each requirement onto a worksheet or typing into a spreadsheet or table.

Shredding the RFP offers the following benefits that can improve your chances of winning the bid:

» Provides you with a tool to clearly address each requirement and assign requirements to a subject matter expert in your in-house kickoff meeting

» Supplies a checklist to guide contributors on what content to include and exclude

» Enables internal reviewers to thoroughly assess the compliance of your proposal

» Simplifies updates if the customer amends the RFP

» Helps you rearrange content if you have to change the proposal outline

» Enables the proposal writer to effectively manage and follow up on responses from different stakeholders by creating accountability for each requirement

Resist the urge to save time by shredding RFP requirements only by section or paragraph. By lumping multiple requirements into the same row within your compliance matrix, you significantly increase the risk of inadvertently omitting a compliance element from your final proposal.

Watching out for gotchas: Instant disqualification

As you shred the RFP (refer to the preceding section), pay special attention to any requirements that you deem as disqualifiers. *Disqualifiers* are customer "must-haves" that can instantly eliminate you from winning the bid. If you don't fully comply with this type of requirement, the evaluator will read no further, regardless of your proposal's other merits.

Here's an example:

> Will this product or service be substantially produced in the European Union? (Yes or No)

This question can disqualify the bidder if the answer is no. Interestingly, the qualifier *substantially* isn't quantified, and the question's format allows no degree of compliance. These aspects of such questions are dead giveaways that the requirement is a disqualifier.

What if you don't have a plant or office in the EU? How do you deal with such a deal breaker? You have two choices:

>> **Verify the requirement.** During the question-and-answer period, ask whether this requirement is flexible. If not, refer to the next bullet point.

>> **Don't bid.** Don't waste yours or the customer's time and money on a bid that you'll be disqualified from on page 1 of the RFP.

But imagine that your boss, or your sales manager, says, "We bid, no matter what." Yes, sometimes the disqualifying requirement is dropped, but you know the odds of that happening — next to nil.

Sometimes, the hardest thing for a business to do is not bid on an attractive opportunity that it can never win. All seasoned proposal writers can share stories of the futility and frustration of knowing that the outcome of a huge amount of work will come to nothing. We discuss the *bid/no-bid decision* (a formal milestone in the proposal process that validates that you're properly positioned to win) at greater length in Chapter 6, but understand that this is one instance when you — the proposal writer — can carry a lot of clout in the decision-making process. Show the decision makers the bid requirement, verify that it's correct, and stand your ground for as long as you can.

Creating a compliance matrix: An annotated index of your response

A compliance matrix is a checklist both for you and for the evaluators to make sure you comply with all RFP requirements. You build this matrix from the list of requirements you shred from the RFP (refer to the earlier section "Shredding the RFP: Parse your way to compliance").

The compliance matrix also goes a long way toward preventing the big mistake that can sink an otherwise potential winning bid — the overlooked requirement. The compliance matrix, like the proposal outline, needs to precisely parallel the structure of the RFP. You develop the matrix in tandem with the proposal outline, before you begin content planning and writing. Building your compliance matrix at the end of the writing effort is like waiting until a house is built before drawing up the blueprints.

Proposal team members may fail to prepare a compliance matrix because they believe it takes too much time, but proposal writers and managers know better. Preparing a compliance matrix actually saves time by reducing mistakes and rework. A matrix helps teams visualize and break down requirements and gather them into bundles appropriate for different sets of stakeholders. Doing this helps a proposal lead follow up on everyone's assignments during daily stand-up reviews or status calls (for more on these project management techniques, see Chapter 14).

You can create your compliance matrix in a word-processing table or a spread-sheet, or even on a sheet of paper if your RFP is simple enough. The goal is to list every requirement, its source in the RFP, whether you comply (or to what degree), and a comment as to why you do or don't comply.

TIP

A compliance matrix can make the evaluators' task easier, so we strongly recommend that you include one in every response, even when one isn't specified. Evaluators have duties and responsibilities beyond reviewing yours and other vendors' proposals. A compliance matrix can save the evaluator time and may even generate a little goodwill.

A compliance matrix is simple to build and to use, but it takes a lot of thought. As you build yours, keep the following in mind.

Consider both stated and unstated needs

In an RFP, we classify needs into two major types: stated and unstated. *Stated needs* are requirements that a customer can readily express in an interview or through the RFP (for example, "We need ten nitrous oxide cylinders with automatic shut-off valves."). Stated needs clearly describe what you have to provide or do if you win the bid.

REMEMBER

Customers don't always set a clear requirement in their RFP when such requirements represent more of an emotional need or may be too difficult to express. Sometimes they don't even know that the underlying need exists. These are therefore *unstated needs*, and they play a huge role in responsiveness.

Understanding your customers' unstated needs is difficult work, but it becomes easier if they're already your customers (because you can meet with them, talk with them about their goals, and ask questions about anything that's hindering their progress toward those goals — and all those other questions from Chapter 3). If they're not already a customer, you have to read their RFPs thoroughly and ask clarifying questions if you're given that opportunity. If you're not, you have to guess.

TIP

We talk about how to "read between the RFP's lines" a little more when we discuss responsiveness in the section "Reading between the lines: The problem with unstated needs." We discuss the topic in even more detail when we work on crafting individual responses in Chapters 7 and 9. We bring the topic up now because we're talking about accounting for stated needs to ensure compliance. Part of that accounting process includes recognizing and addressing these unstated needs.

Prepare a compliance matrix for every bid request

The compliance matrix is a must-have planning document. Always create one, regardless of the bid size or timeline. Create it early in the planning process, before writing begins, and continually update it throughout the proposal process, especially anytime you

>> Receive amendments to the RFP (amendments can come anytime throughout the bid period, especially toward the end after all bidder questions have been reviewed by evaluators)

>> Get answers to your clarification questions (refer to the earlier section "Managing questions: When the RFP is unclear")

>> Change your proposal outline (because of a change in aspects of the solution by your company or a clarification by the customer)

If customers can see that your proposal is compliant, it indicates that you're experienced, professional, and easy to do business with.

Insert a version of the matrix in your response before the first section that references the RFP requirements. Sometimes, customers provide a compliance matrix of their own along with the RFP package. In these cases, keep in mind that the requirements listed are generally "must-haves."

Use your compliance matrix to keep your writing on track

While a compliance matrix helps evaluators judge your proposal and locate specific sections of the response, your team members can also use your compliance matrix in different ways:

» The proposal manager can use it as a content-planning document and tool for distributing requirements to the right people for costing, pricing, and responding.

» For the proposal team, the matrix becomes a checklist to ensure that all requirements are addressed.

» Writers can use the matrix as a guide for what they should write in each proposal section.

» Reviewers can use it as an evaluation tool to clearly define what should appear in each section.

» Management can use the matrix as a top-level view of the proposal progress and strategy.

Keep your compliance matrix simple and clear

Whether you use your compliance matrix as an evaluation tool, a development tool, or both, the simpler it is to follow, the more effective it is. You can build a matrix by simply following these steps:

1. **Create a table with four column headings — *RFP Reference, Requirement, Comply?,* and *Comment* — as you see in Figure 4-1.**

2. **Under *RFP Reference,* insert the section, subsection, paragraph, or question number from which the requirement is taken.**

   If the RFP isn't numbered, supply the page number where you can find the requirement and change the column heading to *Page Number* (instead of *RFP Reference*).

3. **Under *Requirement,* list the requirement statements from your shredded RFP (refer to the earlier section "Shredding the RFP: Parse your way to compliance").**

   Start each statement with an action verb (for example, "*Provide* a written escalation path" or "*Average* 99.99 percent uptime").

4. **Under *Comply?,* place a *Y* for yes and *N* for no.**

   You may use any other form of notation you choose, but *Y* and *N* are clearly understandable and sufficient.

   You may want to be more precise and include *F* for "Fully Comply" and *P* for "Partially Comply." Make sure you supply a legend if you take this approach.

5. **Use the *Comment* column to express any distinguishing value for a *Y* marking or mitigating information for an *N* marking.**

   See the later section "Reading between the lines: The problem with unstated needs" for more on this.

If you plan to extend your compliance matrix to provide guidance to writers (that is, to provide a topical proposal outline), you can include information such as the following:

>> Writer assignments

>> Section themes and strategies

>> Discriminators and *proof points* (facts that support your themes or verify your claims)

>> Key customer issues/hot buttons

>> Graphics

>> Pages allowed

>> Possible cross references

>> References to reusable content

See the appendix for access to a template that you can use to build and customize your own compliance matrix.

You have full freedom for how you lay out a compliance matrix, unless, of course, your customer prescribes a format. If you find no guidelines, do whatever you must to make your matrix as user-friendly for your evaluators and internal users as possible. For instance, if you have long, detailed requirements and you list your responses in separate columns, it can result in hard-to-read layouts. One way to work around this is to design a table that lines up the requirement in one row and the response in the row below and then to shade the response a different color than the requirement (see the partial sample in Figure 4-1).

RFP Reference	Comply?	Comment
Section 1.3.2	Y	See Past Performance Example 4 for more details on how the plan has worked for a similar need.
Requirement		Verify provider's software assurance plan meets contractual requirements.
Response		Our software quality assurance plan not only satisfies this requirement but exceeds ITIL standards with both financial and operational tracking.
Section 1.3.3	Y	
Requirement		Provide monthly reports that meet the following specifications:

FIGURE 4-1:
A sample compliance matrix with complex requirements.

Source: APMP Body of Knowledge

TIP

Make your content easy to read and your comments brief and concise. A compliance matrix is a utility, and some say, "Just get it done; it doesn't have to look nice." Don't listen to them. The matrix is a selling tool — don't sell it short.

Follow the customer's lead

Base your proposal content plan or outline on your compliance matrix. Set the order of topics exactly as they appear in the table of contents. Use the numbering system used in the RFP in your compliance matrix and in your proposal.

TIP

Because some RFPs are poorly written, following your customer's numbering can be challenging and repetitive and can confound your sense of a functional proposal narrative. But adhering to your customer's structure makes it easy for an evaluator to compare your matrix with his evaluation checklist and to score your proposal without having to leaf through your response for information.

When you provide a compliance matrix in your response (and remember, this is always a good practice), stating the RFP's requirements verbatim increases the impression that you're totally focused on the customer. Don't paraphrase or substitute your own preferred terms. Begin each requirement with the action verb used in the RFP, such as *identify, list, discuss, show, indicate, demonstrate,* or *describe*. These verbs signal what the customer expects to see in the response.

Double-check your work

When your compliance matrix is complete, double-check your work to see that you've listed every requirement. You can use software to do this (see Chapter 13), but you should never rely on software entirely. Software can't always tell the difference between a real requirement and other information, and even the best software can miss requirements if an RFP doesn't contain the keywords that the software is designed to recognize.

REMEMBER

Whether you use software or shred the RFP by hand, double-check your work. If you use software, consider shredding by hand as your double-check. If you don't use software, have someone confirm your manual shred. Don't trust either method blindly — verify.

Check the completeness of your compliance matrix

After you build your compliance matrix, run through the brief checklist in Table 4-1 to ensure that you've covered all the easy-to-forget details.

TABLE 4-1 **Compliance Matrix Completion Checklist**

Submittal Instructions

If the matrix is required, have you followed the requested format?

Have you arranged for the matrix to be in an easy-to-find-and-reference portion of your proposal?

Is the matrix easy to read and use?

If the submission is digital, have you embedded links to the full response?

Have you included references to any forms and attachments required?

Do you have all required signatures and authorizations?

Have you included entries to ensure that you submit the response to the right person at the right place at the right time?

Requirements

Are you capable of delivering the service required?

Are there any customer requirements you can't meet?

Is the team you propose actually available to do the work?

Do your comments reflect the win themes and address the customer's hot buttons?

Have you double-checked your matrix against your shred list to make sure you've included all *shall, will,* and *must* phrases?

Have you analyzed and commented on unstated customer needs?

Internal Compliance

Have you highlighted any requirements that need legal approvals?

Have you met all internal legal requirements?

Have you shared the matrix with all the right people/organization units/management levels?

Source: APMP Body of Knowledge

USING A SPREADSHEET TO CREATE YOUR COMPLIANCE MATRIX

TIP

If you use a spreadsheet to build your compliance matrix, you can quickly sort and index requirements directly after you shred the RFP. If your customer releases amendments or modifications, or if you need to adjust your proposal outline, you can make the necessary changes and use the Sort function to update the matrix.

If you've included the additional information to help your proposal team write their responses, you can also use the Sort function to toggle between ordering the matrix by proposal section or RFP section. This can be a big time saver. For example, after importing the shredded RFP requirements, the compliance matrix naturally follows the order of the RFP as it's written. To review the proposal for compliance, you want to order the matrix by proposal section. With a spreadsheet, you can do a re-sort on the field in seconds.

The matrix can also help you manage the contributions of a larger proposal team. You can sort requirements by the contributors' names and mail them the items for which they're responsible. You can then create different files for different contributors and follow up with them on the status of their responses.

Spreadsheets also let you quickly and easily hide columns for different users. You can include a *Notes* column for a writer that a reviewer need not see. When you create the final response matrix for the printed response, you can hide any columns that you don't want the customer to see. A spreadsheet allows you to hide these columns before printing, emailing, or uploading so you present only the material that's useful for your audience, while maintaining the integrity of your original matrix.

Don't forget to download the reusable example spreadsheet-based compliance matrix we direct you to in the appendix.

Enhancing Compliance with Responsiveness

Complying with instructions means that you've followed the requested format, answered all the questions, completed all the forms, and submitted your response on time, to the right person, at the right place. Complying with requirements means that you've agreed to meet all requirements as asked for in the bid request. If you're 100 percent compliant, you've got a contract and a happy customer, right?

Maybe yes, maybe no.

You've pulled out all the stops but heard nothing in return. What did you do wrong? You complied with everything you thought your customer wanted . . . but maybe you didn't really understand your customer's underlying wants and needs.

Compliance usually gets you past the gate. Just as complying with the requirements of the PQQ gets you an RFP, complying with the requirements of the bid means that you're in the running for the contract. Getting the contract is something else entirely, and that's where responsiveness comes in.

REMEMBER

If compliance is strict adherence to both submittal instructions and requirements in the RFP, *responsiveness* does compliance one better by addressing both your customer's stated and unstated requirements. Proposals can be compliant without being responsive, and vice versa. The best proposals — those with the highest win probability — are both.

Every proposal is the result of people needing something that they don't have and expressing that need so someone can offer them something to fulfill the need. Even if they can't express the need, or feel uncomfortable for some reason in expressing it, they still have the need, and leaving that need unanswered renders compliance a partial victory at best. You have to win a lot of compliance battles to ultimately win a proposal war. Responsiveness helps you do both, and that makes your proposal a place to

›› Show that you've uncovered those unstated needs and can associate some unstated needs with stated needs

›› Sell your solution in what many consider a mere compliance matrix

›› Demonstrate how well you understand your customer

As you see in the following sections, responsiveness is the proof that your proposal is all about your customer, and not about you.

Reading between the lines: The problem with unstated needs

"Reading between the lines" is a proposal writer's cliché. The idea is simple enough: If all you have to go on is the RFP text, you can find out about your customers' unstated needs only by inferring what's behind their written requirements. So easy to say, but not so easy to do! How do you discover and understand an unstated need? The following sections walk you through the process.

Discover the true unstated need

Years ago, a watchmaker created a commercial where a gentleman gives his lady a watch at a fancy restaurant. He opens the beautiful box and reveals a lovely, diamond-studded watch. He looks at her lovingly and expectantly. She looks at the watch, sort of smiles, and says something like, "Thanks, but I really wanted a (the watchmaker's brand)." You don't get to see the look on his face.

He thought she wanted jewelry that ticks. She wanted a status symbol. *Unstated needs.*

What could the gentleman have done to understand the unstated need without coming right out and asking (like the lady would have told him if he did!)? Talked to her best friend? Looked at the watch her best friend or favorite movie star wears? Looked at the ads in some of her favorite magazines?

Reading between the lines takes awareness, resourcefulness, and empathy. You have to get inside the heads of your customers and imagine what they fear, what they struggle with, and what they hope for. That is responsiveness in a nutshell.

Uncover the "why" beneath the need

You have to address some unstated needs before you can meet your customers' stated needs. Some are just sitting in the back of your customers' minds, waiting for a savvy vendor to discover and express them and alleviate that vague sense of discomfort over any solution for their problems.

These unstated needs can be

>> **Functional:** The physical thing that must be fixed. For example, a roofing system must withstand extreme heat (the unstated need) as well as the specific bout of torrential rains that caused the leak that damaged the customer's equipment room (the stated need).

>> **Emotional:** The pain that results from the physical need. For example, a customer needs assurance that the new wireless antennae (the stated need) are environmentally responsible (the unstated need).

Unstated needs like these can give incumbents the edge over other bidders because they've discovered them through a series of discussions or deduced them by studying a customer's underlying problems over time. An incumbent will, therefore, know how to address these needs.

Know the industry issues and drivers

If you're not the incumbent, you can compete against insider information by understanding the *why* behind the *what*.

Often, the underlying drivers for change are beyond the stated needs of a business. For instance, industry issues like government regulations can be at the heart of a customer's stated need. Try to deduce whether a stated need may stem from a deeper, more systematic need. The following examples identify the stated need from an RFP, and the unstated need stemming from knowledge you'd gain only if you studied the industry or local conditions:

>> The stated need is for a new management system at a doctor's office. The unstated need behind the generic "new management system" is to meet regulations that impose significant fines for health providers that fail to secure their patient information.

>> The stated need is for a full-functioning website with a strong feedback mechanism. The unstated need stems from criticism by consumer watchdog groups and local news agencies directed at companies that delay in responding to customer complaints.

Here are some other ways to help you determine the *why* behind the *what*:

>> **Use information you've gleaned from customers similar to the new one.** If you have an insider relationship with another, similar customer, test a stated need against needs you've met with that other customer.

>> **Focus on implied dissatisfactions.** In stating a need for the RFP, a customer may inadvertently express dissatisfaction with an incumbent's product, support, or even its way of doing business. Read each stated need closely to see whether you can discover a subjective clue to attacking an unstated need.

>> **Look behind and beneath the customer's stated needs.** What are the emotional underpinnings of those functional needs? Try to imagine what your customer is feeling today without the functional need being met, and express that feeling in terms of a benefit. For instance, if you're proposing an alarm system for a home:

- **Functional need** = sound an audible alarm

  Emotional need = feel more secure while sleeping

- **Functional need** = front door camera and monitor

  Emotional need = can leave teen home alone and feel comfortable

Sometimes discovering a customer's unstated needs is a matter of guesswork. But using these approaches can at least make it educated guesswork.

Selling everywhere: The compliance matrix as responsiveness tool

RFPs typically don't specify a compliance matrix format. If they do, follow it explicitly. If they don't, that means you can use the compliance matrix as more than just an index and checklist — you can use it to express responsiveness. In other words, you can use it to sell your solution in part of your proposal usually reserved to only benefit the customer. Here are two ways you can turn the compliance matrix into a responsiveness indicator.

Use the comment box to show what you know

A smart evaluator uses any tool that helps get the job done, and the job of an RFP is to compare and contrast your solution with everyone else's. So your secondary goal in writing a proposal is to make this job easier for the evaluator. This is why we recommend creating a compliance matrix that does the following:

>> States the customer's requirements and tells the evaluators where in the response they can find the answer (meaning that the evaluator has to seek out the answers, albeit with some guidance)

>> Includes a brief comment that establishes the proof of compliance (leading to less work for the evaluator)

>> Reiterates a win theme or discriminator (which makes it easier for your evaluator to say yes)

By taking all three steps to develop your compliance matrix, the evaluators can simply read through the compliance matrix and not only know *what* your solution is but also *why* they need to strongly consider it. The responsive compliance matrix also leaves the impression that you're a customer-focused organization — suggesting that you behave this way in all your customer interactions.

And don't worry: You don't need to make every line in your compliance matrix a selling point, just provide these comments for the lines where you can reinforce your win themes and key discriminators. Your customer-focused responses to each requirement, which we cover thoroughly in Chapter 7, take care of the rest.

REMEMBER

Every proposal is a battle to win. As with all elements of your proposal, treat the compliance matrix as an opportunity to sell to the customer and show that you're thorough, thoughtful, and focused.

Craft comments that say the unsaid

Reading between the lines is a way to get beyond compliance and into the realm of responsiveness. But how do you do that in the confined space of a compliance matrix?

Consider the example about website feedback in the earlier section "Know the industry issues and drivers." You can see the link between the stated need — a strong feedback mechanism as part of a new website — and the underlying and unstated hot button for your customer — that local consumer watchdog groups and news agencies criticize companies that delay in responding to customer complaints. You infer that the need comes with some emotion and maybe a little irrational fear. The customer fears that any delay in getting the requested information or responding to a complaint may damage a carefully nurtured brand. It's a story that unfolds regularly in the papers and on the news.

Your response can subtly but clearly allude to this fear as you discuss the features and benefits of your web design within the RFP response section. Your comment in the compliance matrix has to do much the same, but in a fraction of the space. For example, look at the compliance matrix in Figure 4-2.

FIGURE 4-2:
Crafting a more responsive comment in your compliance matrix.

RFP Reference	Requirement	Comply?	Comment
Section 1.3.1	Feedback loop with 24/7 monitoring and social media feeds	Y	**Make sure you address unstated need:** Our three-way back-up system ensures you respond to all message sources quickly, *reinforcing your reputation for unmatched service.*

Source: APMP Body of Knowledge

The comment provides enough detail to assure the evaluator that the feature can truly meet the requirement (three-way back-up system; ability to respond to all message sources) and addresses the underlying emotional need of providing quick responses to avoid negative impressions. If the evaluators want more detail, they can jump to Section 1.3.1 for your full response.

TIP

Compliance and responsiveness are important contributors to winning proposals, but they aren't the only factors that customers consider. A non-compliant proposal won't necessarily lose, and a fully compliant proposal isn't guaranteed a win. Develop your proposal to be compliant and responsive, but also highlight your solution's discriminators, benefits, and value and work to develop a winning price.

Maintaining a customer focus: Sidestepping obstacles

Responsiveness is all about getting inside your customers' heads and conveying in writing what you know about them and their needs. Yet even if you're the most customer-focused proposal writer, you can get sidetracked by the needs and policies of the organization you work for. Consider these scenarios:

>> **Your own business's leaders may redirect response strategies and win themes to match their own agendas, not the customer's.** For example, a company's goal to become a top provider of cloud services is not terribly important to a customer whose mission focuses on their end users' safety more than its own computing environment.

>> **You may struggle with your organization's branding guidelines that can turn your customer-focused proposal into a propaganda piece.** For instance, you may see that subordinating your organization's brand to your customer's helps counter your key contact's impression that your business is arrogant and self-promoting. Yet your organization's brand police rigidly oppose any deviation from the standard approach.

>> **You may have to work with an engineer who rejects using customer-focused language in your proposals.** He thinks that the evaluators are his technical equals and bristles at what he calls the "dumbing down" of his jargon-laced language, dense, concept-laden descriptions, and pages-long feature lists.

TIP

You may encounter all these scenarios if you write proposals for a long time. You may encounter them all at once. You can't hope to overcome all of them, especially if you're just starting out. You have to choose your battles wisely. Understanding your customer can not only help you be responsive, but it can help you choose which battle to go all-out to win and which to let go . . . this time.

Using knowledge about your customer to win the advantage

Working daily with a customer gives you a considerable competitive edge when it comes to an RFP (if the RFP doesn't stem from your inability to meet the customer's needs, of course). As an incumbent, you understand your customer's unstated needs better than most.

Before an RFP is released, potential solution providers can attempt something called *RFP shaping*, the process of influencing your customers' thinking to get elements of an upcoming RFP to reflect your business's key discriminators. As you get closer to the RFP's release, shaping becomes more difficult. Many customers stop all communication upon, or in some cases well before, releasing an RFP. Unless you're the incumbent, this limits your insight into what the customer is really looking for. And the silent treatment is for all vendors, so even incumbents are normally shut out until the bids are submitted.

REMEMBER

If you want to gain the most knowledge and exert the most influence, start early — many weeks or months (in some cases, even years) before an RFP is released, not after.

Speaking your customer's language

Perhaps the best way to demonstrate responsiveness within the structure of any proposal, reactive or proactive, is to write the way that your customer and your customer's representatives talk.

Using your customer's voice in your proposal narrative and solution descriptions indicates that you *listen*. It shows that you're not slinging jargon and pre-packaged marketing fluff to "blind 'em with B.S." So write down what you hear your customer say, especially if it triggers new insight or even a chuckle.

If you aren't the customer contact, talk to your sales rep to find out the following information:

>> How the customer describes the problem in operational terms

>> What buzz and trigger words keep coming up in conversations about the business and industry

>> Where the customer is from and what colloquialisms he uses

>> How the customer refers to his company and yours

>> What business and trade magazines the customer reads

Reactive and proactive proposals should result from a dialogue between your sales rep and a customer. You should consider your proposal a continuation of that dialogue. In Chapter 3, we said that you want your customers to know, like, and trust you. Getting someone to like you is a sales representative's key strength. Because people are more easily influenced by those they like (and hopefully they like your sales reps!), write in their voice, too, as well as the customer's. Listen closely to how they talk — about the customer, about the solution, about the implementation plan — and mimic those words, phrases and sentences as much as you can when you write about the solution.

REMEMBER

You want your customers to think that their sales reps wrote these proposals exclusively for them. Getting this information helps you to emulate the voice of your customers and their main contacts and, hopefully, subtly, influence the customers to like your proposal as much as they do your sales reps.

Chapter 5

Sizing Up Your Competition

I n Chapters 3 and 4, we show you how you can find out about and build relation-ships with your customers and then express what you've found out in the structure and content of your proposals. Lurking behind all this information are your competitors:

>> Who are they?

>> What kind of relationship do they have with your customer?

>> Do they know what you know?

>> Do they know things you don't?

>> Do you know things they don't?

>> Do you know things about them that your customer doesn't but should?

In this chapter, we discuss your competition — those who try to crash your proposal party with your customer. We talk about what to do if they're the incum-bent. We talk about what to do about them if you're the incumbent. And we talk in either instance about ways to champion your cause over your competitors' while remaining in line with your customer's needs.

We go a little deeper in this chapter, getting to the "putting words on paper" stage perhaps a little early in the game, but the concept warrants the dive. In a proposal, your customers — your readers — are your most important consideration. But customers have little voices over their shoulders — from you and your competitors — that try to sway their opinions and perspectives. Considering, understanding, and even appreciating your competitors as you begin to write your proposal can have a considerable effect on your chances of winning.

Gathering Information About Your Competitors

In business, competition is a constant. Customers may tell you the same thing coaches do: A little healthy competition brings out the best in each player. And to a customer, competition can mean more innovation, better responsiveness, and richer savings.

Because customers love the benefits of competition, you have to prepare to outwit your competition even when you think the deal's a cinch. And on that note, beware the salesperson who says, "We don't have to worry about following that instruction or explaining that process — this is a done deal." That's a sure sign that someone hasn't done the necessary homework. How do you make sure you do?

The following sections explore how you can stay ahead of your competition by asking the right questions. But answers to these questions — real, valuable answers — don't come from mere reflection. You have to research your competitors by using an array of tools and techniques that proposal writers refer to as *competitive intelligence*. So we also look at these techniques here to help you assess what you know about your competitors and use this information to craft a carefully tailored proposal.

Assessing your competition: Asking the right questions

Early on, as you're planning to write your proposal — in big companies, it's part of opportunity planning; in smaller companies, it's simply following up on leads — you must determine the level of competition you face to win the business. The type of competition you encounter changes everything about your proposal — the strategy, tone, structure, and content.

You have to find out whether a company currently owns the relationship with the account (making it the *incumbent*). If so, you have a lot more questions to answer:

>> Does the incumbent have a competitive advantage or disadvantage for this opportunity?

>> Does this opportunity play to the incumbent's strengths?

>> Has the customer benefited from the incumbent's work?

>> How long have the incumbent and customer worked together?

>> Has anything happened recently to either the customer or the incumbent that indicates the two are not a good match right now?

If your answer is no, you need to ask another key question: Are you aware of any other competitors for this opportunity?

Here we're talking about the usual suspects — the companies you compete with every day. You probably know a lot about their strengths and weaknesses from prior competitions.

Ask the first three questions you asked about an incumbent company here, replacing "incumbent" with "competitor":

>> Does the competitor have a competitive advantage or disadvantage for this opportunity?

>> Does this opportunity play to the competitor's strengths?

>> Has the customer benefited from the competitor's work?

You also need to think about any *internal* sources of competition — that is, other projects or special needs within the customer's organization that may conflict with your project. For instance, your potential customer can always

>> Decide to do nothing

>> Spend money on other priorities

>> Do the work in-house

REMEMBER

Whether the competition is internal (from within the business) or external (from an incumbent or competitor business), you have to build strategies in your proposal to counter opposing points of view.

After you consider the internal and external threats to you winning the opportunity, you need to anticipate the unknown by asking: Might any unknown competitors come out of the woodwork at the last moment?

TIP

To answer this important question, you need to put on your critical thinking cap and ask questions such as these:

>> Has the customer tired of traditional solutions from traditional sources?

>> Is the nature of the problem such that the customer may entertain a novel approach?

>> Might a former incumbent have an advantageous position with a company decision maker longing to restore a relationship?

Going through these preliminary investigations can yield great benefits for your proposal. The answers to these questions can help you establish win themes, hone hot buttons, and may even alter your solution in positive ways (refer to Chapter 2 for more on win themes and hot buttons).

Gathering intelligence: The first line of defense

To beat any competitor, you not only have to physically perform better, but you also have to think better. You have to gather and analyze data to turn it into actionable strategies for your solution and clear themes and messages for your proposal. (The data you uncover about your competitors can help you express the difference between compliance and responsiveness that we stress in Chapter 4.) In short, an insight into your competitors can give you an edge when it comes to explaining the *why* behind the *what* of the customer's requirements.

It's not enough to know merely which competitors are planning to bid. You must also gain insight into what they can offer, at what price, and most importantly, what the customer thinks of them. You have three main ways to do this: through publicly available information, through your own colleagues, and from the customer itself.

REMEMBER

Gathering competitive intelligence is an ethical activity — most sources of information are publicly and readily available. Your competitors, if they're any good, are doing it, too.

Using publicly available information

Thanks to the Internet, search engines, and people's (and companies') illogical and insatiable desire to tell everything about themselves to total strangers, you can find out more than you ever thought possible about your competitors in some fairly easy and direct ways:

TIP

>> **Your competitors' website(s):** These contain information about your competitors' product lines and where they do business, not to mention claims of their strengths, their mission statement, and their value proposition. Go to these sites first to get a high-level view of their operations and offerings.

Drill down on menu headings such as About Us and Employment Opportunities. The former can shed light on your competitors' history and their long-range goals. The latter can provide a subtle clue about their new strategies through the roles they're trying to fill and in which location they hope to fill them.

>> **Your competitors' public records:** You can find this information easily — it's readily searchable on the Internet, or you can track it down on your own or with the help of others, sometimes the competitor itself. Check out the following options to get started:

- **Annual reports:** If your competitors are publicly traded, these reports usually have valuable introductions by CEOs that highlight key strengths, accomplishments, and future priorities. They can also cite recent new business that may pertain to your current opportunity.

- **Social media:** Many companies now have and actually maintain and nurture a presence on Facebook, LinkedIn, Twitter, Pinterest, Reddit, and other social media outlets. Scan these sites for insights into your competition's latest claims and accomplishments.

>> **Industry publications:** Sources include technical articles in trade websites and magazines that have been written by your customers' experts or profiles of your customers' thought leaders. These publications can also explain industry trends (not yours; your customers') that may help you pinpoint hot buttons and craft win themes and value propositions (refer to Chapters 2 and 9 for more on these).

TIP

Check out websites for trade shows and industry conferences for lists of presenters and topics related to your opportunity.

>> **Consumer sites:** Watchdog agencies like the Better Business Bureau and consumer advocate sites like Angie's List can lend substance for key discriminator statements and for subtle insinuations about your competitors' weaknesses (we look at this in more detail in the later section, "Ghosting Your Competition").

>> **Historical records:** In some segments, you can find public information about bids and outcomes that can help you understand your competitors' strategies, strengths, and weaknesses. For instance, if you spot a historical trend that your competitor has failed to win business in a certain part of the country, you may discover a distribution or support problem if you dig deeper.

>> **Special information services:** If you can afford outside help, you can buy subscriptions to databases that track the activities and results of a wide variety of businesses and industries. These services often provide summaries of significant deals, product releases, and personnel changes. A few well-known examples include OneSource, Hoovers, Dun & Bradstreet, GovWin, Gartner, and PWC.

REMEMBER

Publicly available information is normally quite reliable, but you can never take it at face value. However, after you corroborate what you discover, you can use public information with confidence to develop *positive discriminators* (those features and benefits that you can provide but your competitors can't). See Chapter 7 for more information about positive discriminators.

Talking to your colleagues

The best sources of competitive intelligence data may be right under your nose. Often you can find out most of what you want to know about your competitors by asking your colleagues. The challenge is figuring out who knows what, where those people can be found, and how to share that information with your writing team.

TIP

Here are some suggestions to help you overcome this challenge:

>> **Ask other salespeople in your company.** Sometimes, sales organizations shake up the account structure and reassign contacts. Make notes of your sales team's organizational changes. Your customer's former account rep may have crucial information about prior dealings with competitors that can help you.

>> **Incorporate teammates into reviews.** Where appropriate, supplement your internal review team with members from your business or project partners. They often have different points of view about customers, competitors, and solutions that can help increase your probability of winning the business and success over the short and long term.

>> **Seek out colleagues who have previously been employed by the customer or a competitor.** Some companies make a habit of enticing away the talent they encounter when competing for business. If you work for such a company, stay up-to-date on the comings and goings of key sales, solution, and executive personnel. You can find no better source than first-hand knowledge!

Talking with your customers

Don't be afraid to talk about your competitors directly with your customers. Think back to what we said at the beginning of this chapter: Your customers love the benefits that come from competition. When customers share their likes and dislikes about another provider, they can influence your solution and offer to their advantage.

WARNING

When your customers share information about a rival, they aren't necessarily looking out for you. They may well be saying things about you to your rivals to wring greater value from both your offers.

Hosting a competitor review

Many companies use the information they discover about their competitors to fuel a *competitor review* before every bid — a review that analyzes and assesses a competitor's strategies and solutions for a particular opportunity. Sometimes the review is formal, sometimes not, usually depending on the size of your company and the value of the opportunity. The purpose of the competitor review is to anticipate the approach, solutions, and strategies that competitors are likely to use and determine ways to include this knowledge in your proposal.

REMEMBER

Competitor reviews normally do this through role-playing. On the formal side, larger companies may contract with a competitor's former employees, consultants, and suppliers to formulate probable solutions, win strategies, and counterstrategies and to test the credibility of their own strategy. A less formal competitor review may entail you serving as "devil's advocate" for your salesperson's solution — for example, by countering a proposed win theme about a perceived competitor's service issues with information you found on the competitor's website that flaunts a big investment in its support desk.

Outputs from the competitor review can help you articulate the weaknesses in your competitors' solutions and craft messages to neutralize their strengths, but this can take time. Ideally, you conduct competitor reviews several times during your sales cycle, even while you're writing your proposal. Hold your first review before you decide to pursue the opportunity. Then, based on the complexity and significance of the opportunity, hold a second review as you begin crafting your proposal.

Your competitor review needs to answer the following questions (and, yes, some questions we ask under the section, "Assessing your competition: Asking the right questions" bear repeating during each review):

>> How should we try to influence the customer's decision?

>> What are our competitors' strengths and weaknesses?

- » What are our competitors' likely strategies?
- » How do we compare to competitors with respect to answering the customer's key issues?
- » How do our technical approach, price, risk level, and past experience compare to those of our competitors?
- » What weaknesses do our competitors have that we can counter?
- » Does the customer prefer one of our competitors?
- » How do we unseat the incumbent?
- » How do we win as the incumbent?
- » What weaknesses do we have to overcome?
- » What actions can we take to strengthen our position?
- » How can we counteract competitors' likely moves to improve their positions with the customer?

In larger companies, your opportunity or account manager may plan and schedule competitor reviews and select team members from both company and external sources. Your team should include individuals from all pertinent business areas, along with solution design, and even consultants, retirees, suppliers, and partners — whoever has *recent* experience with your likely competitors. In smaller companies, consider including customer service personnel along with sales and company leaders. But even if you're the sole creator of proposals, you still need to answer these competitor review questions to help you craft effective key messages from your answers.

Understanding what you know: Two tools for getting a clearer picture

The competitive intelligence you uncover through research helps you know where your competitors excel and where they fall short, but getting that intelligence into your proposal in a meaningful way takes more than just knowledge. You need to analyze this information alongside your own capabilities and the needs of your customer.

In the following sections, we present two tools that can help you see how your capabilities stack up against those of your competitors — the SWOT analysis and the bidder comparison matrix.

Analyzing pertinent information with SWOT

A *SWOT analysis* is a common tool that proposal professionals use to measure you against your competitors. SWOT stands for strengths (yours), weaknesses (yours again), opportunities (their weaknesses), and threats (their strengths). (You could call this a "YSYWTSTW analysis," but it wouldn't be as much fun to say.)

Although almost any SWOT format will work just fine (check out all the varieties with an Internet search on SWOT), we suggest you build a simple, three-column and three-row grid in your word-processing software or a spreadsheet (see Table 5-1 for an example that shows our preferred SWOT format). Always label each SWOT for future reference: Include the competitor's name, the customer's name, and the date you developed the SWOT. Check out the appendix to find out how you can access a SWOT tool example online.

TABLE 5-1 **A SWOT Analysis Template**

Competitor_____ Customer_____ Date_____

	Strength	Weakness
Yours	What can we do to leverage our **strengths** against each item of importance to the customer?	What can we do to mitigate our **weaknesses** against those items of importance?
Theirs	What can we do to counter **threats** (strengths exhibited by competitor)?	What can we do to exploit **opportunities** (weaknesses exhibited by competitor) against those items of importance?

REMEMBER

Whatever format you choose, what you put inside the table is what matters. Depending on the size of and available resources in your organization, your SWOT analysis can be

>> Rigorous, including intelligence gathered from a broad range of internal and external resources, including sales, marketing, business development, finance, and even key executives

>> Cursory, drawing intelligence from a salesperson's prior competitors, published materials about the competitor's products and the company, and news releases, product reviews, and other material from the Internet

You must completely answer the questions in the table if you want to write a proposal that can win business. Don't worry about style here. Your SWOT can include descriptive phrases that cover key issues, quotes from customers or other sources that prove your assertions, or snippets of examples you heard about from key contacts or print/online sources.

If you leave any questions unanswered, flag them for more research. Pull your research findings and start filling out the SWOT analysis as quickly as you can before you start writing your proposal in earnest.

TIP

Fill out your SWOT template and make it available for everyone on the proposal team. Post it on your workroom wall or in your online collaborative workspace (if you have one), use it as wallpaper on your collaborative website, or send it via email to every author before meetings and reviews. Visualizing issues — having them in print for all to see and contemplate — can stimulate collaborations that generate the kind of value propositions and thematic statements that will persuade a customer to choose you over your competition.

When you do start writing, your responses to the questions in your SWOT analysis help to clarify how your company plans for improving your position with the customer. They also help you to write win themes and proposal theme statements and the subtle doubt-seeding comments we call *ghosting* (see the later section, "Ghosting Your Competition"). You may also want to turn to Chapter 9 for more on crafting win themes.

Comparing strengths and weaknesses with a bidder comparison matrix

When you've completed your SWOT analysis, you may want to take the intelligence you've compiled and complete a *bidder comparison matrix*. This "deeper dive" tool scores the strengths and weaknesses of all significant bidders against the *what* and *why* of the customer's requirements.

EXAMPLE

We provide an example of a simple template for the bidder comparison matrix in Table 5-2.

TABLE 5-2 **Bidder Comparison Matrix Template**

Customer_____   Date_____

Requirements and Issues	Customer Weighting	Your Score	Bidder B's Score	Bidder C's Score
On-time implementation	20%	9	8	4
		1.8	1.6	0.8
Total cost of ownership	25%	7	8	10
		1.75	2	2.5
Technical solution	30%	8	8	7
		2.4	2.4	2.1

Requirements and Issues	Customer Weighting	Your Score	Bidder B's Score	Bidder C's Score
Co-marketing of innovations	10%	3	4	7
		0.3	0.4	0.7
Provide "just-in-time" training at implementation	15%	10	9	6
		1.5	1.35	0.9
Total Score		7.75	7.75	7

As you determine points for your matrix, try to objectively reflect the customer's true perception of your team along with its perception of the competition. Otherwise, you may inadvertently skew your evaluation in your favor.

Here's how to fill out the bidder comparison matrix:

1. **Gather a group of co-workers (in smaller settings, even one other brain will help) who know about your customer, its market, and your competitors.**

2. **In the *Requirements and Issues* column, list all your customer's issues, needs, hot buttons, and key requirements.**

   Issues may be those acknowledged or those unstated. As the opportunity matures, your inputs in this column will likely become more specific and, in the case of RFP responses, eventually reflect the evaluation criteria.

3. **Enter weighting factors to indicate what you believe quantifies each requirement's importance.**

   When responding to an RFP, use the weights from the customer's evaluation criteria (RFPs often reveal how much each aspect of your bid "weighs"; for example, Training = 15 percent, Price = 20 percent, Technical solution = 60 percent, and so on).

   If you're in a proactive situation, or if your customer doesn't provide weightings, create your own percentages based on your interpretation of the customer's needs.

4. **Based on your SWOT analysis entries, assign points for your company on a 10-point scale (1 is low, and 10 is high), indicating your strength on each requirement.**

   Enter the points in the upper box for each requirement.

5. **Assign points (in the same way as you do in Steps 3 and 4) for your competitors.**

6. **Multiply each point entry by the applicable weighting factors in the lower box for you and each competitor.**

7. **Sum the weighted points for you and your competitors in the bottom row (*Total Score*).**

The total weighted score reflects the relative standing of your team versus that of your competitors. These scores show which bidder is strongest and highlights the relative strengths and weaknesses of them all — including you.

You can take this new perspective on your competitors and infuse it into your proposal-writing process. In effect, these scores can help guide you or your writers when crafting win themes and ghosting statements.

EXAMPLE

Consider the following examples of writer's guidance based on the information you glean from your bidder comparison matrix:

>> From intelligence obtained by the salesperson, you know that quality of product is very important to the customer. Based on web research, Company B and Company C will fall short.

Guidance: *Write about our reputation for quality and provide relevant proof points to highlight our strengths in this area (for example, JD Powers' award-winning product line, Angie's List recommended, and so on).*

>> Company C falls short in several requirements. It needs multiple vendor partners to bring its capabilities to the same level as ours, which will raise its price.

Guidance: *Write about our full set of capabilities, providing proof points for each requirement. Discuss our ability to deliver all requirements at a lower cost. Perhaps ghost Company C by saying "to merely meet our abilities, other providers have to hire subcontractors or partner with multiple companies, which raises their costs and introduces unnecessary risks of managing multiple partners. We have the expertise and staff to do the entire project with no outside help."*

TIP

Find out what sources your prospective customer uses for information and add them to your research.

Unseating Incumbents

When contracts come up for renewal, *incumbents* (the current providers of the product or service) usually hold many competitive advantages over all challengers. For instance, they thoroughly know the customer (who's who and who matters), the work (especially problem areas), and how much everything costs to support and maintain. However, incumbents often suffer from many self-imposed disadvantages that make them vulnerable.

REMEMBER

Standard sales planning strategies and tactics tend not to be successful when trying to unseat incumbents. You must go beyond the norm to collect enough intelligence to determine how to neutralize an incumbent's strengths and to take advantage of its weaknesses. With patience, smart opportunity analysis, and a persuasive proposal, you can leverage incumbent's typical weaknesses and win its contracts.

To unseat an incumbent, you must determine how to provide better service or product at a lower or comparable price. (With price, watch out for transition and implementation costs. The incumbent doesn't incur these; only challengers do.) You also have to provide evidence of prior success, preferably in a similar industry on a project of equal scope. If your organization can't identify how to do this, you'd be better off walking away from the opportunity.

Follow these steps to unseat incumbents who hold contracts that are up for renewal:

1. **Compile intelligence on the customer and incumbent.**

Do this long before the contract expiration date. Look for signs that the incumbent is being arrogant, taking the customer's business for granted, not listening, slipping into routine performance levels, tolerating rising costs, or generally being unmotivated or unprepared to defend the contract.

Get inside the customer's and the incumbent's organizations to identify and gauge the incumbent's advantages and vulnerabilities. Ask the following questions:

- Is the customer satisfied with the incumbent's contract performance?

- Is the customer looking for change?

- Is the incumbent performing well on all aspects of the contract?

- Does the incumbent's management team lead effectively?

TIP

Where do you find sources for this insider information? Seek out customer insiders like its leaders, staff, SMEs, and former employees. Consider incumbent insiders such as former staffers willing to talk, employees of subcontractors, and consultants who follow the industry. Just be sure to filter the intelligence you collect. Often opinions won't align, and some sources may be feeding you false intelligence for a variety of reasons.

2. **Assess the incumbent's performance and develop improved solutions.**

   Populate a spreadsheet with your findings beneath these column headings:

   - Requirement, Issue, or Hot Button
   - Incumbent Performance (on a scale of 1 [excellent] to 5 [poor])
   - Incumbent Deficiencies
   - Improvements Proposed
   - Gaps in Our Solution
   - Actions to Close Gaps

3. **Qualify the opportunity and decide on your course of action (find out more about this in Chapter 6).**

   Use your assessment spreadsheet to answer the following key questions:

   - Is this incumbent truly beatable?
   - Can you assemble the resources and strategies to unseat this incumbent?
   - Can you do a better job of meeting all the customer's needs (and can you prove it)?

4. **Use a variety of tactics to capitalize on the incumbent's weaknesses and neutralize its strengths.**

   Consider the following approaches:

   - **Develop better solutions.** Tactfully test them on the customer, increasing its dissatisfaction with the incumbent.

     Be careful how you reveal your ideas; the customer may share them with the incumbent.

WARNING

   - **Develop strategies to neutralize the incumbent's advantages.** Hire comparable expertise. Acquire better management tools. Team up with other providers to increase your performance capabilities. Improve your industry reputation by writing white papers, making presentations at industry conferences, and publishing in industry trade publications — and ensure that the customer receives copies. Use social media to build awareness and interest.

5. **Determine the price-to-win.**

   One of an incumbent's most frequent vulnerabilities is cost creep: Wages increase, and new personnel may be added over time. Familiarity can breed indifference and inefficiency. Work hard to understand the customer's budget and cost expectations; study the incumbent's resourcing and apparent pricing; and develop a bottom-up cost estimate by taking a fresh, objective look at resource requirements.

6. **Be vigilant, and be prepared for surprises.**

   You may find a door open to unseat an incumbent, at least initially. When an incumbent sees you as a threat, expect a fierce battle. Be on the lookout for disinformation spread by the incumbent and other tactics to neutralize your own strengths.

7. **Prepare a persuasive proposal that matches or exceeds the incumbent on all evaluation criteria by neutralizing its strengths and capitalizing on its weaknesses.**

   Beat the incumbent question-by-question, issue-by-issue by addressing the customer's dissatisfactions, issues, and hot buttons with understanding and validated improved solutions. And don't forget to include the proof of your prior successes.

REMEMBER

In a tough market, retaining the business you've already earned is just as important and just as difficult as winning new business, if not more so. Don't take existing customers for granted. Follow the same best practices that helped you win the customer in the first place. Pursue contract renewals just as aggressively as new business. Leveraging incumbency without becoming complacent is the key to keeping existing customers. Complacency is the number-one reason customers move to another provider.

Ghosting Your Competition

In proposal writing, the process of subtly and positively undermining the efforts of a rival is known as *ghosting* the competition. Ghosting is not trash talk, nor is it confrontational. As the name implies, the best ghosting statements are subtle, like squeaking doors in the middle of the night; they conjure up a little sense of unease.

REMEMBER

When using ghosting techniques, you never name the competitor. And ghosting isn't always negative. You can ghost others by playing up your strengths and letting the weaknesses of the competition remain implied.

TIP

Ghosting is similar to an assessment technique called *trade-off analysis*. With this technique, you assess alternative approaches and then build a rationale for selecting one over the others. You can use this technique before you write a proposal — use the insight you gain to highlight your and your solution's strengths, plant little seeds of doubt about your competitor's weaknesses and the flaws in its solution, and provide brief advertisements for your way of doing things.

Thanks to your SWOT analysis, you have all the intel you need to take your analysis one step further and assess the trade-offs inherent in the ways that you offer to solve the customer's problems. To hone in on the elements that make good ghosting statements, you need to follow these steps:

1. **Review your organization's (and your solution's) strengths in the top-left quadrant of your SWOT grid (refer to Table 5-1 to get started).**

   Start a new list, prioritizing your strengths in relation to the customer's requirements and preferences. Along with highlighting your good points, consider the strengths you can use to counter your competitor's ghosting of your weaknesses.

2. **Compile your competitors' weaknesses from the bottom-right quadrant of your SWOTs.**

   Note the plural. It's time to consolidate your competitors into one big adversary in your proposal story (which also helps maintain anonymity for your ghosting). While different competitors have different areas of strength and weakness, look for common shortcomings that they all share versus your strengths (for example, no competitor can match your ability to deliver in-person, just-in-time training for the customer's IT staff). List them next to your corresponding strength. Now you have the basis for comparison/contrast ghost statements.

3. **Compile your competitors' strengths from the bottom-left quadrant of your SWOTs.**

   Consider whether they echo your strengths or counterbalance their weaknesses. Cross out any elements in your strengths list that are no longer clear advantages. Do the same for your competitors' strengths (for example, you and your competitors' technologies are essentially the same; whatever solution you create will be similar). Circle any competitor's strengths that you can't clearly diminish with your strengths, their weaknesses, or your customer's particular needs in this instance.

4. **Compare your weaknesses from the top-right quadrant of your SWOT analysis against your competitors' strengths.**

   Where can they attack you? How can you ward off their ghosts? Look for ways to make a particular weakness irrelevant for this specific opportunity (for example, you score lower on total cost of ownership, but the customer has an immediate cash flow problem: You can implement the solution faster at lower initial cost).

When you've finished your trade-off analysis, you've accumulated all the raw material you need for writing ghosting statements.

REMEMBER

Ghosting your competitors is a great way to educate your customer, but use the technique in moderation. Pick the most competitively sensitive aspects of your proposal and use ghosting techniques to gain that slight competitive advantage that may win the day. And always take the high road. Ghosting isn't spreading rumors or telling lies. It's pointing out shortcomings for which you have proof.

The following sections explore different ways that you can ghost your competition to highlight your strengths, point out competitor weaknesses, and minimize your organization's weaknesses.

Highlighting your strengths

Time to conjure up some ghosts. Start with the positives — your strengths in relation to your customer's needs and your competitors' relative weaknesses. There's no end to ways to highlight your strengths at the expense of your rivals, but here are a few techniques to consider:

>> **Identify your competitors' weaknesses in areas where your organization is strong, and write statements that substantiate those strengths.** This way, you can set yourself up as the gold standard for a feature, benefit, or capability with only the faintest reference to your competitors.

For example, "We house maintenance and repair teams within 15 miles of both of your production centers to ensure that we respond to your calls more quickly than anyone else could hope to."

>> **Use your trade-off analysis not only as a preparation step but also as a form of persuasion in itself.** Consider this technique for justifying your solution while subtly positioning your rationale as superior to that of your competitors.

For example, "We thoroughly investigated two other approaches to your need for uninterrupted access. The first, duplicating your entire system to ensure that you stay connected, was far too costly. The second, creating a series of soft switches, brought too much complexity to the solution and created potential failure points. So we opted for . . ."

>> **Create a checkbox comparison chart (in the same way that consumer advocacy groups often do for product evaluations), to compare your solution's features against those of your competitors (you want more checks in your boxes than those of your competitors).** Use generic names for the competitor's solutions if you can, such as "Typical Open Source Solutions" or other general industry names for technologies. If possible, cite a source for the content, such as a trade publication.

>> **Differentiate any shared strengths by pointing to associated discriminators.** For the strengths that you share with your competitors (common technology, for instance), consider ghosting statements that begin with clauses that indicate that the strength is common in the industry, and then point to a related but separate advantage you hold over the competitor.

For example: "Most high-end providers have adopted X technology, so the track record of support you'll receive after implementation is crucial to your success."

Drawing attention to your competitors' weaknesses

Now for the negative side of ghosting — the subtle put-down of your rivals. Everyone has weaknesses, and if you've done your homework, you can put your competitors' weaknesses on display, if ever-so subtly. Here are a couple of ways to cast doubt without disrupting the positive tone of your proposal:

>> **Use a comparison/contrast statement.** You remember this from high school English (hey, school did give you something you can actually use later in life!). Set up your competitors' weaknesses with a conditional clause and deliver a solid, positive statement about your strength.

For example, "While some solutions require local power and backup systems, ours powers itself with centralized backup should you lose power."

>> **Allow the analysts to help out.** Regardless of your industry or market, someone is watching over what you and your competitors do and how you do it. Highlight your opponents' weaknesses by quoting the most reputable of these watchdogs. If you have the best ratings for your services, say so and cite the source. If your main competitor has a lesser rating, bring it to your reader's attention.

For example, "You told us how much being responsive to customers means to your business; a poor reputation with the BBB is like losing someone's trust — it takes a lot of positives to win it back."

WARNING

When ghosting, never preach. Avoid any language that implies you're instructing your evaluator on how to assess your proposal — for example, phrases like, "You understand the importance of . . ." and "Businesses as successful as yours know that financial stability is the most important . . ." Patronizing your customer with overt ghosting statements does far more damage than good.

Compensating for your weaknesses

If you or your solution has a perceived weakness, you need to anticipate that your competitors can attack you just as you can attack them if the roles are reversed. Here are some scenarios and potential comebacks you can use:

» If you're the new kid on the block, your competitor may trumpet its years of experience and play up the risks of going with an unproven provider (you). You can counter by focusing on your newer equipment, leading-edge techniques, and more innovative approaches than the status quo solution.

» If your reputation has suffered from some service issues, your competitor may reference analysts that drop you into a weaker quadrant and cast you as unreliable. You can counter this by acknowledging your problems and demonstrating how you've overcome them with new equipment, improved techniques, or increased training for your support staff. Most customers understand that problems do occur — it's what you do about them that matters (and be sure to cite proof for your claims of improvement!).

3

Planning Your Approach

Customize a standard proposal process to meet your organization's needs. Integrate that proposal process into your organization's larger sales process.

Choose the right strategy for setting yourself apart from your competitors. Discover how to focus your customers' attention on the benefits of your solution. Prove how you can deliver what you say you will and how your solution provides benefits that the competition can't.

Devise a schedule that ensures you have time to do your work as you manage the efforts of your contributors. Find out how to assemble a team with the right skills and how to keep them on message. Find tips for bringing the proposal in on time and within budget.

Chapter 6

Developing Your Proposal Process

P roposals don't happen overnight. Well, bad ones do. Bad ones also happen over weeks, months, and sometimes years when the people writing them don't know what they're doing. Having ample time can reduce some of the stress of proposal writing, but time alone doesn't ensure a winning proposal.

Proposals take a lot of effort — effort to understand your customers, effort to understand your competitors, and effort to create solutions that meet your customers' requirements and outperform those offered by your competitors. They also take — with a nod to Liam Neeson's *Taken* movies — a "particular set of skills." But before you apply these skills, you need to know how and when to.

What separates proposals that win from those that lose is how you blend the skills you have as a proposal writer with the abilities and efforts of your contributors within the time you're given to create the proposal.

Winning business through proposals takes a plan — a repeatable, flexible process that you can implement whether the window of opportunity is alarmingly short or what may seem luxuriously long. The key word is *flexible*, because few proposal opportunities are identical, and you can never rely on the amount of effort you'll receive from your contributors.

This chapter helps you create and customize your own proposal process based on principles that have been collected, tested, and proven effective across almost every market, industry, and locale.

Understanding Where the Proposal Process Fits In

The idea of a "proposal process" is a bit misleading. Writing a proposal is just a portion of the larger selling process or the even larger business development and retention process.

The overall sales process can be brief and straightforward or long and complex. In either case, the sales process has several major stages and the potential for sub-steps and even multiple "swim lanes" for the actions of a variety of participants. Much has been written about these stages and roles, and we have neither the space nor the inclination to discuss them here. You're here for help with writing your proposals, and unless you're wearing all the hats at your organization, you can and should specialize a bit. If you're the salesperson/sole proprietor/proposal writer, you'll likely have your own approach to fitting the proposal steps within your sales steps.

REMEMBER

For perspective, here we provide you with the whole sales process as seen through the proposal writer's lens. Looking through this lens allows you to narrow down your view of the broader sales process to three key stages:

>> **Pre-proposal stage:** Another good name for this stage is the *decision stage*. Here, you spend time searching for and courting potential customers while fending off competing suitors. All the work in this stage leads to the ultimate decision: Do you propose (bid) or not?

We take a brief look at the pre-proposal stage in the upcoming section "Pre-Proposal Stage: To Bid or Not to Bid?"

>> **Proposal development stage:** For a proposal writer, this is the *action stage*. Here, you do all *your* planning and writing work over four major phases:

- Strategizing, creating themes, and kicking off your proposal project

- Outlining the structure and "look" of your proposal

- Writing and reviewing the content of your proposal

- Publishing, packaging, and delivering your proposal

We take you through this central part of your proposal process in the later section "Proposal Development Stage: Delivering on Your Proposal Strategy."

>> **Post-proposal stage:** You can also think of this final stage as the *reflection stage*. Here, you assess your proposal from two perspectives:

- Your customer's, because you may be required to amend or defend your submitted proposal

- Your own, so you can improve your proposal content, tools, and processes for the next go-round

We look at the post-proposal stage in more detail in the later section "Post-Proposal Stage: Getting Ready for Another Round."

Figure 6-1 shows the three-stage proposal process.

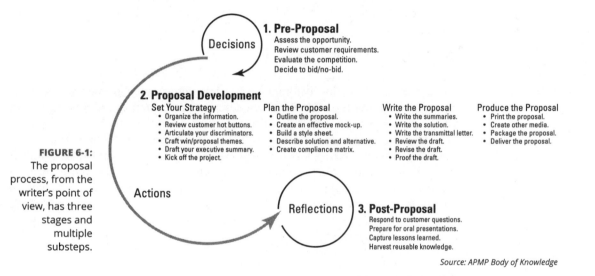

FIGURE 6-1:
The proposal process, from the writer's point of view, has three stages and multiple substeps.

Source: APMP Body of Knowledge

Although some proposal professionals who work the most complex, high-end bids in the world may add a step here, a check and balance there, or a more rigorous review here and there, the process we share in this chapter is comprehensive and doable for even the leanest of proposal operations.

But even the sole proprietor or lone proposal writer may not complete all the steps we outline to the same degree in every proposal opportunity. Sometimes you just won't have the time. Sometimes the step won't yield enough benefits. Sometimes your proposal team will balk at your process and you won't be able to change their minds. Still, you need a process to eliminate chance and chaos — chaos is the last thing you want in your proposal process.

TIP Set up your proposal process to avoid the unexpected by planning carefully. Train your team to follow your process. Use it as often as the situation allows. Look ahead during the project. Anticipate the conditions that may prevent a certain step and plan to work around it, or adjust it to better fit the circumstances. A proposal process isn't an assembly line. It's people working together to achieve an ambitious goal.

Pre-Proposal Stage: To Bid or Not to Bid?

The pre-proposal stage has four distinct parts, three of which we discuss in the chapters leading up to this one:

>> Assess the opportunity.

>> Review customer requirements.

>> Evaluate the competition.

>> Decide to bid (or not to bid).

You decide to pursue the customer, so you find out as much as you can about the customer by using the techniques we describe in Chapter 3, and you figure out what your customer needs, either through your discussions with key contacts or by reading its Request for Proposal (RFP; refer to Chapter 4 for more). You size up the competition by asking lots of questions and searching for information on the Internet and through other public sources (refer to Chapter 5 for more on these competitor analysis approaches). This work leads you to a big decision: Do you go all-out for this opportunity, or do you let this one pass and aim for another? We look at this decision, and how to prepare yourself before you dive into the proposal development stage (if your decision is to go for it!), in the following sections.

Making the bid/no-bid decision

The *bid/no-bid decision* opens the door to you beginning your proposal development process. It's a formal opportunity for you to put all your cards on the table and see how you stack up against the customer's needs and your competitors' capabilities. It's your chance as a proposal writer to see whether you have all you need to create a good proposal.

REMEMBER For a proposal to be successful, you need

>> A winning solution

>> Compelling evidence that you can deliver the solution

>> One or more irresistible win themes that address the customer's hot buttons (refer to Chapter 2)

>> Commitment from your business to dedicate the resources you need to do a quality job

As a proposal manager, you hold perhaps the largest stake in the bid/no-bid decision because it determines whether your efforts will be fruitful or for naught. You can go all-in only if you get total buy-in from your partners.

TIP

The bid/no-bid decision is one of a series of decision milestones in the proposal process. They're defined moments of conscious decisions you must make. Like a gate, they serve as a portal to another stage of the process; like a gate, you can always change your mind and go back out. Hence the frequently heard business term, *decision gate.*

The bid/no-bid decision comes from a series of questions that you ask yourself and your team members to test whether you have what it takes to win this particular business. Winning business is expensive. You have to be willing to accept the risks of bidding for the rewards of winning.

You can use the questions in Table 6-1 to help you make the bid/no-bid decision. Answering yes or no in the *Y/N* column and commenting briefly on why you do or don't meet the criteria in the question will allow you to quickly assess the decision and document your reasons for later reference.

TABLE 6-1   **Bid/No-Bid Decision Table**

Question	Y/N	Comment
Proposal		
Do we clearly understand and can we supply the deliverables?		
Do we clearly understand and can we meet the schedule?		
Will the customer adhere to the published schedule?		
Will our internal and external partners commit to supplying the resources necessary?		
Are our discriminators unique and interesting to the prospect?		
Can the customer justify our selection based on our discriminators and cost?		

(continued)

TABLE 6-1 *(continued)*

Question	Y/N	Comment
Evaluation		
Do we know the evaluation process the customer will use?		
How does our solution rate against the evaluation criteria?		
Do we know who our competitors are and how we stack up against them?		
Competition		
Do we know how the customer perceives our competitors?		
Do we have strong, relevant examples, testimonials, and case studies proving how well we've performed for others?		
Solution		
Does our solution and management approach add value for the customer?		
How does the technical solution differentiate us from other providers?		
How can we fill any remaining solution gaps?		
Price		
Do we know what our price must be to win?		
Is our price acceptable to senior management?		
Are we sure the customer has a budget for the project?		
Incumbency		
Is this incumbent beatable?		
Can we assemble the strategies and resources to unseat this incumbent?		
Can we provide evidence that we'll do a better job of meeting all the needs of this customer?		

Getting your act together

When your organization decides to bid, you can take all the information from your bid/no-bid analysis, plus any historical knowledge you have from prior bids or research, to help you prepare for the proposal development stage (see the next section for this pivotal stage).

TIP

Consider the key activities, depending on whether the opportunity is *reactive* (a solicited proposal in response to an RFP) or *proactive* (an unsolicited proposal that you send because you can see an opportunity), listed in Table 6-2. As the proposal leader, try to stay several steps ahead of the process. This table can help you anticipate upcoming activities during the lull between deciding to bid and launching the proposal effort.

TABLE 6-2   **From Pre-Proposal to Proposal Development: Transition Steps**

Reactive	Proactive
Read the RFP cover to cover.	Search for previous proposals you've given to the customer.
Create the deliverables list.	Meet with the sales team to capture stories about problems and pains.
Shred the RFP.	Meet with developers for solution details.
Assess evaluation criteria.	Map solution features to hot buttons.
Articulate the win strategy.	Articulate the win strategy.
Search for answers to questions.	Research customer for latest news and industry issues.
Draft the executive summary.	Draft the executive summary.
Outline the response.	Outline the proposal (use your standard outline).

Proposal Development Stage: Delivering on Your Proposal Strategy

In the proposal development stage, you apply the knowledge that you acquire during the pre-proposal stage to systematically clarify your customer's problem and your unique solution for that problem. The proposal you write is a written argument that expresses the problem and the solution in a methodical way.

The proposal development stage has four phases. First, you have to finalize your proposal's strategy: How do you plan to use all your newfound knowledge about this customer, this opportunity, and these competitors to build your argument? Second, you have to create a customized plan for this particular proposal: How do you structure your argument and equip your contributors to supply the right information? Third, you must write the argument itself: How do you build all the pieces of the argument and ensure a cohesive and clear message? And fourth, you have to produce the proposal: How do you publish, package, and present the proposal to the customer? The following sections answer these questions for you.

Setting the overall strategy

Proposal writers rarely set strategy, but they often express it. They take the boiled ocean of information — the stuff we detail in Chapter 5, such as data collected from customer visits, competitive assessments, SWOT analyses, Internet research, and from testing potential solutions — and condense it into a clear rationale that the team can refer to and rally behind throughout the long proposal development stage and even beyond to contract negotiation.

With the right information, completing this phase of the proposal development stage isn't that difficult. As Figure 6-1 shows, you have two substeps within the "Set Your Strategy" phase before you're ready to start writing the words that will actually make it into your proposal: Organizing all your information and reviewing your customer's hot buttons. After you've finished these two transitional knowledge-gathering steps, you're finally ready to write — not the proposal, mind you, but the elements that will either find their way into the proposal or serve as models for key proposal elements and sections. These include *discriminators* (features of your offer that differ from the competition and that the customer acknowledges as delivering benefits), win themes (also known as *value propositions*) (high-level statements that express the value of a feature, a benefit, and a supporting proof point), and a draft executive summary. And then, at last, you're ready to kick off the project.

The next sections discuss what you do in each of the six "Set Your Strategy" substeps.

Organizing your strategic information

As a proposal writer, you articulate what others struggle to say. So your first step to writing the proposal is to firm up your business's strategy for winning. It's the unifying element to your proposal's story, and to get the material for this story, you have to get the people who lead your sales and solution development efforts to talk about their strategy. Invite them to a meeting (or at least a conference call, if you can't meet face to face) to discuss the opportunity.

TIP

Prepare yourself by following the guidance provided in Table 6-2, depending on the opportunity type. If you've been part of the opportunity assessment, you already know most or all of the answers to these questions and you can skip this substep. If not, use the information in the table to guide your discussion with the sales and solution experts. During this meeting, you need to make sure you leave the meeting with answers to the following questions:

>> **What does the customer's current environment look like?** Get the team to sketch out what the customer's environment looks like today. Dig to discover the real pain behind the images. Prompt them to retell the customer's own stories about this pain.

>> **What is forcing the customer's hand to act?** These are the hot buttons (refer to Chapter 2 — and the next section — for more on these), and though the customer may have many, you need to know which buttons to press as you craft the overall strategy rationale (but keep up with them all, because you can create multiple win themes from them).

>> **What tactics and actions have you designed that will address all your customer's hot buttons and outclass your competitors' efforts and countermeasures?** The SWOT analysis is the best source for this information (refer to Chapter 5), but your expert's comments will supplement this information.

>> **What will the future look like once your solution is in place?** Your strategy must represent the customer's success more than your own, so have them draw a picture of the changed environment once the solution is in place.

Reviewing the customer's hot buttons

Hot buttons are big issues that motivate customers to buy, so you need to know them, state them clearly, and make them available to all involved with creating the proposal so your team never loses focus. If you're working alone, keep the hot buttons on a sticky note in front of you at all times (these issues are also great sources for win themes).

TIP

Review your customer data to identify all its stated and implied hot buttons — every feature, characteristic, measurement, or objective that the customer uses to identify desirable products, services, or companies. Look for phrases that pop up frequently. Quiz your customer contacts about "trigger" words or buzzwords that the customer uses. These words can help you prioritize the hot buttons and phrase them in ways that immediately resonate in the minds of your proposal contributors and, later, in the minds of your customer's proposal evaluators.

Articulating your discriminators

Discriminators are the features of your offer that differ from those of your competitors. To express them well, you have to consider who'll read them and how they'll perceive the problems and then filter the discriminators through their eyes. We provide techniques for using your discriminators in Chapter 3. We provide ways to use them to quantify benefits in Chapter 7. And we provide ways to make sure they stand out in your proposal in Chapter 10.

Crafting proposal win themes

After you gather all the elements to create powerful proposal messages — your rationale for pursuing the opportunity, the customer's hot buttons, your discriminators, and a solution (what you do or use to solve the customer's problem) that you can logically justify over any others — you're ready to use these to craft your win themes. To use these elements effectively, you use them to do two things:

>> Write a single sentence that summarizes your overall offer and approach — something proposal writers call a *win theme*. Your overall win theme must be

- **Meaningful:** It has to echo the customer's overall problem and your unique approach to solving it.

- **Memorable:** It needs to be your proposal team's mantra — something that they'll remember as they work the solution and write their contributions.

- **Demonstrable:** It has to supply *proof* that you can deliver on your claims.

REMEMBER

The overall win theme is a guide for you (and other proposal writers if you have them) to stay on target as you create your proposal. Keep this single sentence "in your face" as you write. It's also useful for headings and callouts within the executive summary.

>> Create *underlying win themes* — key messages to your customer about the value you bring to individual aspects of the solution. Some call these *value propositions*, but they are built the same way as your overall win theme, and in fact should, if shown side by side, express at least some of the components that make up your overall win theme. You use these underlying win themes to reinforce the value of specific solution components and discriminators within your proposal.

TIP

These underlying win themes don't *have* to echo the overall win theme directly but should provide insight into the supporting benefits of your solution.

In Chapter 7, we show you how to write all this information into win theme statements that not only allow all your contributors to dovetail their thoughts within a unifying concept but also show your customer that you've really got your act together.

Prepping the outline and the executive summary

The executive summary in many ways follows the overall proposal outline. And though outlining is actually part of the upcoming "Plan the Proposal" phase (see the later section "Outlining the proposal"), many proposal writers create a skeleton outline of the bid response or proactive proposal just before the kickoff meeting. This preliminary outline provides direction for the proposal team and assures them that their proposal lead has things well in hand. For proactive proposals, the standard outline refreshes the team's memories on how they'll proceed if it's been a while since they've worked on a proposal.

Many proposal writers believe you should draft an executive summary long before you kick off the project and begin working on the proposal in earnest. An executive summary describes the solution at a high level — usually following the same structure as the proposal — so it can help contributing authors put their responses and messages in context with the overall intent of the proposal. This early draft can coach contributors to present their solutions in relation to your win themes. Along with the style sheet, your draft executive summary can model good behavior, demonstrating good use of win themes, graphics, action captions, and tone.

Kicking off the project

After you've completed the preliminary tasks listed in Table 6-2 and built the thematic underpinnings of your proposal, you're ready to bring the team together in what is traditionally called the *kickoff meeting*. Kickoff meetings are crucial to a successful proposal. Usually, you schedule this meeting with the help of the sales lead or opportunity lead, if you have one.

Invite everyone affiliated with the bid to the kickoff meeting. *Strongly* urge them to attend. Invite their bosses if need be. If the proposal is crucial to the organization's success, invite a ranking company leader.

You need to gather all your resources and customer knowledge together for a successful launch. Of these resources, three documents are most useful:

>> **Overall response schedule:** This is a detailed timeline of milestones, including delivery dates, reviews, and publication deadlines (see Chapter 8 for more on creating this schedule).

>> **Requirements checklist:** This checklist may be your compliance matrix, including all *must, will,* and *shall* phrases (refer to Chapter 4 for more on creating your compliance matrix and turning it into a requirements checklist).

>> **Preliminary proposal outline:** The proposal outline is the skeleton structure of your response or argument (refer to the preceding section, "Prepping the outline and the executive summary").

Table 6-3 lists other materials that you should consider including in your kickoff meeting document package, depending on your situation and your role within your organization.

TABLE 6-3   **Checklist of Kickoff Meeting Documents**

Recommended Items	Content/Function
Proposal project summary	Summarizes the opportunity, its value, relevant dates, contacts, scope, deliverables and source material (RFP)
Customer profile	Customer's needs, issues, hot buttons, evaluation process, and attitude toward your organization (refer to Chapter 3)
Proposal strategy	Overall strategies, win themes, and discriminators, including how to implement these elements in the proposal (refer to Chapter 4)
Proposal/response schedule	Sets dates for key milestones (see Chapter 8)
Proposal outline	Defines sections, headings, page allocation, content owners, and other task deadlines (see Chapter 9)
Writers' packages	Summarizes writer assignments, sets page limits and style guidelines, and includes a compliance checklist
Copy of RFP	Relevant parts or pointers to an electronic source
Draft executive summary	Overall perspective on customer's needs, proposed solution, and win strategy; models good themes, graphics, action captions, and format (see Chapter 9)
Competitive analysis	Competitor profiles and the bidder comparison matrix (refer to Chapter 5)

REMEMBER

As a proposal writer or manager, you're in a kickoff meeting to motivate, inform, and direct. You have the following objectives:

>> Deliver the solution overview to the team.

>> Answer questions about the opportunity.

>> Bring contributors onboard.

>> Deliver the outline, style sheet, and other planning documents to authors (see the next section, "Planning the proposal," for more on these).

>> Describe the logistics of gathering contributions.

>> Gain commitment to roles and the schedule.

>> Create a cohesive team.

However you choose to manage your kickoff meeting, keep it short, informative, and professional. Excuse early anyone who doesn't need to hear details about the solution or information about individual assignments or daily team management. If participants will be calling in, publish the meeting notice with the time, location, and purpose of the meeting as far in advance as possible.

TIP

Structure your kickoff meeting in two parts:

>> **Project overview:** The opportunity leader hosts this part. If the bid is a "must-win" opportunity, try to get a high-ranking executive to speak first to bring gravitas to the project. The opportunity leader can then walk the team through the technical solution, management approach, pricing considerations, past performance and references, and so on.

>> **Response logistics:** You (the proposal writer) host this part. Present the schedule and gain concurrence and commitment from all. Deliver the response outline and compliance matrix. Present your content plans and train participants on how to use your systems or processes to submit their work.

Kickoff meetings can truly make the difference between a winning and losing proposal. But be flexible: Depending on the size and nature of your business, these meetings can be very formal or much less so. For simpler deals, you may combine the strategy meeting with the kickoff meeting. In some cases, you may be the sole participant. Use the information in this section to choose the steps that are right for you, but err on the conservative side when eliminating any actions or outputs.

TIP

In the appendix, we provide a link to a sample kickoff meeting agenda and briefing. This agenda, though aimed for more complex and comprehensive meetings, contains most of the critical segments for any kickoff. Adjust it as your situation and time frame demands.

Planning the proposal

This second major phase of the proposal development stage takes place *during* the strategy-setting phase (refer to the earlier section "Setting the overall strategy"). The output of this phase is the *proposal content plan*. This is an all-inclusive name for the outline, the style guide, page and module mock-ups, and the writing guidance you provide in relation to compliance and themes. The idea here is simple: Think before you write, or plan to write, and write to the plan.

REMEMBER

If you're the sole developer of the proposal, you still need input from subject matter experts. The proposal content plan, extensive or simple, helps you successfully receive and manage this input.

The overall goal of this phase is to help you create proposals that are easy to follow and easy to understand. As you create your plan, remember that well-written proposals

>> Provide a road map to the information reviewers want to see

>> Make key points easy for readers to identify and understand

>> Show that you respect the customer's point of view

>> Highlight important information by using headings, visual cues, and graphics so reviewers can scan your content for what they need

Referring to Figure 6-1, you see the five "Plan the Proposal" steps you have to perform "in the background" as you're getting ready for the kickoff meeting. One of these steps — creating the compliance matrix — we cover in detail in Chapter 4 because it's key to responding to RFPs. The other four steps, however, apply to any type of proposal, and we can't emphasize them enough. Building an outline, mocking-up the proposal layout, creating a style sheet, and clearly describing your solution, any alternatives, and the reasons you chose the solution you did, are all crucial steps in developing a coherent, effective proposal. Each deserves a closer look.

Outlining the proposal

Proposal evaluators often scan to find the answers they need rather than read sequentially. This is reason enough to make information easy to locate and follow. Outlines help you do this, and you can use a couple of outlining techniques to make life easier for you, your writers, and ultimately the customer.

First, you have to generate your *topics* — the things you're going to write about. How you do that is up to you, but you can't go wrong with a blank sheet of paper and pencil or a blank whiteboard and marker. But the first critical step is to structure these topics by using a robust *topical outline*. A topical outline sequences and orders the topics you've generated, normally indicated by a numbering scheme.

TIP

By *robust*, we mean a structure that can support the many demands placed upon it and remain stable as you write and review the proposal. That is, your topical outline should be able to expand or contract, depending on discoveries during the writing phase.

If you're responding to an RFP, you have to base your topical outline on the RFP's exact volume, sections, and question headings. Mimic the RFP's numbering system, naming conventions, and sequence. If the customer doesn't provide explicit instructions, follow the outline of the request and organize within that structure in an order that makes logical sense, given what you've learned about the customer.

WARNING

Challenge anyone who recommends an organizing approach that differs from the RFP. The customer will evaluate your response according to the RFP's structure, and deviating from it may eliminate you from consideration. At a minimum, deviating will annoy your customer.

RFP instructions typically specify an outline down to the first or second level of numbering. To ensure full compliance, create a third level to supply additional detail and address nested requirements (those *wills, shalls,* and *musts* that you picked out when you shredded the RFP; refer to Chapter 4), but take care to sustain the RFP's number scheme.

To improve your chances of winning, add detail to your outline where evaluators place the most emphasis (you can find the evaluation criteria and weightings from the instructions section of the RFP). Provide compelling proofs for your capabilities here, where evaluators look for meaningful, distinguishing traits.

REMEMBER

Pay attention to page and word count limits as you create your outline, allocating content where it can do the most good. Be mindful to create topics for unstated customer concerns that don't appear in the RFP, such as your ability to deliver projects on time and within budget. Place these subtopics throughout your outline wherever your main topic may lead evaluators to think about them.

If you're writing a proactive proposal, prepare a top-level topical outline that reflects the logic of your proposal. Most proactive proposals follow this structure:

>> **Current situation:** Describes the issues, needs, and problems your customer is facing.

>> **Proposed situation/recommendation:** Describes your solution, the benefits it brings, and the methods you use to arrive at the solution and those you'll use to implement it.

>> **Qualifications:** Demonstrates why you're the best choice for providing this solution. The rationale may include past performance plus the technical and managerial expertise of your organization.

>> **Cost:** Explains the cost of the solution in terms of the quality of the solution and the value received.

>> **Implementation:** Shows how you'll deliver the solution and who's responsible for what. Some proposals include an extensive statement of work or explanation of the methodology you'll apply to implement the solution.

Never use these topics as your actual proposal section and subsection headings — these outline headings are for your benefit only. Make your proposal headings descriptive, using a short, informative phrase (for example, "How Our Solution Will Benefit <Company>") instead of a single noun or group of nouns.

At this stage, your topical outline is still just a list of headings. You can now guide your contributors' writing by annotating the outline. An *annotated outline* amplifies a topical outline by further defining the content of proposal sections and subsections. This technique is a simple alternative to more comprehensive content development techniques, like storyboarding and mock-ups, yet still achieves great results.

The best way to annotate your topical outline is in line with each topic. Simply type in your annotations next to the topic or below, maybe using a different color or style of type to distinguish it from the main topic. If your topical outline is in a table, maybe add a new column for your annotations. Typical content-related annotations include

>> Suggested graphics to illustrate topics

>> Proof points to support claims

>> Phrasing for more descriptive, headline-oriented headings

>> Suggested boilerplate for high-level or generic topics

>> RFP requirements that you want to highlight

>> Win themes that relate to the topic

>> Customer terms, style, and usage you want writers to include

Annotations can also be directive, such as page and word count limits or coaching comments to help writers stay on message.

Creating an effective mock-up

Mock-ups are a page-by-page visualization of your finished proposal. In addition to the design implicit in a proposal content plan, mock-ups contain layout information and page space constraints. If you're familiar with storyboarding, think of them as thumbnail storyboards.

COLLABORATING EFFECTIVELY BY USING PROPOSAL CONTENT PLANS

Content plans are essential for collaborative writing efforts, and no document is more collaborative than a proposal. Proposal content plans help writers gather and organize their thoughts before they begin to write. When writers have a view of the entire proposal, they have a better understanding of how to write their individual parts, so a good content plan captures proposal strategies and shows writers where and how to include themes and strategy messages.

Standard elements in a proposal content plan include

- **Topical or annotated outline:** This is your structure for the proposal. With RFP responses (or reactive proposals), you must follow the structure of the RFP. For proactive proposals, build a reusable schema that you can use on every proposal of this type. See Chapter 9 for a standard schema.

- **Business or external style guide:** Most organizations have a writing standard that all employees should follow. These standards include guides for style, format, tone, and usage. If you don't have one, choose an external style standard, such as the *Chicago Manual of Style* or the *Associated Press Stylebook*.

- **Project style sheet:** As proposal writer, you have control over the style and tone of a particular document. Review the RFP or your customer notes to find special words and usages that you want to include in your proposal. Echoing the style of your customers is a great, subtle way of showing that you understand their needs and preferences. For general writing style recommendations, see Chapter 10.

- **Page or module mock-ups:** Writers do best when they know how their content will fit in with the rest of the proposal. They also need to know their limitations. Mock-ups give writers a template for their content and show where they should include theme statements, visuals, headings, and other layout elements. Mock-ups can also enforce page/word count limitations. (See the nearby section "Creating an effective mock-up" for more on this.)

Require writers to complete content plans for their sections. Challenge writers to identify what the message should be in their respective sections. Include your underlying win themes in your content plans. Choose appropriate content planning tools (for example, document templates, past performance, and résumé models) that are familiar to your organization and that fit the bid's characteristics and time frame.

TIP

If you have to submit a hard-copy proposal, mock-ups can help to improve the printing process. For large proposals, mock-ups help the printer establish printing timelines, plan resources for multiple volumes, and anticipate special page requirements like foldouts or oversized attachments.

Figure 6-2 illustrates a mock-up.

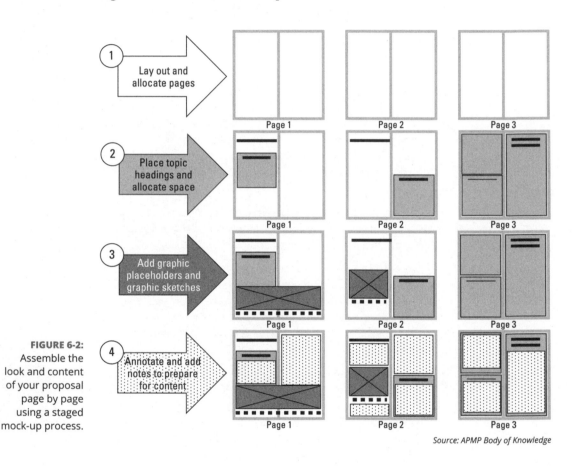

Source: APMP Body of Knowledge

FIGURE 6-2:
Assemble the look and content of your proposal page by page using a staged mock-up process.

Building style sheets

A *style sheet* is a set of standards you develop specifically for a particular proposal that editors and writers can use to ensure consistency in style, grammar, terminology, and mechanics. Style sheets supplement standard and corporate style guides. Simple style sheets are lists of items that writers will encounter time and again while they create content, such as the following:

>> Naming conventions (preferred versions for technical terms)

>> Abbreviations and acronyms, such as MTTR (mean time to repair)

>> Technical notations (such as GB, Kbps, MHz)

>> Products with unique spellings

Style sheets help writers work separately from others and still deliver content that meets a single standard. They can even save time and effort for sole writers of proposals, reminding them of issues easily forgotten. We offer a sample style sheet that can serve as a template for yours via the appendix.

You can also develop design style sheets to control the look and feel of your proposal. Most of the time, you embed these visual style specifications in a document template and set standards at five levels of the document: line level (such as letter and spacing), paragraph level (indentions and bullet formatting), page level (section and page breaks), graphics level (size and resolution), and document level (heading styles and column specifications).

Your proposal template layout standards, defined within your word-processing software, must be

>> **Compliant:** It must follow both customer guidelines and corporate branding or style guidelines. For instance, the customer may specify the paper size, the margins of the paper, the maximum number of pages allowed, and the font to use. If the customer doesn't specify any requirements, use your corporate branding or style guidelines.

>> **Consistent:** Obvious changes in structure, color, font, imagery, layout, or other visual elements suggest a change in meaning. If those changes are unintentional or unexplained, your proposal will appear unprofessional.

>> **Comprehensive:** Your design template needs to prescribe body and heading type and design, bullet and number list symbols and indentions, page margins, column sizes and numbers, marginalia (such as callout boxes), table specifications, graphics resolution and size, header and footer styles and content, branding, color schemes, and the final production format (such as American 8.5-x-11-inch portrait orientation or A3 landscape orientation).

To find out how to access reusable proactive proposal templates and RFP response (reactive proposal) templates, go to the Appendix.

Describing solutions and alternative solutions

A proposal is an argument. An argument states a preferred approach to solving a problem and cites reasons for choosing it over others. Arguments are (mostly) logical, or at least we like to think they are. And while winning proposals include many persuasive elements, they are, at heart, logical arguments.

REMEMBER

Logical arguments accept that a customer can take multiple paths to success. When proposing one solution over others, a smart persuasive technique is to acknowledge those other solutions but then explain why you decided not to offer them. This critical thinking exercise can also help you to create compelling win themes, which you can then elaborate on as you describe your solution and "ghost" the solutions that belong to your competitors (refer to Chapter 5 for more on effectively ghosting your competition).

Creating the compliance matrix

A *compliance matrix* is the tool that helps you and your customer quickly assess whether your proposal meets the customer's specifications. We say *the* tool because it alone can help you assess the validity of your solution before you take the time to propose it, and it can help your customer quickly assess your level of compliance and responsiveness to its needs.

The matrix is a list of specific customer requirements, often splitting complex, multipart requirements into subrequirements, with a notation as to whether you comply fully, partially, or not at all. For a detailed explanation and examples of the compliance matrix, refer to Chapter 4.

Writing the proposal

You're now ready to put "fingers to keys" and write actual content for the proposal. As you recall from Figure 6-1, you have three major elements to write:

>> **Summaries:** The proposal in brief, for various levels of the document

>> **Solution:** Responses for the RFP (the reactive proposal) and the proposal sections in the proactive proposal

>> **Transmittal:** The letter that provides your proposal's first impression

But as the figure indicates, after you're through writing and assembling these parts into your proposal draft, you have to review the draft, revise the draft (as many times as necessary to make it final), and then proofread the final draft for publication. Each substep is crucial to your success, so we discuss each in the next sections.

Preparing the summaries

Depending on the size and complexity of your proposal, you need to write one or more formal *summaries*. Consider your summaries as minute versions of your proposal and your proposal sections.

We can't overemphasize the importance of summaries. You need to have them popping up everywhere in your proposal.

Every proposal of any degree of complexity needs an *executive summary* — a short but persuasive abstract of the main points of the offer aimed at the senior-level decision makers in the customer's organization. Even a five-page proposal is "too much information" for busy decision makers. Highly complex, multivolume reactive proposals need an executive summary plus a summary for every volume. Even larger proactive proposals can benefit from brief introductory summaries for each section to provide road maps for the content to follow and key messages to remember.

All proposal summaries do three important things:

>> They **express win themes** that, because of their position in the document, can influence how readers interpret the information that follows.

>> They **forecast the structure** of the content that follows so readers can decide whether they need to continue or whether they can jump to a portion of greater interest.

>> They **bring important takeaways to the top of the page** so busy, distracted readers get the message, no matter what.

Executive summaries are so important that we devote part of Chapter 9 to how to write them. For now, understand that they're considered to be *formative documents* — that is, you need to draft them early in the proposal process so they can help everyone in your organization understand your strategies, themes, and organizing principles before they ever contribute a word.

Describing your solution

After you have your annotated outline or mock-ups and a guiding executive summary, you can hand them off for your writers to use as they describe your solution, either as a proactive narrative or as individual responses to the customer's questions. (For specific guidance and models to follow as you respond to RFPs and as you craft the narrative for a proactive proposal, see Chapter 9.)

If you're the sole proposal writer, you have to gather the information that your subject matter experts would normally write about. This may be the most difficult and important part of your job. Getting information from experts is a challenge, largely because of the "curse of knowledge." This is the human trait that people all share, regardless of their field of expertise. It's easy to forget what it's like to *not* know what you know. Experts use special terms without considering the effect they may have on people who don't live and breathe their expertise.

Your job as proposal writer is to get all that useful knowledge out of the experts' heads and onto the page — where many non-experts will read them. How on earth do you do that?

Here are a few sources you can use to get started:

>> **Interviews:** Go to where the experts are, sit with them, and ask a lot of questions. And when you get an answer that doesn't make sense to you, ask them to explain it. Remember, these are very busy and important people, so you need to

- Set an appointment (and limit it to an hour at most)

- Come prepared with a set of standard questions about the subject

- Probe for more details and examples after you get your main answers

- Take a humble approach — admit that you need the experts' help and that you may ask "dumb" questions but you're willing to learn

- Thank your experts for their time and let them know that you may need to follow up on some details at a later point

>> **Prior proposals:** Explore this treasure trove of content that's ready for reuse, and is already sequenced and formatted. If your business has a database of prior proposals, search for the most recent ones that address solutions and customer types similar to your new opportunity and pull that information into your annotated outline. Take this information to your experts and have them confirm that it applies to the new opportunity.

WARNING

Make sure you scrub the content for any tell-tale signs of reuse, like other company names and dated references.

>> **Business documentation:** Look to your organization's internal reference sources — the ones that describe your products and solutions (including marketing communications like brochures and product specification sheets), provide technical support for your products (such as manuals), and offer learning resources and training materials for product users.

>> **Industry publications:** Craft effective ways to explain your organization's solutions by checking out similar solutions described in trade journals, blogs, and white papers. If you work for a technology company, you may look to high-tech concept explanation sites like WhatIs.com.

WARNING

As you gather information from secondary sources, remember that copied boiler-plate is easy to spot by evaluators and never specific enough to convince them that you've created the solution just for them. Plus, some of the information you get from the Internet may be copyrighted, so be sure to get permission (if required) to reuse it.

For details about the information you need to get for your proposal or RFP response, see our expanded discussions in Chapter 9 (describing solutions, qualifications, and pricing) and Chapter 7 (presenting benefits).

Writing the letter of transmittal

Every proposal needs a *letter of transmittal,* also known as the cover letter. Although some think this is a relic from an analogue past, the letter of transmittal is another tool for selling, whether in digital form or on good old paper. First off, it's common courtesy. Second, it performs a useful function — it helps get your proposal to the right person. Third, it gets your proposal off on the right note. And fourth, it's one more place to sell your value.

REMEMBER

Write your transmittal letter on your business's letterhead. If you don't have one, use the standard block style (the standard for business letters, which is organized using "blocks" of information, separated by white space) with your address at the top of the page (all parts of your letter should be flush with the left margin), followed by the date, your customer's name, title, and address, a subject line (usually begun with "Re:"), your salutation, the body of your letter, the complementary closing (such as "Sincerely" or "Respectfully"), space for a handwritten signature, and then your name in type. Don't forget to include a line with "Attachment:" or "Enclosure:" followed by the name of your proposal, for the benefit of your reader.

TIP

Start your letter by stating its purpose, but whatever you do, don't say you're pleased to respond to the customer's RFP. You'd be lying. No one is pleased to respond to an RFP — you'd rather sell without doing all this work. So state your purpose here, but do so in a way that will distinguish you from other bidders.

To do this, use a quote from one of your discussions with the customer, or perhaps from a speech made by the customer's president, that summarizes the customer's goals with the procurement. Refer to a significant industry issue that the customer faces and that your solution helps to address. These techniques grab attention and set the tone for the theme-based proposal that follows.

In the second part of the letter, summarize your solution, your offer, and your overall win theme (or multiple, underlying win themes). If your pricing message is favorable and strong, include it. Give your reader every reason to want to know more.

Close by proposing some action or next step. Express a desire for a follow-up meeting. State that you're available whenever the customer wants to answer questions or clarify your proposal. Include the best ways to contact you.

For examples of transmittal letters for reactive and proactive proposals, check out the link in the appendix.

Reviewing your proposal draft

As with most writing projects, the most important part of creating a proposal is reviewing and editing it. Proposal writers and contributors are too close to their work to be able to review it for quality, compliance, consistency, and effectiveness. A fresh look at a proposal by experts who haven't been involved in writing or solution development is essential.

For complex proposals, reviews can consume considerable time in the schedule. First, you may need to schedule different types of reviews: *solution* or *technical reviews* (these provide objective assessments of your solution by qualified experts not on the proposal team), *operational* or *methodology reviews* (these let your project managers or implementation experts evaluate how your implementation plans fit with the customer's environment), and lastly, *final proposal reviews* (these let executives and managers read the entire proposal from the customer's point of view). For a detailed discussion of final proposal reviews, see Chapter 12.

TIP

Reviewers need time to read, understand, and absorb feedback about the proposal. You also need time to determine how best to respond to reviewers' comments. Make sure you allocate plenty of time in your schedule for reviews and the work they spawn.

Everyone's proposals need to be reviewed and edited, even if you're a sole proprietor. Find a trusted confidant who can review your work before you hand it over to your customer.

TIP

Present your reviewers with the closest thing you can get to a final draft. This isn't the time to give them copy with spelling errors and significant content gaps. You want your reviewers to act like customers, so treat them with the exact document you'll present to the customer.

To capture reviewers' comments and suggestions, ask them to make notes on a copy of the proposal or, in more formal reviews, complete a comment form. For bids of significant value, consider creating a scoring summary that mirrors the customer's evaluation criteria.

Revising your proposal draft

Compile reviewer comments into one set of recommendations. Debrief all the reviewers as a team if physically possible, so their comments will spur more discussion and reveal potential issues you may not get from their marked-up copies of the proposal. If not, assign the recommendations to a select core group of contributors to implement, or, for smaller opportunities, implement the recommendations yourself. Arrange for individual reviewers to be available to respond to questions about their comments.

You're now ready to complete a final edit of your proposal. If you can afford it, use a professional proposal editor for making final edits. In smaller enterprises, this task may fall upon you if you're the sole proposal resource. If you're the sole proprietor . . . well, you know it's down to you alone to decide whether to pay for external help.

TIP

If you're doing the editing yourself, allow time in your schedule to set the document aside for a spell — as much as a day or two if possible — to give your eyes and brain a chance to separate from the content and layout. This simple technique can return you to a level of objectivity that can allow you to catch subtle errors. Use spelling and grammar checkers to catch obvious mistakes. Read backward to find embarrassing but hard-to-find errors (such as easily misplaced words like *there* instead of *their* or inappropriate boilerplate/reuse text).

Proofing your proposal draft

If you've done a good job revising and editing your proposal, proofing should be a snap. We used to hold "final eyes" sessions with the proposal team as we prepared to print or electronically publish a proposal. In these sessions, you break the document up into manageable chunks and provide a checklist for proofers to follow to pick up potential errors and inconsistencies. This checklist may ask proofers to check headers and footers for proper page numbers and dates; look for information out of sequence; check graphics and illustrations for errors in labels, titles, and reference numbers; sum figures in pricing tables to make sure they add up; check the table of contents for glitches . . . the list can go on and on.

Proofing is a time for minutiae, not a major overhaul of the text.

REMEMBER

Producing the proposal

The long and winding road is almost at an end. By this time, you probably feel as though you've run a marathon on hilly and twisting paths. You (and your team) have created a compelling argument for your customer to consider. Phase four of the proposal development stage covers *producing* the proposal, and you have four substeps to walk your team through to get to the finish line.

TIP

Start your production plans during the pre-proposal stage, especially for major opportunities. Failing to reserve production resources in advance can jeopardize deadlines. As a rule of thumb, allow 10 percent of your available proposal development time for production, scaling up or down depending on the proposal's size, delivery requirements, and your organization's capabilities.

Producing your proposal takes four substeps: Printing your proposal (or "printing" to PDF format), creating other media as required, packaging your proposal, and then delivering it. Here's more on each of those steps.

Printing the proposal

After you plan, write, and review your proposal, you must turn it into reviewable copy that fulfils the customer's expectations. That may mean publishing it in electronic format, in hard copy, or both. And despite the potential for headaches during this phase, producing the physical proposal is often the most fun you can have in the proposal business — it's when all the hard work comes to fruition.

Always print proposals in color. Colors highlight key information, make images stand out, and reinforce your customers' brands (it's all about them, remember?). Bind your proposals as well — and we don't mean with staples. Create professional bindings, using comb or spiral binding for smaller, proactive proposals and ring binders for larger reactive volumes. Try to print double-sided (it's good for the environment and makes for a less bulky package). The best news: For most opportunities, you can avoid the expense and labor of printing altogether and submit only digital copy (either in PDF format or some other electronic means). PDF is great because you have the convenience of digital and the aesthetic value of a professional document.

Printing a major proposal requires coordination, cooperation, and concerted effort from a team of specialists, including desktop publishers, graphic artists, editors, proofreaders, fact checkers, and either in-house or contracted printers and media specialists. If you're part of a small business or a one- or two-person proposal shop, you may be strapped for time, resources, and specialists. Consider building in requirements for teammates and subcontractors to assist the publishing effort. You may request access to printing facilities, editorial support, desktop publishing resources, or, at minimum, help with assembling books and making "final-eyes" reviews.

For an extensive look at the roles and activities of the final phase of the proposal development stage, see Chapter 12.

TIP

If you're responding to an RFP, carefully re-read its production and delivery instructions and update your publishing plan accordingly. Check to see whether the RFP has stipulated font style, size, and line spacing, all of which can have a dramatic effect on the look and page count of your proposal.

REMEMBER

Be sure to plan for printer and IT support. Your IT staff can save your proposal in emergencies. Know how to contact them 24/7, and be sure that this information is available to all your proposal team, just in case of a crisis (those never happen during production time . . . yeah, right!).

Creating other media

Proposals are no longer just printed. Smart proposers, especially for larger bids, provide searchable media along with print copy to help evaluators find what they're looking for and simplify and speed up the evaluation process. So you may need a media specialist, someone who can turn print documents into PDFs, emails, web pages, and electronic database submissions, not to mention CDs, DVDs, and even flash drives.

TIP

Proposals are evolving with technology, so consider adding video executive summaries, interactive graphics, embedded demos, and other media-driven components of your proposals.

Packaging the proposal

Depending on your customer, *packaging* your printed proposal for delivery (that is, binding your print copy in one or more volumes and creating a convenient and distinctive wrapper for the bundle) may be a walk in the park or a jump through a flaming hoop. Customers may place hard-to-find requirements in their bids to help them quickly separate the pretenders from the contenders — for instance, they may require separate binding for pricing or specify envelopes or boxes. Read each bid's requirements carefully, and follow any packaging instructions to the letter. Packaging digital media can be even more challenging, especially if you're creating multiple volumes or using multimedia. Instead of just attaching a bunch of files to an email, take extra measures to make your proposal package a unified whole.

Delivering the proposal

Nothing is worse than going through the previous phases and steps only to discover that somehow your proposal was sent to Poughkeepsie instead of Paris. Plan your delivery methods (electronic and hard-copy) in meticulous detail.

Contract with two proven delivery companies. Work with them both to prioritize your proposal deliveries. If you outsource your printing, work with your provider to leverage agreements with delivery companies. Building seamless processes across all four areas of proposal production can bring consistency and peace of mind to your operation.

Build in a solid backup delivery plan ready to implement at a moment's notice. Always plan to submit a day early, and train your management to understand the need for this schedule. Accidents, terrorism threats, natural disasters, traffic jams, weather emergencies, severe illnesses, and other problems occur year-round, and late delivery usually means instant disqualification.

TIP

Consciously maintain version control of your documents at all points in the proposal development process. While version control is extremely important throughout the process, it's even more critical during proposal production. You can lose the competition by submitting a non-compliant proposal based on an older version of a proposal section or out-of-date graphics or by committing your organization to performing the wrong services or supplying the wrong products at the wrong price.

Post-Proposal Stage: Getting Ready for Another Round

Submitting a proposal doesn't mean the end of the proposal process. On the contrary, this is the phase where business decisions become even more intense. The final stage of the proposal process has four phases. The first two are closely tied to your submitted proposal and can mean the difference between winning and losing that bid. The second two phases may draw from the just-finished proposal but actually have more to do with looking ahead to success on subsequent opportunities.

Responding to customers' questions

Many customers request clarifications or have discussions with bidders before making a final decision. These conversations may require you to modify your proposal in some way. Your strategy during this phase should be to respond quickly and fully to customer questions and concerns and to reinforce the customer's trust in your solution, your brand, and your people.

As proposal writer, you should be closely involved in preparing the appropriate final revisions, presentations, or other communications that the customer may require to award the business (if you're not already leading this process anyway). While interacting with the customer, your business should refine its sales plan and prepare for customer meetings and live discussions. Overall, your organization's strategy should be to

>> Respond fully to customer questions and concerns

>> Reinforce a customer's trust in your solution and organization

>> Optimize the deal to your benefit and the customer's

Preparing for oral presentations

The oral proposal is like a job interview for your organization. Generally, bidders asked to give oral proposals have made the customer's shortlist and the customer wants a preview of what working with them will be like. The customer may want to see how you solve problems or how you respond to challenges on the spot. Often, a customer will hold a question-and-answer session after the oral presentation. The key is to be ready for anything.

If your proposal yields an opportunity to present your proposal "live," plan your approach carefully before preparing your presentation. For guidance on this step, check out our online resources by referencing the appendix.

Capturing lessons learned

Oddly enough, the two forward-looking steps to close out a proposal opportunity require that you look backward (see also the next section for the other forward-looking step).

TIP

If you hope to create and sustain a strong proposal process, you need to conduct a *lessons-learned review* after completing each opportunity. For detailed information on how to conduct this review, see Chapter 15.

Harvesting reusable content

Every proposal opportunity produces new information — about customers, about solutions, about your own business, and even about yourself. Part of your job as proposal writer is to capture the information that worked and make it available to reuse in a subsequent opportunity.

Mature proposal organizations retain archives of completed proposals. Some even break the content into reusable chunks and store those in a database with tags to help them find what they need. But content reuse can be as simple as keeping a file of topics you know you'll address a second, third, or hundredth time and using that information to pre-populate a draft for a new proposal.

TIP

Follow these guidelines for finding and storing reusable content:

>> **Use your lessons learned to ask about content that worked and content that didn't.** What content caused the customer to ask questions? Think about reworking that information based on how you answered the follow-up questions.

>> **Take a look at the content you reused for the opportunity.** What seemed stale? Would a more recent example or proof point make it more compelling? Would a new illustration help explain the concept?

>> **Refresh your organization's statistics and financial data.** The underlying win themes may stay somewhat the same, but the numbers will change regularly. Set up a schedule for reviewing this information and make contacts in finance and operations to supply updates quarterly or annually, or whenever you deem fit.

REMEMBER

The smallest of proposal operations can benefit greatly from standardized and current reusable content. Make this last proposal step a high priority. You'll look back at future proposals and be very glad you did.

Chapter 7

Setting Yourself Apart From Your Competitors

In this chapter, we start to look at the actual writing of the proposal. Sure, you may have written your topical outline by now (refer to Chapter 6), and if you're not used to writing, that may have felt like a huge task in itself. You may have also worked with your sales lead to boil your customer's hot buttons and your solution's key benefits into a one-sentence, memorable win theme (refer to Chapter 2). And you've supported this cornerstone concept with a number of supporting proposal themes that you'll echo throughout the proposal (refer to Chapter 6 again). But really, you've only just started.

If the win theme is the cornerstone of your proposal, the benefits — those tangible improvements to your customer's business that your solution brings — and the discriminators — those advantages that only you can bring to your customer's solution — represent the framework of your proposal. They serve two main purposes:

>> **They make your solution meaningful to your customer.** Benefits and discriminators reinforce that your solution will take away the customer's pains

that stem from its problem or need. They express the *whys* that persuade customers to buy. They place you and your solution inside the workings of the customer's business, and that makes your solution real to your customer.

>> **They bring structural integrity to your proposal.** Benefits and discriminators echo your win theme and your underlying theme statements. You use them time and again to reiterate your solution's value and your organization's trustworthiness. They add the needed emotional appeal to your argument, touching on matters that mean most to your customers.

And then you have the proofs. They're the underpinning for the entire proposal. Proofs are the evidence that you can do what your win theme says you can. They're the examples that add heft to your logic and the ring of truth to your benefits. They're the confirmation that your solution is the best choice for your customer.

This chapter takes you through each of these three elements: features and benefits, discriminators, and proofs. After you get these key parts of your proposal down, the rest is just a matter of placing them throughout the structure of your reactive or proactive proposal outline so they'll sell your solution from start to finish.

Presenting Features and Benefits

Integral to your proposal is an inseparable pairing. You can call this pairing *feature–benefit statements.* As we explain in Chapter 2, *features* are the physical things or services you offer to solve your customer's problem. *Benefits* are what the feature makes possible in terms of improved process or performance for the customer. You can't have one without the other, so it's best to pair them in your proposal.

TIP

For every feature, you must have a benefit. For every benefit, you must have a feature. Otherwise, forget them — a feature that brings no benefit is worthless, as is a benefit a customer doesn't need.

REMEMBER

Although features and benefits come as a pair in your proposal writing, you need to keep in mind that customers are sold on the benefits they receive from a seller's solution, not the features that the seller touts. With proposals, you always need to think about the customer. Yet many businesses fail to look beyond their own selling perspective to create valid links between their features and the benefits that customers receive. A deeper understanding of your customers' needs, your competitors' offerings and strengths, and your own capabilities (features) and unique characteristics (your *discriminators*) allows you to communicate compelling, trustworthy benefits to buyers.

To grasp how these three aspects relate to each other and to your customers, it may be helpful to think of

>> Features as the *what*, as in "What is it and what does it do?"

>> Benefits as the *so what*, as in "So what does it mean to me?"

>> Discriminators as the *how well*, as in "How do you do things that matter better than your competitors?"

Features and benefits are so critical to a persuasive proposal that we need to look into each more closely. Benefits are so important that we need to qualify them with a special test to be sure we represent them properly. And discriminators — the benefits that mean the most to your customers — deserve a section all to themselves.

Describing your proposal's features

In a proposal, features are the vehicles for providing benefits to your customers. Features are tangible aspects of products that set them apart from your competitors' versions. They're the pieces of equipment that customers can watch you install or calibrate; the functions within a website that your customers can observe working on a screen; the physical aspects of a tool that your customers can handle and use themselves. For services, they're the means by which customers communicate with you; the schedules and processes you follow to meet your customers' needs; the rigor you apply when you solve your customers' problems. Whether product or service, features are normally things that are measurable and demonstrable.

Providing the right amount of detail about your features

How much do customers need to hear about your features? That depends on the type of customer you're seeking and the individual who will make the final decision to buy. Here's a rule of thumb: The higher the managerial level of the person you're writing to, the less about features you need to include.

REMEMBER

Features are what technicians and operators thrive on. They use the product daily and depend on the features to get their jobs done. To win them over, you always have to supply detailed information about the features. Managers just want the features that their workers need to succeed so they can help the business succeed. For managers, listing the feature's name and the function it performs is usually enough.

More and more managers are technically savvy. Make sure that you know your audience's level of technical expertise and that you respond accordingly.

Regardless of your audience, within the proposal, less is more. List only those features that are pertinent to the needs of the customer. If you deem some features as "value adds," discuss them briefly after you list the features that respond best to your customer's requirements.

To make sure your proposal contains the right information for all your potential audiences, place any supporting details in an appendix, or provide a link to a website that provides the details and perhaps even demonstrations, videos, or testimonials.

Determining the best way to present features

If your features require a good bit of explanation, use informative headings to signal to evaluators that you're about to discuss a feature. As you write a heading, try to achieve one or more of the following:

>> **Highlight a major operational element of the feature.** For example, *SureGuard's Phone App: Monitor Your Home Security.*

>> **Link the upcoming feature to a key benefit.** For example, *Arm or Disarm Your System Remotely with SureGuard's Phone App.*

>> **Point out features that are positive discriminators.** For example, *Only SureGuard Feeds Live Video Feeds to Your Phone.*

Check out the later sidebar "Get your headings to shout about your discriminators" for a look at the value of effective headings in more detail.

If your features are fairly simple to explain, use a bulleted list. Order the entries in matching priority to your customer's requirements. You can also consider using a table (as an alternative to a list). Tables can be very effective for setting apart important information that also requires a little explanation. Whichever method you choose, start with the official name of the feature, followed by a brief description of what it's for, what it does, and perhaps how it works.

Here's an example of a feature explanation within a bulleted list (the *what*):

Phone app: Allows you to monitor your SureGuard home security system 24/7, using a simple touch-screen interface. The app is available on all mobile phone platforms and is fully configurable for your needs. It allows you to stream videos from your home cameras and to arm and disarm your system remotely.

Clarifying benefits

Features are the *what* of your offer. But oddly, the *whats* don't really convince customers to buy. Benefits — the *so-whats* — do, especially when you can enhance those benefits with your unique discriminators (something that we explore in more detail in the later section "Quantifying the value of benefits with discriminators").

Benefits are the results that stem from applying features that solve customer problems. They describe the value that the customer can achieve from your solution to its problem. To claim a benefit, a feature of your offer must clearly allow the customer to realize the benefit — it's a one-to-one relationship.

EXAMPLE

To continue with our SureGuard example from the preceding section, here's the *so-what*:

> **Phone app:** If you're stuck in traffic and need to let visiting relatives into your house, you can disarm the alarm from your cellphone just before they arrive, and maintain your home's security until they arrive.

Benefits help customers achieve their goals — goals that go beyond merely solving the problem — because they answer the question, "So what?" The example explains the practical benefit that the phone app's feature supplies.

Benefit statements may be the hardest thing to write in a proposal. Many writers confuse them with features, or even with the new capabilities that result from using the features. Technical experts, who clearly understand the significance of features, have an especially hard time distinguishing the difference.

EXAMPLE

Take, for example, an engineer who claims that a product is made from 93 percent modular components. She may argue strongly that the modularity alone is a benefit. Actually, it's a feature. It only enables a benefit, such as faster repair times and lower maintenance costs. For this reason, always ask someone who doesn't have a technical understanding of your solution but does understand the customer's perspective to evaluate your feature and benefit statements.

Consider the examples in Table 7-1 to help you make sense of the differences between features and benefits.

TABLE 7-1 **The Differences Between Features and Benefits**

Problem	Pain	Feature Statement	Benefit Statement
Secure sensitive information on website.	Your customers are unwilling to purchase tickets online; they're afraid that their credit information is at risk.	Encrypted transactions	Encodes your customers' card numbers and other personal information so they can buy with confidence
Attract new customers with easy-to-use web features.	Your customers give up on transactions because they can't find what they need.	Reconfigured user experience with simplified navigation	Secures transactions so your customers can easily and quickly find merchandise and order or manage tickets

TIP

You must present your features–benefits as complementary — in parallel, in the same order — wherever you present them, whether side by side or in different sections of your proposal.

Applying the "so what?" test

When you look at the problem, pain, feature, and benefit statements side by side (refer to Table 7-1 for some examples), you see how the feature (usually written as nouns and noun phrases — for example, "encrypted transactions") is the working element of the solution that solves the problem. You express features in terms of what they do (the *what* of your solution that speaks to technical evaluators). What makes features become meaningful to less technical evaluators is the benefit that combines the feature (for example, it encodes card numbers) with the business result that it enables (for example, that as a result, people can buy with confidence).

TIP

The benefit statements in Table 7-1 rely heavily on verbs. *Verbs* are words that answer the "so what?" question in your evaluator's heads with actions (for example, "encodes . . . so they can buy . . ."), actively removing the customer's pain as the feature solves the problem. The "so what?" benefit speaks to all the evaluators but especially the decision maker, because not only does the benefit solve the immediate problem, but it also implies a long-term benefit: that customers will keep on buying.

To make sure your benefits aren't just reworded feature statements, ask yourself "so what?" after you read them. A feature statement won't be able to answer the question, whereas a benefit statement will provide a clear answer by expressing the action that your feature performs and the results that the action achieves — which serves to address your customer's specific problem or need.

TIP

To help customers select your offer, don't rely on your benefits to be self-evident. Help customers draw conclusions about the value of your features with a features and benefits table. It can quickly highlight the advantages of choosing your organization based on the value you offer.

Quantifying the value of benefits with discriminators

To test whether your benefit statements truly express benefits and not just features, you ask "so what?" about each one. But to truly convince your customers of your features' value, you need to couple the "so what?" with another question: "How well?" — that is, "How well does your benefit satisfy the customer's most important needs?" The answer lies in discriminators.

REMEMBER

A *discriminator* is a feature of your offer that the customer acknowledges as delivering a desired benefit — it quantifies the value of the feature to your customer. Proposal writers have names for the relative effectiveness of discriminators (they're a little over the top like that). *Key discriminators* are those that the customer acknowledges as delivering important benefits. *Weak discriminators* are only distinct from a single competitor's offer and not from the rest. *Positive discriminators* are benefits that only one bidder can rightfully claim; these benefits are significant enough to customers that they can justify awarding the bid to you on them alone (so positive discriminators are the ones you want!). Still, all discriminators are important — even weak ones show you in a positive light, and key discriminators can at least keep you in the running for the business because customers recognize them as important.

Well-written positive discriminators acknowledge the different roles that readers of the proposal will have and the different perspectives and motivations that each person brings to a collective decision.

EXAMPLE

Take, for example, one of the benefits from Table 7-1:

> Encodes customers' card numbers and other personal information so they can buy with confidence

Imagine that your encoding scheme is world-class, with secret-service-level security. No other competitor can compare. That will resonate deeply with technical evaluators, putting your solution at the top in their minds.

For their endorsement, you can therefore embellish your benefit statement:

> Encodes customers' card numbers and other personal information with the same technology used by government security agencies so customers can buy with confidence

Figure 7-1 shows where your customers' needs, your competitors' capabilities, and your own capabilities intersect — identifying the "sweet spot." Positive discriminators lie in the single segment where you offer something that no one else does and where that something matters to the buyer. No other set of conditions fully qualifies as a discriminator.

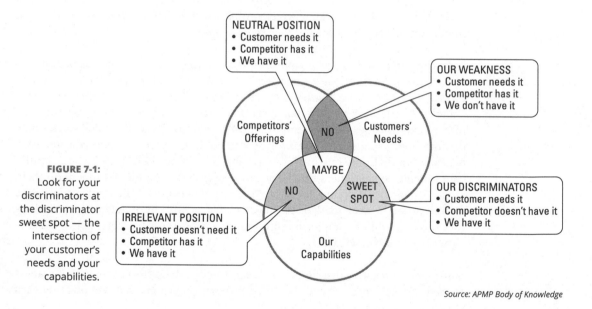

FIGURE 7-1:
Look for your discriminators at the discriminator sweet spot — the intersection of your customer's needs and your capabilities.

Source: APMP Body of Knowledge

Although customers base their buying decisions on benefits (both tangible, like a physical feature, and intangible, like a perceived capability), quantified benefits are more compelling than those that don't deliver a measurable value proposition. But beware: You must also be able to *prove* the quantification claim. If you have no evidence that your encryption scheme doesn't beat the competition's hands-down, find another discriminator.

You want to quantify your benefits with discriminators whenever you can. They're especially convincing if you can convey them graphically, but at the very least, consider adding them to as many of your benefits as possible.

GET YOUR HEADINGS TO SHOUT ABOUT YOUR DISCRIMINATORS

Your solution's win themes, benefits, and discriminators are the most important messages you communicate to your customers. The very best way to make sure they're noticed is to write them into your proposal's headings. Headings stand out — they're bold and they're big. Written correctly, they motivate readers to read on and reinforce the unique attributes that set you apart from your competitors.

Proposal benefits and discriminators are a perfect fit for headings for the following reasons:

- **Headings are active.** Discriminators call out the things that your business does that your competitors can't or won't do.

- **Headings are descriptive.** Benefits describe the value of a solution or its features and how they'll perform in the customer's environment.

- **Headings are vivid.** Win theme statements echo the words that customers have heard from the beginning of their conversations with your salesperson to the present proposal.

- **Headings are helpful.** Your win themes, benefits, and discriminators carry the proofs that evaluators need to make them want to choose your solution.

Consider the following two headings. Which one is most effective?

EDE's New Release of World-Class E-Gates Version 0.6

Our E-Gates System V0.6 Has Reduced Passengers' Check-In Time to Seven Minutes

The second heading focuses on the benefits to the bidder: Reducing passenger check-in time at a highly congested airport, with a precise quantifier that points to proof for the claim. The first simply names the feature with no attending benefit, and readers are left to figure out the benefit on their own.

Backing Up Your Claims with Proof

REMEMBER

Proof points are facts that provide verifiable evidence to support your solution's features, benefits, and discriminators. They also support your organization's win theme and your proposal themes. Without proof points, proposal evaluators may question whether your features work as you claim, whether their benefits can deliver what you promise, and whether your discriminators truly set you apart.

Evidence wins arguments. Proof points make your proposal arguments compelling to a customer. They often describe performance on similar past efforts. A proof point may consist of project data, case studies, customer quotes or testimonials, awards or recognition earned, and more.

REMEMBER

Crafting effective proof points requires that you and your contributors fully understand your win strategy. After you determine your solution, you need to spend substantial effort finding evidence to persuade your readers and add credibility to your claims.

The following sections look at some different ways to prove that your stated benefits can deliver the goods.

Using past projects to back up your claims

Customers prefer organizations that can demonstrate both *relevant experience* in the work that they need to have done and a track record of successful *past performance*. A great way to provide evidence that you can do what you say is to cite examples of how you've done it in the past on projects with similar goals and of comparable size, scope, magnitude, and complexity. Your examples need to illustrate your work on successful projects that you delivered on time, within budget, and to customer specifications.

What parameters of past performance should you include? That depends on your customer's needs. In complex procurements, you may be asked to provide detailed information about a range of categories, such as the following:

>> Contract name, customer name, contact name and information

>> Dollar value/contract type

>> When you performed the work

>> Project objectives and key solution deliverables

>> How the customer benefited from your work

>> Scope of work performed

>> Locale of work performed

>> Project performance

In less complex situations, you may need to provide a customer reference, with a name and number to contact for verification. Sometimes, a mere testimonial quote from a satisfied customer can solidify your claim.

If your prior customers don't want you to quote them or to reveal details of your work with them, you may consider providing a case study that describes your performance on a previous project, using generic language for describing the actual customer.

Some customers may place greater importance on past performance than others. But no matter what the setting, clear descriptions of past performance can help build confidence in your solution and your ability to perform.

Making your proof persuasive

Proof points must be *persuasive* by substantiating the features and benefits that meet or exceed customer objectives and requirements. Here's an example of a persuasive proof point:

> We know that retaining staff is crucial for this project. Our retention rate across the company is 90 percent, compared to 82 percent industrywide for similar IT positions. On helpdesk projects such as this one, our retention rate is 98 percent, because we focus on leveraging Help Desk Institute certifications and best practice processes.

The details in this example help to persuade readers that your proofs are valid.

Avoid using general proof statements that fail to provide the customer with verification. Typical generic proof points include statements (that invite inevitable questions) such as these:

>> We enjoy high levels of customer satisfaction. *How high?*

>> We have low employee turnover. *Compared to what?*

>> We offer relevant experience. *In what?*

Details persuade; generalizations come off as hedges at best and smokescreens at worst. So don't write:

> Some workers will realize productivity gains.

Instead, write:

> Your 28 support staff clerks will reduce their filing and follow-up time by an average of 18 percent, or 1.4 hours per day.

The second statement is much more persuasive. So don't spare the details when you're describing your features, benefits, and discriminators.

Making your proof tangible

Proof points must be *tangible.* They must provide measurable facts and figures. For example:

EXAMPLE

> Our company has delivered 24 software development projects for 13 customers over the past 5 years, all of which were performed at CMMI Level 3 or higher. We are able to staff your project by drawing on 25 ITIL Foundation certified IT personnel.

REMEMBER

Your proof points must be detailed to be believable. But these details must also be accurate. Ensure that all your proof points contain specific numbers as opposed to estimates.

To demonstrate your organization's size and strength, you can present data that shows your locations, divisions, subsidiaries, and programs/projects, preferably through graphics, charts, and tables. If you're the prime contractor working with a partner, pull together the data that represents the combined entities (revenues, locations, employees, projects, certifications, and so on). Merely aggregating data is not effective, however. When you provide numbers, always explain to readers what they mean.

Table 7-2 provides an example to demonstrate how you can provide accurate proof points based on aggregated data.

TABLE 7-2 ## Aggregating Proof Points

Entity	Service Locations	Service Vehicles	Service Technicians
Our Company	14	78	156
Partner A	9	27	48
Partner B	12	66	122
Total	35	171	326

EXAMPLE

As a result of the data in Table 7-2, you can make the following proof point statement:

> Our combined service personnel outnumber our competitors' by 2 to 1. Our combined service coverage places technicians within 25 miles of your branches, and our fleet can arrive for repairs within 30 minutes.

TIP

To provide further tangible evidence, focus your data on objectives met and results achieved. Tangible examples include dollars saved, percentage increases in efficiency, percentage increases in customer satisfaction, and decreased wait times.

Making your proof credible

Your proof points must be *credible.* They must provide verifiable information. For example:

EXAMPLE

We will meet or exceed performance expectations. For the past seven years, we have received the J.D. Power & Associates award for "Best Overall Satisfaction" and "Among the Best" ratings for Performance and Reliability.

Your discerning customer may want to verify your proof points, so make them tangible by identifying all data sources and providing specific customer references and quotes (ask for customer permission before using direct quotes).

Some potential sources for tangible proofs include

>> Case studies reported by trade magazines and sources

>> Citations of industry recognition of innovation or longevity

>> Awards or ratings from external, unbiased third parties

>> Published data that shows size or financial strength

>> Comparisons to show that your solutions meet or exceed industry performance standards (which will also ghost the competition; refer to Chapter 5 for more on ghosting)

REMEMBER

Whether small, medium, or large, all companies must develop proof points to substantiate their features, benefits, and discriminators. Without proof points, your proposal is incomplete. Customers won't be able to verify your claims and will have no reason to believe them.

Chapter 8

Keeping Your Proposal on Track

Many people believe proposal management is a lot like project management, and they're right to an extent. Like projects, proposals have deadlines and milestones. Like major implementation projects, proposals often require you to manage the activities and contributions of a large team of specialists. And, like all major internal or external business projects, proposals can be just as complex, lengthy, resource-sapping, and bottom-line affecting, and can benefit from all the tools that help project managers deliver those projects successfully.

Yet proposal management adds another dimension to the management of a project: Document development and publication. That dimension is a different animal indeed. Proposal projects require scheduling the time of contributors and deadlines for their contributions, making sure all contributors are working off the most current and correct version of the document, establishing the structure of the proposal and associated content (based on either the customer's preferences or yours), developing the order of that content (from declaring your intention to bid to final presentations to close the business), preparing the media used to display that content (from email to paper to a variety of digital formats), and, to top it all off, packaging and shipping the proposal, if required. It takes a master conductor to keep the whole thing on track.

In this chapter, we share how you can bring the proposal project in on time, within budget, and to the delight of a satisfied customer. Because your project's success depends so much on the contributions of others, we also discuss how to build a winning proposal team, with the right people in the right roles with the appropriate skill sets.

Coming Up with a Schedule That Works

Planning, staffing, scheduling, funding, and managing a proposal project, reactive or proactive, is hard, time-consuming yet satisfying work. All this work is crucial to the success of any proposal, great or small. Without the right people doing the right things with the right resources at the right time, all in concert, a proposal will likely fail. And if the proposal fails, the sale will likely fail as well.

Old proposal writers (like us) have a saying: "No proposal ever won a deal all by itself, but plenty have lost them." Proposals lose business all on their own by being ill-conceived, incomplete, or incompetently executed. Managing the time and resources you have can make all the difference. To do this, you must have a schedule — one that does the following

>> Identifies the tasks to be performed for a particular opportunity

>> Assigns a deadline for every task

>> Encompasses each task's essential action steps, their sequence, and their expected duration

>> Balances the workload by maximizing the number of tasks that can be completed in parallel, while minimizing the number that must be done sequentially

>> Ensures quality, compliance, responsiveness, and on-time delivery

You can devise a workable schedule for a proposal of any type, size, or degree of complexity by applying the principles that we discuss in the following five sections:

>> Scheduling from the end to the beginning

>> Breaking large assignments into smaller work units

>> Working in parallel on tasks that don't depend on other tasks

>> Reviewing what works and doesn't as you go along

>> Managing the project day by day, even when milestones aren't imminent

Beginning at the end and working backward

The key to a successful proposal schedule is to be aware of the time frame your customer sets and to begin scheduling milestones and activities at the point when the response is due and work backward to where you stand today (we outline these steps in the proposal process in Chapter 6). And even though that description may sound a little weird, the following sections describe how you can successfully set up the schedule from the beginning — oh, hang on — from the end to the beginning.

Setting (or adhering to) an ironclad due date

REMEMBER

Most reactive proposals have a due date that you can't miss, even by seconds. Remember, it's called a deadline for a reason — and if you miss crossing that line, you're dead.

Many proactive proposals have loose due dates. Your salesperson may convince the customer that a problem needs solving, and so the customer says, "Bring me a proposal" with varying degrees of urgency. Your job is to firm up that date with the salesperson or the customer so you have an endpoint to aim for. Set this date in stone, even if your customer later extends the due date or if your salesperson gets distracted by other opportunities. In both reactive and proactive situations, extensions or delays are a pain to proposal managers because everyone else tends to relax when given more time and milestones are more easily missed. Avoid falling into this trap and the scramble that inevitably results when the due date suddenly looms.

Allotting ample time for production and delivery

Proposal production entails formatting, printing, assembling (sometimes of multiple volumes), and double-checking to ensure that everything is in the package or on the disk and that it complies with all requirements. Not all aspects of the production process are within your control, so you must be conservative when you schedule this activity, and protect this portion of the schedule above all others. Because production (even purely digital production) occurs late in the schedule, any activities that run late affect the production process.

If you're going to adhere to the production schedule without sacrificing quality, you need to establish a firm cut-off time after which no changes can be made to the graphics or text. You must weigh the benefit of additional changes with the risk of faulty production or late delivery and resist editorial changes beyond a pre-established date and time. Maintaining a production checklist like the one in Chapter 16 can help you make the right decisions at crunch time.

Before scheduling tasks that occur earlier, be a little selfish. You need time to ensure a quality product that makes it to the customer on or before its deadline. Consider a range of contingency plans at the production and delivery steps; you never know what kinds of delays can occur if you outsource printing or if you must send the proposal package any significant distance. When you allocate time for production, consider the impact of worst-case contingencies, such as computer viruses, power outages, and equipment malfunctions.

REMEMBER

Setting aside appropriate time for production is a task you normally must fight to keep. Few of your team will understand the amount of work required to prepare a document for production. The work happens behind the scenes, and out of sight is truly out of mind. But no one likes a whining proposal writer, so establish the time, build in a little more for contingencies, and defend the time by repeating how crucial this step is to success.

TIP

To ensure sufficient time to produce professional proposals, schedule your desktop publishing resources well in advance. You may also find it helpful to do the following:

» Format documents parallel to the writing and editing process (as long as they're separated by section or volume and organized in a logical manner that doesn't impede progress or version/configuration control). For example, after you've written Section 1, send it to the production team for formatting while you begin on Section 2. After Section 1 has been formatted, the production staff can return it to you for final editing and formatting checks.

This parallel approach is ideal for large submissions; you or your production team can format smaller proposals after all writing and editing is complete.

» Align document formatting with major review cycles. Remember that reviewed files may require reformatting, particularly if writers, editors, or reviewers introduce errors into electronic files. Generally, the larger the document, the more times it needs to be reviewed and potentially formatted or reformatted.

Most production specialists can format roughly eight pages per hour, using a document template. If you need to format your files more than once, include those iterations in your estimates to create an accurate understanding of how many hours you need in the schedule for completion of this work. Tracking this and other productivity metrics over time can bring huge benefits to your scheduling process.

Allocating time to establish the proposal infrastructure and plan the rest of the project

This is one out-of-sequence task that you should work into your schedule early. Setting up a *proposal infrastructure* (that is, an online or physical workspace for authoring and sharing documents, controlling content versions, communicating with team members, collecting data and artifacts, and managing workflow) and creating realistic plans are critical for a successful proposal because both decrease your overall effort. When responding to an RFP, your planning process can take from 10 to 20 percent of the total time available (this includes preparing for the kickoff meeting, setting up a collaborative workspace or tool, establishing a contact list, defining roles and responsibilities, and developing the detailed schedule).

TIP

To be safe (on a complex project), also reserve 10 percent of the available time to manage unforeseen events, such as a proposal writer with writer's block, a family emergency, or a customer crisis that requires immediate attention.

Allowing sufficient time for proposal reviews

Anyone who works directly on a proposal is too close to the work to be able to review it for quality, compliance, consistency, and influence. To accomplish this crucial task, you need to bring in experts who haven't been involved in developing the solution or writing about it to take a fresh look at the proposal before you publish it.

REMEMBER

Reviews (meetings you hold to assess key activities or deliverables) reduce the overall cost of your proposals and ensure the accuracy and validity of your content. We recommend holding a variety of reviews throughout the proposal process, and we provide guidance for them in several chapters: For competitive reviews, refer to Chapter 5. For final proposal reviews, see Chapter 12. And for daily stand-up reviews, check out Chapter 14.

Beware: Reviews consume considerable time in your schedule. After each review, you must allocate additional time to read and understand the feedback and work it into the next draft. You also need time to determine how best to respond to reviewer comments. Depending on the size and complexity of the proposal, and the number and availability of reviewers, review cycles can take anywhere from half a day to a week. Determine the appropriate number of reviews early, and avoid adding review cycles unless the solution changes significantly or the due date is extended.

The most important review (and in in the case of smaller firms and opportunities, the *only* review) is the final proposal review. For major proposals, allocate a minimum of two weeks before submittal. Allocate at least a day for small proposals. The final document review team determines the proposal's compliance and alignment with your customer's mission, needs, requirements, issues, and hot buttons, and it provides concrete suggestions for improvements.

If you're a lone proposal writer or your proposal opportunities are moderately complex, consider the following alternative review practices:

» **Use a style sheet to ensure consistent content.** Most large organizations have a corporate style reference for business writing. If yours doesn't, use style guides such as the *Associated Press Stylebook* or *The Chicago Manual of Style.* For your projects, create a standard style sheet that denotes your preferred usage, punctuation, capitalization, and use of industry jargon and acronyms.

» **Schedule downtime between writing and reviewing.** A waiting period away from the document allows you to find errors and validate ideas more easily and without emotional baggage.

» **Have your workplace peers edit your work to ensure high-quality content, style, and grammar.** If you're part of a proposal department, ask your peers to review your work and offer to do the same for them. Look for opportunities for substantive, grammatical, and general stylistic improvement.

» **Create functional or technical reviews with your organization's subject experts to ensure accuracy, persuasiveness, and appropriateness.** Try to use objective reviewers not linked directly to the proposal in progress.

Considering your remaining time

After you set your infrastructure, planning, production, and delivery times, list the rest of the tasks that you need to start and complete between planning and production. Check out Chapter 6 for the detailed process steps in the proposal writing element of the proposal development stage to guide you as you list your tasks. At a high level, these steps include the following:

» Preparing the summaries

» Describing your solution and matching it to the customer's needs

» Writing the letter of transmittal

» Writing, editing, reviewing, revising, and proofing the content

We know what you're thinking . . . hey, that's the bulk of the work! And you're right — it is from a labor standpoint. But the ultimate success of the detailed "creative" work really depends on the standard proposal elements we cover in Chapter 9, which provide the foundation for a quality proposal.

Sequencing the tasks and subtasks

As you develop your schedule, include as many levels of tasks as you need to describe the work in detail. Be sure to identify any dependencies for each task (such as supplies, approvals, or other tasks that need to be completed before another can begin or be completed). A detailed task schedule ensures that each activity reflects the best use of time and resources.

Here are some tips for establishing and ensuring accountability:

>> **Set the start and end dates for each major task and subtask.** Set these dates by team member and for the project as a whole.

>> **Post each assignment on the proposal schedule, the project timeline, or in the collaborative workspace.** Note names, task descriptions, task durations, outcomes, and deliverables.

>> **Explain the assignments to all team members.** Make sure they understand their start and end dates and get them to commit to meeting their deadlines. Explain the consequences for your bid if they miss these deadlines.

>> **Ensure that one person alone is accountable for a task or subtask.** That person can, and often must, reach out to others for help, but he must take accountability and ownership for the task. If the owner has to transfer the task to someone else, make the handoff to the new owner clear and explicit.

Be transparent, reasonable, and honest about the schedule with all team members. Respecting team members' time will help you gain their trust.

TIP

>> **Remind team members of their commitments.** Advise them that you'll publicly announce the upcoming start and end dates in team review meetings. Let them know that you'll also remind them privately. Many collaborative platforms allow you to send calendar reminders when task deadlines are approaching. If you don't have such a platform, send "friendly" reminders via email a day or two before the deadline and copy in the boss.

These tactics may irritate some people, but everyone will thank you when the proposal is finished.

>> **Stay focused on the end result.** If you discover that your team members are working on tasks that you haven't placed on the schedule, either assess their value and revisit the schedule to add them or clarify the work assignments for

the team. If your team is working on multiple ongoing tasks or tasks that have long *lead times* (the time between knowing a task must be accomplished and when it's due), set a series of near-term, interim deadlines to drive priorities and keep them on track.

All too often, organizations expand or contract the time frame for a task to fit the available time. Develop and apply standards for common proposal development tasks, based on your experience.

Publishing your schedule in a variety of formats

Your team members can't adhere to a schedule if they don't know it exists. You must ensure that the proposal schedule is visible and clear to the entire team, preferably on a collaborative platform that enables easy access and updates when needed. If you don't have access to a collaborative platform (see Chapter 13 for more on proposal tools), create a timeline in project management software, on a spreadsheet, or in a calendar view.

Not everyone sees a schedule in the same way. Some contributors need to see only certain elements and deadlines for which they're responsible. Some may be constrained by software (they may not have your project management application). Be ready to provide the schedule in an appropriate format for the project's complexity and the individual contributor's needs. If you work in an online system, the format may be set. But you don't always need a Gantt chart or even a spreadsheet to keep people on track (they're great for complex bids with lots of contributors and milestones). For less complex bids, consider using the Word-based, sample schedules for 10-, 30-, and 60-day proposals we provide online via the appendix. You can adapt them easily for your specific needs.

One way to help participants visualize the proposal process in detail is to use action-based plans. Action-based plans are usually based on detailed diagrams. They address specific proposal tasks on time scales, showing specifically when the tasks are to be done and who should perform them. They assume that the readers understand the task and how it needs to be performed.

Gantt charts are the most common format for this kind of plan. A *Gantt chart* is a grid that maps and allocates tasks on the vertical axis against time scales on the horizontal axis. Gantt charts are widely used in both proposal planning and wider project management. (They're also known as *horizontal bar charts*.)

They're not hard to make, even if you don't have project management software (the Gantt chart is a standard output format for these programs). Open a spreadsheet. In the left column, list all the activities and milestones in your project (you may want to number them if your list is long or has multiple substeps or activities). In the next column (to the right), list the names of the people assigned to "own" each activity or milestone. In additional columns, identify the time increments you want to track your project by (days or weeks, usually). Then identify the dates for milestones and deliverables. For an example, head to the appendix.

A well-conceived Gantt chart often underpins and expresses a bid process better than any other document. It typically shows the following elements:

>> Stages of a bid process

>> Start and end dates of specific tasks

>> Milestones, key decision, and review dates (these are sometimes the same thing)

>> Role allocation (by color-coding, shading, and so on) for bid team members and partners

>> Prioritization of tasks (by color-coding, shading, and so on)

>> Leave/vacation arrangements (you can then use a Gantt chart to help define or work around these arrangements)

TIP

Some bid activities depend on the successful completion of prior activities. The process of discovering these dependencies and anticipating what tasks need (and then placing these prior requirements on the grid) is one of the strengths of this type of planning. If activities are time-critical, you can prepare for dates slipping by advancing the completion point on the plan.

Action-based plans typically have several iterations. When starting a new plan, initially start the process away from the grid. Capture all tasks and milestones on blank sheets of paper or on sticky notes. You can then order them on a grid.

Completed action-based plans for large-scale bids can be as expansive as multiple sheets of paper that you can post on a wall. However, a user-friendly, single legal or A4-sized page remains the most useful size for sharing, analysis, and discussion. If you want to record extra detail related to a particular stage, such as preliminary activities for a large, multistakeholder kickoff meeting or the many needs of the final pre-deadline phase, produce an "exploded" version of the plan for that time period.

Figure 8-1 shows an action-based plan in a Gantt chart format with task division and allocation. It also shows an "exploded" final week for mapping more intensive activity detail.

Figure 8-1 (Gantt chart):

	TIME IN WEEKS						DETAIL OF FINAL WEEK						
Bid/Proposal Plan Activity Tasks	6	5	4	3	2	1	7	6	5	4	3	2	1
1. Overall Bid Offer													
• Buyer specification/kit analysis													
• Competitor analysis (and revisit of this)													
• Win theme summary (and revisit of this)													
• Check buyer Q&A responses													
2. Bid Plan Creation and Revisit													
• Share draft 1, seek initial comments													
• Adjust draft (draft 2)													
• Discuss draft 2 at kickoff meeting													
• Make adjustments (draft 3)													
• Issue draft 3 with deadline to agree													
• Confirm plan 3 (final)													
• Revisit plan 3													
• Confirm changes/no changes													
3. Key Meetings (Bid Team/Bid Partner)													
• Kickoff meeting (in person)													
• Mid-term meeting (virtual conference)													
• Final meeting (virtual conference)													
4. Teaming/Partner Issues													
• Brief partners (assume pre-warmed)													
• Agree contacts (bid team and senior staff)													
• Agree terms of partnering in principle													
• Negotiate roles and budgets													
• Content/text inputs													
• Letters of commitment (in principle)													
• Letters of commitment (formal)													
5. Bid Content and Graphics Development													
• Section content plans/mock-ups													
• Graphics commissioned/delivered													
• Sections blocked in full bullet points													
• Sections structured													
• Sections in full text (draft1)													
• Sections in full text (draft 2)													
• Reviews													
• Final revision/proofing													
6. Finalization (*Assume VirtualBid Portal*)													
• Check formatting possibilities/constraints													
• Upload													
• Check safe delivery/valid receipt obtained													

KEY   Bid Team Staff 1 ▬   Bid Team Staff 2 ▬   Partner Inputs ▬   Graphics Staff ▬   Review Team ▬

Source: APMP Body of Knowledge

FIGURE 8-1: This sample action-based plan in Gantt chart format illustrates how tasks can be allocated and executed over the course of a project.

REMEMBER

Use whatever scheduling tool or software makes sense, given the size and complexity of your organization and the proposal you're working on. In some instances, a spreadsheet or a manual scheduling tool is sufficient. Larger proposals often require automated tools that adjust interim deadlines automatically when an extension is given or a material change occurs.

Breaking big assignments into manageable chunks

Many members of your proposal team, particularly writers assigned to respond to whole proposal sections, can be overwhelmed by the size and scope of the tasks they face. (If you're the lone proposal writer, we're also talking about you.)

Think for a moment about what you're asking them to do, all in an abbreviated time frame. They need to

>> Research the content for their topic, either by talking with a subject matter expert or coming up with it on their own

>> Adapt the content to meet your outline and the customer's particular needs

>> Embed win themes, customer hot buttons, proof points, and value propositions within their content to support the solution

>> Find or create suitable illustrations for their content

>> Write their content to the specifications you've set in your style sheet

>> Submit to cycles of edits and reviews

All these tasks become intensified if a contributor lacks proposal writing experience or if deadlines are tight.

TIP

You can make authors and other contributors more effective by breaking large tasks up into smaller pieces, assigning interim deadlines, and providing immediate feedback. Although this approach takes more of your time than allowing your contributors to complete longer assignments on their own, it allows you to check progress early and identify and escalate problems instead of waiting for a proposal section that's overdue, inappropriate, or ineptly written.

Maximizing parallel tasks and minimizing sequential tasks

Think carefully through all your schedule's dependencies when you determine start and end dates for proposal tasks and subtasks. You need to schedule tasks that depend on each other sequentially, and if you have a large number of them, you may run out of available time. To the extent possible, create a task list that includes activities that you can conduct simultaneously, such as writing proposal text and making plans for proposal reviews.

REMEMBER

Many proposal tasks — for example, acquiring forms that require information from finance, operations, or human resources departments, or obtaining legal reviews of contract terms and conditions — have long lead times. Start these activities early and conduct them in parallel with other activities to make the best use of your time.

Make sure you don't assign the same people to tasks that have to be completed in parallel, unless you're certain that they can actually execute them simultaneously. For tasks that have dependencies, check progress every day on the tasks they depend on. For complex proposals, use critical path scheduling to highlight sequential and parallel activities and allocate and track proposal team resources.

However important the deal, resist the temptation to schedule your proposal team to work on weekends and holidays. More work — and constant work — doesn't always yield better work. Even when deadlines are tight, give proposal teams most evenings, weekends, and holidays off to enable them to be more productive during normal business hours. And take care of yourself, too; to be at your best, take breaks, go out and exercise, and get a good night's sleep. Sure, you may have times when you need your proposal team members to work on weekends or even holidays. But if you do your best to protect their personal time, you can more easily get them to work during normal "off" hours if unforeseen events occur.

Using *schedule templates* (pre-ordained proposal plans with set intervals and milestones that you may find on the Internet or through proposal consultants) can make creating a proposal plan easier, but don't enforce their use blindly. Process overkill can hurt your proposals. Be sure to make your schedules flexible, and be ready to customize them based on the needs of each opportunity.

Learning from your experiences

Whether a bid is successful or not, capturing lessons learned is essential to improve your scheduling process and the schedules themselves. You need to build a mindset in your proposal team that allows you to repeatedly assess the effectiveness of your methods. By doing this, you can determine the "right amount of time" for tasks so you not only know how to plan the next similar engagement, but you can also see, over time, the average and optimal time required for these tasks.

Stopping to capture knowledge during your proposal schedule isn't easy. It's even more difficult when you're working with large teams and using intricate processes. But when you supply your proposal teams with a standard to follow, you can more easily assess their performance and how this performance may be improved for next time.

By tracking time spent and activities performed consistently against a standard, you can create an environment of continual improvement in your proposal development process. You can also better assess risks associated with discrete tasks in your schedule. For instance, if you know that your editor can scrub 35 pages of content a day and you've allotted only two days for a proposal that looks to be 150 pages, you know in advance to change durations for other tasks. With this knowledge of time allocated versus time spent, you may even be able to reduce your proposal costs and gain a more competitive position.

TIP

Create time and resource standards for your team to follow. Monitor them and hold brief lessons-learned reviews at key milestones to assess time spent versus time allocated. Use a small part of your daily stand-up reviews to get the team to think about process issues and improvements. Don't fix things here, though (that may take too much time from the task at hand); take a note and follow up after your proposal is complete.

To maximize the benefits of the lessons-learned function, it's helpful to

» Implement a standard lessons-learned process and lead the development of common outputs and artefacts, like follow-up reports and action lists

» Add a lessons-learned review during each stage in the proposal process

» Document recent lessons learned in each new proposal plan

» Cover any changes these lessons learned bring to your standard proposal process in the kickoff meeting

Managing the moving parts

Managing your team's day-by-day tasks is the engine that drives all successful proposals. For even the simplest of proposals, ask your team members to check in daily — preferably at the same time once or even twice a day — so you can check the proposal's status, identify issues and risks, assign and follow up on tasks, and update everyone on any changes that may affect the schedule or elements of the proposal.

When you're working on a complex proposal, you can rarely compress your proposal activities or skip your daily management tasks for any period and expect to succeed. But maintaining a consistent level of discipline isn't easy.

One reason that daily management is so critical (and so difficult) is that proposal team members have limited budgets and time. They need to know how to prioritize activities in the near term. Most participants in the process don't see the full arc of activity, and some may not even understand the strategy and the larger picture, despite your efforts to educate them. Day-to-day management helps everyone to focus on what's important and keeps the entire team moving toward the ultimate objective: Delivering a winning proposal.

REMEMBER

You may have to walk the line between injecting structure and formality where it's needed and knowing when to allow the proposal to run on its own. When in doubt, err on the side of formality.

Budgeting Your Funds and Resources

Proposals are expensive for two reasons. First, they take time from a lot of expensive specialists, people who are paid well to do jobs that in most cases only tangentially include proposal writing. When they work on a proposal team, something has to give, and the loss in their normal productivity can be significant. Second, proposals require resources: physical resources to track the process (such as online proposal management systems and content repositories like SharePoint), human resources to work on the proposal, technical resources to develop the solution and content of the proposal, travel and lodging to transport and house the people working on the proposal, production resources to publish the proposal in digital or (more expensive still) paper formats, and delivery resources to send the proposal over sometimes long distances.

If you're the sole proposal writer or a member or leader of a small proposal team, figuring out the budget for the proposal process falls to you. So you need to be able to budget not only the often paltry sums dedicated to creating proposals but also the time you have to spend on them, because you're likely to be juggling the responsibility of several proposals all at once.

Budgeting your funds

Most large businesses budget for bid and proposal expenses. These budgets define the amount an organization is prepared to allocate for all proposals in a year, and they may allocate funds based on specific opportunities. A proposal budget may include the entire cost of winning the sale or only the cost of developing the proposal.

The following sections explore the proposal budget in more detail, including how to manage budget limitations.

Understanding the proposal budget

The biggest part of any proposal budget is labor, and this aspect of the budget may include permanent titles that are exclusive to creating proposals (for example, proposal manager, proposal writer, proposal editor, graphic designer, and production specialist), people who work in business development roles, and sometimes people assigned to reviewing proposals.

REMEMBER

Labor can represent more than 90 percent of a proposal budget. In addition, the budget includes costs that relate to specialized software and tools, travel, lodging, and meals for remote proposal support, office and production supplies, and printer leases or outsourced production costs.

If you're part of an in-house proposal team, you need to understand how bid and proposal funds are assigned and tracked. The more you know about the funds available, the more you can ensure that you have the funds to get the resources you need most for any particular opportunity. Just be aware that the amount budgeted for an opportunity is usually based on the bid's importance to the organization's growth strategy or its desire to retain an incumbent contract. The more efficiently an organization budgets for its resources, the more money it has to support a bid, maximize the number of jobs it can bid on, or "wedge" in an unexpected opportunity. For this reason, you need to advocate allocating funds to projects based on likelihood of return (read: winning a deal).

Building a proposal budget

TIP

To build a strong budget, use historical expense records and receipts to determine how you spent money in the past to pursue a bid and write, review, and produce a proposal. Then estimate the resources you need to pursue, write, and produce your proposal, including any other direct costs like travel, products, and supplies peculiar to the opportunity.

Table 8-1 provides a list of potential budget-tracking areas.

TABLE 8-1   ## Proposal Budget Categories

Salaries (Loaded)	Tools	Direct Costs
Business developers	Collaboration environments (physical and virtual)	Travel
Contracts manager	Software licenses	Transportation
Pricing analyst	Printers/copiers	Accommodation
Opportunity manager		Meals
Proposal manager		Supplies
Subject matter experts		Paper
Writers		Ink, tabs, binders
Reviewers		Digital media
Graphic artists		Facility chargeback
Production specialists		
Executive overhead		

In the appendix, we provide a link to a sample budget template you can use to record your potential proposal expenses. Any proposal budget is risky, because most proposal expenses are variable. For example, a customer may release an amendment to adjust requirements, which increases your labor costs as you respond to the new requirements.

TIP

Reserve at least 10 percent of your budget to address unforeseen factors.

If you build a budget, you need to track your expenses by it. Track and analyze all your expenses to increase your budget's accuracy over time. Maintain performance metrics, and keep records of budgeted versus actual expenses.

Proving your value

Increasingly, proposal professionals are challenged to do more with less, while increasing productivity and maintaining win rates. Proposal budgets are shrinking while tracking reports and cost justifications are on the rise. Tracking your costs against detailed budgets, and then comparing those costs to the revenue your proposals help generate, can help you demonstrate your value to your organization. At the very least, it demonstrates that you're a good manager of the resources that are allocated your way.

Small businesses usually have limited proposal budgets and limited access to collaborative software or equipment. You may be even more challenged if you're the sole proposal support person because you have to be proficient in numerous competencies (for instance, sales support, proposal writing, and customer service) and with a range of software tools — yet you may not have clearly defined roles or responsibilities and even less authority.

TIP

If you're in this situation, you can partially overcome limited budgets by

>> Setting standards for proposal content through templates and content reuse

>> Relying on proven proposal development techniques that have worked for decades without extensive software and hardware

>> Defining expectations and timelines for other personnel who work to support proposal development

>> Being aware of outsourcing opportunities to provide development or production support in case of emergencies

Budgeting your time

If you're the sole proposal writer or manager in your organization or department, you'll usually be in great demand. When salespeople learn of your abilities and role, they'll come running for your help, especially when they see the quality of the proposals you produce compared to what they can do on their own. And besides, their job is to be with customers, working through issues and presenting information that leads to sales. And, usually, they're much better talkers than writers.

Before long, your time will be your most precious commodity. You'll be tempted to say yes to every opportunity, but you can't. If you do, you'll burn out in months. No lie. Proposal writing is that intense.

It's even intense when you're part of a proposal team, with the right resources like editors, graphic designers, and production specialists. Too much work in succession is a prescription for PSS (proposal stress syndrome). Okay, we made that up. But we're not making up the stress levels involved with the proposal writing process.

Here are three ways you can combat proposal-related stress:

>> **Track your time and overtime (paid or not) and report it.** If you're working 16-hour days consistently, after a while it will start to show in your physical appearance. Don't let it go that far; provide your boss with a weekly report. You'll either get a new colleague or a partner in finding a way to limit the workload. If you don't get either, look for a new job.

>> **Qualify your proposals better.** Keep records of what you win and lose. Debrief sales (or better still, customers) to help you understand why. When you see a pattern emerge, discuss it with the boss or your clients. *Show* how your efforts can be better spent on deals you're more likely to win.

>> **Create a staggered approach to scheduling your jobs.** Proposals, especially less complex proposals, are funny in how they progress in cycles. At the beginning of a project, the work is intense. Then, when your subject experts are gathering material and crafting their solution, the work lessens. It then picks up with a vengeance toward the final days of the project, when the content comes in, reviews are set, and production begins. One person managing three projects can look like Figure 8-2.

TIP

Use the pattern in Figure 8-2 to launch a new project during the lull of the preceding one. Our proposal team did this for all our proposal managers, and they were able to successfully manage more proposals than anyone thought possible. Of course, you need to ensure that your team members get a break after a series of projects, or the burnout will return.

FIGURE 8-2:
Staggering projects for a proposal writer to take advantage of normal peaks and lulls.

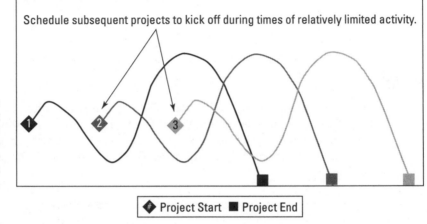

Source: APMP Body of Knowledge

Choosing Your Proposal Team

Even if you're the sole proposal writer for your organization, you can't create a winning proposal on your own. Few people, maybe only sole proprietors or the most grizzled proposal veterans, have the requisite knowledge of the business, the customer, the solution, and the proposal development process to deliver a winning proposal without help. You need teammates to provide the knowledge, skill, and *person-power* to write a compelling proactive proposal or a Request for Proposal (RFP) response of any size. And choosing those teammates wisely can be as important to writing a winning proposal as any process, schedule, or resource. Proposing is a team sport!

To successfully staff your proposal team, you need to know the skills required and who has those skills. Today, the people you need may be spread all over your organization, or even the world. Sometimes your organization may need help from external partners. In this section, we investigate each of these situations in detail.

Understanding roles and competencies

The Association of Proposal Management Professionals (APMP) identifies all the key roles needed to manage the business development function in an organization. Although your business may not require all these specialties, understanding the different roles may help you choose the right people as you become a "proposing" organization.

Table 8-2 shows the common roles within a typical proposal organization.

TABLE 8-2 **Common Proposal Roles**

Role	Description
Knowledge manager	A knowledge manager is responsible for the creation and ongoing maintenance of reusable knowledge databases. Knowledge managers use organization, writing, and information design skills to increase the business strategy value of an organization's intellectual property.
Production manager	A production manager is responsible for planning and directing the printing, assembly, and final check of proposal documents. This role should have specialized skills in both traditional print and electronic media.
Proposal coordinator	A proposal coordinator is responsible for all administrative aspects of proposal development — ensuring security and integrity of all proposal documentation, coordinating internal flow and review of all proposal inputs, coordinating schedules, and directing submission of the final master proposal to production.
Desktop publisher	A proposal's desktop publisher is responsible for designing, formatting, and producing proposal templates, documents, and related materials.
Proposal director	A proposal director is responsible for all aspects of an organization's proposal operations. The proposal director ensures that a formal process exists and is in use. In addition, the proposal director is responsible for ongoing process improvement and may also manage the infrastructure (physical or virtual) within which proposal development functions are conducted. Proposal directors are often involved in broader business development activities, such as strategy development, staff development, and long-term business capability planning.
Proposal editor	Proposal editors are responsible for ensuring that the writing structure and words used in the proposal persuasively convey the offer to the customer. They edit for grammar, punctuation, capitalization, clarity, readability, consistency, and persuasiveness.

(continued)

TABLE 8-2 *(continued)*

Role	Description
Graphic designer	A proposal's graphic designer is responsible for developing customer-focused visual information that highlights an offer's features, benefits, and discriminators. The graphic designer communicates with other members of the proposal/bid team to conceptualize and create visual elements to persuade the customer. Graphic designers may develop multiple deliverables such as proposals, presentations, sales collateral, and brand identities.
Proposal manager	A proposal manager is responsible for proposal development (such as writing, presenting, and demonstrating the solution), including maintaining schedules, organizing resources, coordinating inputs and reviews, ensuring bid strategy implementation, ensuring compliance, resolving internal team issues, and providing process leadership.
Proposal writer	Proposal writers are responsible for creating and maintaining content for common proposal sections, such as past performance, résumés, and reusable product and services descriptions. Subject matter experts that contribute content are also referred to as proposal writers.

Source: APMP Body of Knowledge

Managing virtual proposal teams

In recent years, businesses have come to invest in virtual proposal teams to acquire business. Collaborative working environments are almost ubiquitous, allowing remote access to tools and information as if all resources were co-located.

Proposal teams can plan, manage, and deliver on all phases of proposal development from almost anywhere in the world. To remain competitive and address the work-life balance that employees demand, businesses need to focus on ensuring that collaboration tools provide the needed features and functions their teams need, regardless of where they work, always bearing in mind any security considerations. For more about these tools, see Chapter 13.

Supporting global teams

Global teams must clarify specific terminology that may differ regionally (such as the term *binders* versus *folders*), design concerns (such as color usage in specific countries), and physical production concerns (from paper sizes to production times). These concerns can be mitigated through clear communication early in the process.

Working with external partners

The larger and more complex an opportunity is, the greater the need for bidders (especially small businesses) to join with other organizations to satisfy the requirements of an RFP. This is where things can get very complicated, because assembling a winning team requires a delicate balance of strategy and tactics. While an effective partnering strategy can significantly improve a bidder's win probability, a poorly executed strategy can create serious performance, reputation, legal, and financial problems.

The following sections help you decide on partners should you find them necessary.

Deciding whether you need a partner

As your business assesses opportunities, you collect and analyze a lot of information about the customer's requirements and the competitors likely to bid against you. From that information, you establish win strategies, solution approaches, and price estimates. From that knowledge, you generate a list of required resources (for example, personnel, facilities, and equipment) and capabilities (such as staff skills, technologies, and problem solutions) that you need to have to win. But is your business equipped to provide these resources?

TIP

For large and complex opportunities, most businesses have gaps and insufficiencies. Use your SWOT analysis from Chapter 5 to compare your abilities with that of your competition. If you come up short, you should either look for a partner or decline to bid.

Use the SWOT analysis to assess your organization's relative competitiveness as a solo bidder, as a prime contractor, and as a subcontractor. Honestly comparing your organization's strengths and weaknesses with those of likely competitors (in relation to the customer's needs and expectations) helps you identify potential partnering candidates that can neutralize your weaknesses and improve your firm's chances of winning.

REMEMBER

To work with a partner, you need executive support, whether you're the prime contractor or the subcontractor. And although no executive wants to admit that the business is too weak to win as a prime contractor, few like to share revenues with a partner. You need to show senior management that partnering is the only way you can increase your organization's probability of winning. After all, a percentage of something is better than all of nothing.

Selecting a partner

Select partners first on their ability to increase your chances to win and second on their ability to be a good team player. Find out whether the potential partner has worked with the customer successfully before, or whether they currently work with them. Make sure the potential partner wants to work with the customer and with you. If you've never worked with the potential partner before, ask an executive to reach out peer-to-peer for a preliminary discussion, and follow it up with other peer-to-peer discussions between the departments that will be involved in the bid.

Always investigate potential partners. Some that look good on paper may be serious liabilities if the customer doesn't care for them. Use personal and professional contacts in the customer's organization, industry, and local community to build a clear picture of the firm. Research the partnering organization through Google, Dun & Bradstreet, and industry publications to gauge its performance and reputation. Make sure an organization will be an asset, not a liability, before you invite it to join your team.

When you've identified and vetted the best potential team members, you need to invite and convince each partner to join the team, in priority order. Contact the most appropriate decision maker or influencer and explain the rationale for having his organization on the team, its proposed role in the upcoming contract, and its responsibilities during the opportunity and proposal phases. Avoid detailed discussions of win strategies until the firm has committed to joining the team and signed a nondisclosure agreement.

Before you launch into the invitation discussion, ask whether the organization is already committed to another team. You don't want to share any information that may fall into the hands of a competitor.

Negotiating and documenting partnering agreements

Always thoroughly document the operational, financial, and legal aspects of the negotiated partnering agreement. The terms and conditions of the partnering and subcontracting arrangements need to be mutually acceptable — and perhaps acceptable to your customer. Partnering agreements need to be negotiated by officials with decision-making authority, reviewed and approved by your lawyers, and signed before you proceed.

Partnering agreements should include clearly defined

- **»** Scopes of work, product or service specifications, and targeted work volumes
- **»** Participation levels in proposal activities
- **»** Allocations of proposal costs
- **»** Confidentiality agreements, exclusivity clauses, and other legal liabilities and limitations

4
Creating Your Proposal

Get acquainted with the actual proposal writing process. See how to compose a winning executive summary, strong win themes, compelling value propositions, and concrete benefit and proof statements. Discover why focusing on benefits when presenting prices is the right approach.

Recall the principles of clear, concise, and cohesive writing. Reacquaint yourself with the techniques of persuasive writing and see why headings are a proposal writer's (and evaluator's) best friend.

Understand how graphics can take your proposal to new heights. Review the principles of good design, and see how they can help your proposal persuade your customer to buy.

Uncover the secrets to successful, stress-free proposal production, for both print and digital formats. Ensure a quality product by insisting on multiple edits and reviews. Go beyond the norm by helping your sales team with presenting the proposal orally.

IN THIS CHAPTER

Summarizing your offer for executives

Showing that you understand the situation

Addressing your customer's stated, unstated, and implied questions

Expressing value, not just price

Establishing your qualifications

Making an active closing statement

Chapter 9

Developing Your Proposal

A proposal must meet standards, whether it's a reactive proposal (that is, a response to a Request for Proposal, or RFP) or a proactive one. If you're responding to an RFP, you have to deliver the parts requested, in the order requested, to the specifications requested. If you're writing a proactive proposal, you need to either follow industry standards or set your own. It's best to follow standards because, frankly, they work.

In this chapter, we take you through all the parts of reactive and proactive proposals to help you develop bid-winning documents.

TIP

Reactive and proactive proposals have some sections in common (the executive summary, pricing, and qualifications) and some that differ (how you describe your solution, your recommendations, and your call to action). You may not always follow them in the same order, and you may not even need all the sections for some opportunities, but you can never go wrong if you use them as a framework — a blueprint, so to speak — for all your written proposals.

Crafting the Executive Summary

At the beginning of every proposal is the executive summary. Every proposal needs one. Every proposal without one will fail to reach the decision maker it must reach to win. Is that heavy-handed enough for you?

The fate of your proposal depends on the approval of the executive decision maker. From its very beginning, your proposal must convince key executives that you're the answer to their needs. You have to show them that you're in it for the long run and that you have their organization's best interests at heart.

Knowing what an executive summary is

The *executive summary* is a concise, informational sales document-in-a-document. Its job is to convince your customer's highest-ranking decision maker that your offer is superior to that of your competitors.

TIP

The executive summary is normally a stand-alone section at the front of every proposal. If you're responding to an RFP and the customer's instructions don't allow for an executive summary, you can include the same content you would include in the executive summary as part of your cover letter or introduction. You can't afford to leave it out.

A compelling executive summary is good for evaluators, too. It helps them capture and digest the main messages in your proposal, which in turn improves your chances of winning.

Knowing what an executive summary isn't

Despite its name, an executive summary isn't a

>> Road map to guide readers to what follows, although you can allude to the structure and thoroughness of your proposal

>> Synopsis of your proposal's main points, although you can highlight key aspects of your solution

>> Retelling of your proposal, although it does achieve (in the language and brevity that executives appreciate) the same convincing argument that your proposal does

REMEMBER

The executive summary isn't a traditional "summary" because you write it first, not last. It's your utmost expression of your bidding strategy, so it provides excellent guidance to the proposal team as they write the rest of the proposal (or even you, if you write alone). Write it before the kickoff meeting and review it early with management, before your contributors head down different paths.

Focusing your message on your customer

Your executive summary focuses on your customer, not you. It sells your solution to your reader by demonstrating that you

>> Grasp and can echo your customer's vision and business issues

>> Have aligned your own vision with that of your customer

>> Understand the customer's stated and unstated needs

>> Have a solution that satisfies those needs

>> Offer better financial and operational value than any competitor can

>> Are the most qualified of all those angling to win the business

TIP

Focus on your customer throughout. Borrow your customer's words and echo them in your descriptions of its vision, its issues, and its needs. Scour your customer's website for expressions of its value and mission and apply them liberally.

Use your customer's name often — much more often than you use yours (a three-to-one ratio or a little better is about right). Address your customer directly, using the second person pronoun (you). Write as if you're talking directly to the decision maker. Express how you

>> Understand the customer's motivation when considering a proposal

>> Recognize and appreciate the customer's hot buttons (those compelling reasons to buy, explained in Chapter 2, with more in Chapter 3)

>> Have ensured that the solution satisfies each hot button

>> Grasp that what truly matters are business benefits, not the features that enable them

Building a compelling summary

REMEMBER

Keep your executive summaries brief. Some proposal pundits say they should be 10 percent of the page count of your proposal, but we've rarely seen an effective one be more than two to three pages. If you can't sell your idea to an executive in that amount of space, you're in trouble. Respect your executive reader's time: Get to, and stick to, the point.

If your RFP provides instructions for your executive summary, follow them. If not, here's the most effective approach:

1. Grab your customer's attention.

Here are some options for connecting with a customer and *showing* that you understand its vision, its objectives for success, and the challenges it faces:

- Tell a true story that demonstrates the issues the customer faces.

- Quote a business leader's expression of the organization's vision.

- Cite a big number — a revenue target or potential liability — that demonstrates your understanding of industry issues.

- Provide a "look into the future" regarding the value your solution can bring within the context of the customer's business.

- State your win theme and your "killer" discriminator — that thing you do that no one else can.

2. Explain how you clearly understand your customer's needs or problems.

Use a bulleted list to make each hot-button need visible (for more on hot buttons, refer to Chapter 2). Prioritize each need or problem one by one from the customer's perspective, using your customer's words. Describe them in terms of the business pains they cause. For example:

- Do they make employees less productive?

- Do they anger customers?

- Do they allow revenue to slip away?

- Do they cause unnecessary expense?

- Do they harm the customer's reputation?

TIP

If you're the incumbent, indicate that you see how needs have changed since you started on the job and that your insider knowledge gives you the edge to solving them. If you're the challenger, plant a seed that the old ways of handling these needs won't suffice and that new perspectives are crucial.

3. **Describe your solution and how it solves each hot-button need.**

This may be the most difficult part of the summary to write because you have to distill your solution into a very small space. A bulleted list is appropriate here, too. Here's how to create one:

- Align your solution's features to each of the customer's needs, one by one, in the same order presented in Step 2. Stick to the major ones and only those that address the specific need directly.

- For each solution, state your solution's benefits, followed by brief proof points to substantiate your claims.

- Be sure to indicate how the solution takes away the business pain you identified in Step 2. Consider showing how the future looks after your solution is in place.

- Express why each of these solution elements trumps the competition.

4. **Clearly express your key discriminator.**

This is the most important thing you do better than your competition. Point out this discriminator so your customer knows why it should choose you over your competitors, especially the incumbent (if it's not you).

For more on key discriminators, turn to Chapter 6.

5. **Ask for the business.**

Indicate that you're ready to act. Be as bold with this statement as the situation allows. At the very least, confirm your understanding of the next step in your client's decision-making cycle. At most, you can ask for a meeting to discuss your solution or even finalize the deal.

For a model demonstrating this executive summary structure, see our template at the link we provide in the appendix.

Creating a good impression

Executive summaries may be all that decision makers ever read of your proposal. They are often the only pages a busy evaluator reads in detail before skimming through the other parts of your proposal. If you fail to show value in the executive summary, evaluators may jump to the price page and summarily dismiss the rest.

Your executive summary is like the finishing on a new house: If the molding fits snugly and the cabinets are perfectly painted, a buyer will likely think that the framework, roofing, and plumbing are equally fine. If your executive summary is professional and persuasive, reviewers will assume that the same is true of your solution and support. Make a good impression by

>> **Avoiding excessive boilerplate:** Make sure every executive summary you write is unique to the opportunity. Solutions, client requirements, and competitors differ from one opportunity to the next. If you overuse boiler-plate or "recycle" content from a prior proposal, your customers may think that you haven't thought carefully about their particular situation and needs.

>> **Making the summary visual:** Include graphics to add emotional appeal and use a professional layout that makes the key points easy to see. Use them to reinforce your win themes and your discriminators (we address these elements from a number of perspectives in Chapters 2, 3, 6, and 7).

REMEMBER

In these images (and your words for that matter), avoid excessive technical detail. Focus on benefits and clear discriminators. Illustrate the payback on your solution. If your financial story is positive, include "big-number" or summary pricing and savings.

The executive summary, the cover, the transmittal letter, and the packaging are the most visible parts of your proposal. Each makes a strong contribution to the customer's first impression of your offer, so your message and visuals must be consistent and compelling. For more techniques for creating visually appealing and persuasive proposals, see Chapter 11.

Writing a Transmittal Letter

A transmittal letter is how your proposal gets to the right readers. It's a crucial part of any proposal because it allows you to start selling your solution before your customer opens your proposal. And although it comes first in your proposal package, it's less important than the executive summary in the grand scheme of things (which is why we place it second in this chapter).

Write your transmittal in the form of a standard business letter and attach it to your proposal cover with a paper clip. If your submission is electronic, you normally write the transmittal letter as your transmittal email. It should be more formal than a normal email: Include a descriptive subject line, begin the email formally (Dear Ms. Smith:), and close with a formal signature block (your digital signature, name, company, title, and contact information).

The best transmittals introduce the opportunity, briefly describe the solution, and indicate the next steps. A great model for the transmittal letter is the standard marketing A–I–D–A format:

>> **A is for attention.** Start your letter by reminding the readers why you're sending the proposal. Include an RFP name and number if appropriate. Restate your proposal theme. Echo the enthusiasm that prompted your proposal.

>> **I is for interest.** In your second paragraph, describe the readers' problem or need in the briefest way possible. This piques the readers' interest and pushes them to read the next paragraph.

>> **D is for desire or demand.** Your third paragraph must convince your readers that they want your solution and that it satisfies their needs.

>> **A is for action.** In your final paragraph, ask your readers to read and accept your proposal. You may also offer to meet at a certain date and time to discuss the proposal further and supply contact information to streamline the follow-up process. Some action sentences to consider include

- "I will call you on Friday to discuss next steps."

- "Our team is ready to present our solution to your board next week."

- "To meet the project deadlines and start achieving the benefits, sign the letter of intent today."

Check out our sample transmittal letters (using the A–I–D–A format) in the link we provide in the appendix.

Describing the Customer's Situation

Before you can solve a customer's problem, you have to understand the *situation* — the environment where the problem occurs, the circumstances under which it occurs, and the root causes behind it. If you're ready to write your proposal, you've already completed the preparation for this step (if you need help, refer to Chapter 6).

Unlike the executive summary and transmittal letter, which are key components of every proposal, the customer's situation is a major component of a proactive proposal only. A customer's RFP describes the current situation for you (and you should demonstrate that you understand that situation wherever you get a chance in your response). In a proactive proposal, however, you have to assure the customer that you understand its situation as well as, if not better than, it does.

If you're responding to an RFP, your understanding of the current situation goes in the executive summary. If you're writing a proactive proposal, you must place it in its own section. Believe this: The current situation may be the single most important persuasive element in your proposal. Don't blow it off like there's no use wasting time and words on explaining what the customer already understands — that's not the point. The point is that *you* understand.

The following sections delve into *how* you demonstrate this understanding to your customer in a proactive proposal.

Setting up the scenario

You need to convince your customer that you understand the circumstances that have prompted your proposal. Don't just recount the list of complaints that your customer shared with you. Although you want to describe the situation, using the customer's actual words (see the next section "Expressing the problem and the pain"), you should also do the following:

>> **Express empathy.** Say more than "we understand." Instead, recap the customer's vision and the obstacles to achieving that vision, and acknowledge the difficulty that led the customer to solicit your help.

>> **Mix in a bit of emotion.** This is the argument element called *pathos* (refer to Chapter 2). A great way to bring some emotional appeal into your current situation is to talk about the specific pain the problem causes the customer.

>> **Add insight to what the customer already knows.** You know the customer's problems (refer to Chapter 3), so share your insights about them here. If you're afraid that you'll tip your hand and the customer may share your insights with the incumbent or a competitor, point to the issue and indicate that you've solved this kind of issue before.

>> **Indicate that you'll customize your approach.** Imply that the customer's problem is unique, even if you've solved similar ones a thousand times before (don't solve it yet; that's for the next section of your proposal, which describes the solution you recommend — see the next section, "Expressing the problem and the pain"). This establishes a foundation for your persuasive arguments to follow.

Expressing the problem and the pain

Highlighting your customer's needs and problems is a crucial part of your proposal, because you use them to prep the customer for your solution (which we discuss in the upcoming section "Writing the Solution for a Proactive Proposal"). Make the need or problem statements vivid and as meaningful to your customer as possible. Put them in a bulleted list, and structure your list as follows:

>> **Use verbal labels.** Start each item with a label that concisely describes the need. Write them *grammatically parallel* — that is, write them as nouns or noun phrases, or maybe verb phrases that describe actions that the customer associates with the need. Just write them all the same way.

>> **State the cause.** Follow each label with a brief statement of what you see as the *root cause* of the need or problem.

>> **Point out the pain.** Complete the bullet point entry by describing the business pain resulting from the need or problem. Blatantly appeal to the reader's emotions. Describe the pain in physical terms. Does the problem cause employees to work endless overtime, visibly dampening morale? Does the problem put quotas in jeopardy, reducing employees' compensation and the business's bottom line? Be as graphic as you can.

>> **Prioritize the list.** Align your customer's hot buttons (the customer's most compelling reasons to act) with your list of needs, and prioritize them to match the importance your customer places on them. (Refer to Chapter 2 for more on hot buttons.)

TIP

Readers remember the first items and last items in a list better than those that fall in between. Follow this concept to order your list of needs and problems. And don't forget to limit your list to a *maximum* of seven items.

Illustrating the customer's environment

The best way to show that you understand your customer's environment is to draw a picture that depicts what you know. Although most proposal writers fall back on describing the situation with words, measures, and specifications, pictures can be more effective. Here's why:

>> **They show that you've taken extra care to understand the situation.** Drawing or even photographing the customer's current environment shows that you've put in extra effort to get to the bottom of the customer's problem.

>> **They reduce the amount of content you have to write.** The old adage is right: Pictures do convey more than words. And in proposals, they reduce the amount of detail you have to describe. You still need to write a caption and add references to the images in the text, but you can drastically cut down your verbiage by using images.

Illustrations are so important that we look at them in more detail, including how you can use them in every part of your proposal, in Chapter 11.

Describing problems in the customer's own language

Proposals are all about your readers and their problems, so every word you write in this section needs to apply to your customer alone. A great technique for letting your readers know that you understand their point of view is to echo the very words they use to describe their problems. Nothing says "I get what you said" better than using the exact terms that your customer uses to describe work through scenarios and operational, technical, and managerial problems.

EXAMPLE

You can set up this echo of your customer's words by referring to your visits with the customer's executives and support staff. For example: "In our January 4th meeting, COO Mike Anders said that 'an outage of mere minutes would cripple our operations for days.'"

TIP

If you have established a close relationship with your customer, you can also use the exact words your customer uses when talking about operational woes. (If your relationship is more formal, beware of sounding too familiar.) If your customer uses colloquialisms or colorful local expressions (anything short of profanity is fair game), use those words and phrases in this section. Call attention to them by using italics or quotes.

Answering Your Customer's Questions

Now we come to the solution part of your proposal, and again we must differentiate between the way you describe your solution in an RFP response versus how you do it in a proactive proposal. Most RFPs essentially provide a list of your customers' questions. And proactive proposals basically answer the questions you think your customers have about your solutions, your methods, and your qualifications. So for a proactive proposal, you have to ask yourself the same questions your readers would have asked you. And for both types of proposals, you need to think beyond the customers' simple questions to the unstated questions that lie behind them. Thinking through the stated questions helps you uncover the unstated needs we talk about in Chapter 4. Here are some examples of questions you may hear (the stated needs) and the possible underlying questions that provide insights into unstated needs:

>> How will this work in my world? *Your staging facility is great, but I'm unique, and you can't anticipate my situation and its problems.*

>> Who will do what work? *And why can you do it better than I could myself?*

>> How much will it cost? *And how much will I save, now and in the future?*

>> How can I pay for it? *And can I still make money if I buy it?*

>> Why should I do this now? *Right now, instead of when the economy is a little more robust?*

>> How have you done this before? *Have you done it for someone as individual as I am, or a company I admire?*

>> Why shouldn't I stay with the incumbent? *They're good people; why do you think you'll do better than they have?*

>> How will you stay on schedule and budget? *And how will you prevent scope creep (and it always happens with guys like you)?*

REMEMBER

Many proposals are rejected because the writer makes it easy for the reader to say no. Your job as a proposal writer is to take all the roadblocks to yes out of the way. You can do this by anticipating every point at which your reader may become uncomfortable, skeptical, or fearful.

The following sections explain how to express your solutions: First, in response to questions from a customer's RFP; second, anticipating the customer's questions as you write a proactive proposal; and third, making sure your solution discussions echo your win themes. And although we separate the approaches for your convenience, each approach has insights that may help you with the others.

Responding to an RFP's questions

What's the best way to answer the direct questions in your customer's RFP? *Clearly, directly, and succinctly.* Easier said than done.

You want every response to

>> Express that you comply with the requirement

>> Explain how you comply and why your way is the best way

>> Answer your customer's questions

>> Address your customer's hot buttons and echo your win themes

To help you craft these winning responses, we provide a four-part RFP question-response model for all proposal writers to follow on every deal. Table 9-1 shows the response elements and defines the content that goes in each.

TABLE 9-1   **Four-Part RFP Question-Response Model**

Question Element	Description
Restatement (topic)	Restate the customer's questions in your own words and indicate whether you comply, do not comply, or partially comply. You can enhance your response with a brief value proposition, starting with the preposition *by*.
Brief answer (comment)	In a sentence or two, describe your solution to the problem or tell how you'll fulfill the need. Make this the kernel of your response; if evaluators have only ten seconds to review each answer, make sure they're assured that you comply and that your response supports one of your proposal themes (refer to Chapter 2) or your overall proposal strategy (refer to Chapter 6).
Expanded answer (comment)	For complex questions, use this element to elaborate on, illustrate, and explain your brief response. Add whatever is necessary to fully define what your solution element does and how it works within the customer's environment.
Payoff statement (point)	Give the evaluators a key takeaway for this response. Express how this element addresses a hot button, helps support other requirements, supports a win theme, or brings a significant benefit to the customer.

TIP

Follow this model consistently to ensure that your RFP responses really *respond*, selling your strategy at every level of your response and helping evaluators quickly assess your compliance and responsiveness. To aid you, we supply a link for you to access a template in the appendix and explain how to use it in Chapter 13.

Answering the questions plainly

Some proposal writers weave and bob like a prize fighter. You read their responses to what seem like simple enough questions (okay, they're hard questions but simply stated) and marvel at the evasive tactics. They hedge. They dodge. They redirect to something they find more comfortable to talk about. And they never answer the question. And what does that do? It either disqualifies them for being nonresponsive or prolongs the RFP process by requiring a clarifying stage after all the proposals are submitted.

REMEMBER

You *must* answer your customers' questions. You may as well do it the first time they ask. If not, you'll have to answer them later on paper or in person. Or you never will, because you'll go away empty-handed.

TIP

As a proposal writer, you'll run across colleagues who refuse to answer questions to your satisfaction. They may be salespeople who know a dark secret about how your company failed to support a customer at a crucial time. They may be engineers who see a fatal flaw in your solution. They may be arrogant vendor partners who think they're too special to answer what they deem is a question beneath them. This is when you have to relentlessly pursue a satisfactory response — even if the response won't help your chances of succeeding. No one wins if you can't meet a requirement yet somehow imply that you can.

Linking your answers and win themes

In the earlier section "Responding to an RFP's questions," our RFP response model described two places where you can link win themes with your individual responses to your customer's questions. Every answer affords you an opportunity to reinforce your win themes, but don't limit your win themes to your answers. You can't really overdo this, so look for every opportunity to repeat appropriate win themes wherever you can, such as the following:

>> **Volume, section, and subsection introductions:** Since RFPs usually group questions under categories, address how all the responses in the section support your win themes (provided that the RFP allows you to do this).

>> **Graphics that depict your solution components:** You can illustrate your win themes within images you include to support your answers. See Chapter 11 for ways to do this.

>> **Captions that support your graphics:** These captions echo a win theme as you express the action depicted in your image (see Chapter 11).

Writing the Solution for a Proactive Proposal

Writing the solution section for a reactive (RFP response) or proactive proposal is mostly a matter of answering questions about how you'll solve the customer's problem. Although it's more direct if you're responding to an RFP's questions, you can follow the same approach in your proactive proposals. You just need to create a structure that simulates how your customer thinks.

The following sections show you how to use the questions you believe your customer may have asked in an RFP to write a proactive proposal with a comprehensive portrayal of the work you will do.

Developing a structure that's easy to understand

The questions you need to answer as you're writing the solution for your customer are actually pretty simple. Of course, every answer prompts a new question, so you need to think about your particular customer's needs as you flesh out your solution description. And, for that matter, every main and follow-up question includes an unstated question — "Is what you say true?" For every claim you make as you answer your customer's questions, you need to provide proof that your claim is valid.

If your solution is complex (composed of multiple products and services, or extensive support processes), you will probably have to answer the main questions (and provide proof statements) multiple times. Your need to fully explain that each solution building block is supported by this approach's inherently modular, question-based structure.

To explain a solution fully, you need to answer four key questions (and a number of follow-ups) from your customer's point of view:

>> **What is it?** Define your solution and the products and services that will deliver it. Although you can define your solution a number of ways, a classical definition works well because it places your solution into a class or category of similar solutions and then differentiates yours from everyone else's, as you see in this example:

EXAMPLE

> SureGuard 2.0 is a wireless security system that lets you secure your business from intruders while monitoring and controlling your system from any wireless phone or tablet.

Anticipate follow-up questions like these:

- How is it different from what we have or what you used to offer?
- How is it better than what we have or an alternative?
- How is it especially appropriate?
- What discriminating benefit does it provide?

As an example:

EXAMPLE

> Unlike previous versions, SureGuard 2.0 allows you to view your premises in real-time through webcam feeds while capturing the recordings for later playback. No longer do you have to be on premises to activate or deactivate your system — all functions are available through your iOS or Android device. It's especially valuable for enterprises like yours that hold large sums of money after normal hours of operation.

» **How does it work?** Describe — better still, describe and *show* — the way your solution will work in the customer's environment. Use one of a variety of schematic, conceptual, or metaphoric graphics to illustrate the inner workings of the solution. If you illustrated the customer's current situation, use a similarly styled illustration to show the same scene after you've implemented your solution. Answer follow-up questions such as

- How does it "fix" the problem?
- What are its functional components?
- How do these components work with existing workflows and infrastructure?
- What technology supports the solution?

» **What will it do for me?** Identify and describe the benefits the customer will realize. Now is the time to link individual, specific customer needs with the individual features your solution uses to bring the benefits that will help your customer achieve its business goals. As you craft your benefit statements, anticipate follow-up questions like the following:

- How does that aspect of your solution deliver this particular benefit?
- What immediate benefits may we receive?
- What long-term benefits can we expect?
- How will this solution anticipate future needs?

In Chapter 7, we present a lot of information about features and benefits: What they are (features are the *what* of your solution; benefits are the *so-what*), how they relate, how to tell the difference between them, and how benefits are central to your proposal argument. Earlier in this chapter, in the section "Describing the Customer's Situation," we indicate that you need to create a parallel structure between the problems and needs you describe in the current situation and the features and benefits that solve them in your solution. And now we add the element of proofs: providing supporting evidence that your solution will do what you claim.

One way you can pull all these interrelated elements together as you answer the "What will it do for me?" question is to present them in a table. Figure 9-1 shows the formula for displaying Need-Pain-Feature-Benefit-Discriminator-Proof statements in an easy-to-scan table.

Formatting options abound when you're assembling your Need-Pain-Feature-Benefit-Discriminator-Proof statements. If your statements are relatively simple, you can use the table format from Figure 9-1. If you have complex needs, multiple pains, extensive advantages, comprehensive benefits, and significant proofs, you may need to create short subheadings to introduce each and treat them thoroughly. Usually, you can create a bulleted list and align each statement with the needs you list in the current situation section. You don't have to repeat the need, but if your proposal is longer than a few pages, it's good to remind the reader of the issue that prompted the solution element.

		Current Situation Section		Solution Section			
		Need	**Pain**	**Feature**	**Benefit**	**Discriminator**	**Proof Points**
Principle		Identify every customer need.	For each customer need, describe the physical or psychological pain it causes.	For every state and unstated need, identify a feature that separately or with another feature eliminates the need.	For every feature you have, you must accompany it by describing the tangible benefit it provides the customer.	For every feature you offer, you should express a clear discriminator that, if possible, comes only from you.	For each Feature-Discriminator-Benefit statement, you should supply verifiable evidence that supports your claim — proof points.
Example		You need a reliable, long-lasting roofing system that can withstand the heavy thunderstorms that come every spring.	Your largest tenant just told you that if you can't fix the leaks, it will terminate its lease. Your company will go under if you lose this tenant who provides more than half your monthly income.	Our EnduraBond roofing solution uses a high-density coating to seal and protect your roof and is guaranteed for 30 years.	You will keep more of your profits by retaining your tenants and lowering maintenance costs.	EnduraBond eliminates leaks by adhering to surface imperfections to seal cracks and crevices. No other roofing solution offers a 30-year guarantee.	In the past three years alone, EnduraBond has eliminated roof leaks in 24 buildings like yours. None of our customers have reported issues with the treatment, and seven have agreed to share their results with you.

FIGURE 9-1: The guiding principles behind Need-Pain-Feature-Benefit-Discriminator-Proof statements (and an example of each).

Source: APMP Body of Knowledge

>> **How will you implement it?** Spell out who does what and when. Explain in detail your method for getting the solution up and working for the customer. Use project management tools like a Gantt chart to illustrate how the project will go (we talk about Gantt charts and tracking progress in Chapter 8). Name and justify the key personnel who will deliver each solution component. Anticipate these follow-up questions:

- How will you do the work?

- Who will provide and maintain the service?

- Why did you choose these people to work on our problem?

- Why is your method better than the competition?

- What will happen next?

TIP

For many businesses, the "How will you implement it?" response is a major section, chapter, or even volume of a proposal, known as the *methodology* or *scope of work*. As with the cost question, it's all a matter of degree: The more intricate and expensive your solution, the more detail you should supply.

Creating a vision of the outcomes you'll provide

The solution section of your proposal is all about getting the customer to believe in your version of its vision. You have to align your solution to match the customer's vision, and should your solution not align with this vision, you must provide sufficient evidence as to why altering its vision may be advantageous.

Once again, the best way to confirm this alignment is by illustrating it. Graphics powerfully demonstrate that you "get" your customer's vision and that your vision aligns. The graphics in your solution section influence the following:

>> **Credibility:** People equate visual design with professionalism.

>> **Receptivity:** Readers tend to absorb the main points faster when viewing images versus text.

>> **Stickiness:** Readers recall information more readily when it's presented through or with images.

>> **Responsiveness:** Images trigger emotional responses better than words and, as a result, are more persuasive.

THE POWER OF PROOF POINTS

Proof points are facts that provide verifiable evidence for your solution's features and benefits. They support your company's win themes and discriminators. Without proof points, proposal evaluators may question whether features are proven and benefits are achievable. Proof points ensure that your proposals make compelling arguments.

Proof points often describe performance on similar past efforts. They can be project data, case studies, customer quotes, testimonials, or videos, or awards and recognition earned. Crafting effective proof points requires capturing the knowledge of subject experts and relating it to the solution claim you're trying to substantiate. Proof points must be

- **Accurate:** Use specific numbers instead of approximates.

- **Verifiable:** Cite data sources where possible and provide specific customer references and quotes.

- **Relevant:** Customers should see that a prior success will translate to their unique environment and situation.

Proof points are most effective when they support features and benefits that meet or exceed customer expectations and when they cite quantitative facts and figures. Here's an example of a proof point that persuades by exceeding common performance standards:

> We know that staff retention is an important goal of the project. Our retention rate is 90 percent, compared to 82 percent industry-wide for similar IT positions. On help desk projects such as yours, our retention rate is 98 percent.

Proof points are even more persuasive when they provide information that the customers can easily verify. Help them out by including sources and references when appropriate.

Creating a comprehensive visual strategy that reinforces and enhances your textual messages is a wonderful way to ensure that your readers stick with your solution story and your story sticks in their minds. Recall that "before-and-after" images influence people to start life-changing diets and workout regimens. Use the same approach to show what needs to be changed and how it will change after you deliver your solution. Seeing truly is believing (even if it's not real yet).

REMEMBER

Graphics and illustrations in proposals are a must. See Chapter 11 for more insights into how to make your proposals more visual.

TIP

Demonstrating products or services delivers more tangible proof than mere words, so multimedia simulations of processes and products are more persuasive still. There's no excuse — other than strict customer RFP requirements — for not leveraging modern video, animation, and simulation technologies as "inserts" into multimedia proposals.

Establishing Value in the Pricing Section

Presenting your pricing is a major issue in most proposals. Pricing is tough because it's the "bad news" that goes along with the "good news" of your solution. But it's also the most anticipated part of your proposal, so you have to provide the bad news in context with the good news. When expressing pricing, you answer a simple customer question: "How much does it cost?" And you need to anticipate your customer's follow-up questions, such as these:

>> What's the bottom line?

>> Why is this more (or less) than your competitor costs?

>> How does this price compare to what I'm paying today?

>> When can I expect positive returns?

In other words, your customer wants to know what value it's receiving for this price. This section discusses how to answer your customer's pricing questions and quantify your answers with hard data.

Expressing the value of your solution

Customers scrutinize your pricing section more than any other. That's no deep insight, we know. Every decision ultimately boils down to money. But a proposal writer's job is to present the price within the context of *value*. To do this, you have to

>> Clearly state value propositions that encapsulate the benefits, discriminators, and win themes you've stated elsewhere in the proposal (refer to Chapter 6 and the next section for more on the relationship between win themes and value propositions and Chapter 7 for more on benefits).

>> Illustrate the difference between cost and value by providing graphs and pictograms to help highlight your value and show the return that a price will yield.

>> Provide only the level of pricing detail your customer needs to decide in your favor (or they won't see the forest for the trees).

We explore these three key elements of pricing in the following sections.

Stating your value proposition

In Chapter 6, we urge you to write clear win themes — key messages to your customer about the value you bring to individual aspects of the solution. We state there that some proposal writers refer to these messages as "value propositions." Here's why: While your win themes reiterate value throughout your proposal, in the pricing section, they directly address how aspects of an offer (and the corresponding price for those aspects) can positively affect the customer's business. Well-written value propositions have to describe tangible and quantifiable value because your pricing is now a looming reality to the customer. Your value propositions must clearly show how the price of the solution is offset by the tangible value it brings.

In your pricing discussion, create value propositions to provide a focal point for your solution and its tangible benefits for you and your customers.

REMEMBER

Many proposal experts have built models for writing strong value propositions. We think this one does everything you need it to do:

> You will [*solve/improve/reduce*] your [*problem/need*] by [*time/method qualifier*], because our [*solution/technology/feature/method*] [*delivers/provides/supplies*] [*new capability/problem resolution*] for [*price/price comparative*].

Think about the variables in brackets: They cover the need, the methodology, the outcomes and benefits, the solution, and the cost all in one sentence. In a nutshell, a one-sentence value proposition summarizes the worth of your offer, from end to end.

EXAMPLE

Here's one with the blanks filled in:

> You will *reduce* your *high turnover rates* by *30 percent*, because our *employee assistance program supplies one-on-one counseling* for *a manageable, usage-based fee.*

TIP

You can improve on this model by

>> Expanding it to describe both tangible and intangible value

>> Adding a variable to show how your solution is a better alternative

>> Describing how aspects of your offer positively affect your customer's business

>> Stating priorities and timelines to reinforce your value

When building your value proposition, be sure to avoid the following:

>> Expressing a one-size-fits-all solution

>> Boasting with phrases like "we are the leader" or "our world-class solution"

>> Overselling features without properly describing their benefits

>> Building confusing, complex, hard-to-remember statements

Start your pricing section with your value propositions. Follow them with a recap of your most compelling Need–Pain–Feature–Benefit–Discriminator–Proof statements, before you even bring up the subject of money.

TIP

Place your value propositions in the other parts of your proposal where you know your customer will see them. Display them prominently in your executive summaries. Consider them for callouts and fly-page quotes. Echo them often to make sure they stick in your customer's mind.

Using graphics to clearly show value

A graphic can help persuade your customer that the value you claim truly exists. Using a graph or chart to show the return on investment (ROI) or the payback period on your project is a great way to cement the idea of value. It succinctly reinforces your value proposition and sets the context for the price your customer will pay. Figure 9-2 provides an example that shows how quickly a customer can recoup its investment.

TIP

Graphics, tables, and even thematic pictograms can make dry, complicated monetary issues more understandable, more vivid, and more compelling. And all help you get the message across without your customer getting lost in the details at the wrong time (in the middle of your argument).

For more information about persuading with graphics and other visuals, see Chapter 11.

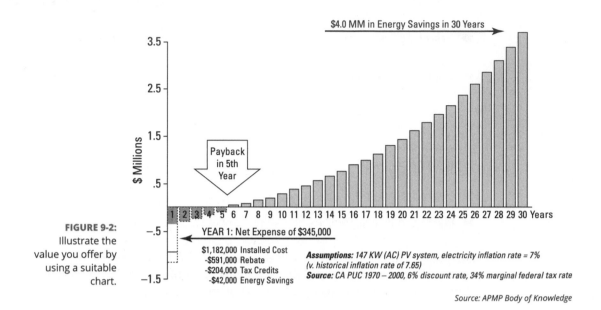

$4.0 MM in Energy Savings in 30 Years

Payback
in 5th
Year

YEAR 1: Net Expense of $345,000

$1,182,000 Installed Cost
-$591,000 Rebate
-$204,000 Tax Credits
-$42,000 Energy Savings

Assumptions: *147 KW (AC) PV system, electricity inflation rate = 7%*
(v. historical inflation rate of 7.65)
Source: *CA PUC 1970 – 2000, 6% discount rate, 34% marginal federal tax rate*

Source: APMP Body of Knowledge

FIGURE 9-2:
Illustrate the
value you offer by
using a suitable
chart.

Summarizing your pricing information

Your proposal will likely be assessed by many reviewers with differing perspectives. The pricing section is no exception. It will be an early target for an evaluator, who will then pass it along to the financial analyst to "crunch the numbers" and verify the value you've claimed. Providing a summary of your pricing detail (in a spreadsheet or table or in a list of item pricing that you can supply in an appendix) makes an evaluator's job easier. It also gives the pricing analyst a simple and quick view of the price, which can speed up comparisons.

REMEMBER

Your pricing summary is the message you want the pricing analyst to deliver to the ultimate decision maker — it's like a mini executive summary, where you can shape the pricing message in the most positive light. Make sure you include as many of these facets of your pricing as possible:

» Total price in narrative and graphic form (many customers want to see the bottom line upfront)

» Pricing assumptions (just the major, most important ones)

» Overall themes (that echo your value proposition)

» Price discriminators (value you offer that no one else can)

> » How you logically established your prices (and any positive price implications of choosing that approach)

> » Any cost tracking and control systems that will benefit the customer further down the line

The pricing summary should tie together details readers will see in the detailed pricing sheets. It should also include your assumptions and estimating guidelines, which will likely need to be tailored from previous programs. Reviewers like to see traceable details as well as summaries of data. An easy-to-review yet detailed pricing reference gives evaluators a reason to award the bid to you.

Quantifying your claims with data

The pricing section can be an argument-clincher by showing that you can do what you say and that you have the facts and the rationale to back up your claims. Your facts not only validate what you're claiming and lend credibility to your organization, but they also provide you and your customer with the details necessary to make informed decisions about your price. And even though price is market-driven, the facts help you build a story that creates confidence in your solution.

You can justify and build your case for your costs by demonstrating that you've done the work before at a certain cost. This is where what proposal people call "past performance" comes into play (you find more about this in the next section). Nothing is more compelling than data showing how you've already performed the work the customer wants done. You may have completed entire projects similar to what your customer needs, so you can fully substantiate your price with verifiable, historical data.

REMEMBER

Although past performance examples are strong evidence that you can meet the customer's requirements, don't forget that most customers still think that their situation (and therefore your solution) is unique. Always indicate the customized aspects of your past performance to assure your customer that your solutions are not "off-the-shelf."

Building the Experience Section

Just as you'd prefer a surgeon who has successfully performed thousands of operations just like the one you need, customers prefer to do business with companies that can demonstrate that they have both experience that is relevant to the work they need done and a track record of success. You write the experience section (sometimes called the qualifications section) to recount relevant know-how and past performance to provide proofs that are hard to argue against.

The following sections help you figure out what to include in this key background information.

Documenting your team's know-how

Have we mentioned that proposal writing is mainly answering a lot of questions? Here's another one: "Why us?" That is, why should your customer choose you over all other vendors? One great answer is, "our people." Although many companies say their people are their greatest asset, a proposal writer has to prove it. And if you can, you can win.

Depending on the type of business you're in and the scope of work in the projects your people perform, you may want to create professional résumés for individuals on your team that highlight their skills, experience, education, and accomplishments. If your company works on major projects, you may need résumés as extensive as, if not more than, traditional job résumés. These may include content categories like Experience, Education (especially technical), Certifications, Awards and Recognition, and Professional Memberships. You need to tailor these résumés for the specific proposal you're writing. Tailor them by rearranging the content to highlight recent projects that match the size, scope, and solution of the current opportunity. You can also include client commendations and even prior work for the customer, if pertinent.

If your proposals are less formal or less complex, you can avoid the full-blown résumé by creating short paragraphs that highlight the knowledge, skills, and experience of your key team members.

As an example:

> David Michaels is the senior project manager we have assigned to direct your project. David has been our most highly sought-after project manager for the past 12 years. He is certified as a Project Management Professional and a licensed electrical engineer. David successfully led the Regional Airport facility upgrade, a project of similar scope and intricacy to yours.

Consider thumbnail photographs of these employees to further personalize your team.

Choosing relevant past-performance examples

The other question customers ask about your qualifications is, "Who else have you done this for?" You want to respond with relevant experience. Relevant experience is simply comparing how you've performed on previous jobs that match the goals, size, scope, and complexity of the new opportunity.

REMEMBER

When it comes to past performance, evaluators have different perspectives. So you have to anticipate the question behind the question. If your evaluators are technical experts, they'll want to know about how you applied your technical abilities and skills on prior projects. They'll also be interested in the technical innovations that you brought to the project. If your evaluators are cost experts, they'll want to hear about how your costs tracked against estimates and if you incurred any penalties for performance.

In general, make sure you answer the evaluators' basic question: "Did you do what the contract required?"

TIP

What goes into your past performance descriptions? Use this list as a starting point (but remember: If you're responding to an RFP, make sure you add any past-performance requirements to the list that you find when you shred the RFP):

>> Customer name

>> Project or contract name

>> Dates of the project and term of contract

>> Customer project lead and contact information

>> Customer's industry

>> Project description (nature of the work performed, number of sites, amount of equipment, types of services)

Some customers may place greater importance on past performance than others. But no matter what the setting, clear descriptions of past performance can help build confidence in your solution and ability to perform. Always present your past-performance descriptions in an attractive, easy-to-understand way, using graphics and proof points as appropriate.

Many RFPs ask for references, and may insist on speaking directly with any companies that you list. Keep an archive of selected customers and customer contacts and ask for permission to use them as references. Help prepare them by supplying a list of questions they can expect to hear, such as "How well did the bidder work with your managers?" and "Did the bidder adhere to its implementation schedule?"

Closing with a Call to Action

In this chapter, we trace the structure of a proposal from beginning to near-end. And you may notice that the experience section, though of significant importance to the customer, may not be the most exciting section to read. You don't want to end your proposal on a low note, so how do you finish well?

REMEMBER

The best way to finish is by starting again. Recall that your executive summary is your proposal in a nutshell — a distillation of your key messages, benefits, and next steps. Your proposal's closing section needs to further distill your executive summary to re-energize your customer with all the positives you can bring to bear. Remember to close with the three Rs:

>> **R**estate your value proposition.

>> **R**ecap your customer's hot buttons and your solution's benefits.

>> **R**einforce the need to act now.

UNDERSTANDING THE ROLE OF ATTACHMENTS

Many proposals — especially RFP responses — seem to serve as an excuse for bidders to include reams (or gigabytes) of attachments — product glossies, spec sheets, case studies, annual reports, kitchen sinks — er, well, you get the idea. Other bidders leave these "extras" out totally, cramming all their content, whether pertinent to the opportunity or not, into the narrative of the proposal. Both approaches are misguided.

Your goal should be to tell your company's story in your proposal. Keep your narrative free from excessive detail. Add an attachments section to the back of your proposal to add details and supplementary references (if you do, and your story will benefit from a proof point in an attachment, direct your reader to the attachment with a clear, direct reference). You can also use hyperlinks to connect your readers to the supporting information that you house on a website, which they can then choose to review or not.

If your vision for your customer differs from the one that an RFP seems to desire, you can use an attachment section to house an alternative response or solution (again, only if the RFP allows it). To make sure you're not disqualified, you should respond to the full RFP as directed, but note that you've included an alternative response in the executive summary.

IN THIS CHAPTER

Structuring your argument

Stating your case clearly

Influencing your readers

Helping readers find what they need

Chapter 10

Applying the Principles of Good Writing: Structuring Your Argument

When it comes to writing, the distance between your head and your hands can seem a lot farther than a couple of feet. Many of you know exactly what you want to say, but you may have trouble getting the words and sentences to cooperate. When you're writing any kind of document, you must be clear or you'll lose your reader. If you lose your reader when you're writing proposals, you lose the sale.

In proposals, you must state what you'll do and how you'll do it in such a way that your customer's evaluators quickly understand and agree with you. Your goal is to persuade, and you can't do that if your reader can't follow your argument.

In this chapter, you find ways to write your proposal so readers can readily understand it. You find techniques on how best to put words together to make clear sentences and how to put sentences together to express clear ideas. You also find out how to creatively express your argument and how to make sure your customer doesn't miss the good parts.

Outlining to Guide Your Writing

In Chapter 9, we lay out the parts of a standard proposal for you in order and discuss ways to ensure that you create a comprehensive and expected argument. We say *expected* because all the parts we recommend make up the schema for a sound proposal argument.

REMEMBER

A *schema* is a mental blueprint that helps your proposal match the way people want to discover and remember new information. All proposals follow such a structural pattern (with variations at times), meeting the expectations of business people — that is, executive summary, current situation, solution/method, financial/pricing, qualifications/experience, and action close.

If you already have a schema (which we follow in Chapter 9 for proposals), why bother with outlines? You have to put content into that schema, and your customer's situation (and yours, for that matter) is unique. So you need a way to organize your content within these schema elements. If you do that upfront, the writing is so much easier.

The next three sections discuss two kinds of outlines that help you write proactive proposals — topical (the simplest and most direct) and descriptive (the one that helps you write better) — and an outlining approach for your reactive proposals (RFP responses).

Using topical outlines to build content

Outlines come in different forms. You probably remember *topical outlines* from your school days — Roman numerals with single nouns that name the major sections of your paper. These types of headings function well and help to organize your thoughts. You can place the topics you need to discuss under each of the major structural elements, as you see in the example section shown in Figure 10-1.

This is the value of topical outlines: They're simple, useful and writer-friendly. They can almost serve as a mind map to cluster your ideas for content into useful categories. If you're the kind of writer who needs just a little organizational help, the topical outline may be your favorite tool. Still, later on, you'll need to take these thought-provoking yet less-informative labels and turn them into descriptive headings (see the next section) that will help readers scan for the information they seek.

```
II.   Current Situation
      A.  Network's Topology
          1.  Major branches
          2.  Regional hub
          3.  Routes and capacities
          4.  External connections
      B.  Network Diagram
          1.  Locations
          2.  Equipment
          3.  Capacities
          4.  Routes
      C.  Network's problems
          1.  Single point of failure
          2.  Choke points
          3.  Aging technology
          4.  Risks of multiple providers
      D.  Network's Importance
          1.  Geological data
              a)  Types of data
              b)  Value of data
          2.  Sensitive client information
```

FIGURE 10-1: A topical outline fleshes out the proposal schema element "current situation" with key components, problems, and implications.

Source: *APMP Body of Knowledge*

Using descriptive outlines to guide your readers (and your writers)

Descriptive outlines are better than topical outlines in two ways. First, as the name suggests, *descriptive outlines* use more expressive headings to bring extra meaning and value to the structural- and subject-based labels of topical outlines. Unlike the nouns and noun phrases that stand in for headers in writer-friendly topical outlines, descriptive headings help to make your content reader-friendly by making your message visible, allowing readers to scan your content and quickly understand your offer. If you refer to your win themes in these headings (refer to Chapter 2 for more on win themes), they can persuade your readers as well as inform them.

Second, descriptive headings also help the writers who are contributing to your proposal understand both the topic they need to write about and the emphasis you want placed on elements within the topic. So they're also writer-friendly — the best of both worlds!

EXAMPLE

Compare the entries for the descriptive outline in Figure 10-2 with the topical ones in Figure 10-1. Nouns and noun phrases, like *Major branches* and *Regional hub* make readers (and writers) stop and think, "What might this be about?" or "How do these relate?" The more descriptive *Connecting your major branches to the regional hub* heading makes the relationship clear and lets a reader or writer quickly establish what content should fall under the heading.

II. Your Network Today

    A. How is your network configured?
        1. Connecting your major branches to the regional hub
        2. Making sense of the routings and transmittal speeds
        3. Linking with the corporate network and with customers

    B. Network diagram (highlight locations, equipment, capacities, and routes)

    C. What problems are you having with your network?
        1. Tempting fate with a single point of failure
        2. Holding back your employees and clients because of choke points
        3. Living on borrowed time with aging technology
        4. Risking a quick resolution because of multiple providers

    D. What happens if your network fails?
        1. Disrupting the transfer of vital data
            a) What kinds of data are at risk?
            b) How much do you stand to lose?
        2. Jeopardizing sensitive client information

FIGURE 10-2: A descriptive outline helps readers scan your proposal and can summarize the key takeaways of your offer at a glance.

Source: APMP Body of Knowledge

Getting your contributors to write what you want can be a big challenge. They tend to recycle what they've done before or, worse, pull technical content from equipment manufacturers' spec sheets and pass that along as their own (or they'll send you the 400-page manufacturer's support manual and expect you to sort through it for half a page of information). Descriptive outlines can get your writers thinking the right way and can act as a catalyst for creating good content.

TIP

Consider the process of developing the outline as an interactive tool for developing proposal content — beneath each heading, plug in notes and expressions you've heard during your planning discussions and let those stimulate responses from your contributors. When they add content, recraft it to meet your style requirements and send it back to them, maybe with some added content or clarifying questions. Repeat this process until you get the content that expresses your value proposition while thoroughly explaining the topic. You'll be doing them and yourself a big favor by putting in the extra effort.

For more on how to write descriptive headings, see the later section "Using Headings to Guide the Reader through Your Proposal."

Outlining the RFP response

When you're responding to an RFP, use the exact headings from the bid request, and include all sections that the customer requires. If anyone on your team wants to digress from the client's format, tell that person that doing so may lower your evaluation score if not outright disqualify you. Remember, customers evaluate your response based on their structure, not yours.

To respond, prepare a top-level outline that mimics the numbering system, naming conventions, and order listed in the bid request. If the customer doesn't provide explicit instructions, follow the general outline of the RFP and organize your response within that structure, using descriptive headings as we just described, in the order that makes most sense, given your knowledge of the customer.

Writing Clearly

Clear writing is as much of a key discriminator for your proposals as a sound technical solution designed to solve your customers' problems. After all, what good is a great solution if your readers can't understand it?

Applying the principles of clear writing makes your technical solution easier to read and understand, which makes it easier for your readers to say yes. If writing doesn't come easy for you, don't fret. You don't have to write a masterpiece. Your goal is to make readers spend less time untangling your meaning and more time thinking about how your solution meets their needs.

REMEMBER

This may come as a bit of a shocker, but the root cause of unclear business communication is style, not format or grammar. *Style* represents the way you put words together at the sentence and paragraph level to express your content and perspective. In this section, we boil style down to its fundamental techniques so you can quickly improve your writing.

Clear writing doesn't "dumb down" ideas; it clarifies them. Clear writing eliminates the mystery of jargon, the ambiguous actions hidden within nominalizations, the shorthand of conceptual shortcuts, and the content density of stacked nouns so ideas stand on their merits and become accessible to all who need to understand them.

TIP

Here's the paradox of writing: If your writing is clear, your readers probably won't notice. (We rarely hear anyone say, "Now that's a well-written proposal!" but we've definitely heard people say, "What the hell do you mean?") Readers can work around bad grammar (but do avoid it, because they may think that you haven't made an effort). But bad style just makes your readers scratch their heads and give up.

A TRUE STORY ABOUT THE VALUE OF CLEAR WRITING

One of our proposal managers wrote a proposal for a large school district that needed a technology upgrade. She'd taken the design specs from the engineering team and written a proposal that spoke to the needs of the district, describing the solution in terms that an educator could appreciate and understand. The design engineers hated it. They told her that she'd "dumbed down" the content and that the customer would reject the proposal.

The sales lead called us in a panic and said that she was now worried that the customer would reject the proposal because the engineers wouldn't stand behind it. We tried to convince her that clearly describing the solution and its benefits without all the technical jargon the engineers wanted would help her win the deal. She asked if we'd confront the engineers; if we convinced the engineers that the content was fine, she'd back our version.

Neil (Charlie was the big boss back then and made Neil do the dirty work) set up a conference call. All the engineers were there. They aggressively restated their position. Neil said, "Let's take it line by line and you tell me what is inaccurate, misleading, or just plain dumb."

Only one engineer challenged the content, saying, "No technical person would say that." Neil asked if a technical person would decide on the solution. He said probably not. He made it about two pages into the proposal before they said, "Go ahead and do it your way, but don't blame us when it fails."

We submitted the proposal "our way." Two weeks later, an excited sales lead called us to say that she'd won the business. "Oh," she said, "and the customer said of the eight proposals they received, ours was the only one they could understand."

Telling stories to your customers

The idea of storytelling has swept the business world. People love a good story. Even stern proposal evaluators love a story. Think of all the ways that storytelling affects your proposal:

>> You hear the stories your customer tells you about its problems.

>> You take those problems and create solutions.

>> You tell your customer how you, a new character in its story, can solve the problems of the main characters in its story.

>> You prove that your story is true by telling more stories about how you've done this before for other companies.

The proposal process consists of one story after another. So when you write your proposal, use all the best storytelling techniques. We cover some of these techniques in the following sections.

Begin your sentences with human subjects

You tell stories through characters and their actions. Because proposals are action-oriented documents, you should try to use human subjects whenever possible. Your proposals need to actively express how you perform for customers, because they pay you for results.

Check out this next sentence:

> Design decisions were made to human factors specifications.

Who is doing what? No actor is named. The verb indicates vague actions. And don't get us started about unravelling that ending cluster of nouns.

Try this for size instead:

> Our engineers design our products to work as you do.

Now you have a human subject — an actor who performs a significant action for your customer's benefit. It's more direct and more personal, so it's more meaningful. And it's worth paying for.

Put sentence parts in the right order

To keep your actors' roles clear and their actions plain, write mainly using an active voice. You learned how to talk using your *active voice*. It's the sentence structure of stories: subject–verb–object (s–v–o). Sentences in active voice position the person doing the action as the subject and place the main action in the verb (the "doing" word), followed by the object or the thing changed by the action.

Here are some examples of the s–v–o sentence structure in action:

> A boy meets a girl.
>
> The parents size up the boy.
>
> The girl defends the boy.
>
> The parents ask, "Where did we go wrong?"

In passive voice sentences, you get the reverse: The subject is the goal of the action, and the action is partially diluted because it's coupled with helper verbs like *is, are, was,* or *were.* If the writer bothers to name the main actor, it's usually the object in a prepositional phrase starting with *by*:

> The girl was met (by the boy).

> The boy is sized up (by the parents).

You get the picture.

REMEMBER

Passive voice is the style of science and technology, where objectivity is a main concern. Although passive voice doesn't necessarily mean that a writer is being objective, in a proposal it can mean three things, none of which are good for winning a bid:

>> You don't know who the "actor" is (not a good thing when talking about what you're going to do for your customer).

>> The reader doesn't care about the actor (usually that's you, and again, not a good thing).

>> You're trying to avoid blame (not a great way of winning customers).

Okay, passive voice is good for one thing in a proposal. Used judiciously, it can help your paragraphs flow and stay on topic (it's all about keeping your topic consistently in the subjects of your sentences). More about that in the upcoming section "Bond your sentences into coherent paragraphs."

How can you tell when a sentence is in the passive voice? The easiest way is to have your word processor's grammar checker look for it. Check the grammar and writing style options in your word-processing software and make sure the function to look for passive voice is turned on.

TIP

Never rely solely on grammar checkers. They still miss a lot, and passive voice isn't hard to spot. Look for three things:

>> A past participle form of a verb (usually ending in *-ed*)

>> A *to be* verb (*is, am, are, was, were, be,* and *being*)

>> A prepositional phrase beginning with *by* (whose object is the true actor)

EXAMPLE

Here's a sentence in passive voice:

> The inspection of the facility was conducted by the security team.

Note the *to be* verb *was*. Then notice the past participle form of the main verb *conducted*. Usually, that's enough to denote a passive sentence. Yet the third sign is also present: the *by* phrase *(by the security team)*.

Now, check out the active voice version:

> The security team inspected the facility.

Not only is this version in active voice, but it also turns the sentence back into a story: people doing something. And better still, the shortened sentence doesn't lose meaning; in fact, it makes the meaning clearer.

Note: The verb *inspected* is in the past tense, which is perfectly okay (you can still express active voice in the past tense). The past participle form of the verb is the same as the past tense form and is an indicator of passive voice when it's coupled with the *to be* verb. If English grammar is your Kryptonite, check out *English Grammar For Dummies*, by Geraldine Woods (Wiley). Or if you really want to dive deep, we recommend Joseph M. Williams and Gregory G. Colomb's *Style: Toward Clarity and Grace* (University of Chicago Press).

TIP

Many technically inclined people tend to write in passive voice. They may have picked this up in engineering classes, where the people doing the thing are less important than the thing itself. But this is business, and business is all about people doing things for other people. So make your proposals about people helping people and avoid the passive voice (unless you really need to use it).

Put action in verbs

Because action drives all but the dullest of stories, use strong, active verbs to avoid abstractions. Technical content often hides complex actions in the form of *nominalizations*, or verbs and adjectives that have been converted to nouns. Nominalizations represent very abstract concepts — *implementation*, *industrialization*, and even *nominalization* itself, to name a few.

REMEMBER

Why do nominalizations exist? Nominalizations help subject experts reduce the number of words they need to convey a complex concept. They work great when subject experts are writing to other subject experts in their field. They don't work so well when they're writing to people without their expertise: You know, the people who make decisions about proposals. And here's the paradox: You want to write concisely in proposals, but you have to be clear. Nominalizations can reduce word counts, but they also make content harder to understand.

TIP

Most nominalizations end in the suffixes *-tion* or *-sion*, but they don't have to. They can also end in *-ary*, *-ery*, and *-ment*, to name a few.

Check out the nominalization in the passive-voice sentence in the preceding section. The main verb is *inspect*. The original sentence used that great, action-oriented verb as a noun — *inspection*. Look at how many more words it takes to finish the sentence after turning the main verb into an abstract noun. First, you have to add a new verb (two, actually) for the sentence to be grammatical: *was conducted*. And what good does the empty verb *conducted* do for the meaning? None, except maybe it formalizes the tone or makes the idea sound grand. You then have to get the actor in there (or the sentence would be worthlessly vague), so you have to create a prepositional phrase to explain who conducted the investigation *(by the security team)*. Eleven words in total when six would do!

Check out this sentence:

> We increase engagement and prevention by implementation of the survey, which enables outreach and increases utilization.

Wow, talk about abstract. Whose engagement? Prevention of what? To whom is the outreach pointed? Utilization of what? It may be easier to start at the end and work backward to figure this one out, first turning the abstract nouns back into verbs and then figuring out what other words they relate to:

>> *Utilization* = *utilize* = *use* (simpler). Use what? You have to uncover a few clues before you can tell.

>> *Outreach* = *reach out*. This is an insidious nominalization — it doesn't end in the usual suffixes — but it's still a verb posing as a noun. Something allows you to reach out. Looks like it's the survey.

>> *Implementation* = *implement*. You implement a survey. Shouldn't that come first? You implement a survey to do what? To reach out to someone who isn't named. For example, maybe it's some people for whom you provide health insurance. Now you're getting somewhere.

>> *Engagement* = *engage*. Another sinister nominalization — this one ends in *-ment*. Who's engaged? The insured? Is that the right word? *Engagement* can mean *participation*. Maybe the survey increases participation in the insurance program (that's a nominalization you may be able to use because most people know what it means).

   Now you can see that *utilization* and *engagement* refer to the same thing. So you need only one of them.

>> *Prevention* = *prevent*. What does the survey prevent? What does the insurance prevent? Can you assume that this word refers to preventing disease?

So what does that leave you with?

> By implementing the survey, we increase program participation, which helps prevent employee health problems.

Now we have an actor *(we)*, and we can clearly identify the cause *(implementing the survey)*, the effect *(increase program participation)*, and the after-effect *(prevent employee health problems)*. Readers can follow the story line more easily when we turn abstract ideas into more concrete actions. And though the passage is not much shorter than the original, it's definitely clearer.

Unfortunately, business and technical content can be full of these abstract nouns. Sometimes writers string them together without words between them, making them even more difficult to decipher. We consider these noun stacks in the later section "Writing concisely."

Eliminating all nominalizations in proposals is probably neither possible nor desirable. Specialists in all fields use nominalizations to label complex concepts that would take many words to explain, and if you're writing to specialists, they already understand the concepts. The problem arises when you're not writing to specialists.

TIP

If you've taken the time to explain an abstract concept to a non-specialist audience, you can use a nominalization subsequently to refer to that concept, reduce your word count, and still be clear. For example, using a nominalization to refer to a process you recently described in detail (an *implementation* process) or a concept that is already understood and accepted by your audience (*participation* perhaps) achieves the original purpose of any abstract noun — to reduce the number of words needed to convey a concept. Because the nominalization has been explained before or its concept is common knowledge, it works.

So what's the takeaway about nominalizations? If your reader understands the concept, use the nominalization. If not, turn the concept into a more concrete action and outcome. After you've explained it, you can use the nominalization later to refer back to your explanation. You know, tell a little story about it.

TIP

To avoid nominalizations, you look for the action verb behind nouns that end in *-tion* and *-sion.* These aren't the only suffixes that nominalize verbs and adjectives, but they're a great place to start your search. For additional endings and tips for finding and converting nominalizations, see the activating nominalizations guide we provide online (via the appendix).

Writing like you talk

People tend to understand you pretty well when you're talking to them face to face. Even when you're discussing heavy stuff — from business to politics to technology — you do a good job keeping your audience listening to — maybe even hanging on to — every word. How do you do that?

Voice inflection and body language helps you to communicate clearly, but when you write, you lose those helpful aids to understanding. Yet you may also tend to write differently than you talk. It's easy to get caught up in the formality of a given situation. You may think that you have to take on a more "proper" set of words and a more distant point of view. When you do, you can lose track of what you're trying to say.

Aim to use the same style of English that you use in conversation to make your proposals more open and accessible to a wide range of audiences. Here are some ways to become more conversational, and clearer, when you write.

Choose simple words

Just as you'd do in conversation, opt for briefer, more common words when you won't compromise your meaning. The following two sentences mean the same thing, but the second one, which uses shorter words, is easier to read and understand:

> We utilize regenerators to provide essential amplification of signals between nodes of a dedicated ring.

> We use regenerators to strengthen the signals between the nodes of a dedicated ring.

You'd probably say this the second way in conversation. The meaning stays the same, but the text is shorter and more direct, which makes for a winning way of writing.

Avoid technical and industry terms

Use jargon only when it's clearly to your advantage to do so. Technical or professional jargon demonstrates mastery of a subject and gains a technical reader's trust, but, because a proposal is usually evaluated by people with different degrees of technical knowledge, be sure to define any necessary jargon you use either right after you first use the term or by including a link to a glossary definition. A better approach is to use nontechnical language unless you're writing only to technical experts.

EXAMPLE

Check out this example of content perhaps too technical for a non-expert audience:

> We proactively monitor our network to guard against a wide range of security threats, including viruses, botnets, worms, distributed denial of service attacks, spam, and other harmful activity.

This passage is perfectly clear to a Wi-Fi expert, but a lesser informed audience may benefit from a few adjustments:

> We monitor our network to prevent security threats from viruses and other malicious attacks that try to overload your system with spam or other data.

WARNING

Beware of acronyms, too. They're the shorthand of technical and industry experts, who instantly translate the often cryptic abbreviations into valuable nuggets of information. Novices or people outside the industry won't understand or, worse, may attach the acronym to another meaning. How bad can it get? The website `www.acronymfinder.com` lists at least 130 meanings for ATM!

Use personal pronouns

Business communications are increasingly less formal. Instead of keeping your customer at arm's length, build intimacy by using personal pronouns and direct address. Using third-person pronouns and collective nouns (for instance, *ABC Company* instead of *we* or *us* and *customer* instead of *you*) puts a distance between you and your reader yet implies no greater degree of objectivity.

TIP

Using the second-person pronoun to address your readers directly is sometimes called the "you attitude." You write just as if you're having a one-on-one conversation. Not only does this approach build on your existing relationship with your reader, but it also reduces the number of words you need and helps you avoid the passive voice.

Tighten your talk with contractions

Along with direct address, use contractions whenever possible to help create an informal, friendly tone. Don't use them if you're writing to someone you don't know or to someone you know is more traditional. Avoid them, too, if you want to create a tone of academic objectivity. But if you want a familiar, personal tone to your proposal — if you're writing on behalf of a salesperson with a long relationship with the customer — contractions can help you mimic spoken English.

Punctuate with punch

To further engage your readers as you write, use a variety of punctuation marks. Although punctuation is more cut-and-dried than style, the examples in this section show you how punctuation can bring emphasis and cohesion to your content.

TIP

The *colon* (:) and *em dash* (—) are both great tools for emphasizing the importance of any content that follows them in a sentence. Use them after complete sentences to point to a single word, a list, another complete sentence, or a series of complete sentences.

EXAMPLE

How do you choose between the colon and the em dash? Use the dash when your tone is informal; use the colon for a more formal look and tone. For example:

Formal: We detected problems in the following areas: accounts receivable, accounts payable, and debit entries.

Informal: We found serious problems — in both accounts receivable and payable and in debit entries.

Semicolons help to join two or more independent clauses when you want to show that they're closely related without having to overtly state that they are.

EXAMPLE

Consider these alternatives:

Less related: The new console has more features. However, the new console does require a separate power supply.

More related: The new console has more features; however, it requires a separate power supply.

Bond your sentences into coherent paragraphs

Readers lose their way in paragraphs for two main reasons:

» They receive new information before they know how it relates to the information that they already know.

» They lose track of the main topic of the paragraph because the subjects of each sentence are inconsistent.

You can improve the cohesion of your paragraphs by placing new information after old information. This allows you to build on what your reader has just read and to use this knowledge as a springboard to the next round of new information.

Notice how the second and third sentences in this paragraph begin with an idea unsaid in the preceding sentences:

> You want to be the best wireless company in the world. To achieve consistently high levels of customer service, your network must perform reliably. We use two redundant management stations that work simultaneously to achieve overall wireless system reliability.

EXAMPLE

To create a more cohesive paragraph, simply start the second and third paragraphs with "old" information:

> You want to be the best wireless company in the world. To be the best, you must delight your customers every time they make a call. To achieve overall wireless system reliability, we use two redundant management stations that work simultaneously to eliminate dropped calls.

You can keep your readers aligned with your paragraph topic by referring to that topic in the subject of each sentence you write.

Notice how this short paragraph seems to hop from subject to subject:

> Your monthly selections should arrive via ground shipping within two business days after we ship. The delivery company will send a tracking number upon picking up the shipment from the winery. Notify us immediately if your selections fail to arrive within the allotted time.

EXAMPLE

By making the subjects of each sentence the main topic (the *monthly selections*), you create a paragraph that truly seems to be about one thing:

> Your monthly selections should arrive via ground shipping within two business days after we ship. When your selections leave the winery, the delivery company will send you a tracking number. If the selections fail to arrive within the allotted time, notify us immediately.

TIP

One last technique: Tie your sentences to others using *transitions* (words, phrases, and sentences that connect one idea or sentence to another). Transitions specify relationships of time, cause and effect, space, addition, comparison, and contrast.

EXAMPLE

A transition after the verb weakens the effect of the transition and sounds awkward, as in the following example:

> The programmers failed to validate the findings with usability testers. Management asked the team lead to retest the routine **as a result**.

Always place transitions at or near the beginning of a sentence:

> The programmers failed to validate the findings with usability testers. **As a result**, management asked the team lead to retest the routine.

Writing concisely

Clear writing is content that respects your readers' time by providing everything that they need in the briefest amount of space possible. People have too much on their plates already, and the information you have to review will continue to grow. The more it grows, the more efficient you (and your readers) must be at conserving your taxed attention for the messages that deserve it most.

When you're writing a proposal, you have to take on the added responsibility of helping evaluators quickly find and take away what they need. The better job you do, the more your evaluators will look upon you with favor.

In the following sections, we introduce seven techniques for writing tightly: the first two at the paragraph level and beyond, and the remaining five at sentence or word level.

Getting to the point

REMEMBER

Clear writing informs readers quickly and unmistakably why they need to read what you've written. State your main idea upfront and make sure everything else in the unit — whether it's a chapter, section, or a paragraph — relates to that main idea. Do the same in your transmittal letter and executive summary; do the same when you introduce each section of your proposal.

When you write, every paragraph you write needs to be about one idea — it should have a topic sentence, and the rest of the paragraph should comment on that one idea. This is sound advice for most writing, but in proposals you need to think beyond this.

You need a way to state your main idea (or your response to the customer's question), provide proof to support it, and then imprint it onto the evaluators' brain.

EXAMPLE

Two American professors in English language, Joseph M. Williams and Gregory G. Colomb, studied the characteristics of effective technical paragraphs and uncovered a model that we think is perfect for proposals. They referred to it in *Style: Toward Clarity and Grace* (University of Chicago Press) as the *issue/discussion/point* pattern. Here's how you do it:

1. **In the first sentence, state your sole topic.**

   Answer the customer's question directly. Here's a simple model for doing this:

   "We provide *[whatever]* because *[why]*."

2. **In the next few sentences, support your topic with comments.**

   Comments are the "proofs" in your proposals, and they should relate only to the topic you stated in Step 1 (that is, sentence one). Be complete but brief: The more comments you make, the more likely your reader will lose your thread.

   To provide proofs, you may use

   - Examples

   - Explanations

   - Illustrations

   - Specifications

   - Testimonials

3. **Close the paragraph with a point statement.**

   In the final sentence, remind your readers why this topic is important to them. Reinforce your win themes (refer to Chapter 2 for more on win themes), differentiate your solution, or echo your main idea and how this particular aspect relates to it.

This logical model inspired our four-part RFP question-response model, which we discuss in Chapters 9 and 13. You can also access additional information online via the appendix.

Unpacking long, dense paragraphs

Shorter paragraphs are easier to read. Shorter paragraphs read like dialogue and reinforce a conversational tone, especially in nontechnical sections of a proposal. Even in-depth responses can be more reader-friendly if you write shorter paragraphs based on the various levels of ideas that you need to present.

The issue/discussion/point structure (introduced in the preceding section) supports a short paragraph strategy and makes it easier for your reader to follow your line of argument. You may even separate the point statement from the main paragraph to make the paragraph shorter and the point more emphatic.

Check out this packed paragraph:

> We approach projects of this scope through a defined program management process. In the initial phase, the ABC Company team identifies the processes and tools required to implement and validate the project. We then systematically develop a resource plan and road map to maximize the potential for success through end-to-end management of the deployment and the associated processes and tools. As a result, you have the defined strategy and experienced resources to help ensure a successful implementation.

You can make the main idea easier to follow while emphasizing the key takeaway by breaking the paragraph into smaller units (in this case, creating bullet points and then separating the point statement from the body of the paragraph):

> We approach projects of this scope through a defined program management process.
>
> ● Phase 1: Our team identifies the processes and tools we need to implement and validate the project.
>
> ● Phase 2: We develop a resource plan and road map to ensure that we control the deployment of the associated processes and tools.
>
> Because we follow this two-phased approach, you have the defined strategy and experienced resources to help ensure a successful implementation.

Separating the paragraph elements makes the content jump out to readers. They get the issue in sentence one, understand the details from the middle two sentences (now highlighted in a bulleted list), and can quickly confirm what you want them to take away from the passage.

Unpacking noun stacks

Watch out for long strings of nouns in succession, or *noun stacks*. When you use two or more nouns to modify another noun, you often force readers to read the string several times to understand which is the main noun and which of the other nouns modify it. Although they're succinct (engineers love them for that), noun stacks create ambiguity and slow down readers.

Here's a challenging noun stack in an otherwise easy-to-understand sentence:

> Our solution applies smart **population health maintenance analytics** to focus our resources where they do the most good.

Sometimes you can get to the gist of a difficult statement by starting at the end and working backward (as you see in the earlier section "Put action in verbs"). At the end of this stack, you have a nominalization: *analytics (analyze)*. What are you analyzing? Another nominalization: *maintenance (maintain)*. What are you maintaining? *Health.* For whom? Another nominalization but an understandable one: *population.* But population of what? In this case, employees.

Unpacking this noun stack yields this idea:

> For our solution, we analyze statistics showing how well your employees maintain their health, so we support those who need us the most.

Still not perfect, but at least you have an idea of what's going on!

Avoiding empty redundancies

To write tight, use only the words that your readers need. Respect your readers' time by eliminating redundant and unnecessary words. *Redundancy* occurs when you use words or phrases that unnecessarily repeat the meaning of other words in the sentence.

EXAMPLE

Here's a terrible example:

> This new routine completely eliminates all errors for a true and accurate count.

When you eliminate something, you get rid of all of it. An accurate account is, by nature, true. So you can rewrite the sentence without losing any of the meaning to read:

> This new routine eliminates errors for an accurate count.

REMEMBER

Wordy phrases add girth to writing with no added value, and with proposals, that can be the difference between meeting page counts and not.

Using concrete images and precise measures

Proposals are a genre of technical communication, and technical writing must be precise. Proposals are also persuasive documents, largely based on logic. Logic depends on concrete proofs, so use exact amounts and measures over indefinite amounts like *some, many,* or *few.*

Applying technical terms consistently

Your readers get confused when you use a synonym or alternative word when referring to technical concepts, providing instructions, or describing equipment.

To minimize frustration or the chance of misinterpretation, create a style sheet (Chapter 6 has more information; check out the link in the appendix for a sample) and list all the technical terms that you'll use in your proposal. Refer to the style sheet often, and share it with all your contributors.

Staying positive

Whenever possible, tell your readers what something is rather than what it's not. Readers comprehend positive statements faster and more easily than negative statements. If you place several negative statements within a sentence or paragraph, your readers may struggle to comprehend. They'll most definitely have to slow down and reread the passage until they untangle the action.

Showing your document's structure

Part of clear writing includes enabling your readers to access your content easily. Because evaluators may look for ways to eliminate bidders, create the most accessible and functional proposal possible as a component of your win strategy (refer to Chapter 2 for more on your win strategy).

Providing a clear view of your proposal's structure can encourage evaluators to choose your solution over submitters who don't. You can make your proposal content more accessible by applying the techniques in the following sections.

Writing informative headings

Knowing that your readers scan, skim, and screen your proposals, write headings that describe the contents of every section and subsection. Consider two guidelines as you write headings:

>> **Avoid single-word headings.** Structure-based headings (for example, *Current situation* and *Recommendation*) are too vague to keep your busy reader from having to read every word that follows. Say something about the current situation that shows you truly understand it.

>> **Use a parallel grammatical structure for headings within a hierarchical level.** This means that you form each heading by using the same grammatical pattern, such as a verb phrase, a noun phrase, or even a full sentence. Using parallel patterns for each level of heading is a subtle way to let readers know where they are in your proposal.

Three strong options for proposal headings include

- **Questions:** Question headings are perfect for proposals, because you're just answering readers' questions anyway. End these headings in a question mark (the only time you should punctuate headings).

- **Appositives:** An *appositive* is a noun (sometimes more than one) followed immediately by words that explain it or rename it to clarify its meaning. This style is a great way to keep structure-based headings and still elaborate on them. Use a colon between the structural element and the description, as in *Current situation: Your network under attack*.

- **Gerund phrases:** *Gerunds* are verbs used as nouns. They end in the suffix *-ing*. They name actions, and you see plenty of them in this book, because the *For Dummies* heading style is to use gerund phrases (for example, this section is titled "*Writing* informative headings").

You can choose from many other heading styles as well: noun phrases, clauses, even complete sentences. All are better than single-word headings. Keep the styles consistent by heading level so your reader can follow the structure of your proposal from table of contents to conclusion.

Check out the later section "Using Headings to Guide the Reader through Your Proposal" to find out more about headings.

Using numbered and bulleted lists

Numbered and bulleted lists are easy ways to open up your documents for easy reading and absorption. Consider these ideas for using such lists effectively:

>> Build numbered lists to highlight items in a sequence. Use numbered lists for procedures, step-by-step instructions, and references to numbered components.

>> Develop bulleted lists to highlight components or elements when no sequential order is evident.

For emphasis, place your most important bullet list items in the first, second, or last positions.

TIP

>> Use hanging indents. Wrapping text around the bullet or number reduces the eye's ability to separate the items in the list.

>> Limit the number of items in your lists. Limit lists to three to seven items (and aim for the lower number). If you have more items to display and can't exclude any, group them into labelled categories (again sticking to three to seven items per grouping) and use them as substeps.

Transitioning smoothly between sections and chapters

Just as readers can get lost within paragraphs, they can easily lose the thread of your message as the pages pile up. To help your readers overcome section and chapter breaks, use visual and verbal transitions that echo your value proposition or key discriminators while promising great value to come.

TIP

Have you ever listened to talk radio? If so, you can think of these transitions as being like the brief teasers that the announcers use to entice listeners to keep listening through an upcoming commercial break. These snippets are known as *packaging*. Instead of saying, "We'll be right back," they plant a little seed to entice listeners to stay tuned for what's to come.

You can use a similar technique to gently push your readers into the next section of your proposal. Use transitions at the end of the current situation section to restate an overall need and set up the promise of the solution section. Push your reader out of the pricing section to your experience section by setting up your staffing plan or past performance as valuable benefits that more than justify the price.

TIP

Consider setting these transitions apart from the body text at the bottom of the last page in a section, allowing any remaining white space to push the reader's eyes to the transitioning message. You can also make the transitions visual, using an icon to lead into the message or a mini sidebar in a shaded box.

REMEMBER

On the flipside, provide a "landing pad" for your transitions as you introduce the section that follows. Pick up the message from the prior page and close out the thought, using a technique such as one of the following:

>> Use cause/effect and comparison/contrast transitions that relate to the transition message from the preceding section.

>> Pull in takeaways from the preceding section that pertain to the new section's line of thought.

>> Preview the new section's structure by indicating how it's parallel to that of the preceding section.

>> Recap prior conclusions.

>> Recast the themes that you established in your executive summary in relation to the purpose of the new section.

Revising your work

If you want your proposals to be clear, you need to include ample time in your proposal process to edit and revise them. By "ample time," we mean allowing for the back-and-forth cycles of reviewing and revising (it's never one-and-done). You need this time not only to make sure your writing is direct and understandable but also to test the validity of your solution.

As you review your writing work, refer to the style sheet for your particular project (refer to Chapter 6 for more on creating style sheets). You need to make sure you're presenting terms consistently and following the usage and punctuation guidelines that you set up for your writers. To access a sample style sheet, check out the appendix.

TIP

Whether you're the sole proposal writer or the editor for a group of proposal contributors, here's one last trick of the trade for writing clearly: Schedule downtime between writing and editing. A waiting period away from the document allows you to find errors and validate ideas more easily and without the emotional baggage that comes with being immersed in a project.

Keep these approaches in mind as you plan to initiate the review of your draft proposal:

» If you're the sole proposal writer, ask your sales team or engineers to review your work. Everyone loves to nitpick, and you'd be amazed at how some people who hate to write love to edit.

Thank them profusely for helping you out, and then ignore any criticism you don't agree with.

» If you're part of a proposal team, ask your peers to review your work and offer to do the same for them. Look for opportunities for substantive, grammatical, and general stylistic improvement.

Writing Persuasively

The purpose of your proposal is to persuade your readers that your solution is the right one for their business. You don't need to be a rhetorician to craft an effective argument, although the principles of rhetoric can provide practical guidance. In this section, we talk about two key principles of rhetoric: knowing your audience, and applying the three modes of persuasion to that audience by appealing to their sense of reason, their emotions, and their ethics.

Knowing who you're writing to

While writers of all communication types have to think about their audience before they write, persuasive writing is *all* about the audience. To write a clear paragraph, you must make sure every sentence relates to the topic. To write persuasively, you have to make sure everything you say is filtered for your audience's style, preferences, and situations.

Analyzing your readers

How do you know what your readers need if you've never met them? How do you know what words to use when you've never heard your readers talk? What if you're a lone proposal writer back at the main office, and your only connection with your readers is the salesperson or service rep who supports them?

You start by posing a few questions to the people who know your readers best:

>> What roles do the readers play in the customer's operation?

>> What are the readers' levels of technical expertise?

>> How urgent is the need for a solution in each of the readers' minds?

>> How does this proposal affect the readers personally and professionally?

>> How do these readers like to receive information?

>> How do these readers make decisions?

>> What special expectations do the readers have?

Aim for specific answers to each of these questions. If you don't get the details you need (such as, what is at stake professionally for each of your readers), you may need to probe deeper. You can't persuade people when you don't know what makes them tick.

TIP If your sales reps haven't met your customer yet, try to persuade your organization to hold off bidding until they do.

Making assumptions about your audience

Some proposal experts go to extraordinary lengths to analyze their audiences. They project roles like decision maker, influencer, advocate, expert, and adversary, and create personas for each. The truth is, all these roles are possible, even likely, in every multi-evaluator situation.

Be specific: Ask your customer-facing contacts who will evaluate, who will influence, and who will decide, and build your approach accordingly:

>> **If your decision maker is an executive,** above all, be brief. State your recommendation at the beginning of your executive summary. Avoid technical terms, and reference the customer's vision and goals as opposed to specific technical problems.

>> **If your decision maker is a middle manager,** focus on *how* the solution will work in the business (a "day-in-the-life scenario, present and future," is a great technique for this reader because it shows exactly how the solution will affect their team as they go about their daily business). Define all technical terms. Speak of processes and outputs.

>> **If your decision maker is a technical expert,** use technical terms but still apply the techniques of clear writing we discuss earlier in this chapter in the section "Writing Clearly." Even technical readers appreciate a clear, direct style (although they tend to talk and write using jargon and noun stacks!).

>> **If your decision maker is a financial expert,** get to the point as you would with an executive and avoid technical terms, but be sure to use terms that illustrate the financial value of your solution.

Should you be writing to all these reader types, write to the least expert reader. You will affirm what the experts already know and you won't alienate the executive or manager who is more focused on business operations.

Applying the principles of rhetoric

Sometimes old is good. In Chapter 2, we talk about three approaches to argument (logical, emotional, and ethical), and we can't talk about persuasion and not bring these approaches up again.

Rhetorical principles were documented thousands of years ago and, for the most part, are still valid tools for the proposal writer. Here, in modern terms, is what we mean by the logical, the emotional, and the ethical approaches to argument, respectively:

>> **Be specific.** Even if you've solved a similar problem for someone else, you still have to show how that success translates to your reader's unique environment and situation. Do your homework to make sure your solution really fits. Don't spare the details — use real scenarios and precise statistics and measures to prove that your solution is right for this particular customer.

>> **Be personal.** Discover what keeps your audience up at night and speculate on the corporate and personal repercussions of not acting or acting incorrectly. The best way to build urgency in a proposal is to make your solution an alternative to real, personal pain.

>> **Be values-oriented.** To create empathy, your audience must see that you care about the same things they do. People like people who are similar to themselves, so look to understand their corporate and personal stances on business, social, and environmental issues to see whether you have common ground.

This doesn't mean to simply say what your reader wants to hear. A proposal is a precursor to a contract, so make sure you can deliver what you claim and that you really care about what you say you care about. A proposal is a true *argument* that aims for a mutually beneficial relationship — the classic win-win situation.

The following sections take a look at these three persuasive approaches in more detail.

Establishing the validity of your proposal by using logic

In proposals, you state claims and provide proofs to support them. This is the most intellectually satisfying of persuasive techniques. The more objective your proofs are, the more compelling your argument is.

Proofs take many forms, ranging from the definitive . . .

>> Technical specifications and standards

>> Test results

>> Certifications

. . . to the more anecdotal:

>> Evidence of past performance

>> Testimonies of satisfied customers

>> Citations of awards and recognitions

To persuade, you must follow every claim with a proof and show how that proof applies in your reader's world.

For more on the logical approach, refer to Chapter 7, where we talk more about the importance of proofs.

Appealing to the emotions of your audience

If you truly understand your readers, you know that they're people of passion as well as of intellect. People — although some don't like to admit it — make decisions based as much on emotion as on logic. A time-tested persuasive technique is to express how inaction or the wrong action can jeopardize your reader's well-being. This is known as the *FUD Factor* (fear, uncertainty, and doubt).

Storytelling techniques can be of great value in a proposal (refer to the earlier section "Telling stories to your customers" for more on this). Telling a story about what may cause an outage or interruption to your reader's business is a great way to bring an acute awareness to a problem and its potential consequences — and a way to bring urgency to a decision.

Another technique for eliciting an emotional response from readers is to use vividly descriptive language. Bring vividness by using the following:

>> **Common words over their formal equivalents:** Listen closely to the words your customers use when describing their problems. Rather than a lot of formal and technical terms, you likely hear words that express the pain behind the technical issues. Repeat these words in your proposals. The more emotion they carry, the better. Use them sparingly, though. In large doses, they may come off as heavy-handed or even unethical.

>> **Concrete words rather than abstract terms:** Language is more persuasive when it helps to build an image in your mind. Concrete words are easier to read and easier to understand than abstractions. Nominalizations are harder to understand than people performing actions. To persuade, use words that accurately describe what *you* see so your readers see it the same way.

Expressing an ethical character

The ethical approach means forging mutual respect with your readers by stating your logical and emotional appeals with sincerity and honesty. Using the ethical appeal adds substance to your argument and reinforces that your solution is a win-win for both parties.

You can win your reader's confidence and convey your integrity by

>> Purging any fallacies from your logical proofs

>> Recognizing issues you may have had in the past, as you explain how you resolved them

>> Showing empathy for people who may be negatively affected by your solution

>> Expressing concern for the environment and a bias for sustainability

Using Headings to Guide the Reader through Your Proposal

Writing descriptive, informative headings as part of your outlining process reaps dividends as you progress through your proposal (refer to the earlier section "Outlining to Guide Your Writing" for more). It's time to pay those dividends. Here's how to write headings that make the key messages of your proposal stand out, allowing your readers to follow your entire offer by merely reading the table of contents or skimming the pages.

Understanding heading styles

Headings do two things: They identify the top-to-bottom structure of your proposal, and they announce the subject of the text that follows. The former are called *telegraphic* headings because they signal when you're moving from

>> One major structural element to the next (major headings)

>> One key point to the next (subheadings)

Telegraphic headings label content but don't describe it — *Solution* and *Financials* are examples. They are, in effect, topical outline entries (refer to the earlier section "Using topical outlines to build content" for more on these).

On the other hand, *descriptive* headings are short, informative phrases, clauses, or even full sentences that forecast the contents of the information that follows or, better still, express it in terms that summarize your story.

Here are some examples, followed by the type of grammatical structure used:

>> What Benefits Can You Expect? *(question)*

>> Solution Benefits for ABC Company *(noun phrase)*

>> Understanding Your Benefits *(gerund phrase)*

>> Nutra-Seed Benefits Your Lawn in Four Key Ways *(sentence)*

Descriptive headings are like newspaper headlines: They create interest that encourages readers to start or keep reading. In proposals, they help evaluators immediately determine both the contents of a section and the benefit to their organization. Along with signaling new topics to evaluators, they can link features to benefits and highlight discriminators.

Good descriptive headings allow evaluators to read only them and still understand your story. Consider this example:

Three Benefits of Our Solution: Lower Costs, Fewer Errors, Less Downtime

It tells the reader that the following content has three parts and that you'll present them in a certain order.

One way to get the full benefits of both telegraphic and descriptive headings is to use an appositive structure (where you immediately expand on your topic after you state it, as in the preceding example). In this instance, use the topical label for major section headings, followed by a colon and a descriptive phrase to provide additional detail for the evaluator. For example:

>> Financials: Reaching payback in nine months

>> Current environment: Where is your network vulnerable?

Accenting benefits and discriminators

The benefits you offer and your discriminators (refer to Chapters 6 and 7 for more on these) are the most important messages you communicate to proposal evaluators, so use descriptive headings to catch their attention and explain what sets you apart.

Of the following two headings, which is more effective?

EDE's New Release of World-Class E-Gates Version 0.6

Our System at LAX Reduced Passenger Check-In Time to Seven Minutes

The first heading has lots of details, but they're focused on the bidder, not the customer, and the heading doesn't describe much. The second heading describes the benefits to the customer — reducing passenger check-in time at a highly congested airport.

Making sure your headings work

Follow these guidelines to help make sure your headings work for your customers:

>> **Limit the number of heading levels to three (unless you're directed otherwise in an RFP).** More than three levels can confuse your readers.

>> **Make your headings grammatically parallel by level.** Use a different structure for different heading levels, but keep all headings for each level the same. This allows evaluators to move quickly through your proposal without being slowed by awkward shifts in structure.

>> **Ensure second- and third-level headings relate to their parent headings.** Unrelated subheadings confuse and frustrate readers.

>> **Number your headings.** Use numbering in proposals longer than ten pages to help evaluators find responses to their requirements.

>> **Present headings consistently.** Distinguish heading levels typographically (use the same font, type style, size, and color by level) and spatially (create left-hanging headings with ample white space).

>> **Avoid all caps.** They're harder to read for older folks like us.

>> **Never underline a heading.** Underlining denotes hyperlinks.

IN THIS CHAPTER

Capturing attention with design

Understanding the basic principles of design

Making your solution memorable with graphics and charts

Chapter 11

Making Your Proposals Look Good

Personal computers have made everyone a desktop publisher. Whether you use bundled word processors, Microsoft Word, Google Docs, or even high-end publishing packages like Adobe Creative Suite, you have the power to create proposals with magazine-quality design and layout. This is both a blessing and a curse. Though many have the software to create professional-looking documents, fewer know the principles and techniques for designing documents to meet professional standards. Moreover, nothing screams "unprofessional" like a proposal with a cluttered, unbalanced layout and cheesy clip art.

Because you're reading this book, we assume that you don't have in-house graphics and publishing resources. But if you have a PC or even a tablet, you have the power to incorporate textual elements, photos, graphics, tables, and word diagrams that bring a higher level of professionalism to your proposals. All you need is a set of principles and guidelines, which is what this chapter is all about.

Designing Eye-Catching, Accessible Documents

Most businesspeople understand that the overall design and layout of your proposal helps to make a positive early impression on decision makers and evaluators (if the proposal looks good, the solution's probably good, too). But did you know that good design is essential for communicating your information and persuading your audience that your information is the best?

REMEMBER

Proposals are a unique hybrid of several types of documents: part persuasive sales pitch following a clearly delineated structure; part technical description calling for clear and accessible explanations; part procedural requiring distinct steps; and part contract, demanding precise terminology and logic. The way you visually depict this information on the page or screen can mean the difference between an evaluator grasping your message or missing it entirely.

Before you begin designing your layout, creating your graphics and images, and selecting your packaging — and you should do this early in your proposal process — answer the following questions:

>> **Does your customer provide instructions or guidelines for the layout, visual elements, medium, or length of your response?** If so, get the specifications into the compliance matrix so you don't forget them. (Refer to Chapter 4 for details on the compliance matrix.)

>> **Does your customer set specific criteria for the physical packaging of your proposal?** If so, make sure you secure the appropriate resources before you begin the production process. (We identify key resources for your proposal team in Chapter 8.)

>> **Do you need to adhere to your organization's style and branding standards?** Check with your marketing or branding gurus and get a copy of your branding guidelines.

>> **Does your proposal need to appeal to a variety of readers in appropriate professional ways?** Identify the audiences you need to reach and think strategically about how you present special information for each group (refer to Chapter 10 for more about analyzing your audience's needs).

>> **What design techniques can help you highlight specific content that your customer needs to see and understand?** Think about how you can display your value proposition (refer to Chapter 9), benefits (refer to Chapter 7), and win themes (refer to Chapter 2) visually as well as in words.

All these issues affect the physical representation of your proposal. From now on, we refer to the collective physical and visual attributes of your proposal as "the package." In this section we discuss the "wrapper" for the package (the cover) and the stylistic attributes of the proposal itself.

Designing right . . . from the start

Sometimes you can judge a book by its cover. The best way to lead off your proposal package is to design a customer-focused cover. Even if your proposal is short — as in, only a few pages — a cover adds an element of professionalism while distinguishing your proposal from most other items on the evaluator's desk or in their email inbox.

Keep the tips in the following sections in mind as you craft the perfect proposal cover.

Show how you understand your customer

Take a photo of your customer's building, a worksite, or other representative locale. Place it prominently. Allow it to stretch across the cover, or even take up the entire cover if enough "empty" space is available for the customer's logo and your title. Make sure the image relates to your major win theme (refer to Chapter 2). The focus should be on the customer's perspective, not your own.

Preview the story line

Just as a good movie title enables you to anticipate the story, your proposal title needs to advertise the content to come. Your title should never be an afterthought. If you're responding to a Request for Proposal (RFP), make sure your title references the document (the RFP probably asks you to do this anyway). Whether you receive direction or not, find a way to create an active, engaging title. Because the title is the first thing the customer reads, you want to make it meaningful and memorable. Consider using it to highlight your win theme or value proposition for the first time.

REMEMBER

Be sure to avoid generic titles, such as "Proposal for Company XYZ." That shouts, "Ho, hum . . . just another bid." A good title needs to

>> Indicate the problem you're solving (including the main hot button; refer to Chapter 2 for the scoop on hot buttons)

>> State what your solution solves (customers pay for benefits; refer to Chapter 7 for how to identify your features and benefits)

>> Omit your product's name (customers care about solutions, not products)

>> Avoid business clichés (eliminate "best-in-class" from your vocabulary!)

TIP

One approach is to use a two-part title (unless instructed differently in the bid instructions). This is similar to the appositive heading style we introduce in Chapter 10. This approach allows you to identify the problem and solution while also identifying the provider and any customer-required information, for example:

> Eliminating Test Lab Worries While Lowering Costs: XYZ Company's Solution for ABC Company

> Building a Network to Withstand Next-gen Assaults: XYZ Company's Response to ABC Company RFP 10-2016N

Brand your proposal, customer first

The most effective proposal covers feature your customer, not your own organization. Use the customer's name, logo (with the customer's permission), and colors, if your own organization's branding guidelines allow. If not, ask the branding gurus to make an exception — it's worth it. Place the customer's name or logo in the top-left corner of the cover. Make the logo large enough to command attention.

TIP

It's relatively subtle, but if you place your organization's logo in the bottom-right corner of the cover while allowing your customer's logo to dominate the top-left corner, you hint to your customers that your proposal is all about them, not you (and a proposal *should be* all about them).

Check out Figure 11-1. It shows the relative positioning of logos, titles, and thematic images on a variety of covers. Simple, clean, and distinctive.

Distinguishing your proposals with consistent document styles

If your proposals have a consistent look and feel, you appear more professional to your customers. First-time recipients of your proposals will appreciate how clearly you've structured and laid out the content. Repeat customers will grow comfortable with your consistent, high-quality approach and eagerly await your next proposal. And although this sense of quality is the goal of any publication, it's especially so with proposals.

Insert customer-focused/industry-focused photos or images here

Streem-tv

Scientific
Instruments
Corporation

WHEREVER/WHENEVER:
CONTENT DELIVERY SOLUTIONS

ON-DEMAND SUPPLY INDUSTRIAL
AIR'S RESPONSE TO RFP #022016:
COMPRESSED GASSES

TELECOM CO.

INDUSTRIAL AIR

FIGURE 11-1:
These example proposal covers highlight the customer and its business through thematic images and descriptive titles.

© John Wiley & Sons, Inc.

EXAMPLE

You can find no better example of a distinctive and consistent publication style than the book you're holding. *For Dummies* books have a visual style that is so distinctive that in many aspects, it *is* the brand. Every visual element has its purpose: The bright yellow cover with the familiar masthead promises a new subject that you can clearly understand; the active headings in gerund style (ending with *–ing*) let you know that you'll actively participate in getting the information you need; the guiding icons show you what's important, memorable, or worthy of a closer look; and the sidebars offer more detailed information for those who can't get enough. These are but a few of the visual elements that help you find and use what you need. All *For Dummies* books follow this consistent visual and content style to phenomenal success.

You want your customers to instantly recognize your proposals in the same way, whether your proposal is proactive or reactive (in response to an RFP). Creating a consistent visual style makes this possible. And although an RFP response needs to meet your customer's packaging guidelines, you can still leverage the distinctive and consistent visual style you use for proactive proposals.

So as you design your proposal package, consider the layout elements in the following sections.

Choosing your paper

TIP

Paper? Who uses paper anymore? A lot of businesses still do, and some RFPs still require paper submittals, even if digital submittals are allowed or encouraged. The answer? Always design for paper, but if a digital submission is required, deliver in PDF format (the design will be the same but with the added capabilities of digital, like embedded links). PDF, though far from tamper-proof, is still more secure than a word-processing file for digital submissions. Email isn't safe. An online submission may be, but this is in many ways a new medium, requiring a different response and delivery strategy.

WARNING

If you print your proposal, don't scrimp on the paper quality, especially if you print in color. Black ink on cheap paper smears; colored ink on cheap paper bleeds.

Consider these guidelines for selecting paper for your printed proposals:

>> **Paper size:** If you're writing for a U.S. audience, use standard 8½-x-11-inch paper. If you're writing for an international audience, use the standard A4 portrait size. Though an odd size may be novel, the novelty wears off quickly when it doesn't fit in a satchel or slips out of a stack.

>> **Paper weight:** Select a good quality paper with a weight of 20 to 30 pounds. This way, if you print on both sides of the page (duplex), the ink won't bleed through. Use coated paper when you want the highest resolution possible for your text and graphics.

>> **Paper brightness:** Choose white, ivory, or off-white paper. Aim for a brightness index in the 90s (this may also be called "bright white" or "ultra-bright"). A brighter paper makes colors more vibrant.

Selecting the right font

The *font* (all the letters, numbers, punctuation marks, and symbols of a particular style of type — what has traditionally been referred to as a typeface) you choose for the insides of your proposal can have a significant influence on how your readers respond to your proposal. A clean, distinct font for your copy, clearly legible for bleary-eyed evaluators, can make the most tedious subject easier to bear (and let's face it, not all proposals are a thrilling read).

A proposal is no place for ornate or whimsical fonts that make readers squint or flinch. Your font size and letter and line spacing become major issues for proposal length when multiplied over the span of tens and hundreds of pages. Here's how to make sure your font is right for your proposal:

>> **Font:** Stick to two fonts for your proposals: One sans serif type for titles, headers, table and illustration content, and captions, and one serif type for body copy. *Serif* type (with small lines added to distinguish letters) is easier to read than *sans serif* (without the distinguishing lines) for large blocks of text. Yet some believe that many new sans serif fonts are more legible than some serif designs, especially for online reading. The point is to think critically about the font style you choose. Note the particular characteristics and overall readability of your text.

Your organization may have standard fonts for all publications, so check your branding guidelines for suitable options.

>> **Type size:** Keep your body text font between 10 and 12 points. You may use type as small as 8 points for text within graphics or tables. For headers, follow this rule: Use a type 2 to 4 points larger than your text. For example, if your text is 12 points, go with 16 or 14 points for your heading.

Be aware that 12 points in one font may not be the same height as in another.

>> **Type style:** Instead of underlines or all capital letters, opt for bold and italic styles to distinguish headings and to highlight text. Underlines now denote hyperlinks. All capital letters are hard to read because they lack distinctive ascenders and descenders (the parts of lowercase letters that rise to capital height or drop below the text line, respectively).

Picking an appropriate binding method

When it comes to proposal packages, what's on the outside really does matter. Always bind your proposals if they're more than a few pages long. Never use pocket or cardboard folders because they look cheap and summon memories of high-school essays. Never use *perfect* binding (bookbinding) either. It's too costly, and the pages won't lie flat. Evaluators often break apart your proposal to share with others, so perfect binding will thwart those efforts.

You have several, more appropriate choices:

>> **Wire or plastic spiral binding:** Great for shorter, proactive proposals, these bindings encourage evaluators to keep the proposal together but don't prohibit them breaking it apart. They allow readers to let the proposal lie flat on a table so they can easily reference and compare them. These binding

formats require that you print a sturdy front and back cover to protect the pages, but this adds a sense of professionalism to your proposals. Many print companies offer spiral binding solutions.

>> **Ring binders:** For longer proposals and most RFP responses, use two- to four-ring binders (as appropriate for your location). They come in sizes from ½ to 3 inches (based on the diameter of the rings, not the spine), in either "O" or "D" styles. They're the easiest to take apart and reassemble, both for you and your evaluators.

Most ring binders have transparent sleeves for the front, spine, and even the back that allow you to insert a printed cover that can wrap from front to back.

>> **Saddle stitch binding:** Good for proposals up to 64 pages (32 sheets of 11-x-17-inch or A3 paper), this method uses large staples through the centerfold to bind pages.

Beware: Documents designed for this binding are difficult to lay out using word-processing software. They're also difficult to assemble and take apart.

Designing effective headers and footers

Headers (appearing at the top of each page) and footers (appearing at the bottom of each page) perform three main functions:

>> They tell evaluators where they are in your proposal (the chapter and page number).

>> They protect your content with a legally binding proprietary statement (work with your lawyer to create the appropriate wording).

>> They create a professional frame for your content (showing your customer and yourself in the appropriate relationship).

The left-hand image in Figure 11-2 shows how your header and footer should repeat the same relationship between your customer and your organization that you express on the cover (refer to the earlier section "Brand your proposal, customer first"): Your customer's logo or name should go in in the top-left corner, and your logo should go in the bottom-right corner. We call this single-sided printing (*simplex*), and it's still an accepted approach to printing a proposal, if more costly. When you reverse the image on the left to create the image on the right, you create a *duplex* (double-sided print) layout for facing pages.

Check out your word processor's ability to design for duplex printing. You need to set even- and odd-page styles to make sure your pagination is consistent.

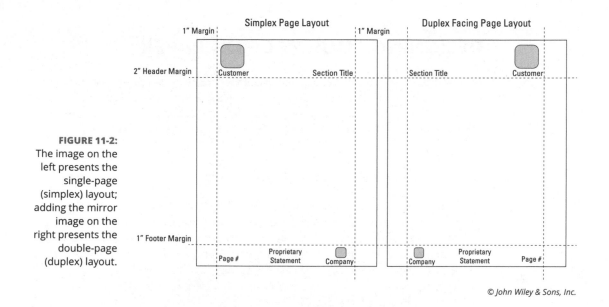

FIGURE 11-2:
The image on the left presents the single-page (simplex) layout; adding the mirror image on the right presents the double-page (duplex) layout.

© John Wiley & Sons, Inc.

Setting your page margins

Standard top, bottom, and side margins for a page are 1 inch (25 millimeters for A4). For a more magazine-style header, double the top margin, but leave the bottom margin at 1 inch.

TIP

Enlarging the header creates a more open layout and allows more room for your customer's identity but does reduce space for body copy. If your customer has constrained the length of your proposal, opt for the smaller top margin.

Designing callouts, pull-quotes, and testimonials

As you create thumbnails for your layout, consider leaving an amount of free space to the right of your text (or perhaps designate this space as another column) to highlight key messages and proofs for your proposal. These highlights are usually peripheral to your primary message. They may be sidebars that address a particular audience who needs information that is more technical or explain certain concepts that only some evaluators need to know. They may be a quote from your text — such as the CEO's comments about the market's biggest challenges — and you want to make it clear to your evaluators that you keep up with everything that goes on in their industry. They may even be proofs of past performance or customer testimonials for the particular subject you're discussing in the main text. Figure 11-3 shows how a page can accommodate any type of marginalia you need to include in your proposal.

DESIGNING YOUR PAGE ON PAPER

Graphic designers say that to create a consistent design within a document or across a series of them, you should first sketch your ideas on paper. Arranging content on a small page representation with an invisible grid ensures that text and graphic elements are evenly spaced, orderly, and easy to follow.

Award-winning graphics designer Jeff Rogers explains how to mock up your page layout. (Check out his website at www.howdyjeff.com.) He says:

> The first lesson in graphic design 101 is *always start with pencil and paper*. When it comes to page layout, using a pencil to organize your thoughts and ideas is the most efficient way to get ideas out of your head so you can see how they work and make better decisions about how you want your page to function before tinkering with the computer. When you draw, you bypass any technical limitations you may have regarding your software, and you are free to quickly come up with the best, most intentional design for your page.
>
> Start by drawing some small rectangles that are about the same proportions as your page. I like to draw a page of boxes that are about one or two inches wide. Making the boxes small helps you focus on general layout ideas rather than getting overwhelmed with smaller details (you can get overwhelmed with details later). Think about the information you need to include and how you'd like to organize it. Thinking in terms of hierarchy will help fine-tune those ideas: Start with headlines, subheads, large bodies of text, and images, and work your way down the hierarchy.

See the accompanying figure for an example of creating these boxes (or *thumbnails*).

Source: Jeff Rogers

Jeff continues:

> When you have some general ideas about how you want your layout to function in the form of thumbnails, you then move to the computer and build the layout grid based on your sketches. Things may shift and change as you populate sections with text, but you'll have a clear idea of the structure of your page if you do the thumbnails before filling a document with text and moving things around from there.

Jeff offers these thumbnail sketching tips:

- Draw rectangles that represent different forms of content — text blocks, pull quotes, section headers — and draw an X inside those rectangles that represent images.

- Stay loose! Don't try to make these sketches beautiful works of art. Just sketch away as you have ideas.

- Resist the urge to erase. If something isn't working or you have a different idea, move to a new box. Focus on getting ideas out and not putting a fine finish on a sketch.

  Jeff recommends using a pen instead of a pencil so you won't be tempted to erase.

- Write notes by the thumbnails so you can remember what you were thinking. These notes will help you as you finalize your work on the computer.

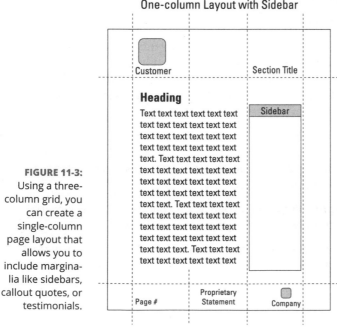

One-column Layout with Sidebar

FIGURE 11-3:
Using a three-column grid, you can create a single-column page layout that allows you to include marginalia like sidebars, callout quotes, or testimonials.

© John Wiley & Sons, Inc.

Turning your mock-up into a digital page

If you have a sophisticated desktop-publishing program like Adobe's InDesign or PageMaker, you can convert your thumbnail into a digital version with ease. But if you have such a program, you probably also have designers trained to use it, so you'd leave the task to the professionals.

If you're working on your own, probably with only a word processor, your grids are limited to setting the number of columns for your document and then living with the built-in grid that the program creates for you. Here's how to set up a professional page layout that you can use repeatedly, all within your humble word-processing program:

1. **Establish your margins, header, and footer (or accept the default).**

2. **Decide on the number of columns.**

   A single-column layout is still the norm for proposals and is perhaps the most flexible style. A two column-format allows you to place more information on a page than with a single-column (but placing larger graphics can be an issue — you'll have to wrap text around the larger figure, and this can cause some readers to lose their place).

TIP

   Avoid using three columns or more. Either the text will be too small or the columns will contain too few words and hyphenated fragments of words, which may hamper readers.

3. **Choose your heading layout.**

   Even in a single-column layout, you can create a variety of heading formats that indicate you've used a grid to design your page layout. Dr Brenda Sims, a University of North Texas professor and author of *Technical Communication*, 3rd Edition (Kendall Hunt), recommends three formats for effective headings for single-column layouts (see Figure 11-4):

   - **Left-hanging headings** are left-justified with related body copy indented beyond the extent of the heading. This format clearly "chunks" content associated with a heading and uses optimal white space to push the eyes to the relevant content.

   - **Over-hanging headings** are flush left as well, but they infringe upon the associated body copy grid to provide more room for text.

   - **Left-justified headings** are as the name indicates, but the associated text is also left-justified. This format relies on line spacing to "chunk" content.

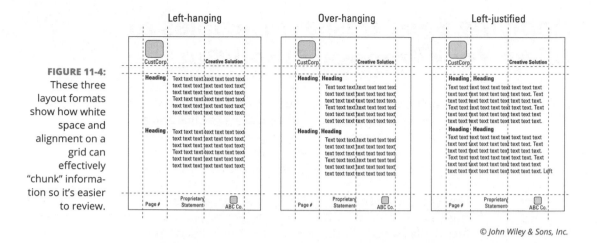

Left-hanging | Over-hanging | Left-justified

© John Wiley & Sons, Inc.

FIGURE 11-4:
These three
layout formats
show how white
space and
alignment on a
grid can
effectively
"chunk" informa-
tion so it's easier
to review.

4. **Establish your heading and text styles.** Your word processor is loaded with different fonts and type styles you can apply and standardize for a particular proposal (and turn into a template so you can easily replicate them in future proposals, as we explain in Chapter 13). In Microsoft Word, for example, under the Home tab, the style window lists built-in styles that you can modify by right-clicking on the style name and illustration. You can then apply the updated style every time you create a new text element.

5. **Set your color scheme.**

If your organization allows you to, go with the colors that your customer uses. Look to its logo and check out its website. Bring visual style to your proposal by coloring your

- Headings

- Bullet icons

- Table and graphic labels/title bars

- Horizontal rule to separate blocks of content

- Shading of tables, sidebars, and callout boxes

WARNING

Be precise and use the eye-drop feature in your word processor, layout, or graphics software to select the exact color matches and then create your color palette from them.

Applying Basic Design Principles to Make Your Proposal Stand Out

You don't need to be a graphic artist to create a useful, attractive, and persuasive proposal. Taking the guidance in this chapter can make your proposals a lot easier to read and much more persuasive than the norm. And although you may never be able to knock out an award-winning design, you can take your design to an even higher level by following six fundamental design principles.

Four of these principles — contrast, repetition, alignment, and proximity — come from Robin Williams's *The Non-Designer's Design Book*, 4th Edition (Peachpit Press). We use them at the University of North Texas to teach technical communicators how to create professional-looking layouts. The other two principles we present, consistency and balance, are common technical writing concepts that enhance the clarity and significance of your content.

TIP

These principles apply not only to page layout but also to graphics themselves — that is, illustrations, diagrams, schematics, photographs, and even tables.

The six basic design principles are as follows:

>> **Contrast** creates emphasis among visual elements and can highlight information (lack of contrast can also bury information you don't want to call attention to, but this can bring into question your ethics). When showing contrast, think big and bold. You can create contrast by using a variety of opposite pairings. For instance, when you place your customer's logo in your header, make it twice the size of your organization's logo in the footer. Show contrast by creating large headings next to small text elements. You can also use reverse type — white text (sans serif) on a black background — for a bold title block for a graphic, a sidebar, or even a chapter or section.

TIP

The stronger the contrast, the more effective the design element will be.

A design element closely associated with contrast is *color*. Color has meaning and affects mood, so your color choices should be deliberate and have a purpose. For example, if your goal is to build trust and illustrate your customer focus, use your customer's colors.

When you create charts, choose your color palette before rendering them and apply colors consistently to data points — a change in color may cause readers to interpret a change in meaning.

WARNING

Colors have different connotations across cultures. When addressing international audiences, make sure you're using the right color for the message you intend.

>> **Proximity**, or physical and visual closeness, establishes a bond between elements on a page and helps readers to understand when two or more pieces of content — textual or visual — are related. The closer the object or block of text, the more related it should be.

TIP

Always place less space between the heading and the text it introduces and more space between that text and the next heading. Readers will quickly see that the preceding topic is complete and the new one has begun. A key feature of proximity is *white space* — unused space on the page that gives pages breathing room, provides a visual break to readers from constant text, and pushes page elements together or apart.

Balance how much white space you use with any customer-imposed page limitations.

>> **Balance** is an artistic concept that you can apply to your page layout to arrange elements so no one section overpowers another. Balance is the main reason designers start with a grid (refer to the earlier sidebar "Designing your page on paper" for more about designing your layout).

TIP

Think of each of your content "chunks" as a shape. Use the *rule of thirds* (the principle of dividing your vertical and horizontal page into nine boxes — three across and three down) to arrange text columns, graphics and illustrations, tables, sidebars, callout quotes, and icons on your grid. You can then position your content and supporting visuals to emphasize your message.

Graphics achieve balance when their left and right sides and, to a lesser extent, top and bottom visually "weigh" similar amounts, giving a sense of equilibrium. The size of an object, along with its thickness and boldness of line, make it heavier than a smaller object and one with finer lines. Two or three smaller, finer objects may offset a larger, darker, bolder object.

REMEMBER

Balanced layouts and graphics convey stability and harmony. Unbalanced layouts and graphics make readers ill at ease — not something you want in a proposal.

>> **Consistency** means using design elements — fonts, colors, icons within graphics and illustrations, and table formats — in a uniform manner to help evaluators navigate your proposal more efficiently. For instance, using italics to identify technical terms listed in the glossary can help readers remember them, along with prompting them to seek definitions. Consistently alternating black with blue text can signal the difference between a question and an answer within an RFP response. These design elements are known as document *conventions,* and if their meanings aren't obvious, you can leave some room in your introduction to explain how you use them.

>> **Alignment**, or the relationships of the parts of a page (text, headers, graphics, tables, and so on) to each other, can make a layout easier or more difficult to read and can influence readers' perceptions of written content. Here's where

the grid lines come in handy. Always align your text and graphics on the invisible lines of your grid: Start and end text on the same horizontal lines on facing pages. Manually tweak your ragged-right margins (the default right margin if your text is left justified) so you maintain a semblance of an edge without the harsh, artificial, and annoying spacing of fully justified text (a ragged-right margin helps readers locate subsequent lines of text, but if it's too ragged, it looks less professional).

Like proximity, alignment can help you tie information chunks together. For instance, if you use white space to separate subtopics on a page, you can use alignment to reinforce that all subtopics are part of a major topic.

» **Repetition** of certain shapes, graphic elements, and even text styles can bring a sense of cohesion to your layout. Repetition is especially helpful for bringing a sense of unity to longer proposals; it also helps bring unity to a page. For instance, imagine that your customer's logo is a triangular shape. Echoing that shape in bullet symbols, using the customer's primary colors, can subtly unite elements on a page. Using that same shape to conclude a section or chapter or even house page numbers in the footer can also quietly reinforce your design.

As you can see in Figure 11-5, good designs use all or most of these six principles. They're essential to creating a professional proposal that will enhance your ability to win.

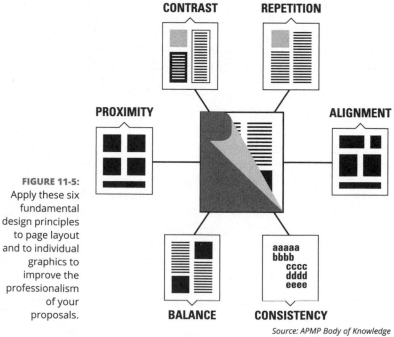

FIGURE 11-5: Apply these six fundamental design principles to page layout and to individual graphics to improve the professionalism of your proposals.

Source: APMP Body of Knowledge

The style of your proposal package communicates your organization's culture along with your approach to customer service, problem solving, and inventive thinking. For example, a modern design sends the subliminal message that your company is young and innovative. Aesthetically unappealing or unprofessional graphics may communicate that you, your solution, and your business are inferior, unprofessional, or simply out of step with the times.

REMEMBER

Have a purpose for every aesthetic decision you make. Avoid design choices that are inconsistent with your audience, your message, or your subject matter. Your design needs to guide readers through your proposal and your individual graphics need to reinforce your message, with the goal of improving comprehension and building trust.

Using Graphics to Help Readers Understand Your Proposal

Readers respond favorably to stories in your proposals (refer to Chapter 10 for more on this); they respond even better when you illustrate those stories with relevant images. In fact, clear, compelling, reader-focused graphics, combined with text and captions that express the action occurring in those graphics, improve your chances of winning the business you seek.

Persuading better than with words alone

Graphics are one of the most effective and efficient ways to persuade because they convey facts (logic) and emotion (which we discuss in more detail in Chapter 10). They're especially effective in proactive proposals because they're more informally solicited. Busy readers will scan and then read further if something captures their interest.

In Chapter 10, we present techniques for writing more clearly and persuasively. But words alone don't come close to the persuasive power of the right words coupled with the right image. Research shows that graphics

>> Grab readers' attention and may influence how well they pay attention to the rest of a story

>> Provide a sense of professionalism, which increases your credibility with readers

>> Enhance or affect emotions and attitudes, which influences even rational thought processes

>> Help information to stick in readers' minds more readily than straight text alone

>> Lead readers to a more profound and accurate understanding of presented material

EXAMPLE

In his book, *Do-It-Yourself Billion Dollar Graphics* (PepperLip, Inc.), APMP Fellow and author Mike Parkinson cites a 3M-sponsored study at the University of Minnesota School of Management by Douglas R. Vogel and colleagues, which found that presentations that use visual aids are "43 percent more persuasive than unaided presentations." Parkinson also provides evidence that graphics improve recollection up to 86 percent and communicate information faster than text alone.

Quickly clarifying and reinforcing your proposal's message with the right visuals not only helps your customer understand your solution and its value, but it also creates goodwill. An underlying theme of any proposal is to convince your customer that you have its best interests in mind. Including professional graphics shows that you're willing to take the extra time, effort, and resources to explain your solution the best way possible.

Making abstract ideas more concrete

As we explore in Chapter 10, the more concrete your language, the more effective your content. Unfortunately, it's very difficult to write well enough to convey complex concepts by words alone.

Think about the abstract ideas you have to convey in your proposals: your customer support model, your implementation process, and even your sales support hierarchy. Think about how many words you would have to use to convey these concepts. Then, consider how much more effective and memorable these ideas would be if you could *show* how they work as well as explain them.

REMEMBER

Graphics aren't better than text. As APMP Fellow and author Mike Parkinson explains, "The combination of graphics and words has a communicative power that neither singularly possesses. Without graphics, an idea may be lost in a sea of words. Without words, a graphic may be lost to ambiguity." Similarly, in his article, "A Transfer-Appropriate-Processing Perspective of Pictures in Prose," Joel R. Levin points out that "Pictures interact with text to produce levels of comprehension and memory that can exceed what is produced by text alone." Understanding how to use a combination of graphics and text effectively can make the difference between winning and losing a bid.

Enhancing the power of your graphics

You can think of the technique for persuading your customer with a proposal as a three-legged stool. You need the following:

>> **Text:** The rationale in words as to why your solution is the best solution, and the proofs to support your claims

>> **Graphics:** The charts, images, and illustrations that illustrate those proofs and clarify and reinforce your verbal messages

>> **Reinforcement:** A succinct and direct explanation of the graphical element so the evaluator's takeaway is memorable

The reinforcement leg of the stool is where a tool called the *action caption* comes in. Larry Newman, PPF, APMP Fellow, and author of *Shipley Proposal Guide*, 4th Edition (Shipley Associates) defines an action caption as a brief sentence that "interprets a graphic for an evaluator."

TIP

Include an action caption with every graphic — every illustration, photograph, table, and chart. And always follow this three-part structure:

>> **Figure number:** A sequential number, preceded by the word *Figure* that identifies the graphic so you can easily refer to it in text or in reference aids. If you have many figures in your proposal, or if you'll be updating the content multiple times, consider placing the volume, chapter, or section number before the figure number (as in "Figure 13-2") so when you revise by adding a figure, you'll have to change the numbers for only figures within a single volume, chapter, or section.

>> **Informative heading:** A descriptive title for your graphic that follows the figure number.

>> **Action caption:** One complete sentence that explains the relevance of the graphic to the evaluator, linking benefits to features. The simpler you can make an action caption, the better.

Avoid listing more than three benefits in a single action caption. Succinct, customer-focused action captions result in better graphics. When applicable, include proof and a discriminator in your action caption. Figure 11-6 provides an example of a benefit-driven action caption.

Proposal graphics help your proposal to be more accessible and persuasive. The following sections help you decide on which graphics to use and how and when to display them.

FIGURE 11-6:
Customer-
focused,
benefit-driven
action captions
improve the
persuasive power
of your graphics
and proposal.

PROOFS validate   **DISCRIMINATORS** tell "how well?"

Increase search speeds by 82%   using our iFind™ software.

BENEFITS give the customer   **FEATURES** tell how the customer
a reason to care   will get the benefit

Source: APMP Body of Knowledge

Using action captions to kick-start content development

TIP

To ensure that you maximize the persuasive power of the text–graphics–reinforcement (caption) three-legged stool, start creating graphics and action captions before you write your proposal. You can then use the graphics and captions as a road map for writing.

Develop your content in this order:

1. **Write action captions that express the messages you want to communicate to your readers.**

2. **Use action captions to develop graphics that convey these messages visually.**

3. **Write your proposal content using conceptualized graphics and action captions as a guide.**

This technique echoes the time-honored approach to proposal writing called *storyboarding,* where you create page-size modules for your proposal that incorporate chapter and section headings, thematic statements, body copy, illustrations, their captions, and any notes to help your contributors write their parts. Although many small businesses today can't afford the time and resources needed to storyboard every proposal narrative, this scaled-down process of describing, illustrating, and then explaining provides many of the benefits of storyboarding without the costly overhead.

TIP

Creating graphics before the intense writing begins ensures that your proposal team is on the same page, that the solution is complete, and that the proposal tells a coherent story.

Knowing when and where to use graphic elements

Proposal graphics are especially important in these three situations:

>> **Your information is too complex for words alone.** Often a graphic can communicate complex concepts more succinctly than text alone. Consider including network diagrams, quantitative charts, dashboard graphics, Gantt charts, organizational charts, and process diagrams as appropriate in your proposals.

>> **The information is critical to your proposal's success.** Some information, if missed or misunderstood, can mean the difference between a win and a loss. In this instance, presenting the information graphically, on top of a well-written description, can help evaluators understand and remember the key details that can win the bid.

>> **You want to influence emotions.** Like it or not, graphics represent quality in the minds of decision makers and evaluators, just like today's CGI animation trumps the cheesy special effects of the '70s. The more professional your artwork, the more evaluators will think of the quality of your solution and the trustworthiness of you as the provider of the solution.

Making sure your graphics meet customer needs

To ensure that your graphics are truly meaningful and appropriate in every instance, develop them according to this eight-stage process:

1. **Write the action caption.**

   Because an action caption clearly defines the content of a graphic in a single sentence, write it before drawing the graphic to ensure that the graphic is about one idea.

2. **Test.**

   Make sure the action caption reflects the customer's requirement.

3. **Conceptualize the image.**

   Create a pencil sketch of the graphic.

4. **Test.**

   Reconfirm that the graphic clearly communicates the message stated in the action caption.

5. **Convert to digital format.**

   Rebuild your sketch in your graphics software.

6. **Test.**

   Ensure that the graphic's message and style is compatible with the design of your proposal package.

7. **Import the graphic into your layout.**

   Embed the graphic, along with the action caption, in your proposal text, making sure to provide a textual reference preceding the graphic.

8. **Test.**

   Evaluate how the graphic fits with the text reference and the action caption.

Going through this process will help you find and fix any inconsistencies between your body copy, your graphic, and your action caption.

Connecting your text and graphics

Although many evaluators may prefer getting their information from graphics over text, they still read the proposal first. In a proposal, text carries the main information and graphics reinforce or enhance that information. Always place your graphics as close as possible to the information that they enhance — always on the same page, and preferably alongside or directly following.

UNDERSTANDING COPYRIGHT LAW

If you don't have permission from the owner of an image, you can't legally use that image in your proposal. The only exceptions to this rule are images in the *public domain* (owned by the public or not under a copyright). If the image isn't in the public domain, you need to secure permission and, if required, pay for rights to reuse the image.

All images are immediately protected under copyright law in almost every country. A copyright is normally valid whether the image has a visible copyright notice or not. After an image has been created, the owner holds its rights. If the owner hasn't given you the right to reuse it, you may not legally use a photograph or graphic from the Internet (for example, a photograph or graphic you found during an Internet search).

You may legally use photographs and graphics that you get from stock image websites and websites that grant the right of reuse for commercial use (that is, for profit).

UNDERSTANDING GRAPHIC FILE FORMATS

Embed the graphics you use in your proposal or presentation in a flat, un-editable file format, such as JPG, PNG, GIF, or TIF. (By *flat*, we're referring to how graphic design programs allow you to build your images in separate layers, which the program overlays transparently for increasingly sophisticated images. When the design is complete, you "flatten" the file to prepare it for embedding into documents.) If you're printing your proposal, use a print resolution of 150 to 300 DPI (dots per inch). If you're presenting or posting your proposal online, match your image resolution to the size of the space it inhabits on the screen. For example, if your computer screen's resolution is 1,024 x 768 pixels and you want an image to fill the screen, create your image to 1,024 x 768. If you want the image to take up a quarter of the screen, divide the pixel counts by 4 (256 x 192).

As you prepare to create and insert graphics into your proposals, you need to know about the two types of graphics: *raster* and *vector*.

- Raster graphics (also called *bitmap* graphics) are made up of pixels. How tiny the dot is defines the lowest resolution of the medium. For comparison, think about HD televisions that display at 1080p (1,080 pixels) across the screen.

  Raster graphics are only as detailed as their original medium allows, which is why when you stretch raster graphics you often blur the image — you stretch the pixels further than they were designed to stretch.

- Vector graphics use mathematical calculations to build an image's outline and interior details. That means you can stretch the image to different sizes without sacrificing image quality (the computer recalculates based on the original mathematical relationships among points that define the image).

  Vector files are typically smaller than raster files. Most presentation software and data graphics software use vector graphics.

Some file formats, like JPG, allow you to compress an image to decrease the file size but do so at a cost — it reduces image quality. To keep your graphics as close to the original as possible, avoid compressing files excessively. To avoid font and file-size issues, create graphics to the same dimensions as they'll appear in your proposal.

Always refer to your graphic in your text before presenting it. You usually need to use a figure reference, such as "as you see in Figure X" or "(see Figure X)." If you have only a couple of graphics, you can use a phrase like, "as you see in the figure below."

TIP

Don't make readers flip pages to see the illustration of an idea — embed each graphic with the associated text.

Chapter 12

Getting Your Proposal Out the Door

In Chapter 8, we show you how to schedule your time backward from your due date so you leave plenty of time to put the finishing touches on your proposal. In Chapter 6, we preview the work you have to do to produce your proposal. The list of tasks is formidable for such a short time span: reviewing, revising, iterating, proofing, printing (or exporting), packaging, and delivering (or uploading).

You can stack to the ceiling all the reasons for making sure you have plenty of production time at the end of your proposal schedule, and not just those in the preceding paragraph — you can handle that laundry list of activities if everything goes right! But no matter how well you plan, something can and usually will go wrong. If something goes wrong in a proposal, it may create a situation where you can't deliver your best, or maybe even deliver at all. And that makes for an unhappy outcome.

So read on to get the insider account of all you have to get right as you try to get your proposal out the door.

Getting Fresh Eyes On Your Proposal

If you want your proposal to be successful, you can't just scribble out your main ideas and call it done. As you do with any important document, you have to *craft* a proposal. You have to review it, revise it, and edit it and then inspect it, sand off the rough edges, and inspect it again before it's presentable. No one wants to believe what the experts say, but we know they're right: Good writing is revision. And proposals are no exception.

REMEMBER

Final reviews and revisions are so important for proposals because so much rides on them, including money, relationships, and reputations. They're the formalized expression of your offer. In some segments, they become public records. Even if they're private, a bad proposal may rear its ugly head later on if a new opportunity with that firm or agency arises. Winning proposals can live even longer. They last as long as a contract and have a second life when it's time to renew them.

TIP

When the time comes to review your proposal, get help. Whether you're the sole proprietor, the lone proposal writer, or the salesperson with no back-office support, you can't afford to review your own work because you know it too well. Even if you can put it aside for a while before it's due and review it with a relatively fresh perspective, you'll catch only a few mistakes. You won't see what a pair or more of truly objective eyes will see.

Big companies that do business with other big companies and government agencies know this. They have extensive proposal resources and review programs to match. They have separate reviews for the technical solution, the managerial solution, and the financial volume (some even have colorful names for each type). They solicit their own company executives to role-play as customer executives to assess the executive summary and other parts of the proposal. They hire consultants to "wear black hats" and play devil's advocates for the solution and the pricing. And if the big kids go to these lengths to review their proposals, you need to take heed.

But you don't have to go review crazy. A proposal review can be as simple as the heading to this section suggests — all you may need is a fresh perspective. When our proposal organization was just getting started, we always let one of our peers review even our simplest proposals before we printed them. We were amazed how much our peers found that we had missed and how a different perspective shed light on better ways to express our offer.

This section is dedicated to the final proposal review — it expands on the summary of reviews we provide in Chapter 6 and covers how to structure the review, how to scale it to fit the circumstances, and how to get the proposal ready to be reviewed.

Structuring your final proposal reviews

Final proposal reviews are the capstone to your proposal management efforts. They are where you not only assess how well your proposal meets its objectives but also validate the rigor you've insisted on since the beginning of the project. No matter the size of the proposal, your final proposal review should be structured, objective, realistic, comprehensive, and scaled to fit the value or complexity of the opportunity:

- » **Structured:** You need a formal plan, including the following items, for setting up, managing, and collecting findings from the review:

  - Firm start and end times for the review

  - Formal invitations to reviewers (sent well in advance)

  - Specific assignments for each reviewer

  - A secure and quiet place for the review so reviewers can reduce if not eliminate distractions and interruptions

  - Clear and firm rules for participation and behavior

  - A format to collect your reviewer's recommendations so you can quickly implement them

- » **Objective:** Your reviewers need to be a group of independent and impartial critics who can take the perspective of the customer's evaluators.

- » **Realistic:** Your proposal needs to be as close to final as you can make it. You don't want your reviewers being distracted by incomplete content, haphazard layout, or sloppy copy editing. You want them to review, as much as possible, the exact proposal that your customer will evaluate.

- » **Comprehensive:** Your reviewers should assess your proposal's

  - *Readiness* for publication

  - *Responsiveness* to the RFP (Request for Proposal) or problems found by the sales team

  - *Effectiveness* in conveying your win strategy, win themes, value propositions, and discriminators (refer to Chapter 6)

  Reviewers need to also assess how well you've ghosted the competition (refer to Chapter 5).

- » **Scaled:** You have to match the rigor of your review to the importance of the deal. (This aspect of the review deserves a deeper look, so we cover this in the next section.)

Scaling final proposal reviews

As part of our overview of the proposal process in Chapter 6, we stress the value of reviewing your proposal draft periodically and from different perspectives so you can ensure that your solution, your implementation, and your messaging are complete, accurate, and effective. Your final proposal review is your most important review of all because it's your final chance to ensure a quality solution and document.

In Chapter 2, we first mention the "accordion process," an expanding and contracting process based on a project's particular circumstances. This, too, is what we mean here by "scaling" the final proposal review — you adapt your review to the extent that this particular proposal requires. The number of final proposal reviews you need depends first on how good the initial draft is. But as you determine how extensive your final review should be, you should also consider the following, and expand or contract your review accordingly:

>> **How complex the solution is:** Some highly technical proposals require a special review of the solution description. You need to bring in technical experts who are unfamiliar with the opportunity but have deep knowledge of the solution or technology to make sure the solution is not only appropriate and functional but also understandable. For less complex solutions, a single, comprehensive appraisal with experts reviewing from a variety of perspectives (technical, managerial, financial, and so on) will usually suffice.

>> **How much the business is worth:** If the fate of your business rests on this bid, you really can't afford to spare any measures or expense to get it right. Some organizations even hire consultants to perform final reviews to ensure complete objectivity on must-win deals.

TIP

If the proposal is one of hundreds you intend to submit this year, or if it's one that you're uncertain you'll win, you may opt for a more cursory review (run a spelling and grammar check, at least).

>> **How much time you've held in reserve for final reviews:** Even if you schedule your project backward as we suggest, things can and will go wrong along the way. Sometimes your review time will be squeezed by circumstances.

>> **Who is available to review the proposal:** If you're a sole proprietor, an elaborate final review process may seem excessive. Still, you need a second pair of eyes to review your proposal — a business associate or a supplier, perhaps. You need an objective opinion on whether your proposal achieves what you've set out to achieve. Perhaps invest a few hundred dollars in the services of a freelance editor to make sure.

TIP

If you're the proposal writer in a small or medium-sized business, seek objective reviewers early, get their commitment, and schedule the final proposal review when the response is 75 to 85 percent complete. Work your schedule to meet theirs as much as you can.

>> **How much work you ask your reviewers to do:** Unless your proposal is very brief, you can't expect every reviewer to read and evaluate your proposal end to end in one review session. On longer proposals, have all reviewers assess the executive summary and then assess the most important parts in relation to their expertise.

Putting together the final proposal review

You need to make your review session more than an appointment on the review team's calendars. To ensure your final proposal review's success, you need to

>> Get the proposal into *final draft* shape (that is, as close to publishable as possible) before sharing it with reviewers

>> Make sure that you have the right people and that they're prepared to review the proposal and recommend clear, actionable improvements

>> Accommodate your executive reviewers

>> Allow ample time for implementing any recommendations

We explore these requirements in the following sections.

Getting the proposal ready to review

To get your proposal in final draft form, you need a number of skills. In large proposal teams, these skills are usually distinct positions and roles (see the sidebar "Proposal team roll call"); in smaller shops or even solo situations, the tasks may fall to you and perhaps one other. Again, the idea of scale comes into play: You need to review only what's necessary for this particular proposal. And while you may not have the skills of a professional desktop publisher or graphic artist, you can use the skills we present in Chapter 10 and 11 to get the document in the best possible shape before reviewers assess it.

REMEMBER

Here's a list of the tasks you need someone (if not you) to perform so you can get your proposal ready to review. We also add the skills and the standard job titles of the people who handle these tasks in the most professionally run proposal organizations. But don't be intimidated: We've known individuals who could handle all these tasks and more.

1. **Create a document template that complies with customer instructions; lay out all proposal text into the template.**

   Skills: word processing; role: desktop publisher

2. **Insert, label, and number graphics in the proposal.**

   Skills: word processing and file management; role: desktop publisher or graphic designer

3. **Create the table of contents, index, and a list of figures and tables (if appropriate).**

   Skills: word processing; role: desktop publisher

4. **Coordinate with editors, writers, and graphic designers to ensure consistent styles.**

   Skills: word processing, interpersonal skills, and limited editing; role: graphic designer, proposal coordinator, or production manager

5. **Produce deliverables, including printing, binding (plus tabs and fly pages), and creating electronic files.**

   Skills: printing, file management, and multimedia; role: desktop publisher, graphics specialist, or production manager

6. **Proofread copy for stylistic, grammatical, punctuation, and capitalization errors.**

   Skills: technical writing and editing; role: technical writer, editor, or proposal manager

7. **Develop a feedback form for reviewers.**

   Skills: form development and technical writing; role: technical writer, editor, or proposal manager

TIP

For bids of significant value, you can create a scoring summary that mirrors the customer's evaluation criteria (as included in the RFP). You can then ask reviewers to evaluate and score sections in the response against those criteria.

Preparing the right reviewers for the job

Your proposal reviewers must not be members of the proposal team, and they must aim to represent the customer's perspective. Your list of reviewers should include experts on the customer, the industry, your competitors, and your solution approach. In addition, they should be familiar with best practices on preparing and presenting winning proposals.

Make a majority of your reviewers people who performed any previous technical or operational reviews (refer to Chapter 6 for more on various reviews you can hold throughout the proposal process) to help prevent contradictory guidance from newcomers, which can derail the project. You may add new reviewers to represent additional perspectives or subject matter, but the core group should remain as constant as possible throughout review cycles.

Your task, skill, and role elements for choosing and preparing your reviewers are as follows:

1. **Assign roles and content sections to the relevant reviewer.**

   Skills: understanding of reviewer's expertise and functions; role: proposal manager, opportunity manager, or sales manager

2. **Prepare reviewers to give you what you need.**

   Skills: persuasion and leadership; role: proposal manager, opportunity manager, or sales manager

Before beginning the final proposal review — through your pre-review communications and again as you kick off the session — explain to your reviewers what you need them to do along with the things you'd prefer they not do. Table 12-1 lists some helpful guiding principles for your reviewers.

TABLE 12-1 **Guidelines for Reviewers**

Things to Do	Things Not to Do
Read your assignment with the purpose and needs of the customer in mind.	Edit for grammar — leave that to the editor.
Review material that falls within your area of expertise.	Criticize writing style — you're looking for accuracy and persuasiveness.
Consult with other final review experts for more information.	Recommend ways to redesign the pages.
Offer suggestions for presenting information instead of saying "rewrite this."	Revise material so it just sounds better to you.

Even seasoned reviewers need guidance. You should always set expectations in your opening remarks to kick off your review. To help you do this, we provide a checklist of standard review items you can access through the link we provide in the appendix.

PROPOSAL TEAM ROLL CALL

Most professional proposal organizations have the following roles to ensure top-quality output (many of these responsibilities are shared by individuals on smaller teams — for example, in a large business development organization, roles may be specialized, and each role may be a separate job title; in medium-sized organizations, roles may be combined such that a particular job title may perform multiple roles; in small settings, all proposal roles may be assigned to only one or two individuals):

- **Proposal manager:** Leads the development of written, oral, and demonstration-related content. Maintains schedules, organizes resources, coordinates inputs and reviews, ensures bid strategy implementation, resolves internal team issues, and leads process development and implementation.

- **Proposal coordinator:** Leads administrative aspects of proposal development. Ensures security and integrity of all proposal documentation. Coordinates internal flow and schedules. Reviews all proposal inputs. Directs submission of the final master proposal to production.

- **Technical writer:** Writes proposal content, creates style sheets, and delivers just-in-time training for contributors. Often writes reusable content for knowledge bases, builds taxonomies for storage and retrieval, and updates content as required.

- **Production manager:** Plans and directs the printing, assembly, and final check of proposal documents for both print and electronic versions. Helps assemble hard-copy proposal volumes, checks for completeness of each volume or copy, and ensures each page/tab/insert/cover/spine is printed and inserted correctly into the proposal binder.

- **Graphic designer:** Develops customer-focused visual information that highlights an offer's features, benefits, and discriminators. Communicates with other members of the proposal/bid team to conceptualize and create visual elements to persuade the customer. May develop multiple deliverables, such as proposals, presentations, sales collateral, and branding content.

- **Editor:** Ensures the writing structure and words used persuasively convey the offer to the customer. Edits for grammar, punctuation, capitalization, clarity, readability, consistency, and persuasiveness.

- **Desktop publisher:** Designs, formats, and produces proposal templates, documents, and related materials.

Note: Because leading the efforts of all these specialists is challenging, some businesses have created a special role — the *bid manager* — to own the entire proposal opportunity and direct the work of proposal and sales efforts. The bid manager oversees bid strategies, price setting, partnering decisions, and proposal strategies, managing the transition from business opportunity to award.

Running reviews with executives in mind

One of the hardest things we've ever tried to do was to keep our executive-level reviewers in their chairs long enough to read the proposal. Everyone's busy, but no one is busier than an executive reviewer.

All your reviewers are doing you a big favor by agreeing to help, but multiply that tenfold for executives! So try to make it as easy on them as possible by following these tips:

>> Get commitment from them (and their executive assistants — even more important!) to allocate the needed time and attention to the review.

>> Give them enough to review but not too much. They want to know that their input is useful, but do be smart about their available time.

>> Push all participants to start and stay on time, and remind technical reviewers that your executive reviewers are present (and to behave accordingly).

>> Limit access to smartphones and tablets.

>> Run interference for them as much as possible. They'll appreciate your extra efforts to isolate them from interruptions.

Allowing ample time to implement recommendations

When the final proposal review process is complete, you'll have a variety of comments, all reflecting the various personalities and perspectives of your reviewers. If you've created an evaluation form, you can more easily compile their recommendations into an actionable plan. If your reviewers have worked less formally and annotated the proposal itself, you have a larger task on your hands.

Your task, skill, and role elements for implementing recommendations are as follows:

1. **Compile all findings into one set of recommendations.**

    Skills: knowledge of proposal content and structure; role: proposal manager

2. **Implement the recommendations.**

    Skills: solution and offer knowledge; role: selected proposal team members or proposal manager

3. **Review the content before reprinting or production.**

    Skills: technical editing; role: technical writer, editor, or proposal manager

4. **Perform a page-by-page "turn-through" inspection before packaging (called the *white glove* review in some markets).**

Skills: sharp eye for details and knowledge of proposal content and structure; role: proposal manager or sales manager

Readying Your Proposal for Delivery

When you've revised your proposal for the last time, you're ready to produce it in digital copy, hard copy, or both so you can submit it. In Chapter 6, we cover the production process in detail, but now we look at some tips for ensuring efficient and successful production activities in the following sections.

Scaling production to meet your needs

In Chapter 6 we urged you to put your proposal production plan in place early because of the many activities that must take place during a normally tight time frame. This plan includes the activities you see in Figure 12-1. You need to consider including all of them in your plan, but also with a mind to scaling them depending on how big and complex the project (the nearby sidebar "Scaling your production plan" considers how to approach your plan no matter the size of your organization or the proposal).

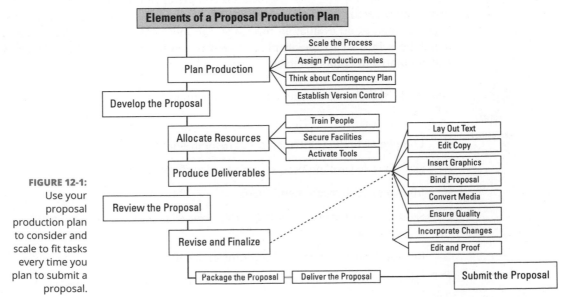

FIGURE 12-1: Use your proposal production plan to consider and scale to fit tasks every time you plan to submit a proposal.

Source: APMP Body of Knowledge

TIP

Here are a few production activities you need to perform every time to ensure a smooth production phase:

» Confirm that your proposal style and layout specifications comply with your customer's instructions.

» Make contingency and backup plans for all aspects of production, especially those relying on computers and their networks or on the schedules of executives.

» Establish a way to implement *version control* (a system for recording changes to content files over time so you know which versions are the most recent) of all proposal text and graphics. Poor version control has undermined countless proposals and created hordes of hoary-headed proposal managers.

» Set a *content freeze* date, after which authors and managers can't make changes unless not doing so would create a non-compliant proposal.

» If you're responding to an RFP, confirm instructions and any amendments before producing the proposal. You don't want to overlook a key requirement that you then don't notice until it's too late.

Planning for production activities early helps you identify gaps in your production capabilities, tools, equipment, facilities, and personnel. If you find gaps early, alert management to supplement your resources while you can still make a difference.

Using checklists to ensure quality

One of the greatest and simplest tools to ensure quality processes is the checklist. Surgeons use them before every operation. Airplane pilots use them before every takeoff. Smart proposal people use them on every deal (even grizzled old veterans like us). Checklists remind you of what you need to do and provide you with a record that you did.

TIP

We talk about some helpful editing and production templates in Chapter 16. You can scale them to match an individual proposals' requirements and complexity as well as your organization's resources and capabilities.

SCALING YOUR PRODUCTION PLAN

You need to apply the steps in your production plan to all proposals, whether you work for or are bidding for work with a small, medium, or large organization or commercial- or government-focused environments. Use your judgment to balance the actions you perform based on the size, time frame, and delivery method for each proposal, alongside the size of your organization:

- **If you work in a large company with a formal proposal organization:** Proposal teams generally manage and produce multiple proposals concurrently with many people performing the distinct roles we list in the earlier sidebar "Proposal team roll call." These proposal organizations must develop a comprehensive production plan for each proposal so they can create compliant proposals for all these opportunities.

- **If you work in a smaller business with an ad-hoc proposal organization:** You and certain of your colleagues may perform proposal-related duties as your "second jobs." Aim to develop a simple yet comprehensive production plan that you can all follow and support alongside your primary jobs. Assess the size and complexity of the opportunity and scale your production plans to match.

- **If you're the lone proposal resource:** The best way to survive and thrive is to establish a production plan that offers you the most flexible schedule for pulling everything together without spending the night (or even several nights) burning the midnight oil. Set and enforce firm deadlines for content submissions and a hard content freeze date. Spend time upfront on building a strong outline that allows you to plug in reusable content for contributors to reference. Consider outsourcing the printing, media development, packaging, and delivery to a reputable vendor-partner. Ruthlessly drive your proposal schedule. You may still have a few late nights, but you'll keep them to a tolerable minimum.

Planning for the worst

What can go wrong in the final stages of your proposal process? Computers and printers can break. Files can go missing. People can disappear. Here's a partial list of production and delivery mayhem (all of which we've experienced firsthand):

>> The master word-processing file becoming corrupted (or, *why you need to back up your files automatically, every hour at least*)

>> Someone writing over a file of edited content with new material, which reverted the edited content to a previous version (or, *why you need version control*)

>> A sales director coming in at the 11th hour with substantial changes to the proposal (or, *why you need to loudly enforce your content freeze date*)

>> A bomb threat occurring at a nearby building, forcing evacuation of proposal center on production day (or, *why you need a Plan B*)

>> A must-win proposal package intended for Sacramento being shipped to Cincinnati instead (or, *why you need a backup delivery plan*)

REMEMBER

Have an emergency backup production and delivery plan ready to implement at a moment's notice. Always plan to submit your proposal a day early (that actually saved us in that last scenario in the list), and train your managers to understand *why* they need to heed your schedule. Maintain and distribute all relevant contact information and directions to the entire proposal team in case you lose electricity, computers, equipment, network, or a facility. And be vigilant: Accidents, threats, natural disasters, traffic jams, and severe illnesses occur when you least expect them, and late delivery means no delivery.

TIP

Get to know your IT staff. Educate them about the critical nature of your proposal work and how their software and systems — especially backup systems — are a crucial link for achieving corporate revenue goals. IT staff can save your proposal in emergencies. Know how to contact them 24/7 in case of emergency, and be sure this information is available to your proposal team.

Responding to Electronic Submissions

Many businesses are replacing traditional RFP responses with electronic proposal submissions, often through third-party vendor applications known as online auction sites. Note the word *auction* — these sites are the *bizarro*-eBay of procurement, awarding business to the *lowest* bidder. Some businesses are so taken with the concept that they've developed their own systems for procuring products and services in secure, web-based applications.

Although a boon to procurers, these online systems can be a nightmare for responders for the following reasons:

>> **Few if any response standards exist.** Each vendor uses a different format for receiving content, and responders must scramble even more than with RFP-based procurements to meet specifications if they are to be compliant.

>> **Many weigh decisions solely on price.** This approach commoditizes products and eliminates the value-adds that distinguish many superior providers from their competitors.

>> **Responses are tightly constrained.** The response system provides little opportunity to persuasively argue for the value of your unique approach or methodology.

>> **Time can be a factor.** Start submitting your response as early as possible. Working with these systems can be time-consuming because of their sometimes non-intuitive interfaces.

These systems are a natural evolution to the proposal business, considering the influence technology has had on business communications in the last two decades. We believe that proposal writers can adapt and even thrive inside this new environment by mastering the fundamentals of proposal development that we share in this book.

As you encounter these systems, keep in mind the following differences between them and paper submissions and some messaging techniques that can help you adapt.

Understanding how electronic submissions differ from paper

When we started our proposal careers, we published exclusively on paper. Then we moved to digital media: CDs, DVDs, email, PDF, and even HTML. Then, some of our customers had us upload digital documents to secure extranet sites, which led to electronic procurement systems. We can't wait to see what happens next.

Today's electronic procurement systems have these key functions:

>> They advertise and communicate the proposed offer.

>> They set the format for and manage a vendor's submissions.

>> They facilitate the review and rating of submissions.

>> They announce the winner of the procurement process.

>> They provide a mechanism for debriefing the bidders.

On the surface, you'd think that everyone would welcome these systems. They lower the cost to bid and to award. They conserve resources for bidders and procurers. They're quite secure. They speed up evaluations and awards. What's not to like?

Well, they take digital sophistication, for one. All organizations have the technological ability to respond to an RFP on paper. However, not all organizations have databases of content that they can upload into an online auction site. They can't all create videos and online demos to meet multimedia requirements (which aren't the norm right now but surely will be in the near future). But maybe digital sophistication is just the new qualification standard. If you can meet the technological requirements of submittal, you're likely savvy enough to have strong technology solutions for the customer's problems.

On the other hand, electronic submissions may eliminate many of the competitive advantages that bigger organizations have traditionally held over their smaller rivals — for example, their unlimited resources for printing and distribution and their vast human resources for adapting to last-minute amendments.

Adapting your messages accordingly

Electronic submission portals, particularly those where automated tools help evaluators assess bids, frequently impose rigid structures on proposal content. When content is limited to text answers pasted or uploaded into an online questionnaire, you need to focus on compliance and responsiveness in the text. How do you prepare for or adapt to this new trend in procurement?

TIP

In Chapter 10, we advocate a clear, concise, direct style for your proposal content. This approach works for electronic submissions as well as for hard-copy RFP responses. If you're writing clearly and concisely, explaining actions by using verbs and eliminating all unnecessary words and marketing fluff, you're already prepared for the kind of rigorous electronic submissions that are growing in number and scope each year. Still, if you thought some RFPs were overly stringent in word and page counts, you ain't seen nothing yet. For instance, databases allow you to restrict the number of characters (letters and numbers) in a response field. You may be required, as with Twitter, to constrain your response to 140 characters. This is where bidders who can write clearly, directly, and concisely will rule!

Giving an Oral Presentation

If you've responded successfully to an RFP, you may be asked to "defend" or expand upon your proposal in an oral presentation for the customer. The oral proposal is like a job interview for your organization. Generally, if you're asked to give oral proposals, you've made the short list and the customer wants a preview of what it will be like to work with you. The customer may want to see how you solve problems or ask you to clarify certain aspects of your proposal (if questions remain after the standard clarification stage). Often, the customer will conduct a question-and-answer session after the presentation, which is akin to an oral examination for an advanced degree and just as nerve-racking. So you need to prepare thoroughly for this next hurdle in the procurement process.

REMEMBER

Oral presentations can challenge the best proposal writers. Those called upon to present are usually the potential staff who will deliver the services set out in the bid or members of the original proposal team.

Don't take the oral presentation lightly. It's every bit as important as the written proposal. You must prepare fully for the presentation. If you present poorly, you may lose the opportunity — wasting all your efforts on the written proposal.

The following sections help you plan your presentation, craft a memorable message, and prepare yourself to speak so that you make the most of this important opportunity to reinforce your proposal.

Planning your approach

Presenting your proposal requires almost as much planning as the proposal itself. Before you start creating your presentation, you need to

>> Identify how much time you'll have to present

>> Understand the setting and circumstances

>> Determine which team members will attend and whether in person or virtually

>> Review the RFP's evaluation criteria (refer to Chapter 4) to remind you of the customer's priorities

>> Review all bid requirements in relation to your compliance matrix (refer to Chapter 4)

>> Revisit the win themes and key discriminators to ensure your presentation conveys a consistent message (refer to Chapter 6)

REMEMBER

You and your sales lead write the presentation script, oversee the reuse of visuals from the proposal and any new illustrations needed, and assign presentation roles. It's also up to you to conduct several practice sessions and then a final dress rehearsal with the entire team. By properly preparing and rehearsing the presentation, each speaker can refine his or her persuasive message and practice the presentation skills needed to be successful.

TIP

Seasoned oral presenters recommend that you do the following when giving your presentation:

>> **Get off on the right foot.** Your customers are busy; they have other meetings to attend and other projects to implement. Don't waste their time by arriving late, fumbling with the projector, or making long introductions. Be ready to go when it's your time to speak.

>> **Get to the point.** State your recommendation, preferably in the first minute. Your customer is itching to interrupt you with questions, so get to your main point before the customer commandeers your presentation.

>> **Sell a vision first.** Don't walk into the meeting and immediately start talking about yourself, your business, or your products. If you do, your client will immediately focus on cost and product features, which can derail the meeting before you've had a chance to make your pitch. Instead, focus on selling a vision first. Your clients want to know how they can beat their competitors, reach new customers, retain existing customers, and increase their profit margins. So paint a vision for how you're going to help them achieve these goals.

>> **Ask questions.** After you've spoken for a few minutes, stop and ask your customer a question. This is a great way to stay in control of the meeting while allowing your customer to become part of the presentation. Some questions you may ask include

- Does my description track with your vision of success?

- Have you used this or a similar approach in the past?

- Have I prioritized your goals correctly?

- Have I adequately summarized this challenge for your company?

>> **Lead with stories, not data.** Although your customers value data, they're also realistic about what data can — and can't — tell them. They've seen many projects fail despite the glowing research results, and they've seen projects succeed despite the lack of any data to back up the solution. Therefore, tell stories about your solutions first; you can then present the data to back them up.

Come to the presentation armed with customer experience data and your views on competitors' moves. Your customers are far more interested in what their customers are saying and what their competitors are doing than they are in the latest research study in your field of expertise.

>> **Use presentation software wisely.** If you're going to use presentation software, use it for what it's meant to do — enhance your oral presentation. Most slides are far too complex and include too much text, distracting designs, and unrelated images. Limit a slide to one image and one line of text, if any (some say no more than six words per slide). Your clients can absorb only so much at once, and if they're too busy trying to sort out the objects and words on the screen, they may miss most of what you say.

>> **Keep it short.** Keep your main presentation as short as possible, but keep a close eye on the time limits and directions your customer provides. Remember: The more you try to tell your clients, the less they remember. Beware the glib speaker who goes on long after the customer stops listening. Instead of a monologue, engage your audience with questions.

>> **Say why the customer should choose you.** Your qualifications cement your vision and solution. Support your qualifications with testimonials from your other customers and stories of your successes in similar situations.

>> **Have a clear agenda.** Your presentation needs to have a clear and compelling agenda. Begin with compelling reasons to consider your proposal and culminate with a specific request for the business.

TIP

If you can't afford to lose, consider hiring someone who can improve your chances of winning. Just as a college can upgrade a sports program by hiring the right coach, you can improve your ability to score big on the oral presentation by hiring a qualified coach to help prepare your team.

Although the team may be made up of highly intelligent people, they may not be experts in oral presentations. A professional orals coach will conduct formal training to bring your team up to speed in all aspects of the presentation: script writing, stage presence, slide development, and question fielding. Orals coaches can help proposal teams deliver the most effective and persuasive oral presentations possible, and they are well worth the extra cost.

TIP

So many organizations have won business through oral presentations that several successful models exist to help you build a logical, responsive, consistent, and persuasive presentation. Your customer's preferences will always trump your designs, but if the customer doesn't provide a structure for your presentation, you can use one of the approaches we outline in our oral proposal template, which you can access through the link we provide in the appendix.

Helping your message stick

In a proposal, carefully selected visuals have a powerful effect on evaluators — and the effect is even greater in a proposal presentation. Visuals help listeners remember key messages, particularly after a series of oral proposals presented in one mind-numbing day or over a series of equally mind-numbing days. (Chapter 11 looks at the impact of visual elements in your proposal documentation in more detail.)

TIP

Use these ideas to integrate graphics into your oral presentation:

>> Scan your proposal response for visuals appropriate for the presentation. If they're not too detailed, use them as is. This visual link to your proposal, plus your statements, creates "instant recall" and doubly reinforces your key themes.

>> Display a partial or enlarged image (if possible) to highlight a key message from the original visual that calls to mind the original while offering a different or more focused perspective to viewers.

>> Create a story graphic that summarizes your offer at a high level. Your executive audience will appreciate the big picture, and you can then drill down into each "chapter" of the proposal story to support your presentation structure.

>> Illustrate your proofs by using images of your solution in action at other customers' work locations. Unless you have permission, use images that don't identify other customers directly. Instead, allude to the customers indirectly in your presentation.

Ensure that your presenters rehearse with the visuals projected behind them, coaching them to always speak to the audience, not the visual. Consider using blackout slides, a la Steve Jobs, to focus listeners' attention on the message, not the visual, and let the visuals introduce or reinforce the spoken message.

Practicing good public speaking skills

Public speaking is a common fear, and non-sales presenters often aren't that keen to put themselves out there. This is why practice is vital. All presenters, regardless of their skill level, need to practice their individual parts on their own 10 to 15 times out loud before they practice with the team. The team then needs to practice under conditions similar to those they'll face in the final presentation.

TIP

Follow these tips for making practice perfect:

>> **Write a script.** The best way to stay within a time budget, deliver all the points you plan to, and sustain a conversational tone is to write your presentation out in script form, just as if it's a short play. You can then read it out loud, cutting out words that you stumble over and any others that detract from your main points. The more you read it, the more conversational you'll make it (you'll hear any artificial-sounding phrases), and the more you'll imprint it in your memory. Then you can toss the script and rely on a few notes (with trigger words and phrases).

>> **Set a timer.** Staying within set time limits is crucial to success, but keeping the presentation to an effective length is even more crucial. Strictly hold all presenters to their time limits during each practice session. No exceptions.

>> **Practice your handoffs.** Nothing wastes time or looks less professional than fumbling transitions during a presentation. Paradoxically, they don't sound natural if you don't rehearse them. Pre-determine and practice how you'll introduce your team members and move from presenter to presenter.

>> **Demand clarity and concision.** How you practice is how you'll present. Don't accept presenters who fail to take their roles seriously. Call them out and put the pressure on them to do the work to help the team succeed.

>> **Film each speaker.** The only good feedback is immediate feedback. You can use a smartphone to create clear video and audio references and then critique each presenter's performance.

>> **Invite a tough audience to your dress rehearsal.** Larry Tracy, author of *The Shortcut to Persuasive Presentations* (Imprint Books), recommends that you present to a "murder board," where colleagues role-play the worst-case audience and, as the name suggests, brutally critique the performance. We bet you know just the right people to invite to your murder board!

Before we close our remarks about oral presentations, we take a look at how you make your words and your actions align and how you normally close out your oral presentations: handling questions from your audience.

Aligning verbal and nonverbal messages

Nonverbal messages either reinforce or contradict your verbal message. Your messages need to be on point, but you also need your body language to be in agreement with your words.

TIP

Here are some ways to assess and improve nonverbal presentation skills:

>> **Watch your pace and tone.** Speak too quickly and you sound nervous. Speak too slowly and you sound wary or uncertain. Speak in a monotone and you risk boring your listeners.

Speak like you talk (not a typo) — that is, as you express something exciting, speed up a little; when you relate technical matters, slow down and be deliberate.

>> **Punctuate with your hands.** Gestures emphasize words and ideas and help your listeners stay focused on you. While distracting movements hinder communication, using your hands to act out certain expressions can aid comprehension.

>> **Look them in the eye.** Early in your presentation, make eye contact with someone (perhaps even address that individual at some point), and then seek others to become your conversation partners. Return now and then to your original target. (**Note:** An old recommendation to look over your audience just makes you look spacey.)

>> **Express yourself.** Your face is the window to your message. Use the appropriate facial expressions for your messages. When you have good news, smile and throw your eyes wide with enthusiasm. When you talk about serious issues, don't frown, but do look concerned.

Preparing for questions and answers

Although a question–and–answer period isn't part of every oral presentation, be prepared for it just the same. Make sure you

>> Know your material thoroughly so you can respond with authority and without hesitation

>> Anticipate specific questions and rehearse your answers — be especially prepared to address risks and other contentious issues

>> Conduct several question-and-answer practice sessions apart from your presentation run-throughs — answering questions is a different skill to presenting

>> Field questions in a consistent manner by

- Responding fully to one question at a time

- Listening carefully to the full question (don't interrupt or jump the gun)

- Repeating the question to confirm that you have it right and that others have heard it as well

- Focusing your attention on those asking the questions — look directly at them and lean or step toward them as you respond

- Deferring to someone else on your team if you don't know the answer, or admitting that you don't know and telling your audience that you'll find the answer for them

» Practice handing off to specialists for complex questions requiring technical answers

5

Taking Your Proposal to the Next Level

IN THIS PART . . .

Understand the tools and systems available to help you automate your proposal development process. See the value of templates and checklists for creating a consistent, repeatable proposal experience.

Discover ways to motivate and lead your proposal team — not just manage it — from your kickoff meeting to your final reviews. Find out how to make sure everyone is on the same page and stays in sync over the life of the project.

Look at how to seek, harvest, and distribute lessons learned from every proposal. Find out how to improve your personal skills through certifications and professional networking. Know where to find mentors, coaches, and other resources for getting better every time.

Chapter 13

Using Tools and Templates to Accelerate Your Proposals

When you've been writing proposals for a while, you find that you do a lot of rework. From deal to deal — small or large, simple or complex — you'll find yourself performing a task, sending a reminder, training a newbie, describing a product, or defending an action, and you'll say to yourself, "I've been here before."

It's therefore reasonable to seek a way to avoid these constant, mundane repetitions and focus your energy on making a difference to each new and vitally important deal.

Whether you're experienced or just starting out, commercially or governmentally focused, you need a suite of tools to help you win more business through proposals. These tools may be as fundamental as a single laptop with word-processing software and an Internet connection. They may be as straightforward as a set of home-grown templates that streamline your page layout. Or they may be as sophisticated as an end-to-end Request for Proposal (RFP) response management system that serves hundreds of concurrent users. Tools are necessary for every proposal writer because you simply have too much work to accomplish without help.

Because new proposal and project management tools come out all the time, you need to understand the different approaches these tools take for enhancing your efforts during the proposal process. That's what this chapter is all about — helping you choose or build the ones that you need, wherever you are along the volume and complexity scale.

Tooling Around with Proposals

Online dating sites are amazing. They help you build a profile to show yourself off at your best (or even maybe better than your best — but that's another story). Then they help you plan your strategy for finding your mate and assist you with your search for your dream date — identifying suitable candidates based on their profiles. They do everything but ask someone out for you.

And wouldn't you know it — oddly similar tools are out there that help you identify business prospects, find out about what they like and don't like, narrow down those prospects to those most likely to buy from you, and then guide and keep tabs on your progress. And although online dating tools can't actually woo your date for you, some of the selling tools we're talking about can help you generate professional proposals to win your prospects over.

REMEMBER

The bigger your business gets and the more you acquire business through the proposal process, the more you should consider getting the help that these tools provide. But they're a big step — they can be costly, and they may not work the way you want or need them to.

Figure 13-1 lists the kinds of tools available to support your efforts through the three stages of the proposal process (pre-proposal, proposal development, and post-proposal; refer to Chapter 6 for details). Your options at each stage deserve a little discussion — some a bit more than others — so you know what's out there for you when you're ready to take the plunge.

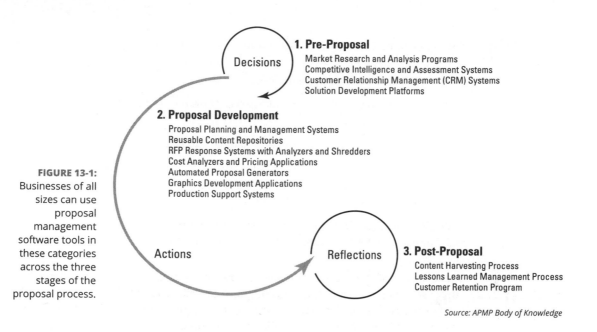

FIGURE 13-1: Businesses of all sizes can use proposal management software tools in these categories across the three stages of the proposal process.

1. Pre-Proposal
Market Research and Analysis Programs
Competitive Intelligence and Assessment Systems
Customer Relationship Management (CRM) Systems
Solution Development Platforms

2. Proposal Development
Proposal Planning and Management Systems
Reusable Content Repositories
RFP Response Systems with Analyzers and Shredders
Cost Analyzers and Pricing Applications
Automated Proposal Generators
Graphics Development Applications
Production Support Systems

3. Post-Proposal
Content Harvesting Process
Lessons Learned Management Process
Customer Retention Program

Decisions

Actions

Reflections

Source: APMP Body of Knowledge

Mechanizing the pre-proposal process

During the first stage of the proposal process, you're trying to get organized and find out as much as you can about the prospect, its situation, and your competition. Special systems and tools can help you find, assess, qualify, plan, and manage new sales initiatives. They put you in the best position to get the most out of your proposal activities. And they can even help you manage your relationship with the customer after your proposal wins.

Researching and evaluating markets

As you look for new business, you need information about the markets you want to sell to. You can use a variety of tools and services for researching and analyzing markets. Commercial market research firms offer software that

>> Alerts you and offers insight to upcoming opportunities

>> Researches market conditions and trends

>> Identifies, qualifies, and tracks opportunities

>> Surveys potential customers to identify specific information

You can conduct your own online market research by using

>> Internet-based keyword searches

>> Surveys (web-based, social media–based, or telephone-based surveys, or through focus groups)

>> Data mining, using spreadsheets or database software

>> Government-sponsored sources such as the U.S. Small Business Administration (www.sba.gov), Eurostat (ec.europa.eu/eurostat), and other government agency websites

>> SWOT analyses (which look at strengths, weaknesses, opportunities, and threats — refer to Chapter 5 for the full story on SWOT)

Make sure that the market knowledge you gather from these sources flows into any systems or resources that your proposal contributors will use as they write the proposal. Also, get into the habit of citing the sources of your information so you can trace back and respond to challenges or audits.

Safeguarding this information is paramount (you don't want your hard-earned intelligence walking out the door), so make sure that only the right roles have access to this information and the permission to view, edit, and apply it.

Gaining and assessing competitive intelligence

You can help your executives make the right bid decisions by gathering and analyzing information about competitors, their products and services, and their existing customers. (Refer to Chapter 5 for ways to gather competitive intelligence.)

Larger companies often employ competitive intelligence professionals (some even have entire departments performing this function) who do this research as their main function. Smaller companies can hire analysts or subscribe to services that do the same work, which may include

>> Assessing and ranking your competitors

>> Briefing you on customer and competitor status

>> Creating models for estimating competitors' pricing

>> Developing win theme strategies

>> Identifying potential partners for your deals

>> Performing the SWOT analysis (more on this in Chapter 5)

>> Reporting "talk on the street" about procurements and competitors

Competitive intelligence professionals can also do primary and secondary online research and telephone research, which they store and analyze by using customer relationship management (CRM) systems (see the next section for more on these), *relational databases* (these let you store data by categories so you can easily determine relationships), and even spreadsheets.

TIP

Many resources on the web provide information on the practice of competitive intelligence. A quick search reveals professional organizations and consultants who can improve your thinking and processes on this subject.

REMEMBER

Effective research enables stronger, more compelling proposals, so study your competition by using these information sources. At the very least, become acquainted with publicly available sources for customer analysis and competitive intelligence. More come online all the time. And don't forget social media (Facebook, Google+, LinkedIn, Pinterest, Reddit, and many others).

Managing customer relationships

To win business, you must get inside your customer's head. Your main goal is to understand where your customer is really coming from — and to get the customer to know, like, and trust you more than your competitors. You do this best by using a simple concept with a fancy name and acronym: *customer relationship management (CRM)*.

REMEMBER

In simple terms, CRM is the process of managing all aspects of your relationships with customers so they

>> Know who you are and what you can do for them

>> Come to know, like, and trust you

>> Choose you over your competitors

The keyword in CRM is *management*: You can't fully know your customers without working hard at it. You need a thorough and well-considered action plan that you can execute every day, which is where automation can help.

A CRM system electronically captures and stores all your accounts, contacts, calls, meetings, tasks, emails, documentation, marketing campaigns, and more. All of this information resides in a centralized database so everyone in your organization who needs it can access it with a few mouse clicks.

TIP

CRM tools are available to fit every budget. If you're a small business or just starting out, you can build your account and contact plans in a spreadsheet. You can record meeting notes and calls in a word-processing file. You can store them in shared folders with a customer-based file structure. As you grow, you can move to a relational database and ultimately switch to sophisticated, specialized software.

What else do you put in CRM systems? After you have added the basic information (the customer name, industry, locations, not only key decision makers but also the contacts who will influence the decision makers, contact numbers, products/services they offer, organization charts, contact notes, purchase preferences and history, service feedback, budgets, and so on), also focus on information that helps you determine your winning price. This means tracking as best as you can what your competitors charge. But vital for this as well is intelligence about what your customer can afford to spend. Other important information to seek and save includes the customer's

>> Buying history

>> Executive stakeholders and influencers

>> Organizational hierarchies

>> Favored suppliers

>> Opinions of its suppliers

>> Financial decision-making criteria (that is, lowest price or best value)

Developing solutions with software

Depending on your industry, you may have specialized software for developing the solutions you create for your customers. In telecommunications, for instance, software tools help reduce the time and resources needed to design and engineer customer networks and configure equipment. They also reduce errors and provide professional-looking outputs for proposals and presentations. These solution-development tools may be the first on your list of computer-aided tools that help you do more with less.

But you may be more in need of tools for the supporting tasks required to create solutions in any industry — tasks like allocating resources; developing schedules; estimating costs (including labor rates and loadings); managing project phases, deliverables, and work packages; and developing contracts. For such tasks, software is a true blessing. Although you can handle much of this work with databases, spreadsheets, and project management software, you may also benefit from the following "thinking" tools:

- >> **Mind-mapping software** to help you generate ideas for solutions

- >> **Graphics or presentation software** to help you depict ideas, processes, and concepts through flowcharts, workflow diagrams, and organization charts

- >> **Computer-aided design (CAD) software** to create 3-D models, blueprints, floor plans, and network diagrams

- >> **Business process management (BPM) software** to help you structure processes and methods for a wide range of programming and business functions

TIP

Integrating the output or, better still, the workflow of these tools with a proposal management system or collaborative environment can increase their value exponentially.

Using tools to enhance the proposal development stage

Thanks to advances in technology, tools abound for automating many aspects of the proposal development stage. Although pre-proposal support tools bring you many benefits as a proposal writer, those benefits pale in comparison to those you get from collaborative workspaces, content development and management, and document generation in this stage. In this section, we review six categories of tools that can enhance your proposal development efforts.

Managing and developing proposals online

Proposal management systems (an all-encompassing term for online environments with a variety of tools for responding to RFPs and building proactive proposals) have been available commercially for more than 20 years. Some companies have had proprietary, self-built systems for even longer. As technology has evolved, so have these systems.

At first, they were mere file repositories, places where contributors could check out and check back in files to preserve version control. Later, they began to facilitate team communications and schedules. Using *parsing technology* (the ability of computer programs to "read" content and identify content elements), they evolved into RFP analyzers and content shredders (we discuss "shredding" your RFP in Chapter 4). As the Internet evolved, they became development environments where contributors from around the world could work on a deal day and night.

What's the difference between proposal management systems and collaborative workspaces? They're expressly designed to help the proposal professional manage the various tasks, techniques, and procedures unique to the proposal development process that we've discussed throughout this book, including

>> Shredding an RFP into its component numbered sections

>> Revealing buried *wills, shalls, shoulds,* and *musts*

>> Creating proposal outlines, content development plans, and storyboards

>> Developing your compliance matrix

>> Generating a calendar of major and minor milestones

>> Assigning writing duties and due dates for content contributors

>> Communicating, tracking, and notifying pending and missed milestones

CHOOSING THE RIGHT TOOLS FOR EFFECTIVE COLLABORATION

Proposal development is intensive, time-consuming work. To remain competitive and address the work–life balance that employees desire, companies must ensure that collaboration tools provide the needed features and functions for their teams, wherever or however they work.

Collaboration tools are even more crucial because companies now rely on virtual proposal teams to win business. Nearly everyone involved in writing a proposal has a full-time role elsewhere in the business. These busy professionals have to work collaboratively, with access to proposal tools and information resources through VPN connections, web portals, and mobile devices, or they'll never get all the work done. They must be able to contribute to the proposal whether working from a corporate or field office, local coffee shop, home office, airport, or car.

Before you propose to buy or build a set of collaborative tools, get your sales and business development managers on board. Better still, enlist the support of senior executives to provide the time, funding, training, and other resources needed to develop and maintain the systems and software you need. To help drive adoption, encourage management from all participating units to integrate the use of these tools into their own daily business practices.

Regardless of your organization's size, without access to effective tools that support and reinforce best practices, you can't maintain a managed, repeatable proposal development process — and that will reduce your overall chances of winning business.

Pulling content from a formal repository

Perhaps the most valuable tool for proposal writers is the content repository. *Content repositories* provide standardized, structured, and approved information ready to include in your RFP responses and proactive proposals. This tool provides excellent return on investment in the proposal development field. It pays for itself in a year by reducing duplicative, redundant work, lowering your costs and increasing your team's efficiency. Even if you have to copy and paste from content repositories, this collection of previously used chunks of content (be they chapters, sections, paragraphs, or even sentences and phrases) will improve your ability to respond to tight deadlines with vetted content. However, the more you rely on old (or should we say "pre-used") content, the less customized your responses become. But for chunks of information that change little, if ever, why reinvent the wheel?

TIP

If you do reuse content but worry that you're filling your custom proposal with boilerplate text, remember that you don't have to reuse it verbatim. Writing improves with revision, as you see in Chapter 12, so continually improve your content by reusing and revising it.

REMEMBER

You want your content repository to be a collaborative tool, with easy network access from anywhere, at any time. The best tools are integrated with proposal management platforms for a seamless user experience. Your repository should have the following:

>> A search function supporting *Boolean operators* (which allow you to perform more sophisticated queries by including *and, or,* and other conjunctions to limit or expand search terms), keyword, text, and question-and-answer searches

>> The ability to store "clean" content without formatting codes so you can apply the content to any medium

>> A single version of each content chunk so you can easily update it and maintain consistency across your messaging

The content in your repository needs to have the following:

>> Metatags based on content type, subject, and application

>> Links to related content based on your search criteria

>> A common style so it all sounds like it was written by one person and therefore complements other material from the repository (refer to Chapter 10 for more on effective writing)

TIP

What kinds of content can you store in your repository? The sky's the limit, but here are a few ideas:

>> Product and solution descriptions and specifications

>> Processes and methods

>> Archived proposals

>> Reusable graphics, including tables, charts, photos, illustrations, flow charts, organization charts, and diagrams

>> Résumés and personnel information (such as skills inventories)

>> Past-performance write-ups

>> Corporate history boilerplate

>> Oral presentations and scripts

Analyzing costs and calculating prices

Many companies have such complex pricing that they require unique spreadsheets (and in some instances, whole software suites) to identify costs, generate item-by-item and summary pricing, and apply volume or bundled product discounts.

TIP

Proposal management systems rarely include costing and pricing capabilities, but many allow you to import the outputs of these systems into templates for delivery to customers within the proposal.

Activating reusable content with automated proposals

Automated proposal generators enable your sales force to click a few buttons and create small, (usually) proactive proposals that can approximate the quality of "from scratch" proposals. This level of quality is possible because proposal writers supply the core and reusable content (in your content repository). These easy-to-use programs help salespeople respond quickly to requests from customers. They reduce proposal writing time from hours or days to as little as 10 or 15 minutes. They can improve the quality and consistency of messaging while freeing limited proposal resources to work on the most valuable opportunities.

WARNING

As you may imagine, quality can vary across commercial proposal generators. Some spit out standardized proposals that have as much customer focus as a mass market brochure or a form letter. Some won't let you edit the output, so you run the risk of missing specific customer requirements or including content that just doesn't address the needs of a particular customer.

The best of the breed, however, do an amazing job by allowing you to

>> Specify the needs of your customer and perfectly align the corresponding features and benefits

>> Select the industry of your customer and apply appropriate terminology to describe the current and future situations

>> Upload schematics, images, tables, and graphics from other applications to customize your offer and reinforce your message

>> Preview and edit reusable content chunks before you insert them to ensure they're appropriate

>> Generate custom covers and artwork that reinforce selectable themes

>> Export output to different media (including multiple print formats, email, HTML, XML, PDF, and so on)

REMEMBER

The quality of your automated proposal depends on the quality of the content in your repository, not on the software's bells and whistles. And quality content depends on having a trained proposal writer to develop and maintain that content. In large proposal organizations, this is usually a full-time role. In smaller teams, it's shared by all, with the best editor finalizing the content for reuse.

Illustrating your solution with graphics software

As you see in Chapter 11, proposals need visual elements that clarify the written material, echo its win themes (refer to Chapter 2 for more about win themes), and improve its readability. However, the software that enables anyone to build vibrant graphics is a double-edged sword: Few have the design skill and experience that you need to get the most out of these applications. Still, you can't have a professional proposal without graphics, so you need a strategy for using these tools.

To conceptualize and render proposal graphics, including tables, figures, and illustrations, you need

>> Professional-level illustration software (such as Adobe InDesign, Microsoft Publisher, QuarkXPress, and others)

>> Professional-level diagramming software (such as Microsoft Visio, Google Draw, SmartDraw, and others)

TIP

These examples of software are merely suggestions; a variety of programs are available that can meet your needs and your budget, and what's preferred today may fall out of favor tomorrow.

To mock up simple versions of graphics, your contributors can utilize some easy-to-use illustration and diagramming alternatives. Although a pencil sketch will usually suffice, using software for roughing out ideas is much more transportable if your contributors work remotely. After you finalize your mock-ups (refer to Chapter 11 for insights on how you can become proficient at mock-ups for page layouts and graphics), you can ask a graphic designer to render these mock-ups in professional-grade software. If your organization doesn't have in-house resources, or maybe can't justify the cost of these types of programs, freelance graphic designers can really save the day.

TIP

Make sure your software can create and work with the following:

>> Design and layout grids

>> Imported graphics, photos, and CAD drawings

>> Multiple templates and styles

>> Table functions and tools

>> Text and typographic functions and tools

Other key features you need include a WYSIWYG (what you see is what you get) interface, the ability to export to multiple formats and versions, a review and comment function, and the ability to create macros to speed up repetitive actions or functions.

Producing proposals to customer specifications

Change is slow in the proposal world. Ten years ago we talked about building an XML schema to standardize online procurements. Recently, a proposal expert said it may be time that we revisit the proposal XML concept — ten years later!

Slowly but surely, the proposal world is progressing. Paper submittals are still prevalent, but most bids are developed, delivered, and assessed digitally (via email, digital media, and online procurement sites). To meet changing customer requirements, you must be able to deliver your proposal in the customer's preferred medium, so your production toolkit needs to include

>> Word-processing or desktop-publishing software

>> PDF creation software (so you can submit documents that look identical regardless of the computer or display platform)

>> Video and audio production software with *closed-captioning features* (which provide text transcripts of audio for hearing impaired viewers)

>> CD, DVD, or Blu-ray authoring, burning, and copying software

Preparing for the next one

Just because the proposal is out the door, it doesn't mean your work is over. You may need to work with the sales team during the question-and-answer period. You'll also likely help create the best and final oral presentation. But four tasks remain to get ready for the next proposal, which often is already on your doorstep, if not already underway. We discuss these tasks in the next sections.

Harvesting content for reuse

In proposal lingo, *harvest* means to review, extract, and organize valuable content from prior proposals to add or update entries in a content repository. Harvesting is a continual improvement process that helps ensure that your proposals reflect your organization's thinking in a fresh, accurate way.

To harvest efficiently, you need a way to determine

>> Which chunks of content need refreshing or revising

>> What gaps you need to fill in your content repository

>> When a new section of content is better than a stored version

REMEMBER

With your criteria set, harvesting involves combing through the latest proposal and extracting the content chunks that fit your needs. You (as proposal writer) are best suited for this work because you're most familiar with the recent proposal and you may have used content from the content repository to write it. Look for content that

>> Was missing when you originally searched the repository

>> Was questioned by technical contributors during the project

>> Was deemed out of date or incorrect during reviews

Capturing lessons learned

Not all tools are mechanisms or software programs; many are simple but powerful processes that help you get better with each subsequent opportunity. One great example is a *lessons learned management process* (LLMP). An LLMP is a knowledge management discipline, used in progressive companies around the world to instill a culture of continual improvement. It's a way for you to capture the good and not-so-good things that happened during the proposal process so you can make the good things part of your standard process and prevent the bad things from happening again.

LLMPs come in several types, the following two being very effective for proposals:

>> **After action reviews (AARs):** People learn best when you can reinforce or correct an action shortly after it occurs. Conduct AARs periodically throughout a proposal project.

In an AAR, participants assess whether a proposal activity was truly as effective as it was supposed to be. The review has four parts:

- **Intent:** What did we plan to accomplish?
- **Outcome:** What actually happened?
- **Gap:** What were the differences and why did they happen?
- **Learn:** What would we do the same or differently next time?

>> **Postmortems:** As the name implies, postmortems give proposal participants an opportunity to slice and dice a proposal after the fact. After you submit the proposal, you gather the key participants and document the good, bad, and ugly that happened during the proposal process. Your postmortems should be formal but non-threatening: You want honest opinions without fear of recrimination. This is why you set clear guidelines for the discussion, using a structured approach that inspects the following:

- What you did well
- Where you need to improve
- What may help to streamline the process
- What particular trouble spots or misunderstandings you experienced

Holding a lessons-learned session with your customer during debriefing is ideal but difficult to accomplish, especially if you lose. If you can get your customer to agree to one, you need to hold it after the customer has made its decision. From the customer debriefing, you can find out

>> What really mattered to the customer

>> How this particular customer evaluated your proposal

>> How you can improve early customer interaction

To access a sample lessons learned management process template, check out the appendix.

Celebrating success

Proposal writing is a tough job. The minute you finish one proposal, you hardly have time to take a breath before you have to start another one. Sometimes it's a thankless job (after all, a proposal never wins a deal outright, but it sure can lose one). This is why you need to celebrate each milestone you reach, especially when you submit the proposal and definitely when you win.

TIP

Do your part to create a culture of appreciation. At the beginning of each proposal meeting, acknowledge team members who've met deadlines or contributed something special to the process. Acknowledge the team for a successful review. Send e-cards for personal celebrations and accomplishments. Hold a virtual reward ceremony at the close of the proposal. Then, maybe, your sales team will invite you to the victory party.

Planning to keep the business

In a tough and competitive market, retaining old business is as difficult as winning new business — maybe more. You must pursue contract renewals as aggressively as you do new business. And here, tools can help.

TIP

Start planning to retain the business on the day you're awarded a contract. Although the processes for initially winning and for retaining business are similar, you now have something to tout that your future competitors don't: actual project performance for this customer.

REMEMBER

Plan to keep the business by implementing three phases to your account plans:

>> **Performing to win:** Create a performance tracking form that documents successes, failures, and what you did to correct these failures. Use customer feedback, metrics, and performance trends as proofs. Create a special section of your lessons-learned repository to store these performance tracking forms.

>> **Preparing to win:** Turn your performance proofs into requirements that will influence the next solicitation. Keep these issues top of mind with your customer's leadership by equipping your sales contacts with communications vehicles (for example, executive briefings and routine presentations).

>> **Proposing to win:** Write a compelling proposal aligned to the evaluation criteria, which you've hopefully been able to influence. Don't assume that the evaluator knows your performance history; use it as a prominent theme, which you have the proofs to support.

Creating Foolproof Processes and Outputs

REMEMBER

Templates are the lifeblood of any proposal organization. They allow you to perform consistently well from one bid to the next. They give you models to follow as you plan, kick off, and manage a new project. They allow you to store and manage information in a standardized, reusable format so you can retrieve it faster and more easily. They allow you to insert content into proposal documents more efficiently, because they enforce predetermined *styles* (defined sets of formatting parameters for document elements such as headers, footers, captions, and headings). Beyond question, templates make your job easier and help you do it better.

Templates come in many forms. They may be

>> Word-processing "shells" that provide a header, footer, and placeholders for headings and body copy

>> Worksheets — word-processing tables or spreadsheets — that prompt you to provide details about actions or values

>> Charts that identify sample organizational structures or process flows

>> Checklists with standard elements and room to add customized elements

Whatever their form, they can improve your efficiency and your output at every stage of the proposal process. We provide ten samples to help you plan, develop, and produce your proposal in Chapter 16, and you can find many more on the Association of Proposal Management Professionals (APMP) website at www.apmp.org.

For the rest of this chapter, we focus on some specific types of proposal templates and how you can create them.

Planning smarter with templates

During the pre-proposal stage, you need to quickly establish a sense of professionalism within your proposal team. After all, you're usually dealing with stressed-out sales professionals and preoccupied engineers, and they may not automatically treat you as a peer (Dilbert's "Tina the Tech Writer" springs to mind). So you need to show your sales team and technical colleagues that you're prepared and you have everything for the project organized and ready to roll. The templates we look at in the following sections help you do that.

Communicating consistently

Establish an email template that will help contributors instantly recognize communication about the project and the level of urgency to the message. Create a standard subject line (for example, "<CUSTOMER> RFP: Addendum Review Call at 4:30 p.m. EST").

Add a line in the body of the email before the salutation that expresses the urgency, like URGENT! or CRITICAL! for instance.

Use plain text for your template, because emails are read on a variety of platforms and not all support formatting. Define and document when and how the team can use emoticons to clarify the emotional meaning of an email.

Many proposal development systems include intra-team emailing and instant messaging within the application, so encourage your team to use this feature, if available.

Tracking action items to resolution

Proposal plans are largely long lists of actions that you must doggedly track if you're to meet your milestones. For example, successfully moving forward after key decisions depends on recording and following up on action items that result from periodic reviews. Deciding to proceed comes with a series of critical actions that the team must complete before the next review, and it's often your job to clearly define, assign, and track the status of each item. You can use a simple template like the one in Figure 13-2 to track action items and keep everyone informed.

To make information easier to see and digest, add color to the status column fields — for example, green for 100 percent complete, yellow for 50 percent complete, and red for little or no progress.

Assigning and tracking responsibilities

As you kick off your proposal project, you can use the proposal outline you create (refer to Chapter 6) to help generate a proposal responsibility matrix. The *responsibility matrix* is a document that identifies proposal team members and their specific proposal section responsibilities. It maps authors with specific section- and response-writing assignments. And though each proposal outline is different, the other elements of the matrix make it a great candidate for a template.

Action	Person Accountable	Status
Follow up with the two subcontractors who have not yet submitted bids	Subcontracts Manager	In process; waiting to hear back from the subcontractors
Confirm vacation dates of author of Volume 2	Proposal Coordinator	Not yet started
Notify printer of schedule	Proposal Coordinator	Complete
Find out correct spelling of product referred to in figure on page 6	Proposal Coordinator	Not yet started
Approve design for proposal cover	Proposal Manager	Complete
Rephrase question about requirement 5.3.7 and send question to customer	Contract Manager	In process
Get details about degrees and certifications from proposed program manager	Volume 3 Author	In process; waiting for program manager to return from overseas trip
Set up room for review teams	Proposal Coordinator	Complete
Find additional person to format the proposal in the week after red team	Proposal Manager	In process; person identified but assignment not confirmed

Source: APMP Body of Knowledge

For example, the responsibility matrix assigns a responsible party to each uniquely assignable item in the outline. The responsibility needs to be unique so you have one accountable person for each section or requirement. Figure 13-3 offers a sample template for your responsibility matrix.

Headings for Responsibility Matrix
Customize the content of your responsibility matrix to customer instruction and the opportunity.

Section (section number of each question)	Section/Subsection Title (identifies each question or requirement)	Page (where each question is found)	Response Reference (references name and page number of documentation that you supply as part of the response)	Comments

Source: APMP Body of Knowledge

TIP

You can convert your compliance matrix into a hybrid "compliance/responsibility matrix" that will kill two birds with one stone. If you do, you need to remove the internal responsibilities before including it in your proposal.

Writing to spec with templates

Although templates can simplify planning and tracking tasks, they're most valuable for creating content for your proposal. Templates can help you overcome a number of major challenges in proposal writing, including

>> Ensuring that authors address the appropriate topics

>> Building consistency in style and topic treatment across multiple authors

>> Coaching authors to include themes and value propositions in responses

>> Keeping authors in line so you can meet page count constraints

As you see in the following subsections, templates can improve the quality of your RFP responses, your proactive proposals, your graphics and illustrations, and more.

TIP

You may want to create templates for special proposal sections such as résumés, past performance, corporate experience, or executive summaries. In all your templates, use tables to organize frequently referenced information (such as dates, project names, or staff titles). Tables also provide an easy structure for concepts like questions and answers, features/benefits, and customer/competitor, which you can use throughout the proposal.

Creating your templates

You need to create at least two authoring templates: one for RFP responses and one for proactive proposals. Our proposal team created two new ones each year, mostly to ensure that we complied with company branding guidelines (we received new typefaces and icons every year) but also to stay current with publishing and design trends. Although we wanted to maintain a consistent image for the benefit of our customers, we didn't want to look like yesterday's proposal. As a result, our templates always focused on the customer, with placeholders for customer-specific images and thematic references.

Most word-processing and design software applications allow you to create document templates. You just have to make sure everyone who contributes to your proposal is using the same software and the same version (this may be an issue if you partner with other firms on solutions).

Select the appropriate template to match the opportunity. Introduce and distribute your proposal template to your team during the kickoff meeting. If you're writing a proactive proposal, review the templates section with the authors. Set expectations so each author follows the set styles and structure.

TIP

If you're working on an RFP response, merge the customer's RFP into your response template and adjust it to include all the customer's guidelines you discovered during your shredding process. You want your template to carry your response but also respect your customer's formats and specific requirements.

REMEMBER

Your proposal template must first be compliant. For instance, the customer may specify the paper size, its margins, the font, and the number of pages allowed. Follow these requirements to the letter. If the customer has no specific requirements, comply with your organization's branding or style guidelines. If none exist, follow the standards used most commonly in your industry.

TIP

Your template must reinforce consistency, not only in reflecting stated customer requirements but also in communicating your organization's professionalism. Any inconsistencies in structure, use of colors, fonts, imagery, or layout orientation suggest a change in meaning. If you fail to explain any intentional shifts, you may appear unprofessional, inept, or lazy.

Designing effective RFP response templates

Templates give you a head start on every RFP by predefining key structural, design, and layout criteria. Your RFP response template can be little more than a header and footer shell, because you usually have to follow the stipulations of the customer's RFP. Plus, you never really know what's coming unless you've responded to a customer or consultant's RFP before. So for an RFP response template, less is truly more.

Even so, your templates should reflect the best practices we laid out in Chapters 10 and 11 (like the customer's logo — if approved by the customer — or name in the header and your organization's logo in the footer), corporate styles (that you may have to comply with to publish your work), and other limitations (such as physical production or electronic file sizes). Train your response team so they know how to use the template and meet your expectations.

Although you may not be able to fully control the layout, typographical, and graphic elements of your RFP response, if you're responding to a question-and-answer-style RFP, you can use a template for consistently answering the customer's questions. In Chapter 9, we describe a four-part RFP response model (five, if you include the customer's question) that makes a nifty template for these types of proposals, as you see in Figure 13-4.

In your kickoff meeting, demonstrate how to write within the response model template, distribute the template to your authors (insert the customer's question to make life easier), and set a short deadline for a few submissions so you can review them and provide specific feedback to the authors. Your responses will then have a cohesive framework.

Section	Directions
Question/Customer Requirement	*Include the customer's question or requirement as a search device, highlighting key words and potential metatags.*
Respondent should describe in detail its general approach, strategies, and methodologies used to assess and develop a successful implementation plan for this type of initiative.	
Restatement (TOPIC)	*Recast the customer's question in a topic sentence that indicates your understanding of the question/context and expresses an affirmative or negative response.*
<COMPANY> has proven strategies and methods to assess and develop a successful implementation plan for this project.	
Brief Answer (COMMENT)	*Write comments that support your restatement assertion. This section may be the extent of your proof or a set-up for greater detail in the Expanded Answer section.*
We approach projects of this scope through a defined program management process. In the initial phase, ...	
Expanded Answer (COMMENT)	*Write comments that support your restatement assertion. This section expands on your proofs, provides a pertinent example of past performance or capability, or describes an illustration in detail.*
After the initial phase, we develop the following: • Current state assessment design and roadmap • Project roadmap and project plan Then, the <COMPANY> team will execute against the project plan. <COMPANY> uses key personnel to manage the work of the project...	
Payoff Statement (POINT)	*Write a key takeaway for your reader to one of these ends: summary, conclusion, restatement, transition, resolution, deduction, emphasis, consequence, enumeration of benefits, or differentiation.*
By following <COMPANY>'s approach, you will have the defined strategy and experienced resources to help ensure a successful implementation.	

FIGURE 13-4: This four-part question-and-answer template not only ensures consistent responses from authors, but it also creates a model for answering questions in your content repository.

Source: APMP Body of Knowledge

Designing effective proactive proposal templates

Your proactive proposal template needs to define all layout and typographical elements. Create your ideal proposal structure, save it as a template in your word processor, and post it so other proposal writers, your sales reps, and other contributors can use it. To get you started, we provide a sample proactive proposal template you can access through the link we provide in the appendix.

Your template needs to define the following:

>> **Final production information:** How will you print and bind the proposal? Will you send it electronically? What is your preferred page size and orientation (8.5 x 11 or A4; portrait or landscape)? What limits will you set for the number or type of design elements?

>> **Page margins:** What margin widths do you want on the top, bottom, left, and right of your pages? Will you need a wider interior margin to accommodate certain types of bindings?

>> **Column size and number:** How many columns do you want for your text? One column is the most common and easiest format to work with, but two columns can increase visual interest and the amount of text you can put on a page. Do you need to plan space for tables, callout boxes, or graphics?

>> **Header and footer style:** Apply headers and footers to the top and bottom of every page. You may want to include identifying markers such as a company logo, the name of the proposal, the chapter or section name, and the submission date. For two-sided printing, create mirror-image headers and footers for a professional appearance.

>> **Font family or typeface:** Specify the font family by using your word processor's style function. You need to further define how to treat the following types of textual information:

- **Body or normal text:** Used for most text-based information.

- **Headings:** Used to break up large blocks of body text; these may be a different font family, color, or size depending on heading levels.

- **Bulleted lists:** Used to highlight content that is otherwise buried in paragraphs; these lists need a consistent symbol before each item, such as a small ball, square, or dash.

- **Callout or testimonial style:** Used to emphasize textual messages from body text; this may include design elements, such as a color or a box around the text.

TIP

Choose fonts based on your customer's instructions or your organization's style guide. If no guides are available, choose a common and legible *serif* font (such as Times New Roman or Cambria) for body text and a *sans serif font* (such as Arial or Calibri) for titles, headings, and captions. Use type no smaller than 10 or 12 point (outside of graphics or tables, which may be as small as 8 point).

>> **Colors:** Use color to bring needed contrast to typographic and design elements. Many layouts use a colored line to separate headers and footers from body copy. Color is also effective in tables to highlight headings or stubs and in headings to denote hierarchy.

TIP

Choose your customer's color palette when possible.

>> **Graphics styles:** Specify how you want graphics to integrate with text. Generally, design your graphics to physically fit within the margins or columns of the document, size them for appropriate resolution (for print or online viewing), and place them to appear after you reference them in the text. Include an action caption beneath each graphic placeholder (refer to Chapter 11 for the scoop on action captions).

TIP

Don't edit or resize graphics within your word-processing or desktop-publishing software if you created them in a separate program. Doing this will distort them. Refer to Chapter 11 for more on maintaining graphic quality.

Creating images with templates

A graphic template is a great tool for quickly developing consistent, quality graphics. It also eliminates the need for reformatting. When working with a team, your template ensures that all graphics look as if one person or organization created them. The resulting graphics demonstrate that the solution provider is acting as a team with a consistent vision.

REMEMBER

To follow your template, choose a color palette, image or icon style, arrow style, font, line spacing standard, and capitalization scheme — and stick with it.

Proposal graphics must, above all, be understandable. Your template needs to take into consideration the following variables:

- ❯❯ The size of the graphic
- ❯❯ The medium on which it will be presented (printed or projected)
- ❯❯ Any emotions you want to elicit
- ❯❯ Your branding requirements or intentions
- ❯❯ Special considerations (for example, a vision-impaired audience, graphics duplicated in black and white for review)

Chapter 14

Leading Proposal Teams Effectively

E ven if you're a sole proprietor or lone proposal writer, your role as a proposal professional is a lot more than just writing a good proposal. For every proposal project, someone has to

>> Coordinate the efforts of a number of people with differing levels of expertise and experience

>> Massage the substantial egos of specialists and bosses (who sometimes have conflicting agendas)

>> Motivate busy people with other priorities to drop everything to contribute to your project

>> Troubleshoot problems under stressful time constraints and scrutiny

>> Ensure the consistency, accuracy, and timeliness of the proposal

Most proposal professionals do all these things while performing the majority of the writing, editing, revising, and publishing work. And sometimes these issues are compounded by a challenge of the globally connected economy: virtual teams and transglobal customers. With all of this on your plate, you may think that to be a proposal professional you have to be some kind of superhero. You don't, but you do have to be a leader — oftentimes even when you're not the *anointed* leader.

This chapter helps you meet the challenges of proposal leadership — from leading pre-proposal efforts, to guiding a team of proposal professionals and project contributors, both local and remote.

Leading Long Before the Project Begins

The engine that drives all successful proposal projects is the individual who guides other leaders and the team of contributors day in and day out, through the major crises, minor setbacks, and humdrum routines that are part of every proposal project. But proposal leaders have to think bigger than that. As you grow in the profession, you need to think beyond daily management and start thinking strategically, aligning yourself with the salespeople in your organization, getting people engaged before an opportunity appears, and anticipating what you'll need not only in the next proposal but also in those you'll be leading years from now.

The following sections take you through the key areas you need to think about in advance so you can hit the ground running when a new project arises.

Leading by doing

The best leaders of proposals are proposal professionals who can do every job that they expect others to do. We know that flies in the face of some management theories, but proposals require specialized skills — planning, researching, writing, editing, visualizing, troubleshooting, orchestrating, and production — and a good chance exists that on any given proposal you won't have all the people with the skills you need to get the job done right. That's why knowing all the aspects of proposal development is your last line of defense for saving a proposal project that's landed in the ditch, or simply for ensuring that everything is done right. Plus, you lead by example: Being with the final reviewers at 11 p.m., turning pages, and fixing little mistakes speaks a lot louder than wishing everyone success and heading home at 5 p.m.

Most proposal executives, leaders, and consultants start off as proposal writers. They prove their value and take on more responsibilities (such as editing and project leadership) until they become indispensable. As their organizations learn to appreciate their value, they bring on specialists and protégés as they create and lead a proposal center. Or they become consultants who help companies learn how to create winning proposals. Wherever they end up, they all have one thing in common: They can write one hell of a proposal.

Engaging your colleagues at every level

Proposal leadership goes in three directions: Up, across, and down. Your leadership is always under scrutiny because so many have a big stake in your success. To ensure your success, you need to guide the following people:

>> Your bosses — as high as you can go — to help them understand and advocate for your function, your processes, and yourself

>> Your peers in other departments — to help them follow your lead on proposal issues while you follow their lead in their areas of expertise

>> Everyone on your proposal team — to train and coach them into the culture and craft of proposal development

The following sections look at these three directions in more detail.

Getting executives on your side

The best way to build a professional proposal function is to have a genuinely supportive executive sponsor. Developing proposals the right way takes high-level skills. Too many companies still believe that proposal writing and production should be part of a salesperson's job or that it can be done by low-skilled office workers — on top of what they already do! The resources with the skills you need are hard to come by: They and their tools will add cost to the business and require coordination across departments to succeed. Without an executive sponsor — someone high enough in the organization to influence where the money goes and who can articulate your real value — changing that perspective is almost impossible.

Depending on the size of your business, your tactics for getting executives on your side will differ:

REMEMBER

>> **In large organizations, approach leaders of the business development function.** If your organization lacks a separate department for this function, look to sales or marketing. You have to align with those groups who understand that the customer is top priority, not your organization.

The customer is the force behind the proposal function.

To reach out to executives successfully:

● Arm yourself with success stories, internal and external, that demonstrate the value of a strong proposal development team.

● Do the math and show how the relatively small additional cost can add significantly to the organization's win rate and revenue.

- Show that you think like they do and focus your efforts on deals led by the best of their organization. Let their own people introduce you as an invaluable resource.

>> **In midsize organizations, you likely work within the sales organization.** You're the resource they choose to handle the writing work. You may not have much pull at first, but over time you'll have chances to instill standards into each proposal you write and demonstrate your value.

To demonstrate the value of your work:

- Use sales meetings to showcase your work. We say *showcase,* because leaders need to *see* what you do and how it differs from the proposals created without your help.

- Find opportunities to show your strategic thinking. Offer ideas on how to streamline the proposal process and put salespeople in front of customers instead of sitting in an office building proposals.

>> **In small businesses, you have greater access to the leader.** Aim to champion a few improvements, but always follow his or her lead. Change in these situations usually consists of gradual, hard-won improvements, such as a customer-focused cover and message instead of your organization's standard fare. Choose your battles, though — give and take is the rule.

Joining forces with your peers

If proposal writing has become a recognized function in your organization, make sure you lead across the organization — coordinating with your peers in other groups that contribute to winning new business and retaining existing business. Groups that are upstream or downstream from your process flow can have significant influence on how well you and your team get your work done. For instance, a finance group may impede your progress by requiring that you follow lengthy procedures for acquiring bid bonds, even though you come to them every other week for a new proposal. Your proposal writer doesn't have time to continually wrangle the content from the source. As a leader, you have to go to your peers in other groups to work through the kinks and streamline processes so that your specialists stay on task.

TIP

You may find it helpful to align with the following departments:

>> **Competitive analysis:** In Chapter 5, we talked about how some companies have full departments for tracking the efforts of competitors. These specialists are indispensable in helping you ghost the competition and forge messages that counter their competitive strengths. Create relationships with your peers to establish routine knowledge-sharing sessions and specialist-to-specialist relationships.

>> **Contracts:** Your peers in this department can save you a lot of time with legal reviews by anticipating problem terms and conditions (they know what your company has agreed to in prior contracts). Bring them on board for your first RFP response read-through.

>> **Finance:** If your finance department sets prices and margins, work with them to establish vivid and detailed expressions of value. Show them how you can write and illustrate key financial arguments on their behalf. They can help you not only create compelling value propositions for customers but also convince sellers that they don't have to always try to win on price.

>> **Marketing:** You may not have graphics support when you start writing proposals, so connect with the organization that usually has the budget and the resources to make your proposals more visual. But be careful: You don't want them turning your customer-focused proposals into mass market brochures.

>> **Procurement:** Make friends with those on the "other side of the table." The people who buy products and services for your business have a wealth of knowledge about buying trends and purchasing techniques. They can help you build tactics for better communications with their peers in your client companies.

>> **Sales:** Your organization's best sales reps are your main allies. Build relationships with them; find out how they win business proactively and how they respond to RFPs to see where you can add value. If they handle their own proposals, show them you're willing to do the things they don't like to do or don't do well.

Advocating for effective proposal team training

People at your organization who contribute skills or content to your proposals need to understand how your tools and processes work. This means not only your proposal specialists but those contributing experts who come from sales, engineering, finance, and operations. Your job as proposal lead is to see to it that all these specialists are trained to deliver their expertise in the way you prescribe. But deciding what they need to know and how to train them isn't as easy as it sounds.

REMEMBER

Have you heard about *just-in-time (JIT)* training — teaching users how to use tools and follow processes right before they need to work in them? This beats just-in-case (JIC) training every time (*JIC training* is like classroom training presented only once or once a year — unfortunately, students forget most of what they learned by the time they need to use it). But in the throes of a proposal, it's hard to stop and deliver JIT training or even squeeze it into a tight schedule. And some seasoned veterans don't need the full training package — they just need a refresher or an update on lessons learned.

What can you do? You have options, and we introduce these in the upcoming section. But training isn't the whole story or always the best approach, so we also tackle the importance of mentoring to take your team's expertise to the next level.

BUILDING A VARIETY OF TRAINING OPTIONS

Train people the way they learn best. Put together a training plan with documentation for all proposal development processes and software that offers a variety of approaches and matches the needs of your participants.

Your training plan may include:

>> **Classroom-based training:** Prepare a half or full day of comprehensive training that you can offer new hires as part of their onboarding process.

TIP

A shorter version of your classroom-based training can serve as JIT training for all proposal team participants. This is another great way to assert your leadership at the beginning of a project. If you're working with a lot of newcomers on a project, you can work this into the kickoff meeting (refer to Chapter 6 and to our kickoff meeting agenda and kickoff meeting briefing you can access through the link we provide in the appendix). Look on the list of activities and place your training session in the optimum slot for all attendees. If you have only one or two newcomers, you can hold a session before kickoff.

>> **Online training:** Create some simple videos or webinars that participants can review in their own time. Playing a role in these presentations also reinforces your proposal thought leadership.

TIP

Point your team to the links in the project kickoff meeting email invitation. Good leaders promote learning and preparedness every chance they get.

>> **Reference materials:** Develop some helpful process-based materials, including a list of frequently asked questions, process flow diagrams, and quick-start guides. Post them online or include them in a kickoff package. Be ready to reference them in your kickoff opening remarks (refer to Chapter 6).

>> **JIT lessons learned:** Schedule time in the kickoff meeting to bring everyone up-to-date on recent improvements in the process or new features in the proposal process tools. This again shows leadership by promoting continual improvement in your processes.

>> **Checklists and templates:** Introduce these items in your kickoff meeting and indicate where the team can access them online. Demonstrate how to use them once, and your team will take it from there. These items enforce standards and can even direct actions and outputs without you having to be involved.

TIP

Checklists and templates are a great starting point for providing help wherever and whenever a participant needs it. Make sure your checklists are comprehensive and easy to follow. Include instructions in your templates so your contributors can work independently and still meet your specifications. For examples of checklists and templates, check out Chapter 16 and the appendix.

But perhaps the best way to train your proposal team members is to have them learn from the experts as they go!

TIP

The Association of Proposal Management Professionals (APMP) offers a wealth of JIT training material in the APMP Body of Knowledge. For information about how to access the Body of Knowledge, go to www.apmp.org.

FINDING MENTORS FOR KEY ROLES

Not to shoot ourselves in the foot here, but learning how to do a proposal strictly from a book or in a classroom without hands-on reinforcement is a fairly futile endeavor. Proposal writing is definitely one of those things best mastered by doing. When we trained newcomers to our proposal center, we had them "ride along" with seasoned proposal managers to learn beyond the training material: cultural things like checking egos at the door, doing whatever it takes to make the sales client happy, and staying positive during stressful periods. You have to practice to do all these things, plus be a good writer, collaborator, and problem solver. But practicing without coaching may only reinforce bad technique. That's why mentoring is the best way to bring people along in their roles on proposal teams.

REMEMBER

Mentoring works in two ways. First, it allows new proposal writers to discover the proper procedures from seasoned professionals while offering a firsthand view into the correct ways to behave in a variety of real-life situations. Mentoring reinforces the lessons that new writers pick up in their training at the moment they'll do the most good. Second, mentoring allows mentors to practice their leadership skills on individuals before applying them to teams. A win-win situation!

EXAMPLE

In our company, we had extensive mentoring programs that developed new generations of proposal writers who discovered "our" way to prepare proposals and quickly found out how to innovate and move the organization forward. We looked at it this way: Training creates specialists; mentoring creates leaders.

Knowing where your resources lie

REMEMBER

Proposal resources are normally scarce within a business (especially if you're the only resource!). Even if you're part of a major proposal operation, you rarely have enough resources to work every opportunity your clients want you to. And here's a great conundrum: Many proposal pundits will tell you that to be successful you must be very selective about the projects you undertake (some say to avoid working on deals you aren't sure you can win!). Yet every time you fail to support a project, you risk the stigma of being regarded as unreliable or, worse, unhelpful.

LEADING WITH METRICS

Many of the metrics that companies use to grade their proposal operations are less-than-reliable indicators of value. A lot of the standard measurements, like win and close rates, tell you little about how well the proposal writer has performed. Michael Lewis's book *Moneyball* (W. W. Norton & Company) shows that you can't reliably rate baseball players based on statistics that include outcomes that are beyond a player's control. In the same way, you can't base a proposal writer's effectiveness solely on a measure that's influenced by the efforts of so many team members. For example, sometimes the best proposal is undermined by a salesperson's lousy relationship with a customer. Sometimes a service issue from years ago will taint an evaluator's perspective about your company.

Proposal leaders understand this and aim to set the story straight. And while you still want to capture and analyze traditional measures like pull-through revenue and cost-to-revenue ratios, keep them to yourself as points of comparison or to supplement other, more appropriate measures that provide a more comprehensive picture of your value, such as the following:

- **First-time clients:** Track the number of new salespeople who ask for your support. This measure indicates that their leaders and peers are recommending you.

- **Repeat clients:** Track the number of salespeople who come back with additional deals for you to support. This measure indicates satisfied clients. Create a ratio of first-time to repeat clients to understand your client base better.

- **Person-hours per proposal:** Track the hours you spend on each proposal, preferably classified by the type of work you're doing (writing, editing, administration, production, and so on). Capture ancillary statistics about each proposal (size, solution complexity). This way you can better estimate how much time succeeding proposals will take and better schedule resources.

- **Percentage reuse:** After you create a reusable content database, track what percentage of questions from a new proposal you can pre-populate with prior content. Share this with your sales leaders so they can see firsthand how you're freeing their salespeople to spend more time with customers.

These are but a few of the measures a proposal leader can use to track individual and team performance, but they give you an idea of the kinds of measures that can provide a more useful view of the value of your work.

TIP

The best way to be selective and still be seen as a ready and willing asset to your business is to work closely with sales so you know what's in their funnel. If you collaborate with sales managers and planners, you can anticipate when major RFPs will be released and when customer buying cycles are optimal for writing proactive proposals. You can then reserve resources for the deals that mean most to your sales partners, and they can come to rely on your services when they need them most.

Sometimes leadership is subordinating your role to that of others. Knowing when to do this, and when to stand strong for your methods and your team, is crucial to proposal leadership. We realized early on that proposals are part of the sales process, which is part of the business development process. It's a crucial part, but placing it ahead of the others will not win you favor. If you're the proposal lead, you have to work the system to your advantage.

If you're not already a part of the sales organization, work to be considered an extended part of their support staff. Your goal is to get into their leader's staff meetings and planning sessions. If they hold sales kickoffs, ask to present, or at least to attend. Often you can get an invitation after impressing them with your work supporting a key project. Use the invitation to identify and meet top sellers while you build deeper relationships with existing clients.

Guiding Your Team from Start to Finish

If you're managing a proposal, you have to start leading before the opportunity officially becomes a project. Your presence and leadership is crucial at several early decision-making points:

>> **During strategy and planning sessions:** You have the historical perspective to cite specific previous projects as evidence for embracing or avoiding certain approaches. Stay close to the sales team and prove yourself by taking on important fact-finding and analysis tasks, which sets the tone for the role you'll assume during the proposal (refer to Chapters 3 and 4 for opportunities to contribute thought leadership).

>> **During the bid/no-bid decision:** You have the insight and experience to determine whether the time is sufficient to win, the resources are available to win, and the commitment of the participants is sufficient to win. Come to the meeting prepared with metrics and cost figures (refer to Chapter 6).

>> **While assessing the business's readiness to bid:** You can objectively evaluate the health of projects nearing kickoff by testing how well the deal leads understand your customers' issues, how much progress they've made

developing the final solution, and how well they've resolved outstanding action items and resource issues.

>> **During the kickoff meeting:** You above all other leaders are able to quickly assess the readiness of proposal team contributors. Have their profiles ready, showing how much process and tool training each will need, what expertise each will bring, and which combinations will help establish effective sub-teams (refer to Chapter 6).

>> **During solution development:** You have an end-to-end view of the proposal, so you can best understand all content requirements. You need to devise a content plan that will identify and supply previous content that solution developers can apply verbatim or with slight modifications to fit with completely new material.

The preceding list covers the times when your leadership is crucial. The following sections present ways to lead while your proposal is in development.

Embracing the leadership role

Proposal management is daily management. Every day — heck, every *hour* — of a proposal project can mean the difference between success and failure. And everyone involved will be looking to you to keep every activity on schedule and everyone on task.

The following sections explore how you can keep track of your team, know who's doing what at every stage of the proposal process, resolve issues without breaking a sweat, and work with your team to monitor project and personal progress.

Aligning daily activities with a written proposal plan

The best-led projects start with a written plan that everyone on the team agrees to follow. This plan is basically a highly detailed view of your standard proposal process that you customize for a particular project (refer to Chapter 6). A written proposal management plan establishes a common framework of justifications, assumptions, constraints, and criteria that eliminates the need to repeat information when new people join the team. Every task that a proposal team member performs must relate to an assigned task documented in the proposal management plan.

REMEMBER

The project leader's job is to keep the plan, a living breathing document throughout the project, up-to-date. You must document any changes to the plan, especially those that affect the schedule, proposal outline, or information about the customer and the solution.

The proposal plan is your blueprint for managing the team day by day. If you discover that team members are spending time on unrelated or unproductive activities, you can use the plan to bring them back on task. If you find that the solution requires activities that weren't anticipated in the plan, you have to update the plan and see to it that all team members are aware of the changes. The plan is your daily touchstone as you create a culture of collaboration, consistency, and camaraderie.

TIP

Even if you're part of a small proposal team (or you're the *whole* proposal team!), first off, write down your plan. You must have a written plan that you (and your team, or clients, or bosses, if appropriate) can refer to. And after you've written one proposal plan, you can adapt it for future projects.

Clarifying roles and responsibilities

One of the biggest risks to successful proposal completion is confusion or uncertainty about who's supposed to do what.

WARNING

Never describe roles and responsibilities in general terms. Set your expectations clearly and specifically. Write them out to avoid confusion. Make them part of the proposal plan. These "mini-contracts" can be tiresome to prepare and communicate, but you'll be glad you took the time and effort. They will help you create a climate of accountability on the team, especially if everyone publicly agrees to follow them.

TIP

These mini-contracts are reusable, so keep a repository for future pursuits.

Wrapping an iron fist in a velvet glove

A proposal leader has to walk the line between strictly enforcing structure and formality where it's needed and knowing when to allow the proposal to run on its own. Consistent daily management is the only way to achieve this delicate balance.

Unless you work in the largest of proposal operations, many of your contributors will be moonlighting when they participate in your proposal. They have day jobs that siphon their time and attention from your project. You need to manage their efforts closely and help them to prioritize their activities daily, while still giving them opportunities to check in with their usual work groups. Indeed, most contributors outside the core team (sales, solution development, and proposal management) don't see the arc of activity on the project, and some may not understand the strategy and the larger picture, even with the help of the written proposal plan. Be firm when you need to be, but also get to know each member's situation so you can customize your management approach.

TIP

Tracking the status of proposal activities of numerous contributors in minute detail can consume all your energy and time. Early in the proposal, create a simple, visual tool to track progress on major tasks and explain how this tool works during the kickoff meeting. The tool can be as simple as a stoplight chart that shows a red, yellow, or green status for each major activity (to access a sample stoplight chart, check out the appendix).

WARNING

Don't try to capture the status of subtasks and embedded activities, the complexity behind every task, or all the possible contingencies when tracking or reporting status. Instead, use the tracking tool to share the status of major proposal tasks so the whole team stays aware of progress and setbacks.

Making daily stand-up reviews work for you — and your team

Day-to-day management helps everyone focus on what's important and keeps the entire team moving toward delivering a winning proposal. Checking in with your team daily is essential for identifying issues and risks, assigning and following up on actions, and updating the team on any changes from your customer or to your solution.

REMEMBER

In Chapter 8, we first mention the value of daily, mandatory stand-up reviews, conference calls, or videoconferences to check on your proposal team's progress (*stand-up* implies that the meetings should be short enough that everyone can easily remain standing for its duration). A daily stand-up review is like a *scrum* (to use agile software development-speak), in that it focuses on the status of key proposal activities, particularly those with imminent interim deadlines, those with long lead times, and those that are prerequisites to other critical activities. They're also a time for proposal team members to identify problems or roadblocks for the day's priorities.

The stand-up review is one of a proposal leader's best management tools, but you have to use the concept appropriately or your team will come to dread them. Leadership tips for stand-up reviews include

>> Stress them in the kickoff meeting as mandatory.

>> Keep them short to respect everyone's time and increase participation. Get a quick status check from team members responsible for proposal sections and functions and any supporting team members with pending deliverables.

>> Use them to announce changes in the schedule or priorities (don't rely on email or group messaging).

>> Allot a little time at the end to field questions to reduce one-on-one communications during the workday. Everyone will thank you for respecting their time when the project is completed.

>> Schedule them at the same time (or times) every day. Consider holding two stand-up reviews during crucial phases in the schedule — one first thing in the morning and another at the end of the day. This may seem like overkill, but we've seen many major issues avoided because we took the time to check the pulse of the project twice daily.

When contributors identify simple problems, address them right away. If they bring up complex or cascading issues, defer addressing them to a second, closed meeting. Invite only those who need to resolve or escalate the problem and set an acceptable time frame for resolution. Be prepared to read out the status of the issue at the next stand-up review meeting.

TIP

You can't check the status of every activity every day, so use your schedule and plan to ask for progress reports on milestones with near-term deadlines and progress made since the last check-in. When contributors know that they have to report on progress daily, they're more accountable and more forthcoming with problems.

But don't just think near term. Reserve part of each daily stand-up review to focus on activities that have long lead times, such as requests for information from teaming partners or clarifications from the customer.

TIP

Sometimes getting the real status from team members during a daily status update can be difficult. If any team members repeat their status on subsequent updates or never seem to identify problems, contact them privately to probe further. Do the same should you fail to hear from participants who have critical path deliverables. Sometimes they just don't want to indicate problems in front of other team members. Giving them a pass will only increase the risk of failure when you have less time to recover.

For smaller, embedded subtasks or action items that aren't major milestones but are on the critical path, use an *action-item tracking matrix* like the one we introduce in Chapter 13 to document progress and close out issues. For activities that aren't on a critical path, convene check-ins with only those contributors involved to check the status and resolve any problems.

WARNING

Skipping management chores for several days and then trying to catch up or regain control is nearly impossible. At the same time, maintaining momentum if you interfere too much is also difficult. Be sensitive to comments during check-ins and follow up privately when you sense reluctance or receive any pushback.

Timing your feedback

Giving feedback to contributors is always a tricky subject. You want to provide affirmative or corrective feedback as close to an incident as possible, but you rarely can afford to stop momentum.

REMEMBER

Years ago, we held a postmortem review after every proposal to determine what went right, what went wrong, and what we could do to reinforce good behaviors and correct bad ones. They had their value, but because the proposal had already been delivered and many from the contributing team had moved on, they weren't as effective as more immediate feedback may have been.

For all major milestones and interim deliverables, we recommend holding an AAR (after action review). The AAR is immediate: It happens quickly after an event, so it's fresh in the minds of the participants. It is brief: It usually takes less than 30 minutes (unless some major catastrophe has occurred). It's focused on outcomes, not individuals. It's positive, always pointing out successes before tackling failures. And best of all, it can be implemented as part of your process. We discuss AARs in Chapter 13 as part of capturing lessons learned and provide a template for holding AARs and capturing their findings.

Before you kick off the project, look at your proposal plan and schedule and identify the most critical activities and milestones. Schedule a formal AAR immediately after each milestone on the timeline. Quickly accumulate sufficient details about everyone's performance and the outcome of the event so you can discuss what went right and what went wrong in the briefest time possible. Then distribute your findings in a brief, formal report that

>> Identifies the milestone or deliverable

>> Identifies contributors to the milestone or deliverable

>> Summarizes the planned objectives, the actual outcomes, the reasons for the outcomes, and any lessons learned

Tracking your team's progress

In Chapter 4, we present the idea of a compliance matrix, an at-a-glance summary of how your solution matches your customer's needs. It's essentially the outline of your proposal (more usually an RFP response) that you can adapt or extend to become a project management tool: the *responsibility matrix*.

The responsibility matrix is as valuable for you as the compliance matrix is for your customer. In it, you will be able to see who is responsible for delivering content for each section of your proposal and validating compliance to the customer's requirements. You can also track due dates and even internal deliverables and tasks by adding more parameters to the matrix. To access a sample responsibility matrix, built upon a sample compliance matrix, check out the appendix.

TIP

Add your proposal responsibility matrix to the proposal management plan. You can use the matrix for daily check-ins, or, in less complex projects, you can use the stoplight chart described in the earlier section "Wrapping an iron fist in a velvet glove."

Motivating your team

The best proposal leaders are followers first (they lead within a culture of trust and mutual respect, hearing all voices before determining the path forward — and they lead by doing as well as directing). Remember, almost everyone on the team has other responsibilities. Although most recognize that the proposal is important to the organization, they may need reminding that it can also determine whether they have regular jobs to return to. But avoid the heavy-handed approach. As their project manager, you can't just tell team members what to do (you're not their real boss). You have to motivate them to care and work as diligently as you.

Consider these approaches to motivating your teams:

>> **Tell each contributor early on *why* their contributions are so important.** Understanding why is a key to motivation. When your contributors see the role their work plays in the value of the deal to the organization, they'll motivate themselves.

>> **Recognize (in a public way) the contributors who go the extra mile to complete assignments on time.** Daily check-ins are one avenue for doing this, and this opportunity for recognition may further motivate everyone to attend.

>> **Provide team members with the tools and information they need to complete their assignments**. This will help maintain motivation. Knock yourself out to get them what they need; they'll usually reciprocate.

>> **Adjust the workload whenever possible among contributors to avoid burnout.** If your proposal schedule goes longer than ten days, do whatever you can to respect your contributors' personal obligations.

Taking a Virtual Approach to Proposal Team Leadership

As companies adopt communications technology, such as mobile devices, video-conferencing, web conferencing, and cloud computing, you'll often have team members working remotely. Although some companies continue to concentrate resources in one locality and physically sequester proposal teams for the duration of a project, that is no longer the norm. As companies seek the best talent, sometimes they have to take that talent where it prefers to work. And that can add new wrinkles to how they prepare proposals.

A *virtual team* is a team in which permanent proposal team members along with subject matter experts, teaming partners, and account leads are geographically distributed and interact primarily through telecommunications. Virtual teams are governed by the same fundamental principles as traditional proposal teams — the difference lies in how the team communicates. Instead of context-rich, face-to-face exchanges, the team relies primarily on emails, file transfers, teleconferences, videoconferences, collaborative tools, and virtual meeting spaces. This means that you have to spend more time planning and paying extra attention to communication and team building.

The following sections explore how you can lead an effective virtual team.

Considering the positives and negatives

With great technology and enhanced capabilities come great opportunities, challenges, and added responsibilities for proposal leaders. Virtual proposal teams offer you several advantages. They

>> Increase your team's productivity by leveraging time-zone differences so distant team members get work done during local team members' downtime

>> Lower your overall costs by eliminating the need for physical work spaces and travel

>> Help you staff proposal teams with qualified resources because you can draw from talent wherever it is located

>> Increase your team's knowledge sharing by tapping resources from around the organization or the world

>> Support your corporate sustainability goals

But with the good come some leadership challenges, such as the following:

» Limited social interaction with your team, which can undermine your authority

» Reduced nonverbal, face-to-face communication, which can create misunderstandings and mistrust

» Additional personnel issues stemming from differing cultures and work styles

» Diminished team spirit, caused by feelings of isolation or insignificance

» Increased contributor burnout, because you can't see the symptoms developing and take early action

» Compounded version control issues because of software incompatibility

REMEMBER

If you're leading a virtual team, you must be the bridge between team members to overcome these challenges, build trust, and create cohesion.

Creating a virtual proposal center

Because virtual teams rarely interact face to face, they need a single, easy-to-access place to share resources and information. This platform — a *virtual proposal center* — can take many forms, but the proposal process remains largely the same for virtual proposal teams as it is for co-located teams. Your job as proposal leader is to make the platform work as seamlessly as if your team is co-located.

Here are some guidelines for leading virtual teams supported by a virtual proposal center:

1. **Before you hold your kickoff meeting, evaluate the RFP.**

   Bring in some contributors to evaluate the nature of the opportunity as it will affect the virtual team. You have to make sure everyone will be on the same page.

2. **Define what your virtual proposal center will look like for *this particular project*.**

   Define what features and functions the platform will support: document sharing, scheduling and tracking, version control, review cycles, or estimating and pricing.

3. **Determine the trade-offs.**

   What's most important to the business and to the team: low cost, full functionality, or ease of use? Opting for the latter is always a good idea.

4. **If you can, establish your virtual center on a website that can push information, such as announcements, calendar features, and reminders, to team members.**

   If you don't already have the capability, find tools that meet your budget and have good reviews from organizations like yours.

5. **Document what each feature does and how to use it.**

   Create a welcome packet that provides user instructions, identifies team roles, defines the process steps, and publishes team contact information.

6. **Consider all the following functions to ensure that you have the tools for effective team communication.**

   Some may be embedded in the virtual proposal center and some may be ancillary:

   - **Conference line:** If not already available, find out whether a team member has access to one. Otherwise, research available services, including Internet-based telephone services.

   - **Screen-sharing tool:** This tool lets you share and display computer screens among team members. Teams can use this to comment on and confirm content in real time.

   - **Cloud computing/centralized document sharing:** Many services are available. When selecting a cloud service, consider storage capacity, accessibility, version control, and especially security.

   - **Shared calendar:** Calendar functions for simpler proposals may mean the ability to send meeting invitations. For larger teams or more complex proposals, a shared calendar reminds contributors of critical milestones. This can be a stand-alone application or may be a feature of your cloud-computing tool.

   - **Instant messaging (IM):** IM can help a team build instant connections as members trade ideas, brainstorm, or even share personal messages. Make sure all team members can install your IM tool on their devices.

   - **Video screen capture:** This is a great tool for training team members. Digitally record step-by-step instructions, including audio. The team can then download and play videos as needed.

   - **Virtual video meeting:** Virtual meetings allow everyone to visually interact. Speak slowly and clearly, and wait for everyone to finish speaking, as other team members may experience lags in the conversation due to connectivity levels. Encourage participants to speak up and ask for clarification if they miss something.

Laying the groundwork for clear communication

When your team is virtual, you have to make sure all team members can access the reference information they need to do the job within your schedule. But it's really not that different from leading any proposal team: You need to create a master schedule that the team can access and keep the schedule updated in real time should priorities shift.

REMEMBER

When you're working up the schedule for virtual teams, you need to ask all team members a few critical questions:

>> **What hours will they work?** What hours are team members available and what is their time zone? Do they have a different definition of a work week? For example, in the Middle East, the work week runs Sunday to Thursday. Plan for four or more overlap hours for team interaction and schedule meetings during that time. Set office hours when the team can reach you during these overlap hours and notify everyone on the team.

>> **When will they take vacations or holiday?** Note these dates on the team calendar so you can plan work around schedules and everyone can enjoy time off.

>> **What is their experience with technology?** Not all team members have the same technical competency. Find out what their comfort level is so you can choose tools that everyone can use.

>> **What version of software do they run?** To save major formatting issues and ensure document stability, know what version of software each team member is using. Use the most common one as the standard and tell everyone to "save down" to that version, if possible.

>> **How do they prefer to communicate: via telephone, email, IM, or text?** Find out each team member's preference and use that method. You'll get a quicker response, and they'll know you listened.

Increase the times and ways you communicate with your team and individual teammates. Schedule regular meetings at the same time and use the same medium (for example, every Monday at 10:00 a.m. EST on the team conference line). To ensure maximum attendance, take time zones into account. If some simply can't make regular meetings because of time differences, have someone take notes and share them.

TIP

Email is still a great way to communicate, especially when you share detailed information and the receiver may need to retrieve that information at a later date (it also allows you to keep an audit trail). To improve email communication, follow these tips:

>> **Create a distribution list.** Having a distribution list saves time every time you send an email to the whole team. Keep the list up-to-date by removing team members after their contribution has finished (also a good security practice).

>> **Create a standard email template.** Use a standard structure, in plain text, including a subject line. Team members may read emails on a range of platforms, and not all support formatting. Instruct on when and how to use emoticons to clarify the emotional meaning of an email.

>> **Clearly identify the project in the subject line.** People usually scan incoming emails and trash those that don't grab attention. Clearly identifying the proposal project in the subject line helps to reduce accidental deletions.

>> **Put the key message in the body of the email.** Team members will access information on a variety of platforms and may not be able to open attachments. If they can't open them immediately, they may never see the information embedded in them.

TIP

Because virtual teams rarely have the opportunity to form in-person relationships, proposal professionals must use different techniques to strengthen communication and build rapport among teams. These techniques include

>> **Picking up the telephone:** Place a call to all team members — those you already know and those you don't. Show that you're ready to listen to them. Get to know team members and what issues or concerns they have. Find out what they do both in and out of the office.

>> **Acting like you're speaking face to face:** During a conference call, get up from your desk. Walking around or simply moving your arms greatly improves the sound of your message. Voice opinions as you would in a regular meeting. This encourages the rest of your team to do likewise.

>> **Setting reasonable expectations:** Get all team members' buy-in on project goals. Articulate the common goal. Explain how you intend to manage the bid to reduce their overtime. Set the schedule, and keep it.

>> **Celebrating each milestone:** At the beginning of each meeting, acknowledge team members who've met deadlines or celebrated a special event. Acknowledge the team for a successful review. Send e-cards for personal celebrations and accomplishments. Hold a virtual reward ceremony when the proposal is finished.

Conducting virtual kickoffs and reviews

Virtual kickoff meetings and reviews don't differ in kind from those of a regular proposal team except in the methods you use to conduct them (for guidance on running a kickoff meeting, refer to Chapter 6). The following sections explore some helpful methods for running successful virtual kickoff meetings and reviews.

Kicking off the proposal virtually

Your virtual kickoff meeting has the same structure as an in-person meeting, but it may be even more important for virtual teams (see our kickoff meeting agenda and kickoff meeting briefing package that you can access via the appendix). As you would for any kickoff, prepare a clear agenda and distribute all the necessary documents electronically, in advance.

REMEMBER

But here's where your approach has to differ. With a virtual kickoff, you have to demonstrate your enthusiasm through your tone of voice and the words you choose. Your delivery must convey a strong sense of organization and calm resolve while at the same time being upbeat about winning. Start by stating the strategic benefits of success to the participating organizations and your customer. This gives the team confidence in your leadership and encourages them to share your enthusiasm for preparing the winning bid, even though they may be on the other side of the world. A dull or tentative presentation, in contrast, may begin a tide of negativism.

At a minimum, schedule a teleconference line and a screen-sharing tool for the kickoff. If you can, use videoconferencing so the team can match names with faces. Add training to the agenda to demonstrate how the team will use the virtual proposal center and how to access training tools or 24-hour support. Training on your content plans, including how to use style guides and templates for inserting descriptive content, win themes, competitive ghosting, and graphics, is also appropriate. This will help team members develop content by using a single voice, even though they're not physically working together.

Running virtual stand-up reviews

Depending on the schedule, team availability, and complexity, virtual stand-up reviews can take several forms (refer to the earlier section "Making daily stand-up reviews work for you — and your team" for more on these). For small or fast-track proposals, the review can simply be a daily email (you can color code or use bold text to indicate upcoming deadlines; for example, bold red text may indicate an overdue deadline).

TIP

For larger teams, use a teleconference line and screen-sharing tools, or for more formal reviews, a videoconference.

"Live" daily stand-up reviews ensure that everyone stays engaged. Conduct them just as you would in-person stand-up reviews.

Reviewing documents virtually

The type and frequency of the reviews you hold depend on the schedule and complexity of the proposal. You can hold full virtual meetings (like the regular reviews we discuss in Chapter 12 but held using your collaborative toolkit) or peer-to-peer reviews, in which reviewers independently evaluate documents and send them back to the virtual proposal center for collating and final edits.

After you define the number, types, and methods to use for your document reviews, confirm the reviewers' availability, their familiarity with the review format, and their proficiency with review tools or software. If a team member can't use a particular tool, work out another way for him to submit his comments, or excuse him.

Final proposal reviews can be a challenge for leaders when you can't work face to face with your reviewers. Before the review, send an email with clear instructions to reviewers on how to meet your expectations. Better still, call them, introduce yourself and explain your role, thanking them for their willingness to help make the project a success. Clearly define the purpose of the review, the process the review will use, and what the final product should look like. Close the call by explaining how the reviewer will receive documents and the process for you to receive their input and for any clarifying follow-ups. After the review, be sure to send a note of thanks and inquire if the reviewer will be willing to review other proposals after a suitable time has passed.

If your virtual review is less formal (for instance, a peer-to-peer review) email your reviewer instructions on how to send comments and when you need them back. Give reviewers 24 to 48 hours to respond. After you send the email, call all reviewers and confirm that they received your instructions and can meet the deadline.

The usual methods for reviews will also apply to virtual reviews. Refer to Chapter 12 for more in-depth discussion of final proposal reviews.

REMEMBER

Communicating with team members from different cultures is often a challenge. Culture influences writing style, sentence structure, and spelling. Avoid using acronyms or local references in your own communications.

Chapter 15

Making Each Proposal Better than the Last

I n Chapter 13, we talk a lot about tools and systems that can help you develop your proposals more efficiently and effectively. Although tools are great, they're no substitute for knowing how to develop proposals the right way so you can create them regardless of the number of tools or amount of support you have at your disposal. This chapter is all about strategies and techniques to improve your processes and proposals every time you write a new one.

Most of our recommendations come from the Association of Proposal Management Professionals (APMP) — that group of proposal "nerds" (and we mean that in the most respectful way) that we found early in our proposal careers. They're the gurus who trained us, the hard-headed traditionalists who argued with us, the eggheads who humbled us, the mentors who coached us, the sponsors who persuaded us, and the giants who let us stand on their shoulders so we could make great livings developing proposals and then distill all that experience into this book. You could say that we're saving the best for last, because making each proposal better than the last is the mark of the true proposal professional.

Improving with Every Opportunity

In Chapter 12, we encourage you to build in periodic reviews along your project timeline to ensure that you're getting everything done that needs to be done at the appropriate times, to evaluate the quality of proposal components, and to identify problem areas so you don't forget them or disregard them after you complete the proposal. But these reviews alone won't necessarily mean that you do a better job on the next proposal. You need a concerted effort — a *lessons learned management process,* to borrow a term from knowledge management — to make sure you continually improve.

TIP

Add two kinds of lessons-learned reviews to your proposal process: external and internal. *External* reviews with your customers are sometimes harder to establish because they mean asking them to tell you what you did right and wrong, and customers rarely have the time to sustain relationships beyond the one they have with the provider they select. But *internal* reviews are no cakewalk, either: Many of your proposal contributors go straight back to their day jobs and gladly leave the added work and stress of the completed proposal behind. Some may have moved on to the next one, too (like you, the proposal writer).

Still, you can't get better if you don't reflect on what you've done. So take the initiative and set up a lessons-learned process to review what worked and what didn't, standardize what did work, and discard or retool what didn't. In the following sections, we look at external (customer) and internal (colleague) reviews in detail.

Learning from your customers

The best feedback you can get — the best lessons learned — are those you get from your customers. A customer-focused lessons-learned review eliminates the guesswork and internal politics. It lets you know whether your team effectively captured the customer's perspective as you were planning the solution and whether the customer actually noticed it.

TIP

Ask for this review as soon as possible after the customer reaches a decision, because as with any internal review, the closer to the decision or action, the better the intel. During the review, your focus needs to be on how you can

>> Better analyze an opportunity.

>> Improve your methods of collecting opportunity-specific information.

>> Incorporate that information into a proposal.

REMEMBER

Every win and loss is a chance to improve your processes and deliverables. Not all customers will work with you this way; when they do, make the most of the opportunity.

Here are two approaches to getting the information you, your contributors, and company leadership needs to perform better on subsequent opportunities with specific customers (and with all potential customers, for that matter).

Debriefing with your customer

Customer lessons-learned reviews provide substantial information that can increase your organization's effectiveness. In some settings, a customer may offer to conduct a review for all bidders. In others, your sales team may need to specifically request one.

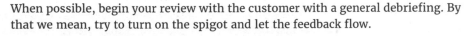

TIP

When possible, begin your review with the customer with a general debriefing. By that we mean, try to turn on the spigot and let the feedback flow.

REMEMBER

When are these reviews most useful? The logical situation for a review is after a loss. Your customer lets you know where you fell short and lends insights into how to improve your chances of winning its next opportunity. However, debriefing with your customer after a win is just as important. The post-win review may be the only way you'll ever fully understand what you did right (and the reasons may be different from what you think). And, because "win" reviews are laser-focused on the most recent proposal (and not the new relationship), they're the best way to confirm whether the discriminators that you communicated in that particular proposal were as powerful as you planned.

A professional proposal writer is usually not the customer contact, so your sales team probably sets up and organizes the customer debriefing. And though the sales team can learn great lessons from a customer review, no one will discover as much useful information as you. So do whatever you must to influence the decision to ask for a review. Promise the sales team anything — free proposals for life, free cold pizza at every deal, or shorter stand-up calls. If the session is delayed — and this happens all the time — continue to follow up with the sales team so the review doesn't fall off their radar.

Even if the review isn't their idea, most customers will dictate the method and medium for feedback. Campaign for a face-to-face meeting, but settle for a phone debriefing if that's what the customer requests. Because of their ongoing relationship, encourage the sales executive in charge of the opportunity to lead the meeting for your organization.

Support your sales executive by sharing these review process suggestions:

1. **Prepare for the customer review as thoroughly as if it were a crucial sales presentation (because it is).**

   If the customer has provided written feedback, use that to prioritize your list of topics for the review.

2. **Accept and record the feedback as is (don't become defensive).**

   Formally document the feedback so you can share it with the proposal team before subsequent bids (build your customer review using a standard list of questions like the checklist of questions for customer debrief that we point to in the appendix).

3. **Compare the feedback you receive in the review with any written comments you received after the bid (try to clarify any inconsistencies).**

4. **For strategic bids, send copies to your managers and your organization's leadership (their influence will help change future behaviors).**

5. **Send a thank-you note to the customer after the session is over.**

If your customer agrees to a formal review, allowing for the customer's preferences, encourage the following members of your team to attend:

>> The sales executive responsible for the opportunity

>> Key customer contacts from the sales team

>> The solution designer

>> A senior executive (especially for strategic opportunities)

Following up with a questionnaire

Even if your customer doesn't extend you the opportunity to review the outcome of a bid "live," you can still follow up and suggest alternative ways for feedback. Sometimes a simple email will elicit the important feedback you need. Sometimes a brief questionnaire will work, while showing that your business is all about getting better with every opportunity. Even if you don't get the feedback, you may leave a positive impression on the customer.

If the customer does respond to your query, request a debriefing by phone. This offers you an opportunity to clarify feedback and to re-engage with the customer — one more chance to turn a loss into an eventual win.

Learning from your colleagues

Our old buddy Socrates said that "the unexamined life is not worth living." We say that the unexamined proposal process is not worth repeating.

Some of your best insights into your proposal process come from the people who actually participate in it. Soon after you complete your proposal, schedule an internal lessons-learned session to analyze what went right and not-so-right.

TIP

Although you want to let the team rest a little before you hold the review, don't wait too long. You want the bid experience to be fresh in their memories, but you also want to provide your team with sufficient time to reflect. If the project was particularly stressful and trying, grant them a little more time to decompress.

It's your job to plan and lead the session and to sustain a constructive and positive approach throughout the review (after all, it's *your* process). To help participants provide constructive feedback, create a nonthreatening atmosphere — focus discussions and critiques on the project, not the people.

We present some guidelines and techniques in the next two sections to help you create more effective lessons-learned capture sessions with your colleagues.

Shaping your lessons-learned sessions

A defined structure helps to make external lessons-learned sessions more productive (refer to the earlier section "Learning from your customers"). The same applies to internal reviews.

TIP

To formalize the structure of an internal session:

>> **Notify participants in advance by sending email invitations and copying in everyone's bosses.** In your email, include these high-level questions. They set the tone of the session, direct attention to the proposal itself, and hopefully pre-empt personal attacks.

- How well did we understand the customer's business?

- How well did we understand the expressed requirements?

- How well did we anticipate unstated needs or secondary issues?

- Did our strategy align with the customer's vision?

- Did we accurately assess the market and competitive landscape?

- Did our price match the customer's budget and expectations?

- How did our approach, our discriminators, and our value proposition compare to those of the winner?

>> **Attach to your invitation a form for capturing lessons learned (get access to a sample in the appendix and see the next section, "Collecting internal lessons learned") so participants can prepare.** This form will prepare them to discuss all aspects of the bid, including the following:

- New insights into your process and people's strengths

- Honest assessments of your process and people's weaknesses

- Specific examples of what went right with your process

- Definite process steps where your team needs to improve

REMEMBER

Coupled with lessons learned from the customer review, the internal review provides a complete picture of the project that can spur a culture of continual improvement. To achieve this lofty goal, you need to

>> Instruct participants to offer remedies to balance each criticism.

>> Encourage all voices to speak up — keep an eye out for introverts and ask for their input.

>> Intervene to focus feedback on issues, not people, if any feedback gets personal.

>> Press for agreement on the lessons learned so you can close the meeting with a list of next steps you can deliver.

>> Document all approved recommendations in the lessons-learned form, and share with the appropriate process owner.

TIP

Make sure that someone with authority distributes and follows up on recommendations so they become part of each participating department or workgroup's improvement plans. Change management works best with an executive sponsor.

Collecting internal lessons learned

For your lessons-learned form, you need a simple but effective tool to collect and store the knowledge the team generates during the internal review. All these approaches can succeed:

>> **Word-processing form:** You tab through form fields to capture the team's responses and suggestions and then file these in a shared-access folder.

>> **Relational database:** You capture input in columns and rows so you can search for all comments by category, opportunity, or any number of search criteria.

>> **Web survey:** These collate individual inputs and place them into a single report.

Whichever approach you take, the tool must do the following:

>> **Identify** specific problem areas.

>> **Capture** sufficient detail to help you correct those problems.

>> **Categorize** problems to help you track particular problems over successive proposals.

>> **Share** the knowledge with all process owners and participants.

TIP

Include questions like these as part of your lessons-learned tool:

>> How effective were our sales planning and proposal processes?

>> Were senior managers involved at appropriate points?

>> Was the proposal compliant, responsive, persuasive, and clear?

>> Did we budget correctly for the opportunity (people, time, and money)?

>> Did we manage review and decision milestones properly?

>> Did we hold appropriate reviews? Were they effective?

>> How well did we meet deadlines and milestones?

>> How well did the teams work together?

REMEMBER

Lessons collected are not lessons learned. You must have a process for harvesting, tracking, and communicating lessons learned to responsible stakeholders. A perfect time to review the resulting process changes is in future proposal kickoff meetings or pre-proposal training sessions.

COMPARING YOUR PRACTICES WITH THE BEST

If you can't get your customers or even your colleagues to participate in lessons-learned reviews, you can continually improve your proposals by comparing what you do with what the best practitioners do. In fact, smart proposal writers do this anyway. It's not that hard to do, and you'll reap the benefits of probably thousands of internal and external lessons-learned reviews that have over time established these best practices.

You can find best practices for proposal development from a variety of sources. You can search the web, using simple text-based searches. You can join professional associations like the APMP, which provides you with unlimited access to its Body of Knowledge (the source of much of this book; the APMP's Body of Knowledge is a living, changing summary of best practices gleaned from proposal professionals from around the globe, in every industry you can imagine). You can go back to school: Many colleges and universities have business and technical communication programs that offer courses in proposal writing. You can create benchmarking studies (to systematically compare your processes with those of other recognized leaders) or reference studies created by analysts that give insights into how the best in your industry win business through proposals.

Both lessons learned and best practice comparisons offer great benefits, but they can take a while to implement and, as they mature, require enabling technology (for example, consider how many proposals you submit each month and how quickly your database of lessons will grow). Smart proposal writers start thinking this way early in their careers, and as their organizations grow, they find their careers trending upward as well.

Collecting Content for Reuse

The more proposals you write, the more you realize that you've done it all before — the product description, the organization's history, the need, features, and benefits statement, and even the value propositions. How can you stop the merry-go-round?

Most proposal professionals are able to stay on the merry-go-round by implementing *knowledge management* (the practice of getting the right information to the right people when and how they need it). The following three sections will help you understand the intersection of proposal management, proposal content management, and proposal knowledge management.

Building your content repository

When you reach the tipping point of not having enough time to write each proposal from scratch, it's time to build and manage your proposal content repository. Many proposal organizations create repositories so they can store content to eliminate rework, reduce search time, and, if the content is *clean* (devoid of formatting and customer-identifiable references and edited for clarity, concision, and completeness), improve quality.

A successful repository does the following:

TIP

>> **Follows a thorough classification scheme:** Unstructured content is useless — the knowledge can neither be easily found nor readily reused. Building a *taxonomy* (a hierarchy of terms where lower-level terms are more specific instances of higher-level ones) for your content based on your particular business requirements and proposal content categories (like features, benefits, and implementation steps) is crucial for finding your knowledge assets after you've stored them.

>> **Takes an object-oriented approach:** A good repository is built up from the most distinct level of content units you can create and still manage. We like to call these content nuggets *fundamental content objects* — your FCOs, the kernels of information you have ready to apply to your next project. If you respond to Requests for Proposals (RFPs), your best FCO is the question-and-answer pair. If you primarily create proactive proposals, your FCO may be a particular proposal section or subsection that you use in every proposal or content that's even more distinct and precise.

TIP

Don't confuse an FCO with that bad word of proposal writers, *boilerplate.* Because they perform discrete communication functions (like answer questions, define terms, or describe benefits), you can easily customize FCOs for new audiences or purposes while retaining the fundamental content you want to express.

>> **Uses a robust search engine:** If users can't find the right knowledge, they can't reuse it. Even if your repository is a file share, your taxonomy will help. But at some point, you'll want a searchable content repository — one that uses a search engine. So, from the beginning, create a list of keywords that describe what the content is about or what it does. Associate keywords with all your FCOs to help users narrow their searches. If your organization allows you to, opt for a search engine that also searches text by using single words, strings of words, and *Boolean searches* (that is, adding words like *or, not,* and *and not* between search terms, as in "benefit *and not* feature") to further streamline their searches.

>> **Includes a way to measure the usage and effectiveness of your content:**
A content repository can be an administrative nightmare if you can't determine what content is useful and findable. As soon as your resources permit, use an analytics program that can tell you

- Who your users are

- What they search for

- How long they take to search

- What content they take away

- Which keywords work and which don't

>> **Has a rigorous implementation and update plan:** Without guidelines for governance, repositories can quickly become unwieldy data dumpsters — holding some of the information you need and a lot you don't, with no way to tell the difference. (Think "needle in a haystack.") Decide who's responsible for managing and updating content. If you're the lone proposal person, it will be you. You'll thank yourself later for doing this (and any who follow you will think you're a genius).

EXAMPLE

Content repositories are for every size of enterprise and proposal team. Our first proposal content repository was a Microsoft Word file with headings to label each reusable content chunk. As it grew and became unwieldy, we moved to a database program on a desktop computer. Our peers heard about it and we sent them content when they asked for it. The repository kept growing, so we moved it to a file-sharing site where the entire proposal team could access it. Over time, we transformed it into a web-based content gathering, authoring, storing, and repurposing system that generated tens of thousands of proactive proposals each year and pre-populated hundreds of RFP responses in question-and-answer format. That took years. Today, technology makes doing this easier and cheaper than we could have imagined possible.

Choosing your content objects

Here's a blinding flash of the obvious: Reusable proposal content comes from proposals. Well, that's not always the case, but it's how it usually starts. You write proposals, and you realize you're reinventing the wheel on certain topics time and again. Therefore, you save content objects in your repository and use them until they get old and lose their value.

What you put in your content repository depends on what you need. What do you reuse most often? What would keep you from searching through prior proposals? What would save you time?

TIP

Start small and watch your collection grow. Group objects with similar topics (start shaping your taxonomy right away). Find key facts you can reuse that won't go stale for a year or more. Many proposal writers start their repositories with reusable proof points that cross operational boundaries, such as number of employees with certification (human resources), incidences of superior past performance (project or contract management), financial reports and projections (finance), your organization's history and philanthropy (public relations), and performance commendations, testimonials, and success stories (sales). Even reusable nuggets like tax identification numbers and banking information can save you a lot of time and have a place in your repository.

REMEMBER

Some content objects are *evergreen* — that is, they don't change very often, if ever. Some change so often that you need to verify their accuracy with each succeeding proposal. When that happens, start talking with the sources of these objects and work out a deal to have them update your repository routinely. Then you're really in business.

To help you visualize how a content repository works, look at Figure 15-1. This *knowledge map* (another term borrowed from knowledge management) shows common sources for proposal content on the left and top and how their information flows to the proposal manager, through the review process, and on to the customer via a proposal. Notice the box labelled *KM Team.* This stands for *knowledge manager* — the person who reviews the final proposal content and harvests reusable content from it. The KM Team then populates the content repositories (after a while, you'll probably need to create special collections of reusable content such as frequently asked questions and answers, full versions of published proposals, special requirements from consultant-led RFPs, incidences of past performance as those shown in the figure, and more as your needs require), and these in turn provide a source of reusable content to the proposal manager for the next deal.

TIP

For a comprehensive list of potential reusable content objects, see our proof points tracking checklist by referencing the appendix. You can use this checklist to inventory and maintain a repository of reusable proof points. Check out, too, our tools in Chapter 13, especially those that support content reuse while helping you manage the proposal process.

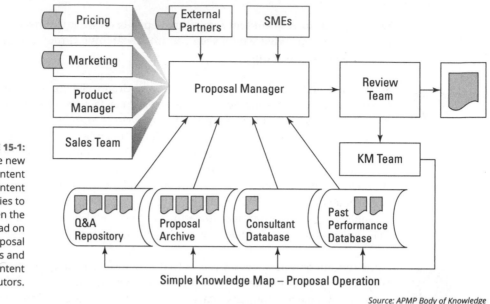

FIGURE 15-1:
Move new
proposal content
into your content
repositories to
lessen the
workload on
proposal
managers and
proposal content
contributors.

Simple Knowledge Map – Proposal Operation

Source: APMP Body of Knowledge

Applying knowledge to the next proposal

Most proposal writers have stories about how a customer's name from a prior bid made an accidental guest appearance in a new proposal for another customer. This oversight is obviously not cool. But it can happen if you pilfer directly from prior proposals. You're in a rush. You cut and paste. You don't notice it, or you say, "I'll catch this in the review," and move on. You edit and miss it again. Your reviewer misses it. The customer doesn't.

TIP

To successfully apply reusable knowledge to your next proposal, follow this process:

1. **Scrub all content for specific references to customers: names, locations, times, and terms from the customer's industry.**

2. **Check recent proposals to see whether a different wording of the content nugget exists, and compare to make sure you use the best version.**

3. **Insert your reusable content into your proposal or response template.**

4. **Apply a distinctive format (bold, italic, color) to any reusable content chunks you use so your contributors can quickly identify them.**

5. **Confirm with your expert contributor that the content nugget is appropriate for this solution and still accurate.**

6. **Note any shortcomings or alterations your expert contributor makes to the content so you can update the nugget in your repository.**

   Consider adding a second version of the content nugget if your expert contributor says the original still has value.

7. **Scan your proposal for your formatted reuse chunks to make sure they're ready for final review.**

8. **Reformat the reused content to match the format of the rest of your proposal text.**

9. **Use your word processor's Find function to perform a final global search for rogue words/terms in the proposal before you send it out.**

TIP

Many repository managers use a placeholder or variable name like *<CUSTOMER-NAME>* to replace actual customer names in reusable content nuggets. This helps to eliminate the problem of using the wrong customer name and allows you to use a global Find command to ferret out unedited content flaws.

Getting and Staying in Proposal Shape

After reading this book, you'll have a solid foundation for writing commercial proposals and managing proposal teams. But if you want to make proposal writing a career, you need ways to keep up with new tools, techniques, and processes in the profession. Business moves way too fast to rely on what you've done before. For instance, in a matter of months, our proposal team changed from printing proposals to delivering almost all of them digitally. Decades-old practices can change radically in the blink of an eye.

REMEMBER

Proposal training is good for you and for your business, so talk to your boss about picking up the tab. The benefits to your organization include keeping up with the best practices of other companies (maybe even your competitors) and improving business development processes that increase revenue and lower costs. Benefits to you and your peers include enhancing your personal skills and professionalism while improving morale and job satisfaction.

Fortunately, you have many informal and formal options for getting better at your job, so we take a look at your options in the following sections.

Joining a professional organization

Professional associations offer important services and resources for people who want to rise to the top of their field. In the proposal business, the APMP has defined best practices and offers training programs that build competencies and skills, drawing from the work of more than 7,500 members in over 100 countries. The APMP sponsors training through an approved network of training organizations. These organizations ensure that learning is current and based on proven adult learning theory.

APMP membership prepares you and your staff for a higher level of winning. The APMP defines the path to improving your organization's business development, proposal management, writing, and graphics skills. Keep on top of industry strategies and stay ahead of industry trends through affordable education and member networking opportunities.

Membership benefits include

>> Free, unlimited access to the APMP's Body of Knowledge (refer to the earlier sidebar "Comparing your practices with the best"), which includes best practices, templates, and resources.

>> Free, monthly access to APMP webinars (12 per year), which provide ongoing training on timely proposal topics from acknowledged experts.

>> Free access to APMP compensation studies that identify where your salary ranks with other professionals in your role.

>> Free access to the APMP Job Bank, which lists career opportunities within the proposal industry. It also allows potential employers to search for individuals' CVs and résumés that match their needs.

>> The opportunity to attend the APMP's annual international conference, featuring keynote speakers, more than 50 educational sessions, an awards program, and the industry's best networking opportunities.

>> Regular networking and educational events organized by local APMP chapters, which offer both face-to-face and virtual networking opportunities for your convenience.

TIP

APMP live events deliver affordable opportunities to reach contacts and prospects who are, otherwise, hard to access. Local chapters around the world provide consistent-quality forums and networking opportunities.

Earning professional certifications

Organizations recognize when you enhance your capabilities and skills through continued education and professional certifications. For you to progress as a proposal writer, you need to be able to differentiate yourself from others. Certifications demonstrate that you're

>> Taking personal responsibility for improving your skills

>> Adopting the best proposal development practices

>> Improving continually to help your business succeed

>> Credible, competent, and ready to lead

REMEMBER

The APMP offers the only industry-recognized certification program for bid and proposal professionals in the world. APMP certification is the standard for developing and demonstrating proposal management competency. (Refer to the preceding section for more on the benefits of APMP membership.)

APMP's certification syllabus is a catalogue of competencies that correspond with the skills needed to handle situations that proposal professionals commonly encounter. After you're certified, you'll know and understand best practices in every aspect of business and proposal development. You'll also be able to sustain your certification status and stay up-to-date with changes in the field through continuing education credits.

REMEMBER

APMP certification has three levels — Foundation, Practitioner, and Professional:

>> **Foundation certification** is for professionals who are relatively new to the bid and proposal world. Foundation certification focuses on 22 early career competencies that proposal writers need to know to perform their jobs effectively. To achieve Foundation-level certification, you need to be an APMP member, have at least one year of experience in proposal development, and pass the Foundation level certification exam. APMP offers in-person training courses, printed study guides, and online resources to help you prepare for the exam.

>> **Practitioner certification** is for proposal professionals with three or more years' experience. It validates real-world mastery of 35 mid-career competencies based on industry best practices and the ability to lead others in using

them. To achieve Practitioner-level certification, you must be an APMP member, have achieved Foundation certification, provide a reference to verify your experience, and respond to the *Proposal Practitioner Assessment Questionnaire,* an assessment that validates your abilities against those of equally experienced professionals.

» **Professional certification** is for Practitioner-level APMP members with at least seven years' experience in the field. Individuals who reach this level of certification are known as thought leaders, change managers, and exemplary mentors in their organizations. To achieve Professional-level certification, you must provide a reference to verify your performance on behavior and attitude competencies and deliver a *Proposal Professional Impact Presentation* that demonstrates your contributions to the profession along with your communication and leadership skills. Candidates offer their impact presentations to a panel of independent evaluators.

Figure 15-2 shows the three levels of certification and key milestones in achieving them, along with continuing education requirements at each level.

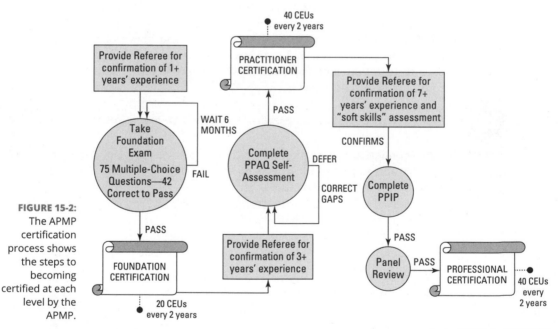

FIGURE 15-2: The APMP certification process shows the steps to becoming certified at each level by the APMP.

Source: APMP Body of Knowledge

Getting trained by the best

Adults learn best by being actively involved in the learning process. Luckily, proposal professionals have at their disposal a wealth of resources that specialize in interactive learning for the practitioner. These training organizations provide training through a variety of methods, including in the classroom, through video, and interactively online. They supply theory and practice through experiential learning based on hands-on exercises, role-playing scenarios, and case studies. Many of the finest of these training organizations work hand-in-hand with the APMP to stay current with best practices and trends while influencing advances in the profession.

The APMP lists these training organizations on its website and in its resource directory and encourages you to check them out as your training needs grow.

Mentoring and coaching for leadership

If you find yourself leading a team of proposal professionals (which this book helps you do), an integral part of your job is developing your team. Although training organizations and the APMP can provide a great foundation, true development takes place one on one, day by day, again and again.

REMEMBER

One of the most powerful types of professional development is *mentoring*, where job knowledge, experience, and skills intermingle to help a person develop. Through a mentoring program, leaders at all levels can provide useful and timely counsel to their colleagues. Usually, mentoring sessions are at set times, weekly or monthly, when less experienced mentees bring their issues to their mentors and "learn at the master's feet." Often, mentors establish a curriculum of topics, based on observations by a manager or through an initial dialogue, and systematically work through them. Mentors and mentees form strong bonds; some that last lifetimes. Some of those relationships become partnerships for innovation and mutual success.

Coaching is another strong approach to training, especially when training isn't affordable or appropriate. *Coaching* specifically aims to help people develop mastery of the knowledge they already have. It helps them develop their critical thinking and decision-making skills. Coaching usually happens one on one in an informal, unstructured environment. The goal of coaching is to improve performance and behavior on the job. Unlike mentors, coaches talk more than they listen, asking pointed questions of the people they coach.

TIP

Both mentors and coaches need to follow good management practices. These generally accepted methods may help you get started:

» Assess employee performance continually to confirm that methods to identify areas needing training and new job skills are up-to-date.

» Set definite goals that an employee can realistically measure and reach.

» Motivate the employee through assignments that contribute to the organization's mission.

» Give positive and constructive feedback so the employee knows what skills to apply or what behaviors to correct.

For more on the role of the mentor and proposal leadership skills, turn to Chapter 14.

6

The Part of Tens

Acquire, apply, and adapt ten templates and checklists to keep your proposal projects on track and your output professional. Link to online resources for even more tools that can help you do more and do it all better.

Review ten myths of proposal development that you're bound to hear at some point in your proposal career, and find out about the best practices that debunk them.

Chapter 16

Ten Templates for Building Your Proposal

The Association of Proposal Management Professionals (APMP) provides the collected best practices of the world's leading professionals in proposal, bid, and opportunity management, and business development, in its Body of Knowledge (BoK). This book is an outgrowth of the APMP BoK, and we provide a collection of references and tools online that contain a portion of the BoK's contents.

The web page that we provide includes downloadable templates for you to use and adapt that we know will streamline your proposal writing efforts. (You can find out more about the templates we provide, plus the URL, in the appendix.) We know how busy you are as a proposal writer, and these templates will take a load off your plate and your mind. They cover everything from proposal process management tools to content models. This chapter summarizes the purpose and value of ten of them.

Creating a Compliance Matrix

A *compliance matrix* is a simple, effective tool that helps you in two ways:

>> It summarizes and shows your level of compliance to the customer.

>> It keeps track of your team's approach for responding to the Request for Proposal (RFP).

A compliance matrix is basically a checklist both for you and for evaluators to make sure you comply with all RFP response requirements. The compliance matrix maps the requirements of the RFP down to the location in the response where you answer them. Because it organizes sections and subsections of the RFP, a good compliance matrix also serves as a plan of action for writers.

If your customer provides a compliance matrix as part of the RFP package, follow its format and place it in your response where the customer specifies. Insert a version of the matrix in your response before the first section that references the RFP's requirements.

Even when not specifically required, consider including a compliance matrix to make the evaluator's task easier. After all, you'll have to track your team's compliance in some way — why not share that with the evaluator?

We explain more about the compliance matrix in Chapter 4. Check out the appendix for more info on a useful template to help you build your compliance matrix.

TIP

As a bonus, we also include an expanded compliance matrix that serves as an internal responsibility matrix (refer to Chapter 14), so you can track your team's progress in responding to each requirement in the RFP.

Proving Your Past Performance

In a proposal sense, *past performance* is any favorable outcome from a solution you've implemented to solve a similar customer's problem. Past performance provides proof that you can stay within budget, stick to a schedule, and do what your customer expects you to do. And although some customers place greater importance on this than others, providing clear descriptions of your past performance can help build confidence in your solution and in your ability to perform to a customer's standards.

The best way to use past performance data is to build a file or database that classifies projects by industry, solution, or outcome and summarizes each incident so you can merely copy that information for appropriate proposals. For more information about past performance, refer to Chapter 7.

The template we recommend is a model that you can customize to create a standard for your organization. Check out the appendix for more on accessing this past performance template.

Standardizing the Proposal Model

A *standard proposal template* is a blueprint that helps contributors follow a prescribed structure and apply consistent formats and styles for their portions of a proposal. Templates with built-in styles, protected to enforce compliance, save you time and effort. They eliminate rework and the mundane work of formatting content submitted through a variety of media, such as differing word-processing programs or email formats. They standardize fonts for headings, sidebars, titles, captions, headers, footers, and body text. They can even coach writers how to craft everything from descriptive headings to action captions to product descriptions.

TIP

Use a standard proposal template with a proposal-specific style sheet and insist in the kickoff meeting that everyone contributing content uses the template and its styles.

We offer two standard proposal templates: one for responding to RFPs and another for building proactive proposals (refer to Chapter 2 for more about the two types). Check out the appendix for more on how to access these templates online.

Keeping Up with Your Costs

Large and midsize organizations usually designate a specific budget for *bid and proposal (B&P) expenses,* which defines the amount these organizations allocate annually. Then they divide the annual amount into budgets for specific opportunities. A B&P budget may include the end-to-end costs of winning the bid or only the cost of developing the proposal.

The biggest part of a B&P budget is labor, based on the number of hours or work units that the proposal team spends on a particular effort. Labor costs for proposals include the wages, salaries, and *loadings* (the overhead for benefits, administration, and facilities that go in to accounting for the total costs for employees) for a business developer, an opportunity manager, the proposal manager, all proposal writers, proposal editors, graphic designers, production specialists, and reviewers. Labor represents a big part of a proposal budget. The remainder is made up of software, equipment, travel, lodging, meals, supplies, and production costs.

We talk about proposal budgets in detail in Chapter 8. Check out the appendix for details on how you can access our sample budget template.

Tracking Your Customer Contacts

The *account plan* is an essential tool for managing your relationships with customers. A contact plan is usually a key part of an account plan. It is a digital or paper reference that lists your targeted customers, along with pertinent details, such as

>> Who in your organization will visit them

>> What information you want to find out from them

>> What messages you want to communicate to them

>> When and where you will meet with them

>> How you will communicate your messages to them

The plan can also allow you to document the important information you gather during your meetings. We discuss this plan and other pertinent customer information in Chapter 3.

To access a sample contact plan, check out the appendix.

Scheduling Your Process Milestones

In some markets, a proposal that is one minute late is rejected. In any market, on-time proposal delivery is the prime objective of your proposal process.

Your *proposal schedule* is a plan that outlines major milestones spanning the opportunity assessment and proposal development processes. The principles your schedule follows parallel those of project management: The schedule identifies major milestones and intervals for their completion along with any contingency plans you derive from the uniqueness of the opportunity, your organization, and your resources.

TIP

Depending on the complexity of your project, you can develop and work this plan on anything from a sheet of grid paper to a spreadsheet or project management application. The templates we recommend demonstrate how easily you can establish and manage the schedule of a simple to complex proposal.

For more on the proposal process, check out Chapter 6. To access sample schedule templates on calendar schedules for 10-, 30-, and 60-day projects, check out the appendix.

Deciding Whether to Bid

Bid decisions help disqualify sales leads or proposal opportunities that you probably won't win so you can focus on opportunities that you can win. You should re-evaluate a decision to bid before and throughout the proposal process. Because every organization has finite proposal resources and funds, smart businesses find ways to pursue opportunities they have a reasonable probability of winning.

One of the most important of these decisions is the *bid/no-bid decision*. It occurs before the proposal kickoff meeting and is the final "okay" before your business starts spending serious money to pursue the business. And while larger businesses surround the bid/no-bid decision with a series of other key decisions, like whether to enter a market or further investigate or develop an opportunity, smaller organizations can usually succeed with a single bid/no-bid decision.

REMEMBER

The bid/no-bid decision can include any factors you've gained from experience but usually includes probability of winning, long-term value to the business, cost to acquire the business, payback period, strategic fit, customer relationship, and other hard and soft measures. We explore the bid/no-bid decision in detail in Chapter 6.

To access a sample bid/no-bid decision template, turn to the appendix.

Checking Off Production Activities

After you finish your proposal, you have to produce it in an electronic format, hard copy, or both. *Production* includes all the tasks required for formatting, publishing, and delivering your proposal to a customer. Although production is always one of the final steps of a proposal process, you should plan for it at the very start of the project.

TIP

The production template we recommend outlines all the elements, processes, and considerations that can help you deliver a quality proposal. You need to include all of them in the plan with more or less detail, depending on the magnitude of the production effort. Customize the checklist to include any unique requirements for a specific proposal. (Chapters 6 and 12 consider the production process further.)

For help in making sure you have the right resources and activities for production, turn to the appendix. Two templates should prove useful:

>> A list of all the human, equipment, and monetary resources you may need (production resources checklist)

>> A checklist of standard production tasks (production checklist)

Checking the Checker

If you're lucky enough to have a professional editor on your team, this checklist may not be necessary. (If you do, you know to include your editor in your kickoff meeting and in periodic reviews so he or she isn't blindsided by a massive edit as you frantically near production.)

Still, some proposal and general documentation standards are routine enough to list and provide a road map for your editor to follow. Even the pros feel better when they can check off that last editing chore and avoid the 3 a.m. panic attack that they've forgotten to review some aspect of the proposal that will go out at 8 a.m. And this way, you can feel better that your editor has done the job as thoroughly as possible. (Chapter 12 considers the importance of bringing an editor on board to assist with finalizing your proposal.)

To find out how to access a handy editing checklist, check out the appendix.

Capturing and Sharing Lessons Learned

After you've won or lost a bid, you need to create a record of the things you did well and the things you did poorly so you can continually improve your process. We call these *lessons learned,* and you need a standard way to solicit, capture, and share them.

REMEMBER

You have two main sources for these lessons: your proposal team and your customer. Reconvene the proposal team one last time to debrief them as soon as possible after you submit your bid. Ask to debrief your customer after it has awarded the bid. Each type of debrief provides valuable but different lessons learned — and each is key to improving your win rate.

Your internal debriefing should focus on how efficiently you operated and the strengths and weaknesses of your proposal process. Your customer debriefing should try to find out how the customer evaluated the proposals, what mattered the most, how you can improve early customer interaction, what you did well, and where you can improve.

TIP

The most important first step in creating a lessons-learned program is to standardize how you capture the information. The template we recommend provides a task-focused, outcome-driven approach that will put participants' minds at ease that you're not on a witch hunt. (Chapter 15 looks at how lessons learned can add value to future proposals.)

Check out the appendix to access the lessons learned template.

Chapter 17

Ten Common Misconceptions about Bids and Proposals

When you've been a proposal writer for a while, you'll hear a lot of advice, usually from people who aren't as well versed as you in the craft of proposal management. Smile, listen, nod, and . . . *run away as fast as you can!*

Be wary of these ten misconceptions about bids and proposals, proposal processes, and proposal techniques — following any of this misjudged advice will jeopardize your and your proposal's effectiveness.

Engaging the Customer Early Isn't Important

Reacting to an opportunity — caused by when you're unaware of an RFP being released or a problem that your customer is having — is never good practice, if only because it usually gives your competitors a jump on the business. But it's worse than that. Scrambling to assemble a solution and a team to respond puts your whole organization behind the eight ball, disrupting normal business operations and siphoning resources from other important projects. And, because a proposal opportunity normally has a hard deadline that you dare not miss, a delayed start can mean a frantic finish.

TIP

Start early and be consistent. *Front-load* your projects by making proposal planning an integral part of your sales planning and business development processes. Scanning ahead for pending opportunities can give you that all-important extra bit of time to develop a responsive proposal rather than a merely compliant one. Positioning products and services early and building strong customer relationships improve your chances of winning a contract.

REMEMBER

Many believe that a compliant, responsive, and well-written proposal will win the contract. On the contrary, a proposal is more often the final step in affirming a customer's buying decision. Effective marketing, positioning, and selling — all key elements of a successful proposal process — are critical to winning business. The proposal then can do what it does best: Demonstrate the best solution.

Because proposals are all about your customers, we discuss customer relationships throughout the book. However, Chapter 3 focuses on developing strong relationships with your customers, and Chapter 4 offers in-depth strategies for understanding and responding to customer requirements.

An Executive Summary Only Summarizes Your Proposal

An executive summary is so much more than its name implies. A strong *executive summary* is a brief, targeted business case and value proposition to convince your evaluators' bosses to select you.

Unless your proposal is a page or two, always include a well-written executive summary. An effective executive summary demonstrates that you understand the customer's business, have worked with the customer to define its issues and needs, and can use the customer's own language as you describe its problem, your solution, and your unique discriminators. (See Chapter 9 for details on developing an effective executive summary.)

A customer-focused executive summary does the following:

>> Demonstrates that you understand the customer's motivation and vision

>> Recaps the customer's hot buttons (refer to Chapter 2)

>> Confirms that the solution satisfies each hot button

>> Focuses on benefits to the customer, avoiding technical content that obscures those benefits (refer to Chapters 7 and 9 for features and benefits)

>> Uses the customer's name more frequently than your organization's name

>> Is written concisely and clearly in the decision maker's preferred manner

>> Ghosts the competition (refer to Chapter 5)

Don't include your corporate history in your executive summary. If you feel (or are) compelled to include it, add it as an appendix.

Features and Benefits Are All the Same

Features and benefits are *not* the same. *Features* describe what your product or service does. *Benefits* describe what that product or service will help the customer accomplish.

How can you tell the difference? Apply the "so what?" litmus test as you review your feature and benefit statements. To make sure that your benefits aren't just reworded feature statements, ask yourself "so what?" after you read them. A feature statement won't answer the question, whereas a benefit statement will provide a clear answer. Benefit statements will clearly show not only how features solve the customer's problems but also what happens to the customer's business when it uses them.

Don't stop there — stating the benefits of a proposed feature is mandatory but still insufficient. Unless your benefit statements include verifiable proof, customers may not believe that they'll realize the benefits you claim.

REMEMBER

You have to detach yourself from your organization's usual stance on a product and look at it from the customer's perspective. If you can't, ask someone who doesn't have a technical understanding of your solution but does understand the customer's perspective to evaluate feature and benefit statements. And if you're the incumbent, don't assume that you already know the customer's needs; be as sensitive to the customer's request as your most urgent competitor.

Chapter 7 gives you all the detail you need to create feature and benefit statements that help set you apart from your competitors.

If You're the Incumbent, You've Got Nothing to Worry About

Ever suffer from the heartbreak of *incumbent-itis*? It's the arrogance and complacency that, when you're the current supplier, leads to a false sense of security, meaning you underestimate the competition. You may think that your customer won't risk changing providers because of the higher cost or the disruption of operations. Lately, this mode of thinking has proven disastrous. Incumbent win rates are on the decline, and customers are more willing to change contractors than to automatically pay a premium for retaining one.

REMEMBER

In a tough competitive market, retaining the business you have is just as difficult as winning new business, if not more so. When you have to compete to retain your business (the fact that a business is releasing an RFP should tell you something), follow the same best practices you do when you don't already have the business. Being complacent is the number-one reason customers oust incumbents.

TIP

Start earning your next contract on the day your customer awards you the first one. Start documenting your performance and make those records the key proofs to support your retention efforts. But don't stop there: Failing to push for innovation is another pitfall of incumbents. Avoid phrases like, "This is how we're doing it" or "We will continue to do these things." You must challenge yourself to offer your customers the best solution to their problems instead of simply continuing the work you do now.

We offer advice for unseating an incumbent in Chapter 5. If you're the incumbent, look in the mirror as you read the section.

Always Use Business Speak and Buzz Phrases in Your Proposals

"Our solution is award-winning, best in class, state of the art. . . ." Do any of those boasts bear any burden of proof? Hasn't your customer heard those empty adjectives a million times already? A proposal isn't a high-school essay that you need to pad to make ten pages. Cut the fluff, jargon, and clichés. Nobody wants to read that anymore (as if they ever did).

REMEMBER

Proposals are all about the audience — your customers (in particular, their evaluators and decision makers). To persuade them, you have to make sure you filter everything you say for them. A proposal steeped in business speak persuades your audience to move on to the next proposal.

So how do you set those filters? Consider the following:

>> Talk to the people in your organization who know the customer and ask them what words they use to describe the customer's problems and your potential solutions.

>> Address your customer's problems, but make sure you respond to any personal stake a decision maker or evaluator may have in the outcome. Put your solution into its business.

>> Supply enough concrete details (recognizable scenarios and precise statistics) so the customer perceives your solution as real.

>> Refer to your customer's corporate and personal perspectives on business, social, and environmental issues, and show that you have common ground.

TIP

A lot of overworked proposal writers take the easy path and repeat the same tired platitudes and catchphrases and recycle dull and impersonal boilerplate. Break the bad habit and craft a targeted, meaningful message to your audience. Refer to Chapter 10 for advice on writing effective and compelling proposal content.

Sales Is a Game of Numbers, So Bid on Everything

It's true that you can't win the lottery if you don't play, but responding to bids you have little hope of winning yields only slightly better odds. You'll hear this notion with a twist from some sales leaders: "If we bid more, we'll win more." This is a costly mistake that many businesses make, and as a result they spend way too much money for no reward, diluting already strained resources, so they can't perform as well on bids that they're better suited to win.

Successful businesses leverage the power of effective initial and ongoing bid decisions and reviews, scheduled along the proposal schedule, to make sure winning is still possible. Make the tough no-bid decision rather than waste money on a marginal opportunity. (Refer to Chapter 6 for factors you need to consider when making the bid/no-bid decision.)

You Can Skip the Reviews if You're Short on Time

Having impartial reviewers test your work throughout the proposal process is often the difference between a win and a loss. Too much rides on your proposal's outcome to leave its quality to chance or to people with a bias toward the status quo. Unless your project has reviews at its start, in its middle, and at its end, you won't be able to catch problems in time to do something about them. Nothing's worse than realizing in a final review that your solution has gaps, your contributors have ignored your style guidelines, or your executive summary simply doesn't persuade.

What can go wrong if you skip the reviews? Everything. When you skip reviews, you

>> Rely on a single editor to catch all the mistakes in the content

>> Are stuck with quality assessments that come from the people who performed the original work

>> Miss out on the expertise of your business's leaders and critical thinkers

>> Can't protect your organization's bottom line from poor pricing decisions

>> Can be blamed for any and all shortcomings after a loss

REMEMBER

Stress the importance of reviews at the kickoff meeting. Highlight them on your schedule. Have experienced reviewers assigned from the start. Provide guides for each role in the review stages: contributor, reviewer, editor, and project lead. Walk participants through their responsibilities either at the kickoff meeting or in a separate session afterward.

If you're short on time, drop the bells and whistles — anything but the reviews.

Chapter 12 looks at the review process in detail, and Chapter 6 considers how to schedule reviews throughout your proposal process.

Collecting Information about Your Competitors Is Unethical

Competitive intelligence is an ethical business practice guided by written rules from the association of Strategic and Competitive Intelligence Professionals (SCIP). Its website provides a wealth of guidance and training for gathering competitive intelligence in legal ways. Use it to supplement your organization's internal guidelines for ethical conduct.

TIP

You can find most of the competitive intelligence data you need among colleagues and online. Hold a brainstorming session with sales and service personnel. Check to see whether you've hired anyone from your competitor, and pick his or her brain for information. You can then verify the data you collect by using SCIP and online sources.

Check out Chapter 5 for more ways to size up your competition.

After You Decide to Bid, Stick to Your Decision to the End

We stress the need for initial and ongoing bid decisions and reviews in your proposal process because you have to be prepared to cut your losses if you discover reasons a bid is unwinnable. This realization can come during many stages in the process:

» **Opportunity qualification:** Review your decision here to confirm whether the opportunity merits expending resources for research and assessment.

» **Bid pursuit decision:** Review your decision here to determine whether to commit resources to developing opportunity plans and influencing the customer to prefer your solution.

» **Bid/no-bid decision:** Review your decision here to determine whether you have positioned yourself favorably enough to justify planning to develop a proposal.

» **Bid validation:** Review your decision here to determine whether the opportunity is still worth pursuing and the proposal worth preparing, considering any amendments or changes in an RFP.

» **Final review:** Use your final review to decide whether to submit the proposal as prepared, considering the anticipated financial reward and level of risk.

The success of the proposal process depends on deciding yes or no at each review milestone. Making these decisions can stop investment early in opportunities that you have little chance to win. Using decision reviews consistently demonstrates to your organization that you're fostering a truly professional proposal operation.

Debrief Sessions Help You Single Out Underperformers

Some people think that after action reviews (AARs), lessons-learned reviews, and postmortems are nothing more than witch hunts for identifying people who underperformed. This goes against the spirit and principles behind these knowledge management best practices. These reviews should be about the decision points, information flow, system performance, and resource allocations that contributed to a winning or losing bid. And if you find that someone needs additional training, the only acceptable course of action is to focus on the individual's behaviors and outcomes, not on the individual.

If you do these reviews right, beginning when the opportunity is first identified and ending after the contract is signed, you eliminate a lot of unsatisfactory behavior along the way, and a witch hunt is unnecessary.

Lessons collected are not lessons learned. You need a plan to harvest, store, track, and distribute lessons learned so they get to the responsible stakeholders and do their job — to continually improve the proposal process.

Chapter 15 looks at debriefing to discover ways to improve the proposal process. Chapters 13 and 14 also discuss other types of reviews — all of which are designed to improve the process, not invoke an inquisition.

Appendix

Online Resources

We wrote *Writing Business Bids & Proposals For Dummies* for people who write a few proposals each year in the commercial market — that is, small business owners, salespeople, and lone proposal writers. This book will help you understand how to write customer-focused, persuasive proposals that win more business.

We want to give you more than just ideas and instructions, however, so here we provide details on how you can access some practical tools and examples for improving your proposals. This appendix details the collection of all the online resources, tools, and templates that we reference throughout this book. We hope that you'll use them, adapt them, and improve them (and when you do, we'd love to hear from you and use your ideas to make them better). That's what the Association of Proposal Management Professionals (APMP) is all about: being better proposal writers and managers every time out.

For more information about the APMP, go to www.apmp.org. To access the resources you need, simply visit www.apmp.org/page/proposalsfordummies.

In Table A-1, we map each resource to the chapter (or chapters) of this book where we refer to it.

TABLE A-1   **Proposal Resources**

Chapter(s)	Resource	Description
2	Example of RFP	Representative model of a commercial Request for Proposal (RFP). A document from a customer or funding source calling for proposals for a specific program, project, or work effort.
2	Example of RFQ	Representative model of a commercial Request for Quotation (RFQ). Often a brief RFP that focuses on a few key requirements and asks for a price quote.
2	Example of RFI	Representative model of a commercial Request for Information (RFI). A customer document used at an early stage of a procurement to create a list of viable bidders who will later be invited to render an offer or respond to an RFP.

(continued)

TABLE A-1 *(continued)*

Chapter(s)	Resource	Description
4	Customer question tracker	A table to help you track the questions you and your competitors ask the customer during an RFP period.
4, 16	Compliance matrix	A list of specific customer requirements from an RFP. The matrix often splits complex, multipart requirements into sub-requirements. It also helps proposal managers and internal reviewers verify that the RFP response meets all the customer's requirements.
5	Strengths, weaknesses, opportunities, and threats (SWOT) analysis instructions and template	An analysis that bidders perform to assess their competitive positioning and identify the steps they must take to develop a compelling, winning proposal.
6, 14	Kickoff meeting agenda	A schedule for leading the meeting that starts the proposal effort for all contributors. It includes activities such as answering questions about the opportunity, assigning writing tasks, setting milestones, and creating a cohesive team.
6, 14	Kickoff meeting briefing	Collection of references, templates, and tools to help the proposal team write a proactive proposal or RFP response. It includes customer profile, draft executive summary, opportunity overview, customer background, competitive assessment, proposal strategy, proposal schedule, and solution approach.
6, 10	Style sheet	Writing guidelines for authors so they can work separately from others and still deliver content that meets a single standard. Saves time and effort for lone proposal writers because it reminds them of issues easily forgotten, such as word usage, formatting, grammar, and spelling.
6, 13, 16	Proactive proposal template	A preformatted word-processing file with predefined headers, footers, headings, and text blocks to guide users as they write proactive commercial proposals.
2, 6, 16	Reactive response template	A preformatted word-processing file with predefined headers, footers, and other standard elements that allows users to insert a customer's RFP and then respond as directed.
6, 9	Transmittal letter for a proactive proposal	A model for introducing a commercial proposal to a prospective customer.
6, 9	Transmittal letter for a reactive response	A model for introducing a commercial RFP response to a customer.

Chapter(s)	Resource	Description
6, 12	Oral proposal template	A model for developing a live proposal presentation following a successful submittal.
8, 16	Proposal schedule	Three sample "calendar style" templates, including key deliverables and milestones, for delivering proactive proposals or RFP responses.
8	Example Gantt chart	A sample management tool (horizontal bar chart) for identifying and tracking progress on activities, milestones, and deliverables over the life of a project.
8, 16	Budget template	A preformatted worksheet with standard expense categories to forecast and track potential proposal expenses.
9	Executive summary template	A preformatted word-processing file with predefined headers, footers, headings, and text blocks to guide users as they write proactive commercial executive summaries.
9, 10, 13	Four-part RFP question-response model	Structured writing model for answering RFP questions consistently and clearly. (Based on the issue/discussion/point pattern concept devised by Joseph M. Williams and Gregory G. Colomb; refer to Chapter 10 for more).
10	Activating nominalizations guide	Job aid to help writers identify and eliminate nominalizations and improve the clarity and concision of their text.
12	Final review checklist	A list of requirements so proposal reviewers can effectively assess the entire proposal — its compliance, readiness, and responsiveness, plus its effectiveness in conveying the proposal's themes, fulfilling its strategy, and depicting its discriminators.
13, 15, 16	Checklist for internal lessons-learned review	This template guides you as you get feedback (both positive and negative) from your internal team so you can continually improve the capture and proposal processes.
14	Stoplight chart	A simple chart showing a red, yellow, or green status for each major activity during a project.
14	Responsibility matrix	An extension of a compliance matrix that identifies proposal team members and their specific proposal section responsibilities.

(continued)

Chapter(s)	Resource	Description
15, 16	Checklist of questions for customer debrief	This template guides you while obtaining positive and negative feedback from your customer on how your proposal scored in its evaluation.
15	Proof points tracking checklist	Provides a comprehensive list of potential reusable content objects to support your claims.
16	Past performance template	A structured format for creating and retaining knowledge about previous projects so you can provide proofs for your claims.
16	Customer contact plan	A reference document that lists the customers you plan to contact, who in your company will visit them, what you want to find out, what you want to communicate, when and where you'll meet, and how you'll communicate your messages. The plan also includes a placeholder for the information you gather during a customer meeting.
16	Bid/no-bid analysis	A guided assessment template to use after you've completed the opportunity plan that validates whether you're properly positioned to win.
16	Production resources checklist	An accounting of all the human, equipment, and monetary resources you may need to produce and deliver your proposal to the customer.
16	Production checklist	A list of document attributes that your published proposal should meet.
16	Editing checklist	A list of criteria that an editor should ensure a proposal meets before submission. The checklist covers grammar, punctuation, capitalization, clarity, readability, consistency, and persuasiveness.

Index

A

abstract ideas, 268
accordion process, 45, 80, 278
account plan, 368
accounts, planning, 70
account team, 66
action-based plans, 177–178
action caption, 21
  in content development, 270
  in graphics, 269
action-item tracking matrix, 315, 335
action stage. *See* proposal development stage
active voice, 229
Adobe Design, 309
after-action reviews (AARs), 312, 336, 378
alignment, design principles, 265–266
Angie's List, 107
annotated outline, 140, 141
annual report, 107
APMP. *See* Association of Proposal Management Professionals (APMP)
APMP Job Bank, 358
appositives, 241
Arial font, 321
Associated Press Stylebook, 141, 174
Association of Proposal Management Professionals (APMP), 22–23, 329, 345, 352, 358
attachments, 220
audio production software, 310. *See also* software tools
automated proposal generators, 308–309

B

backing up claims
  credible proof, 166–167
  with past projects, 164–165
  persuasive proof, 165
  tangible proof, 166–167
balance, design principles, 265
benefits of proposal
  clarifying, 159
  defined, 156–163
  features, compared with, 160, 373–374
  headings, 249–250
  misconceptions, 373–374
  overview, 153–154
  presenting, 156–163
  qualifying value of, with discriminators, 161–162
  "so what?" test, 160
Better Business Bureau, 107
bid and proposal (B&P) expenses, 367
bidder, 9
bidder comparison matrix, 112–114
bid manager, 9, 187
bid/no-bid decision
  customers' requirements and, 87
  decision-making points, 331
  described, 18
  pre-proposal stage, 128–130
  sticking to bid decisions, 377
  template, 369
bid pursuit decision, 377
bid validation, 377
binding method
  plastic spiral, 257–258
  ring, 258
  saddle stitch, 258
  selecting, 257–258
  wire, 257–258
Blu-ray burning software, 310
Body of Knowledge (BoK), 22–23, 329, 352, 358
body or normal text, proactive proposal templates, 320

boilerplate, 62, 200, 353

bookbinding, 257

Boolean operators, 307

Boolean searches, 353

brand, 254

brief answer, 206

brightness, paper, 256

budget

building, 183–184

categories, 183

limited, overcoming, 184

overview, 183

time, 185

understanding, 182–183

value to organization, proving, 184

bulleted lists

proactive proposal templates, 320

using effectively, 241

business development life cycle

accounts, planning, 70

eight-stage, 68–69

market, finding, 69

negotiating and closing the deal in, 73–74

opportunities, identifying and qualifying, 70–71

opportunities, planning for, 71–72

overview, 67–68

proposal, writing, 73

proposal plan, developing, 72–73

relationship, sustaining, 74

business documentation, 146

business process management (BPM) software, 305

business proposals

defined, 10

types of, 10, 25

C

calendar, shared, 340

Calibri font, 321–322

callouts

designing, 259

proactive proposal templates, 321

call to action, 220

Cambria font, 321

CD burning software, 310

celebrations, 313, 342

centralized document sharing, 340

chapters, documents, 242

charts templates, 314

checklists

quality, 285

templates, 314, 370

training, 328–329

Chicago Manual of Style, 141, 174

claims, backing up

credible proof, 166–167

with past projects, 164–165

persuasive proof, 165

tangible proof, 166–167

classroom-based training, 328

clear writing. *See also* writing the proposal

described, 225

paradox of writing, 225

revising work, 243

showing document's structure in, 239–242

storytelling in, 226–231

using conversation style in, 232–236

value of, 226

clients

asking opening questions, 57–58

communications, 75

concerns, in proactive proposals, 39–40

current environment, 62

debriefing, 347–348

describing situation of, 201–204

early engagement with, 372

echoing needs of, 62–63

first-time, 330

focus on, 99–100

getting to know, 56–66

hot buttons, 16, 42, 64, 133

instructions of

following, 78

overview, 78

pre-qualification questionnaire, 78–80

reading, 81–82

unclear RFP, 82–84

knowing the business of, 56–57

knowledge about, 100–101

language of, 101

learning from, 346–348

making the message about, 61–62

managing relationships with, 74–75

metrics, 330

needs of, 58–61, 62–63

in opportunity planning, 71

questions of

  answering, 204–207

  answering plainly, 206–207

  answers and win themes, 207

  brief answer, 206

  expanded answer, 206

  payoff statement, 206

  responding to, 152

  responding to RFP's questions, 205–206

  restatement, 206

repeat, 330

requirements of

  compliance matrix, 88–94

  disqualification and, 87–88

  list of, 86

  overview, 84–85

  shredding the RFP, 85–87

situation of

  describing, 201–204

  describing in customer's own language, 204

  environment, illustrating, 203–204

  list of need, 203

  problems and pain, 203

  scenario, setting up, 201–204

  verbal labels, 203

support to, 66

types of requests, 27

winning

  by differentiating offers from others, 65–66

  by echoing their needs, 62–63

by focusing on benefits, not features, 64–65

by making the message about them, 61–62

using discriminators, 66–67

close captioning, 310

cloud computing, 340

coaching programs, 360–361

collaborative workspaces, 306

Colomb, Gregory G., *Style: Toward Clarity and Grace*, 229

colon (:), 234

colors, proactive proposal templates, 321

color scheme, 253

columns,

in digital mockups, 262

in proactive proposal templates, 320

competition

  assessing, 104–106

  ghosting, 117–121

  internal sources of, 105

  opportunity planning and, 71

  overview, 103–104

competitive analysis, 17, 326

competitive intelligence

  described, 104

  gaining and assessing, 302–303

  misconceptions, 377

competitors

  annual reports, 107

  bidder comparison matrix, 112–114

  collecting information about, 377

  consumer sites, 107

  gathering information about, 103–104

  ghosting

    compensating for your weaknesses in, 121

    competitors' weaknesses, 120

    defined, 117–121

    described, 117

    by highlighting your strengths, 119–120

    SWOT analysis, 118

  historical records, 107

  industry publications, 107

competitors *(continued)*
  intelligence-gathering on, 106–109
  publicly available information on, 106–108
  public records, 107
  questions about, 104–106
  reviews, 17, 109–110
  social media, 107
  special information services, 108
  strengths and weaknesses, 112–114
  SWOT analysis, 111–112
  talking to colleagues, 108
  talking with customers, 109
  unseating incumbents, 114–117, 374
  weaknesses of, 120
  website of, 107
compliance matrix
  comment box, 98–99
  completion checklist, 93
  creating, 88, 144, 365–366
  defined, 85
  double-checking work in, 92–93
  following customer's lead, 92
  keeping writing on track with, 90
  preparing for every bid request, 89
  as responsiveness tool, 98–99
  simple and clear, keeping, 90–92
  stated needs, 89
  template, 365–366
  unstated needs, 89
  using spreadsheet to create, 94
compliance/responsibility matrix, 317
computer-aided (CAD) software, 305
conference line, 339–340
consistency, design principles, 265
consumer sites, 107
content
  freeze date, 285
  lean and concise, 37
  outlining, 36–37
  plans, 141
  size of proposal and, 47–48

content repositories
  building, 353–354
  classification scheme, 353
  content effectiveness, 354
  content harvesting, 311
  content objects, 354–355
  implementation plan, 354
  moving new proposal content into, 356
  object-oriented, 353
  search engine, 353
  update plan, 354
  usage measurement, 354
contracts, 327
contrast, design principles, 264
copyrights, 272
cost, 71
cost analysis, 308
cover letter. *See* transmittal letter
current environment or problem, proactive proposals, 12
current situation, proactive proposals, 43
customer relationship management (CRM) system, 70, 303–304
customers
  asking opening questions, 57–58
  communications, 75
  concerns, in proactive proposals, 39–40
  current environment, 62
  debriefing, 347–348
  describing situation of, 201–204
  early engagement with, 372
  echoing needs of, 62–63
  first-time, 330
  focus on, 99–100
  getting to know, 56–66
  hot buttons, 16, 42, 64, 133
  instructions of
    following, 78
    overview, 78
    pre-qualification questionnaire, 78–80
    reading, 81–82
    unclear RFP, 82–84

knowing the business of, 56–57

knowledge about, 100–101

language of, 101

learning from, 346–348

making the message about, 61–62

managing relationships with, 74–75

needs of, 58–61, 62–63

in opportunity planning, 71

questions of

  answering, 204–207

  answering plainly, 206–207

  answers and win themes, 207

  brief answer, 206

  expanded answer, 206

  payoff statement, 206

  responding to, 152

  responding to RFP's questions, 205–206

  restatement, 206

repeat, 330

requirements of

  compliance matrix, 88–94

  disqualification and, 87–88

  list of, 86

  overview, 84–85

  shredding the RFP, 85–87

situation of

  describing, 201–204

  describing in customer's own language, 204

  environment, illustrating, 203–204

  list of need, 203

  problems and pain, 203

  scenario, setting up, 201–204

  verbal labels, 203

support to, 66

types of requests, 27

winning

  by differentiating offers from others, 65–66

  by echoing their needs, 62–63

  by focusing on benefits, not features, 64–65

  by making the message about them, 61–62

  using discriminators, 66–67

Cyrano de Bergerac (Rostand), 75

D

data mining, 302

day-to-day tasks, 181

deadline, 13, 46

decision gate, 70, 129

decision stage. *See* pre-proposal stage

delivery of proposal

  checklists to ensure quality, 285

  electronic submissions

    adapting messages in, 289

    disadvantages of, 287–288

    functions of, 288

    overview, 287

    versus paper submission, 288–289

  getting ready for, 284–287

  overview, 151

  planning for the worst in, 286

  scaling production, 284–287

  scheduling, 171–173

descriptive headings, 248

descriptive outline, 223–224

design, proposal

  binding method, 257–258

  branding in, 254

  callouts, 259

  consistency in, 254–263

  customer-focused, 253

  designing page on paper, 260–261

  design principles, 264–267

  document styles, 254–263

  font, selecting, 256–257

  graphics, 267–274

  headers and footers, 258

  overview, 252, 254–255

  page margins, 259

  paper, choosing, 256

  pull-quotes, 259

  questions to answer in, 252

  storyline preview in, 253–254

desktop publisher, 187, 282, 310

developing the proposal
  answering customer's questions, 204–207
  call to action, 220
  executive summary, 195–200
  experience section, 217–219
  pricing section, 213–217
  proactive proposal, 208–213
  transmittal letter, writing, 200–201
development stage, proposal. *See also* post-proposal stage; pre-proposal stage
  compliance matrix, 144
  discriminators, 133–134
  executive summary, 134–135, 195–200
  getting ready to propose, 19
  kickoff meeting, 135–137
  mock-ups in, 140–141
  organizing strategic information in, 132–133
  outline, 134–135
  outlining the proposal, 138–140
  overall strategy, 132–137
  overview, 18, 126–127, 131–132
  planning the proposal in, 20, 137–138
  producing the proposal in, 149–152
  resources, 19
  reviewing customer's hot buttons, 133
  scheduling in, 20
  solutions and alternate solutions, 143–144
  strategizing in, 19–20
  style sheets, 142–143
  tailoring the process in, 19–20
  transmittal letter, writing, 200
  win themes, 134
  writing the proposal, 144–149
digital page, turning mock-ups into, 261–262
director, proposal, 187
discriminators
  articulating, 133–134
  headings, 249–250
  in headings of proposals, 163

  qualifying value of benefits with, 161–162
  sweet spot, 162
  using, 66–67
disqualification, 87–88
disqualifiers, 87
distribution list, email, 342
document styles
  binding method, 257–258
  callouts, 259
  consistency in, 254–263
  designing page on paper, 260–261
  font, selecting, 256–257
  headers and footers, 258
  overview, 254–255
  page margins, 259
  paper, choosing, 256
  pull-quotes, 259
  testimonials, 259
  turning mock-up into digital page, 261–262
Do-It-Yourself Billion Dollar Graphics (Parkinson), 268
dots per inch (DPI), 273
double-sided print (duplex), 258–259
draft
  proofing, 149
  reviewing, 148
  revising, 148–149
dress rehearsal, 294
due dates, 46–47, 170
Dun and Bradstreet, 108, 190
duplex (double-sided print), 258–259
DVD burning software, 310

E

editing the proposals, 174
editor, 187, 282
electronic submissions
  adapting messages in, 289
  disadvantages of, 287–288
  functions of, 288

overview, 287

versus paper submission, 50–51, 288–289

email

body, 342

communicating with team, 342

distribution list, 342

subject line, 342

templates, 342

em dash (—), 234

emotional need, 96, 97

English Grammar For Dummies (Woods), 229

ethical character, establishing, 247–248

ethos, 44

evergreen objects, 355

Example icon, 4

executive summary

avoiding excessive boilerplate in, 200

building, 198–199

costumer-focused, 197

creating good impression in, 199–200

defined, 196

described, 145, 196–197

misconceptions, 372–373

proactive proposals, 12

in proactive proposals, 43

proposal development stage, 134–135

visual, 200

win theme in, 42

expanded answer, 206

expenses, bid and proposal (B&P), 367. *See also* budget

experience section

described, 217–218

documenting team's know-how in, 218

past-performance examples, 219

external reviews, 346

F

feature-benefit statements

defined, 156

features, describing, 157–159

presenting, 156–163

features

benefits, compared with, 160, 373–374

defined, 156–163

details, 157–158

misconceptions, 373–374

presenting, 158

feedback, timing, 336

figure number, 269

file formats, 273

final production information, 320

final proposal reviews

comprehensive, 277

deciding to bid or not to bid after, 377–378

for executives, 283

getting the proposal ready for, 279–280

guidelines for reviewers, 281

objective, 277

preparing right reviewers for, 280–281

putting together, 279–284

realistic, 277

recommendations, implementing, 283–284

scaling, 278–279

structuring, 277

finance department, 327

first-time client, 330

fonts

in proactive proposal templates, 320

selecting, 256–257

type size, 257

type style, 257

footers

designing, 258

proactive proposal templates, 320

formative documents, 145

Foundation certification, 359

"4Cs and P" in opportunity planning, 71–72

free-form RFP, 38

front-loading, 372

FUD (fear, uncertainty, doubt), 58

functional need, 96, 97

functional reviews, 174

fundamental content objects (FCOs), 353

G

Gantt charts, 176–178

Gartner, 108

generators, proposal, 308–309

gerunds, 241

getting ready to propose, 18

ghosting the competition

  compensating for your weaknesses in, 121

  competitors' weaknesses, 120

  defined, 117–121

  described, 117

  by highlighting your strengths, 119–120

  SWOT analysis, 118

GIF file format, 273

global procurement

  cultural differences, awareness of, 50

  overview, 49

  rules, 49

  subtleties in, 49

global teams, 188–189

Google, 190

Google Draw, 309

GovWin, 108

graphic designer, 188, 282

graphics. *See also* images

  abstract ideas and, 268

  action caption, 269–270

  connecting text to, 271–273

  copyrights, 272

  customer needs and, 271

  defined, 269

  enhancing power of, 269–272

  figure number, 269

  file formats, 273

  informative heading, 269

  in oral presentations, 293

  persuading with, 267–268

  in proactive proposal templates, 321

  raster, 273

  in storyboarding, 270

  vector, 273

  when and where to use, 271

graphics software, 305, 309–310

H

headers

  designing, 258

  proactive proposal templates, 320

headings

  appositives, 241

  benefits and discriminators in, 249–250

  bulleted lists, 241

  descriptive, 248–249

  discriminators in, 163

  gerunds, 241

  guidelines, 250

  informative, 240–241

  layout, 262

  numbered lists, 241

  parallel grammatical structure, 240

  proactive proposal templates, 320

  question, 241

  single-word, 240

  styles, 248–249

  telegraphic, 248

holidays, 341

Hoovers, 108

hot buttons

  asking questions, 57

  issues, 64

  motivators, 64

  pushing, 16, 64

  reviewing, 133

  win themes, 42

I

icons, explained, 4

images. *See also* graphics

  creating with templates, 321–322

  GIF file format, 273

  JPG file format, 273

implementation plan, proactive proposals, 43

improving proposals

  applying knowledge to next proposal, 356–357

  collecting content for reuse, 352–356

  debriefing customers, 347–348

  following up with questionnaires, 348

  learning from colleagues, 349–351

  learning from customers, 346–348

incumbents

  misconceptions, 374

  unseating, 114–117, 374

industry publications, 107, 146

instant messaging (IM), 340

instructions of customers

  following, 78

  overview, 78

  pre-qualification questionnaire, 78–80

  reading, 81–82

  unclear RFP, 82–84

intelligence-gathering, 106–109

internal reviews, 346, 349–350

Internet research, 302

interviews, 146

Invitation to Bid (ITB). *See* Request for Proposal (RFP)

Invitation to Tender (ITT). *See* Request for Proposal (RFP)

J

jargon, 225, 232–233

JPG file format, 273

just-in-case training, 327

just-in-time training, 327

K

key discriminators, 31, 65–66

kickoff meeting

  documents in, 135–136

  objectives in, 136

  project overview in, 137

  response logistics in, 137

team leadership during, 332

  virtual, 343

knowledge management, 352, 355

knowledge manager, 187

knowledge map, 355

L

leading proposal teams

  aligning daily activities with written proposal plan, 332–333

  bid/no-bid decision, 331

  business's readiness to bid, 331–332

  daily management, 333–334

  daily stand-up reviews, 334–335

  embracing leadership role in, 332–335

  engaging colleagues at every level, 325

  feedback and, 336

  getting support of executives, 325–326

  joining forces with peers, 326–327

  kickoff meeting, 332

  leading by doing, 324

  mentoring programs, 329

  motivating team, 337

  overview, 323–324

  before the project begins, 324–331

  resources, 329–330

  roles and responsibilities, clarifying, 333

  in solution development, 332

  strategy and planning sessions, 331

  training and, 327–329

  virtual approach to, 338–344

  wrapping an iron fist in velvet globe, 333–334

leads, 92

left-hanging headings, 262

left-justified heading, 262

lessons learned management process

  after-action reviews, 312

  best practice comparisons, 352

  collecting lessons learned, 350–351

  debriefing customers, 347–348

  defined, 311, 345

lessons learned management process *(continued)*

following up with questionnaires, 348–349

internal sessions, 349–350

learning from colleagues, 349–351

learning from customers, 346–348

misconceptions, 378

postmortems, 312

template, 370

lessons learned review, 74, 153, 180–181, 378

letter of transmittals

AIDA format, 201

in proactive proposals, 43

win theme in, 42

writing, 147, 200–201

Lewis, Michael (*Moneyball*), 330

life cycle, business development

accounts, planning, 70

eight-stage, 68–69

market, finding, 69

negotiating and closing the deal in, 73–74

opportunities, identifying and qualifying, 70–71

opportunities, planning for, 71–72

overview, 67–68

proposal, writing, 73

proposal plan, developing, 72–73

relationship, sustaining, 74

loadings, 367

logos, 44

M

manager

bid, 187

proposal, 9, 188, 282

market, finding, 70

market research software, 301–302

meeting, kickoff

documents in, 135–136

objectives in, 136

project overview in, 137

response logistics in, 137

team leadership during, 332

virtual, 343

mentoring, 329, 360–361

methodology review, 148

metrics, 330

Microsoft Publisher, 309

Microsoft Visio, 309

midsize organizations, 326

milestones, 342, 368

mind-mapping software, 305

misconceptions

bidding on everything, 375–376

collecting information about competitors, 377

debriefing sessions, 378

engaging the customers early, 372

executive summary, 372–373

features versus benefits, 373–374

incumbents, 374

skipping the reviews, 376

sticking to bid decisions, 377–378

using business-speak and buzz phrases, 375

mock-ups, 140–142, 261–262, 310

Moneyball (Lewis), 330

motivation, 337

motivators, 67–68

N

nested requirements, 35

Newman, Larry (*Shipley Proposal Guide*), 269

Next Steps section, proactive proposals, 43

nominalization, 229–231

non-verbal messages, 294–295

noun stacks, unpacking, 238–239

numbered lists, 241

O

OneSource, 108

online market research, 301–302

online resources, 379–382

online training, 328

operational review, 148

opportunities
    identifying, 70–71
    planning for, 71–72
    qualifying, 70–71
opportunity qualification, 377
oral presentations
    agenda, 292
    asking questions during, 291
    getting to the point in, 291
    graphics in, 293
    keeping it short, 292
    leading with stories in, 291
    overview, 289–290
    planning approach in, 290–292
    practicing public speaking skills for, 293–296
    preparing for, 153
    selling vision in, 291
    software, 292
    supporting qualifications, 292
outline
    annotated, 140, 141
    of content, 36–37
    descriptive, 223–224
    preparing, 134–135
    of proposal, 138–140
    of RFP response, 225
    schema, 222
    topical, 138, 141, 222–223
    writing the proposal, 222–225
over-handing headings, 262
overtime, tracking, 185

P

packaging the proposal, 151
page margins
    proactive proposal templates, 320
    setting, 259
paper
    brightness, 256
    choosing, 256
    size, 256
    weight, 256

parallel tasks, maximizing, 179–180
Parkinson, Mike, 268
partners
    deciding the need for, 189–190
    negotiating and documenting agreements, 190–191
    selecting, 190
    working with, 189–191
PAS 75, 49
past performance template, 366
past projects, as proof, 164–165
pathos, 44, 202
payoff statement, 206
PDF creation software, 310
percentage reuse, 330
personal pronouns, using, 233
person-hours per proposal, 330
persuasive writing
    analyzing the readers in, 244
    Aristotle's fundamental elements of, 44
    assumptions about audience in, 244–245
    being personal in, 246
    being specific in, 245
    being values-oriented in, 246
    described, 243
    emotions of audience, appealing to, 247
    ethical character, 247
    rhetoric in, 245–248
    validity of proposal, establishing, 246–247
planning phase, 18
plastic spiral binding, 257–258
PNG file format, 273
portfolio, in opportunity planning, 71
Portny, Stanley, *Project Management for Dummies*, 46
postmortems, 312, 378
post-proposal stage. *See also* development stage, proposal; pre-proposal stage
    lessons learned review, 153
    oral presentations, 153
    overview, 127
    responding to customers' questions, 152
    reusable content, finding and storing, 153–154

Practitioner certification, 359–360

pre-proposal stage. *See also* development stage, proposal; post-proposal stage

  bid/no-bid decision, 128–130

  competitors, analysis of, 17

  customers, 16

  deciding to bid or not to bid, 18

  gathering and providing right information in, 16–17

  getting act together in, 130–131

  overview, 14–15, 126

  proposal as communication platform, 17

  right opportunities, 15–16

  trusted advisor, 15

pre-qualification questionnaire (PQQ)

  information in, 78

  overview, 78–79

  preparing response to, 80

  requirements, 28

pre-sales process, 14

presentations, oral

  agenda, 292

  asking questions during, 291

  getting to the point in, 291

  graphics in, 293

  keeping it short, 292

  leading with stories in, 291

  overview, 289–290

  planning approach in, 290–292

  practicing public speaking skills for, 293–296

  preparing for, 153

  selling vision in, 291

  software, 292

  supporting qualifications, 292

presentation software, 305

pricing

  calculations, 308

  cost analysis, 308

  expressing value of solution in, 213–214

  in proactive proposals, 12, 42

  quantifying claims with data in, 217

  summary, 216–217

  using graphics to show value in, 215

  value proposition in, 214–215

printing the proposal, 150

prior proposals, 146

proactive proposals

  adjusting process for, 12–14

  answering for key questions in, 208–211

  customer concerns in, 39–40

  deadline, 13

  defined, 10, 25

  graphics in, 211

  organizing, 43

  outcome vision in, 211

  versus RFP responses, 11–14

  rules, 12–13

  sections, 43

  strategies in, 40–41

  structure of, 12, 208–211

  templates

    body or normal text, 320

    bulleted lists, 320

    callout or testimonial style, 321

    colors, 321

    column size and number, 320

    final production information, 320

    font family or typeface, 320

    graphics styles, 321

    header and footer style, 320

    headings, 320

    page margins, 320

  timeline, 13

  win theme in, 41–42

  working around competition in, 13

  writing, 38–44

  writing the solution for, 208–213

procurement

  cultural differences, awareness of, 50

  electronic versus print, 50–51

  global, 49–50

  overview, 48–49

  rules, 49

  subtleties in, 49

product features versus product features benefits, 65

production
  plan, scaling, 284, 286
  scheduling, 171–173
  template, 369

production manager, 187, 282

professional certifications, 359–360

professional organizations, 358

professionals, 22–23

progress of team, tracking, 336–337

Project Management for Dummies (Portny), 46

project overview, in kickoff meeting, 137

proof points. *See also* software tools
  aggregating, 166
  credible, 167
  defined, 164
  described, 212
  past projects, 164–165
  persuasive, 165
  tangible, 166–167

proposal coordinator, 187, 282

proposal development stage. *See also* post-proposal stage; pre-proposal stage
  compliance matrix, 144
  discriminators, 133–134
  executive summary, 134–135, 195–200
  getting ready to propose, 19
  kickoff meeting, 135–137
  mock-ups in, 140–141
  organizing strategic information in, 132–133
  outlining the proposal, 134–135, 138–140
  overall strategy, 132–137
  overview, 18, 126–127, 131–132
  planning the proposal in, 20, 137–138
  producing the proposal in, 149–152
  resources, 19
  reviewing customer's hot buttons, 133
  scheduling in, 20
  solutions and alternate solutions, 143–144
  strategizing in, 19–20
  style sheets, 142–143
  tailoring the process in, 19–20

transmittal letter, writing, 200
  win themes, 134
  writing the proposal, 144–149

proposal-development tools
  automated proposal generators, 308–309
  collaborative workspaces, 306
  content repositories, 307–308
  cost and price analysis, 308
  customer specifications, 310
  graphics, 309–310
  online, 305–306
  proposal management systems, 305–306

proposal director, 187

proposal editor, 187

proposal generators, 308–309

proposal infrastructure, 173

proposal management systems, 305–306

proposal manager, 9, 188, 282

proposal plan
  aligning daily activities with, 332–333
  developing, 72–73

proposal process
  development stage, 18–21
  overview, 125–126
  post-proposal stage, 21–22, 127, 152–154
  pre-proposal stage, 14–18, 126, 128–131
  proposal development stage, 126–127, 131–152
  scheduling, 20
  tailoring, 19–20

proposal professionals, 22–23

proposal reviews, 173–174

proposals
  attachments, 220
  benefits of
    clarifying, 159
    defined, 156–163
    features, compared with, 160
    headings, 249–250
    overview, 153–154
    presenting, 156–163
    qualifying value of, with discriminators, 161–162
    "so what?" test, 160

proposals *(continued)*
  budget, 182–186
  as communication platform, 17
  content plans, 141
  continual improvement of, 21–22
  creating in other media, 151
  deadline, 46
  delivery of
    checklists to ensure quality, 285
    electronic submissions, 287–289
    getting ready for, 284–287
    overview, 151
    planning for the worst in, 286
    scaling production, 284–287
    scheduling, 171–173
  developing
    answering customer's questions, 204–207
    call to action, 220
    executive summary, 195–200
    experience section, 217–219
    pricing section, 213–217
    proactive proposal, 208–213
    transmittal letter, writing, 200–201
  electronic submissions, 286–289
  headings, 248–250
  oral presentations, 289–296
  outlining the proposal, 138–140
  packaging, 151
  persuasive elements in, 43
  plan, developing, 72
  planning, 137–138
  preparing, 14–20
  printing, 150
  prior, 146
  producing, 149–152
  production plan, scaling, 284, 286
  publishing, 21
  scheduling, 169–181
  size of
    content and, 47–48
    due date and, 46–47
    overview, 45
    scaling, 45–47
    small versus large, 45–48
  small versus large, 45–48
  strategy, 72
  structure of, 240–243
  templates, 314–322
  writing
    avoiding technical and industry terms in, 232–233
    clear writing, 225
    cohesive paragraphs in, 234–236
    compliance matrix, 90
    concisely, 236–240
    describing solutions in, 145–147
    outline, 222–225
    overview, 221–222
    persuasive style in, 243–248
    proactive proposals, 38–44
    proofing draft, 149
    in proposal development stage, 18, 144–149
    proposal stories, 20–21
    punctuations, 234
    reviewing draft, 148
    revising draft, 148–149
    in sales process, 73
    summaries, 144–145
    transmittal letter, 147
    using contractions in, 233
    using conversation style in, 232
    using pronouns in, 233
    using simple words in, 232
proposal team
  competencies, 187–188
  global teams, 188–189
  members of, 187–188
  motivating, 337
  overview, 186
  roles, 187–188
  tracking progress of, 336–337
  training, 327–329
  virtual, 188, 338–344

proposal writer, 21, 188
proximity, design principles, 265
public domain, 272
public speaking skills, practicing
  clarity ad concision, 294
  dress rehearsal, 294
  expressions, 295
  eye contact, 295
  filming, 294
  hand gestures, 295
  handoffs, 294
  overview, 293
  pace and tone, 295
  questions and answers, 295–296
  script, 294
  timer, 294
  verbal and non-verbal messages, 294–295
publishing, 18, 21
pull-quotes, 259
PWC, 108

Q

qualifications, in proactive proposals, 43
QuarkXpress, 309
question-and-answer style RFPs
  challenging questions, working with, 34–35
  classifying the questions in, 32–33
  easier questions, answering first, 32–33
  fine-tuning responses into narrative, 36–38
  getting ahead of the curve in, 31
  most important questions, responding to, 35–36
  overview, 30
  reactive mode in, avoiding, 31
  win strategy in, 30–31
question headings, 241
questionnaires
  following up with, 348
  pre-qualification questionnaire (PQQ), 28
    information in, 78
    overview, 78–79
    preparing response to, 80
  reader analysis, 59–60

questions and answer process
  managing, 82–84
  practicing for, 295–296
questions of customers
  answering, 204–207
  answering plainly, 206–207
  answers and win themes, 207
  brief answer, 206
  expanded answer, 206
  payoff statement, 206
  pre-qualification questionnaire
    (PQQ), 28
    information in, 78
    overview, 78–79
    preparing response to, 80
  responding to RFP's questions, 205–206
  restatement, 206
questions to ask, 57–58
quotes, 9

R

raster graphics, 273
reactive mode, 31
reactive proposals, 10, 25, 26
reader analysis questionnaire, 59–60
reading between the lines, 94–97
recommendations
  described, 42
  implementing, 283–284
  proactive proposals, 12, 43
redundancies, avoiding, 239
reflection stage. *See* post-proposal stage
relational databases, 303, 351
remaining time, 174–175
Remember icon, 4
repeat clients, 330
repetition, design principles, 266
repositories, content
  building, 353–354
  classification scheme, 353
  content effectiveness, 354
  content harvesting, 311

repositories, content *(continued)*
  content objects, 307–308, 354–355
  implementation plan, 354
  moving new proposal content into, 356
  object-oriented, 353
  search engine, 353
  update plan, 354
  usage measurement, 354
Request for Information (RFI), 27
Request for Proposal (RFP)
  adjusting process for, 12–14
  compliance with customer's requirements, 28–29
  customer requests in, 27
  defined, 10
  free-form, 38
  overview, 26–27
  pre-qualification questionnaires, 28
  question-and-answer style, 30–38
  reasons for, 13–14
  responding to, 26
  responsiveness in, 29
  shaping, 100
  shredding, 85–87
Request for Proposal (RFP) responses
  answering customer's questions in, 205–206
  content requirements, 81
  deadline, 13
  defined, 9, 10
  delivery requirements, 81
  format requirements, 81
  four-part RRP question-response model, 206
  outlining, 225
  packaging requirements, 81
  versus proactive proposals, 11–14
  requirements, 81
  rules, 12–13
  sections, 11
  structural requirements, 81
  structure, 11–12
  templates, 318–319
  timeline, 13
  working around competition in, 13

Request for Quote (RFQ), 27
requirements of customers
  compliance matrix, 88–94
  disqualification and, 87–88
  list of, 86
  overview, 84–85
  shredding the RFP, 85–87
resources, 19, 329–330
response logistics, in kickoff meeting, 137
responsibilities, assigning and tracking, 315–316
responsibility matrix, 315–316, 336–337
responsiveness
  compliance matrix as tool, 98–99
  customer focus and, 99–100
  customers' language and, 101
  enhancing compliance with, 94–101
  knowledge about customers and, 100–101
  overview, 94–95
  reading between the lines and, 94–97
  unstated needs and, 94–97
restatement, 206
retaining businesses, 313
reusable content, finding and storing, 153–154
reviews
  after-action, 312, 336
  comprehensive, 277
  for executives, 283
  external review, 346
  final proposal
    comprehensive, 277
    for executives, 283
    getting the proposal ready for, 279–280
    guidelines for reviewers, 281
    objective, 277
    preparing right reviewers for, 280–281
    putting together, 279–284
    realistic, 277
    recommendations, implementing, 283–284
    scaling, 278–279
    structuring, 277
  getting the proposal ready for, 279–280
  guidelines for reviewers, 281

internal, 346, 349–350

misconceptions, 376

objective, 277

overview, 276

preparing right reviewers for, 280–281

putting together, 279–284

realistic, 277

recommendations, implementing, 283–284

scaling, 278–279

scheduling, 173–174

skipping, 376

stand-up, 334–335

structuring, 277

virtual, 343–344

revisions, 243

RFI. *See* Request for Information (RFI)

RFP. *See* Request for Proposal (RFP)

rhetoric in writing

being personal, 246

being specific, 245

being values-oriented, 246

emotions of audience, appealing to, 247

ethical character, 247

validity of proposal, establishing, 246–247

ring binders, 258

Rogers, Jeff (graphics designer), 260–261

Rostand, Edmond, *Cyrano de Bergerac*, 75

S

saddle stitch binding, 258

sales process

accounts, planning, 70

eight-stage, 69

market, finding, 69

negotiating and closing the deal in, 73–74

opportunities, identifying and qualifying, 70–71

opportunities, planning for, 71–72

overview, 67–68

proposal, writing, 73

proposal plan, developing, 72–73

relationship, sustaining, 74

sales reps, 327

sans serif type, 257, 321

scaling, 45–47

scheduling

breaking big assignments into chunks, 178–179

day-to-day tasks, 181

downtime between writing and reviewing, 174

due date, 170

formats of schedule, 176–178

lessons learned review, 180–181

overview, 20, 169–170

parallel tasks, maximizing, 179–180

production and delivery, 171–173

proposal infrastructure, 173

proposal reviews, 173–174

remaining time, 174–175

sequential tasks, minimizing, 179–180

staggered approach, 185

tasks and subtasks, 175–176

template, 368

templates, 180

schema, 222

screen-sharing tool, 340

search engine, 353

sections, documents, 242

semicolon, 234

sequential tasks, minimizing, 179–180

serif type, 257, 321

shared calendar, 340

Shipley Proposal Guide (Newman), 269

The Shortcut to Persuasive Presentations (Tracy), 294

shredding, 85–87

simplex (single-sided print), 258–259

Sims, Brenda, *Technical Writing*, 262

single-sided print (simplex), 258–259

size, paper, 256

size of proposals

content and, 47–48

due date and, 46–47

overview, 45

scaling, 45–47

small versus large, 45–48

Small Business Administration (SBA), 302

small businesses, 326

SmartDraw, 309

social media, 107

software tools
  audio production, 310
  CD, DVD and Blu-ray burning, 310
  collaborative workspaces, 306
  competitive intelligence, 302–303
  content harvesting, 311
  content repositories, 307–308, 311
  customer relationship management, 303–304
  desktop publisher, 310
  for developing solutions, 304–305
  graphics, 309–310
  market research and evaluation, 301–302
  overview, 301
  PDF creation, 310
  in preparing for next proposal, 311–313
  proposal-development, 305–310
  proposal management systems, 305–306
  screen-sharing, 340
  version, 341
  video production, 310
  word processors, 310

solicited proposals, 10, 25

solution review, 148

"so what?" test, 160

spreadsheet, 94

standard proposal template, 367

stand-up reviews
  tips for, 334–335
  virtual, 343–344

stated needs, 89

statement of work, proactive proposals, 12

storyboarding, 270

storytelling in proposal
  active voice, using, 229
  beginning sentences with human subjects, 227
  described, 226
  nominalization, avoiding, 229–231
  passive voice, avoiding, 228–229

putting actions into verbs, 229–231
putting sentence parts in right order, 227–228

strategizing phase, 18

stress, 185–186

structure of document
  chapters, 242
  headings, 240–241
  sections, 242

style guides, 141

styles, document
  binding method, 257–258
  callouts, 259
  consistency in, 254–263
  designing page on paper, 260–261
  font, selecting, 256–257
  headers and footers, 258
  overview, 254–255
  page margins, 259
  paper, choosing, 256
  pull-quotes, 259
  testimonials, 259
  turning mock-up into digital page, 261–262

style sheets, 141, 142–143, 174

Style: Toward Clarity and Grace (Williams and Gregory), 229

subject line, email, 342

subtasks, scheduling, 175–176

successful proposals, celebrating, 313

summaries, executive
  avoiding excessive boilerplate in, 200
  building, 198–199
  costumer-focused, 197
  creating good impression in, 199–200
  defined, 196
  described, 145, 196–197
  proactive proposals, 12
  in proactive proposals, 43
  proposal development stage, 134–135
  visual, 200
  win theme in, 42

surveys, 302

SWOT analysis, 17, 30, 111–112, 118, 302

T

tasks
  day-to-day, 181
  parallel, 179–180
  scheduling, 175–176
  sequential, 179–180
taxonomy, 353
team, proposal
  competencies, 187–188
  global teams, 188–189
  members of, 187–188, 282
  motivating, 337
  overview, 186
  roles, 187–188
  tracking progress of, 336–337
  training, 327–329
  virtual
    advantages of, 338
    communication, 341–342
    described, 338
    disadvantages of, 339
    document reviews, 344
    email communication, 341–342
    external partners, working with,
      188–191
    kickoff meeting, 343
    managing, 188
    stand-up reviews, 343–344
    virtual proposal center, 339–340
team leadership
  aligning daily activities with written proposal
    plan, 332–333
  bid/no-bid decision, 331
  business's readiness to bid, 331–332
  daily management, 333–334
  daily stand-up reviews, 334–335
  embracing leadership role in, 332–335
  engaging colleagues at every level, 325
  feedback and, 336
  getting support of executives, 325–326
  joining forces with peers, 326–327
  kickoff meeting, 332
  leading by doing, 324

mentoring programs, 329
motivating team, 337
overview, 323–324
before the project begins, 324–331
resources, 329–330
roles and responsibilities, clarifying, 333
in solution development, 332
strategy and planning sessions, 331
training and, 327–329
virtual approach to, 338–344
wrapping an iron fist in velvet globe, 333–334
technical competency, 341
technical review, 148, 174
technical terms, 232–233
technical writer, 282
Technical Writing (Sims), 262
telegraphic headings, 248
telephone calls, 342
templates
  communicating with, 315
  creating, 317–318
  creating images with, 321
  email, 342
  forms, 314
  overview, 314
  planning smarter with, 314
  proactive proposal, 320–321
  proposal-building
    account plan, 368
    bid and proposal (B&P) expenses, 367
    bid/no-bid decision, 369
    checklists, 370
    compliance matrix, 365–366
    lessons learned, 370
    past performance, 366
    production, 369
    proposal schedule, 368
    standard proposal template, 367
  responsibility matrix, 315–316
  RFP response, 318–319
  tracking action items with, 315
  training, 328–329
  writing to spec with, 317

tender, 9

testimonials
   designing, 259
   proactive proposal templates, 321

text
   connecting graphics to, 271–273
   persuasive, 269

themes, win
   answers to customers and, 207
   elements of, 42
   hot buttons, 42
   issues, 42
   main statement, 41
   motivators, 42
   in proactive proposals, 41–42
   in proposal development stage, 134
   in question-and-answer style RFPs, 30
   supporting statement, 41

TIF file format, 273

time management
   breaking big assignments into chunks, 178–179
   budgeting time, 185
   day-to-day tasks, 181
   downtime between writing and reviewing, 174
   due date, 170
   formats of schedule, 176–178
   lessons learned review, 180–181
   overview, 20, 169–170
   parallel tasks, maximizing, 179–180
   production and delivery, 171–173
   proposal infrastructure, 173
   proposal reviews, 173–174
   remaining time, 174–175
   sequential tasks, minimizing, 179–180
   staggered approach, 185
   tasks and subtasks, 175–176
   templates, 180
   tracking time, 185

Times New Roman font, 321

Tip icon, 4

tools
   collaborative workspaces, 306
   competitive intelligence, 302–303
   content harvesting, 311
   content repositories, 307–308, 311
   customer relationship management, 303–304
   for developing solutions, 304–305
   graphics, 309–310
   lessons learned management process, 311
   market research and evaluation, 301–302
   overview, 301
   in preparing for next proposal, 311–313
   proposal-development, 305–310
   proposal management systems, 305–306
   screen-sharing, 340

topical outline, 138, 141, 222–223

Tracy, Larry, The Shortcut to Persuasive Presentations, 294

trade-off analysis, 117

training, proposal
   certifications, earning, 359–360
   checklists, 328–329
   classroom-based, 328
   coaching programs, 360–361
   joining professional organizations, 358
   just-in-case, 327
   just-in-time, 327
   mentoring programs, 360–361
   mentors, 329
   online, 328
   overview, 357
   reference materials, 328
   templates, 328–329
   training organizations, 360

training organizations, 360

transmittal letter
   AIDA format, 201
   in proactive proposals, 43
   win theme in, 42
   writing, 147, 200–201

type size, 257

type style, 257

U

unsolicited proposals, 25
unstated needs
  defined, 89
  discovering, 96
  emotional, 96, 97
  functional, 96, 97
  industry issues and drivers, 96
  reading between the lines, 94–97

V

vacations, 341
vector graphics, 273
verbal labels, 203
verbal messages, 294–295
version control, 285
video production software, 310
video screen capture, 340
virtual proposal center, 339–340
virtual proposal teams. *See also* team leadership
  advantages of, 338
  communication, 341–342
  described, 338
  disadvantages of, 339
  document reviews, 344
  email communication, 341–342
  external partners, working with, 188–191
  kickoff meeting, 343
  managing, 188
  stand-up reviews, 343–344
  virtual proposal center, 339–340
virtual video meeting, 340
Vogel, Douglas, 268

W

Warning icon, 4
weaknesses, compensating for, 121
web surveys, 351
weight, paper, 256
Williams, Joseph, *Style: Toward Clarity and Grace*, 229

winning customers
  by differentiating offers from others, 65–66
  by echoing their needs, 62–63
  by focusing on benefits, not features, 64–65
  by making the message about them, 61–62
  using discriminators, 66–67
win strategy, 30–31
win themes
  answers to customers and, 207
  elements of, 42
  hot buttons, 42
  issues, 42
  main statement, 41
  motivators, 42
  in proactive proposals, 41–42
  in proposal development stage, 134
  in question-and-answer style RFPs, 30
  supporting statement, 41
wire binding, 257–258
Woods, Geraldine, *English Grammar For Dummies*, 229
word-processing form, 351
word-processing templates, 314
word processors, 310
working hours, 341
worksheet templates, 314
writers, 21, 188
writing
  clear
    described, 225
    paradox of writing, 225
    revising work, 243
    showing document's structure in, 239–242
    storytelling in, 226–231
    using conversation style in, 232–236
    value of, 226
  persuasive
    analyzing the readers in, 244
    Aristotle's fundamental elements of, 44
    assumptions about audience in, 244–245
    being personal in, 246

writing *(continued)*
  being specific in, 245
  being values-oriented in, 246
  described, 243
  emotions of audience, appealing to, 247
  ethical character, 247
  rhetoric in, 245–248
  validity of proposal, establishing, 246–247
transmittal letter, 147, 200–201
writing concisely
  getting to the point, 236–237
  noun stacks, unpacking, 238–239
  redundancies, avoiding, 239
  shorter paragraphs, 237–238
  staying positive in, 240
  technical terms, applying consistently, 239–240
  using concrete images and precise measures, 239
writing the proposal
  avoiding technical and industry terms in, 232–233
  clear writing, 225
  cohesive paragraphs in, 234–236
  compliance matrix, 90
  concisely, 236–240
  describing solutions in, 145–147
  outline, 222–225
  overview, 221–222
  persuasive style in, 243–248
  proactive proposals, 38–44
  proofing draft, 149
  in proposal development stage, 18, 144–149
  proposal stories, 20–21
  punctuations, 234
  reviewing draft, 148
  revising draft, 148–149
  in sales process, 73
  summaries, 144–145
  transmittal letter, 147
  using contractions in, 233
  using conversation style in, 232
  using pronouns in, 233
  using simple words in, 232

X

XML schema, 310

Notes

Notes

About the Authors

Neil Cobb, APMP Fellow, is the former executive director of the AT&T Proposal and Knowledge Management Center and currently a lecturer in the Department of Technical Communication at the University of North Texas. He has more than 25 years of experience in proposal development and leadership, content management and repurposing, and marketing communication. Neil holds six U.S. patents for his content authoring and repurposing methods and systems.

Charlie Divine, CPP Fellow APMP, is the director of certification for the Association of Proposal Management Professionals (APMP). He has been closely associated with APMP since 1995. He has been a leader in APMP's best practice research programs to identify the best practices and competencies that lead to successful outcomes for both individuals and organizations. Charlie is certified at APMP's highest level (Professional), and has been honored as a fellow in the organization. Prior to retirement, he worked for SBC Communications (now AT&T), leading its proposal organizations and working closely with Neil.

Dedication

To our wives, Rebecca and Terry, who graciously allowed us to set aside retirement for a little bit longer and reunite to write this book, a long-time dream for us both.

Authors' Acknowledgments

Neil would like to thank Charlie, once again, for giving him his first job in the proposal business and creating a wonderful legacy to follow. He also thanks Brenda Sims for teaching him all about technical communication, and Yeow Loong Lee for helping make his content repurposing concepts a reality. Special thanks to Jeff Rogers and Katherine Seibert for their artistic talents.

We would both like to thank the members of the APMP, whose guidance and collaboration have nourished us over our proposal careers. We also thank the authors of the APMP's Body of Knowledge. Much of the information we present in this book comes from the Body of Knowledge, and any errors in facts or judgment are exclusively ours. We are especially indebted to Rick Harris, who dreamed up this project.

To close, we also thank our former colleagues at the SBC and AT&T proposal centers, who shared their insights for this book. For more than 20 years, we did some pretty remarkable things together: won a whole lot of business; turned the proposal process from a little bit of chaos to a professional, knowledge-driven machine; and created the closest thing to a family that a business could hope to become. We couldn't have written this without all of you. Special thanks to Sam Etter, Mike Peirano, Larry Keller, Lee Cobb, Keith Seibert, and Linda Greenwell for their advice and encouragement.

Publisher's Acknowledgments

Executive Commissioning Editor:
Annie Knight

Project Manager: Michelle Hacker

Development Editor: Kerry Laundon

Copy Editor: Jennette ElNaggar

Technical Editor: Vicki L. Griesinger

Production Editor: G. Vasanth Koilraj

Cover Photos: jijomathaidesigners/Shutterstock

Take Dummies with you everywhere you go!

Whether you're excited about e-books, want more from the web, must have your mobile apps, or swept up in social media, Dummies makes everything easier.

Visit Us

Like Us

Follow Us

Watch Us

Join Us

Pin Us

Circle Us

Shop Us

FOR DUMMIES®

A Wiley Brand

BUSINESS

978-1-118-73077-5

978-1-118-44349-1

978-1-119-97527-4

MUSIC

978-1-119-94276-4

978-0-470-97799-6

978-0-470-49644-2

DIGITAL PHOTOGRAPHY

978-1-118-09203-3

978-0-470-76878-5

978-1-118-00472-2

Algebra I For Dummies
978-0-470-55964-2

Anatomy & Physiology For Dummies, 2nd Edition
978-0-470-92326-9

Asperger's Syndrome For Dummies
978-0-470-66087-4

Basic Maths For Dummies
978-1-119-97452-9

Body Language For Dummies, 2nd Edition
978-1-119-95351-7

Bookkeeping For Dummies, 3rd Edition
978-1-118-34689-1

British Sign Language For Dummies
978-0-470-69477-0

Cricket for Dummies, 2nd Edition
978-1-118-48032-8

Currency Trading For Dummies, 2nd Edition
978-1-118-01851-4

Cycling For Dummies
978-1-118-36435-2

Diabetes For Dummies, 3rd Edition
978-0-470-97711-8

eBay For Dummies, 3rd Edition
978-1-119-94122-4

Electronics For Dummies All-in-One For Dummies
978-1-118-58973-1

English Grammar For Dummies
978-0-470-05752-0

French For Dummies, 2nd Edition
978-1-118-00464-7

Guitar For Dummies, 3rd Edition
978-1-118-11554-1

IBS For Dummies
978-0-470-51737-6

Keeping Chickens For Dummies
978-1-119-99417-6

Knitting For Dummies, 3rd Edition
978-1-118-66151-2

FOR

DUMMIES®

A Wiley Brand

SELF-HELP

978-0-470-66541-1

978-1-119-99264-6

978-0-470-66086-7

LANGUAGES

978-0-470-68815-1

978-1-119-97959-3

978-0-470-69477-0

HISTORY

978-0-470-68792-5

978-0-470-74783-4

978-0-470-97819-1

Laptops For Dummies 5th Edition
978-1-118-11533-6

Management For Dummies, 2nd Edition
978-0-470-97769-9

Nutrition For Dummies, 2nd Edition
978-0-470-97276-2

Office 2013 For Dummies
978-1-118-49715-9

Organic Gardening For Dummies
978-1-119-97706-3

Origami Kit For Dummies
978-0-470-75857-1

Overcoming Depression For Dummies
978-0-470-69430-5

Physics I For Dummies
978-0-470-90324-7

Project Management For Dummies
978-0-470-71119-4

Psychology Statistics For Dummies
978-1-119-95287-9

Renting Out Your Property For Dummies, 3rd Edition
978-1-119-97640-0

Rugby Union For Dummies, 3rd Edition
978-1-119-99092-5

Stargazing For Dummies
978-1-118-41156-8

Teaching English as a Foreign Language For Dummies
978-0-470-74576-2

Time Management For Dummies
978-0-470-77765-7

Training Your Brain For Dummies
978-0-470-97449-0

Voice and Speaking Skills For Dummies
978-1-119-94512-3

Wedding Planning For Dummies
978-1-118-69951-5

WordPress For Dummies, 5th Edition
978-1-118-38318-6

Think you can't learn it in a day? Think again!

The *In a Day* e-book series from *For Dummies* gives you quick and easy access to learn a new skill, brush up on a hobby, or enhance your personal or professional life — all in a day. Easy!

Football Rules & Positions DUMMIES *in a day*
Howie Long with John Czarnecki

Improving Your Golf Swing FOR DUMMIES *in a day*
Gary McCord

Buying & Serving Wine FOR DUMMIES *in a day*
Ed McCarthy Mary Ewing-Mulligan

Getting Started with Crowdfund Investing FOR DUMMIES *in a day*
Sherwood Neiss Jason W. Best Zak Cassady-Dorion

Boost Your Confidence FOR DUMMIES *in a day*
Kate Burton Brinley Platts

Giving a Presentation FOR DUMMIES *in a day*
Malcolm Kushner

Knitting a Scarf FOR DUMMIES *in a day*
Pam Allen, Tracy L. Barr, Shannon Okey, and Kristi Porter

Launch a WordPress.com Blog FOR DUMMIES *in a day*
Lisa Sabin-Wilson

Rugby Union Basics FOR DUMMIES *in a day*
Nick Cain Greg Growden

Cricket Rules FOR DUMMIES *in a day*
Julian Knight

Become More Mindful FOR DUMMIES *in a day*
Shamash Alidina

Running a Great Meeting FOR DUMMIES *in a day*
Bob Nelson, PhD Peter Economy Mark H. McCormack Dirk Zeller

Planning a PRINCE2 Project FOR DUMMIES *in a day*
Nick Graham

Building Rapport with NLP FOR DUMMIES *in a day*
Romilla Ready Kate Burton

Ukulele FOR DUMMIES *in a day*
Alistair Wood

Become More Relaxed FOR DUMMIES *in a day*
Shamash Alidina

Available as PDF, eMobi and Kindle